FRANCIS WILLUGHBY'S
BOOK OF GAMES

Frontispiece   Oil portrait of Francis Willughby by Gerard Soest

Francis Willughby's Book of Games

A Seventeenth-Century Treatise
on Sports, Games and Pastimes

Edited and introduced by
David Cram, Jeffrey L. Forgeng and
Dorothy Johnston

ASHGATE

Published by
Ashgate Publishing Limited
Gower House
Croft Road
Aldershot
Hants GU11 3HR
England

Ashgate Publishing Company
Suite 420
101 Cherry Street
Burlington
VT 05401-4405
USA

Ashgate website: http://www.ashgate.com

British Library Cataloguing in Publication Data
Willughby, Francis
  Francis Willughby's Book of games : a seventeenth-century treatise on sports, games and pastimes
  1.Willughby, Francis. Book of games 2.Games - Early works to 1800 3.Sports - Early works to 1800 4.Amusements - Early works to 1800
  I.Title II.Cram, David III.Forgeng, Jeffrey L. IV.Johnston, Dorothy V.Book of games
  790.1

Library of Congress Cataloging-in-Publication Data
Willughby, Francis, 1635-1672.
    Francis Willughby's book of games : a seventeenth century treatise on sports, games, and pastimes / edited by David Cram, Jeffrey L. Forgeng and Dorothy Johnston.
        p. cm.
    Revision of a manuscript fragment by Francis Willughby held by the University of Nottingham Library.
    Includes bibliographical references and index.
    ISBN 1-85928-460-4 (alk. paper)
      1.Games--Early works to 1800. 2. Amusements--Early works to 1800. I.Title: Book of games. II.Cram, David. III. Forgeng, Jeffrey L. IV.Johnston, Dorothy. V.Title.

GV1201 .W54 2002
790.1'09'032–dc21

2002074540

ISBN 1 85928 460 4

Typeset by Bournemouth Colour Press, Parkstone, Poole, Dorset and printed in Great Britain by MPG Books Ltd, Bodmin, Cornwall.

Contents

List of Figures

Foreword

Francis Willughby, the seventeenth-century naturalist and father of the 1st Lord Middleton, occupies a special place in the Willughby family history. Of the many who played a role on a national stage, his is probably the most familiar name. His life and work was cut short at the early age of 36, but his legacy of papers and specimens, and the interest of his family and friends, ensured that a contemporary record was made of his achievements. His entry in the *Dictionary of National Biography* is witness to his continuing significance for historians. The introduction to this edition of his Book of Games, possibly the most intriguing of his surviving manuscripts, brings together a biographical account which confirms his reputation. It contains much that is new and offers a fresh understanding of his personality and preoccupations. I warmly welcome this publication; the family is grateful to the editors for their interest and the research they have undertaken to make accessible a work which should have been available many years ago.

Willughby's achievements as a scientist have long been overshadowed by the career of his friend John Ray, whose eminence as a natural historian was recognized in his lifetime and remains unquestioned to this day. Historians have debated the issue of their relative contributions to work which in its published form was immediately associated with Willughby in the area of birds and fishes and with Ray on the study of plants and insects. In fact, they worked as partners during Willughby's life and enjoyed a continued form of collaboration in Ray's posthumous edition of Willughby's studies. The loss of so many of the original working papers had made it seem impossible to unravel the true nature of their association, but there is modern correspondence in the family archive which suggests a different view. The circumstances in which Charles Raven completed his outstanding biography of John Ray, written during the war in the face of restrictions on travel and research, meant that he did not know about the surviving Francis Willughby materials until March 1942, when his biography was already in page-proofs. He described his visit to see the Willughby/Ray collections as 'one of the most thrilling experiences of my working life'. As a result, some last-minute additions to the biography were made, but in a letter of 30 April 1942 to my grandfather, then Lord Middleton, he made it clear that much more should be undertaken in the future. 'I'm convinced that Willughby's notes & diaries & memoranda ought to be discoverable. Then it would be clear whether he was the patron or the partner, & how far his knowledge extended. Some day a book on him & his collection must certainly be written.'

In the 60 years since Raven's work appeared more researchers have indeed become interested in Willughby, and his working papers are more readily accessible. Unfortunately, many gaps still remain; it is tantalizing to know that diaries and notebooks once existed that cannot now be traced. A major biographical work would still present a considerable challenge. In these circumstances, the present edition is all the more welcome, particularly in throwing light on an aspect of Willughby's work in which Ray had no immediate hand. At the very least, the Book of Games will introduce Willughby in his own right to a new audience, and will, I hope, stimulate interest in the further study of his life and work.

Michael Willoughby

Preface

Francis Willughby's Book of Games, published here for the first time, is a
work of extraordinary interest. Dating from the 1660s, it was left unfinished
when the writer died in 1672 at the age of 36. Although this circumstance
raises complications in presenting a coherent text, the clarity of the work's
structure and its internal evidence provide unambiguous clues about its
original conception and development. The book's accessibility to a modern
audience is guaranteed by its subject matter – the manner in which games
and recreations of all kinds were pursued. Games of skill and chance,
particularly those involving cards or tables, occupy a substantial section, but
sports, word games and children's games also feature prominently. The
games are for the most part described in sufficient detail to enable the
uninitiated to join the play. Rules are provided, terminology and the words
or phrases used by the players explained, equipment illustrated, and
speculations offered about the origins and significance of obscure aspects.
The information supplied often touches on other features of contemporary
life; the account of cockfighting, for instance, contains much detail about the
care of the birds, and the brief passage on the first games that infants play
provides a rare view of the early development of babies and small children.
In fact, a substantial subsection of the work appears to have been written by
a child, an extremely rare survival of a juvenile voice from the early modern
period. Although there are gaps, in part reflecting the unfinished nature of
the work, Willughby's treatment has a scope and detail which is without
parallel in its period. Its most obvious appeal will be for those interested in
the history of sports, games and recreational pursuits, and for those who in
recent years have extended our understanding of early modern popular and
cultural history.

There is, however, another dimension which will draw other specialists to
this text. Francis Willughby was not writing to educate the gamester
fraternity, but in this as in other enterprises worked as a scientist, a member
of the newly established Royal Society and the friend of eminent intellectual
figures. His educational background at Cambridge and his relatively
comfortable circumstances enabled him to devote his energy and time to
scientific occupation, with the study of the natural world becoming his

principal concern. His best-known contribution was the posthumous *Ornithologia* (1676), edited from his papers by his close friend and collaborator John Ray, whose pre-eminence as a natural historian owed much to the support and patronage of Willughby. The Book of Games shows the application of the same principles of systematic observation, description and classification as developed in his work on natural history. To the enterprise Willughby brought also his mathematical training, particularly in observations on games involving chance. Historians of science, and especially those interested in the Royal Society's work in the 1660s, will find in the Book of Games a number of associations with contemporary scientific concerns.

General questions of interpretation of the Book of Games and its place both in the author's life and work and in the history of writings on games and pastimes are discussed in the Introduction, which also offers a substantial new account of the author's life. Although the main elements in Willughby's life story are well known, the study of this particular text has opened new avenues of approach and made it necessary to re-examine some of the evidence. The intention has been to provide a broad understanding of Willughby within his intellectual circle, and to identify the interests and patterns of working which help our interpretation of the Book of Games. Depending on their individual interests, readers may follow different routes through the Introduction. Some, particularly those pursuing the history of specific games, will find the independent Glossary of Games, which follows the text, an alternative point of access. Those with a more specialist interest in Willughby's scientific contributions are referred to the review of his literary remains in the Bibliography, and the chronological life-table which concludes the Introduction.

The scope and direction of this edition inevitably reflects the background of the editors, who originally began the project working separately and with slightly differing perspectives. Dorothy Johnston, as Keeper of Manuscripts at Nottingham University, first came across the text in the context of the Willoughby family muniments in the Middleton Collection at the University Library and began work on an edition together with David Cram who, as a general linguist, was drawn first to the Collection through research into Willughby's fieldwork on vernacular languages in Europe and his association with the efforts of John Wilkins to develop a universal language based on Real Character. Jeffrey Forgeng, who has worked in lexicography and has a particular interest in the history of sports and games, meanwhile also established a text, with supporting materials concerned particularly with these aspects. The final collaboration of the three editors has not been one of rigid division of responsibilities but has involved each in every section, although some owe more to one hand than another. The partnership has, we believe, enriched the edition itself and the range of ancillary interpretation and illustration. We remain, however, acutely aware that there might have been other approaches and different choices in the focus. We hope that this edition satisfies the interests of a majority of its readers and provides others with sufficient information to support their further study.

David Cram, Jesus College, Oxford
Jeffrey L. Forgeng, Higgins Armory Museum/
Worcester Polytechnic Institute
Dorothy Johnston, University of Nottingham

Acknowledgements

This volume has been in preparation for almost a decade, yielding from time to time to other individual commitments of the three editors. Its completion, and the extent to which it has grown beyond its original conception, is in no small measure due to the enthusiasm and support of friends and colleagues. It would be impossible to name all those who have played their part with encouragement, advice and suggestions – the following acknowledges only the most immediate and general of credits.

Our first debt must be to our institutions which in a variety of ways have assisted our practical needs. Over the years the University of Nottingham, the University of Michigan, Worcester Polytechnic Institute, the Higgins Armory Museum, Massachusetts, and Jesus College, Oxford, have provided travel grants or other resources to enable the project come to fruition.

Advice and assistance has been generously given by staff in the Department of Manuscripts and Special Collections at the University of Nottingham, where the Middleton Collection of Willoughby manuscripts is located, and also by archivists and librarians in many other institutions. We are grateful to all these curators, and particularly to those at Trinity College Cambridge, the Bodleian Library Oxford, the Royal Society, the British Library, East Sussex Record Office, the Record Office for Leicestershire, Leicester and Rutland, and Warwickshire Record Office.

It is particularly difficult to list all those friends and academic colleagues who have in greater or smaller measure participated in this project. We have been acutely conscious that the breadth of possible interest in the Book of Games has taken us into areas beyond our usual expertise, and are grateful to those who in different ways suggested avenues of further investigation, alerted us to related evidence or studies, and commented on early drafts of our own findings. Among those we would particularly like to mention are Thierry Depaulis and Michael Dummet, for advice on the history of card games; Mordechai Feingold, for useful suggestions on early drafts of the Introduction; Werner Hüllen for reading through a draft and making helpful comments; Ruby Reid Thompson, for her guidance on watermark evidence; Peter Seddon, for sharing his extensive knowledge about the Willughby family and Nottinghamshire in the seventeenth century; Narita Pike, for references to ecclesiastical court documents mentioning games in the Nottingham Archdeaconry records; Jackie Stedall and Charles Webster, for comments on mathematical topics. A great debt is also owed to the earlier Willughby biographers, particularly to Mary Welch, formerly of the University of Nottingham, and Michael Hunter, who has revised Willughby's entry for the *Dictionary of National Biography*. In assisting us to publication, we are grateful to Alex MacAulay, who initially took on the project on behalf of Scolar Press, to Tom Gray, who has acted as 'midwife' on behalf of Ashgate, and to Liz Greasby for seeing a complicated text into print.

Finally, an acknowledgement of a different kind must be made to members of the Willoughby family itself, who from the time of his daughter Cassandra Willoughby and his son, Thomas, 1st Lord Middleton, have ensured the survival of a considerable body of Francis Willughby's papers and encouraged interest in his life and work. More specifically, we are grateful to Lord and Lady Middleton and to the Honourable Michael Willoughby for their support of the present project, and most particularly for approving the edition of the manuscript and allowing the use of Gerard Soest's portrait of Francis Willughby as a frontispiece illustration.

Abbreviations

BL	British Library
NUL	Nottingham University Library
DNB	*Dictionary of National Biography*
MED	*Middle English Dictionary*
OED	*Oxford English Dictionary*
Phil. Trans.	*Philosophical Transactions of the Royal Society of London*

Editorial Conventions

The manuscript original of Francis Willughby's Book of Games, written almost entirely in his own clear if idiosyncratic hand, presents few major editorial problems. The text survives in a folio volume with a number of loose sheets and notes attached. It is clearly a work in progress, heavily amended in some parts, and bearing marks referring to other sources or to topics requiring further investigation. The principle behind this edition has been to provide the clearest possible text for a modern reader with the fewest possible changes to the language of the seventeenth-century original. Textual comments concerning authorial changes and uncertain readings are supplied in footnotes, but given the rough and multilayered state of the text we have not attempted to be exhaustive in documenting authorial revision. The footnotes also include a number of interpretative and explanatory notes, primarily to elucidate references in the text; for fuller descriptions of the games in question and for unfamiliar expressions used by Willughby the reader is referred to the Glossary of Games and the Glossary of Technical and Obsolete Terms. In both these glossaries, as in the Introduction, citations of material from the Book of Games use the pagination of the original manuscript.

The transcription has retained Willughby's characteristic spelling patterns, with modifications to capitals and punctuation. His use of capitals is somewhat erratic, even by seventeenth-century standards. With some characters (e.g. *B* or *H*) he regularly uses a capital form, whether the letter is initial or medial in the word; in other cases the capital form of the graph is difficult to distinguish (e.g. *C* or *S* and the problematic digraph *ff*). In the interests of clarity we have normalized the use of capitals at the start of sentences and provided punctuation to clarify sentence breaks and the rendering of numbers and lists. Elsewhere we have not attempted absolute consistency in modifying Willughby's practice; the use of capitals has been restricted to proper names, the names of games and certain game-related expressions, and the introductions of technical terms. Other changes which have been systematically made include the extension of standard word abbreviations (e.g. *against* for *agt*) and the normalization of words with superscript endings (e.g. *which* for *whi^{ch}*). His common rendering of *y^e*, *y^t* and

y^n has been replaced by *the*, *that* and *then*, and his use of *i* as consonant and *v* as vowel has been standardized as *j* and *u*. Any underlining or use of round brackets in the original text has been retained.

The edition does not extend the two common symbols used by Willughby in his text, '*Q*' (quaere) and '*V*' (vide), which indicate points to be further investigated, and references to sources or other parts of the work. The symbol '*X*', sometimes '*X X*', is also rendered as given, indicating either cross-references to other parts of the work or a note to add further information. His use of 'p.', 'P.', 'p:' or 'P:' to introduce page references has been normalized as 'p.'.

Square brackets, without footnote explanation, have been used to indicate text supplied by the editors. Titles are thus supplied in brackets where no name is given by Willughby but its form is provided from his index or description; in addition, on the rare occasions where an identifiable game is not named by Willughby, a constructed title is supplied in italic. To assist reading of what is often presented as crowded notes on a page, line breaks and paragraph formatting have also been introduced. Occasional editorial notes in italic interrupt the body of the text, to explain physical changes concerning the manuscript or the handwriting.

Introduction

The biography of Francis Willughby (1635–1672),[1] author of the Book of
Games, is at once both accessible and obscure. As a member of the Midlands
landed gentry, with estates throughout England, his social identity and
economic base can be examined through his family's archival remains and
other contemporary sources. His family background is well known, and we
can follow in broad outline his ancestral line. We have details of his
educational background and intellectual accomplishments, and can trace his
historical reputation as a natural historian and mathematician. Among his
contacts and friendships we can identify men of influence, themselves public
figures, and know something of their role in his life. A well-rounded picture
emerges from these combined sources, that of a seventeenth-century
'virtuoso' of multi-faceted interests.[2]

At the same time, the surviving evidence falls short, particularly in our
present context. Willughby's premature death at the age of 36 meant that the
two major publications under his name, the *Ornithologia* (1676) and *Historia
Piscium* (1686), were posthumous editions by his more famous collaborator
John Ray (1627–1705). It is no easy matter to establish the extent of Ray's
contribution and the limits of Willughby's; uncertainty on the issue has
engaged historians, with C.E. Raven's authoritative biography of Ray in 1942
establishing an account of their collaboration from the perspective of Ray.
Furthermore, the remarriage of Willughby's widow to Josiah Child
(1630–1699), a man who was unsympathetic if not hostile to Ray, contributed
to the dispersal of Willughby's literary remains. This dispersal was

---

1. Francis Willughby, the naturalist, consistently spelt his name in the form WILLUGHBY, and this
   has been respected in historical sources, although the family name is commonly given as
   WILLOUGHBY. These conventions have been followed in the present edition. Willughby held no
   hereditary title, and was never knighted, although his predecessors were at various times and for
   various reasons dubbed knights. His own father was knighted in Dublin by Sir Arthur Chichester,
   Lord Deputy of Ireland, in 1610 on the occasion of his marriage (Shaw 1906: ii, 150), just one year
   before the rank of baronetage was created by James I to raise money for troops in Ulster. The
   naturalist's eldest son, also Francis, was created baronet in 1677 (*Calendar of State Papers: Domestic
   1677–1678:* 47; patent survives at NUL Mi 4/156/1). No evidence has been found to substantiate
   the claim by Cokayne that the honour was awarded in recognition of his father's writings
   (Cokayne 1904: iv, 85). On his death, the title passed to his brother Thomas, who in 1712 became
   the 1st Lord Middleton.

2. On the notion and identity of the seventeenth-century 'virtuoso' see Houghton (1941b).

compounded by Ray's own efforts to bring his late friend's work to fruition, and his consequent need to have sight of his papers. Further loss continued after the death of Ray, through the well-meaning efforts of William Derham (1657–1735), Ray's early biographer, who industriously sought to acquire relevant correspondence. Cassandra Willughby, daughter of Francis, assisted him by sending letters from her father's study. Derham used such papers selectively, concerned essentially for their relevance to Ray's history, and does not appear to have returned the originals to the family.[3]

These circumstances have combined to impoverish the sources on Francis Willughby, particularly those which would have illuminated his intellectual development. The result poses a particular challenge in approaching Willughby's Book of Games, a work which apparently lacks any mention in the surviving correspondence of his circle and which has, rather surprisingly, been largely unremarked by modern commentators. The Book of Games is in fact a remarkable text, without any precise contemporary parallel, though in conception and execution it is clearly a product of its day. A work of taxonomy written by an original Fellow of the Royal Society, it requires readings at a number of different levels. It reveals him from a variety of perspectives, going beyond his well-known preoccupation with natural history to focus on his curiosity about the human world; it demonstrates his training in making detailed observations and interpreting the results; it exemplifies his interest in a variety of mathematical concerns, including mechanics and probability.

To assist the concerns of different readers, this introduction provides a number of distinct avenues to the text. First, it offers a biographical account, locating the work in the broader context of Willughby's intellectual interests, his methodology, abilities, and associations with contemporary men of scientific inclinations, both eminent and amateur; secondly, it provides an analysis of the text itself, its origins, and its place in Willughby's other works; thirdly, it describes the history of games literature and comments on its relevance for Willughby's study; and, fourthly, it explores the scope of the Book of Games through a survey of associated aspects of the wider intellectual and cultural scene. For ease of reference, a tabulated chronology of the main events in Willughby's life is provided in conclusion.

---

3. See further below Section 2.1, on the fate of Willughby's manuscript papers.

Biographical Background

As a figure of accepted historical significance, Willughby has already been the subject of enquiry, and a number of modern biographical studies are available. The best known are those of G.S. Boulger in the *Dictionary of National Biography* and C.E. Raven in his biography of Willughby's friend and collaborator, *John Ray, Naturalist, his Life and Work*.[4] Two articles by M.A. Welch provide useful supplementary material, particularly concerning the relevant papers in the Middleton Collection now at the University of Nottingham.[5] Together, these accounts have assembled the bulk of the surviving evidence on Willughby's life, drawing on the reports and opinions of his contemporaries as well as archival and printed sources. Central to these discussions has been the question of Willughby's collaboration with John Ray and the assessment of their respective responsibility for the natural history publications on birds and fishes which came out in the name of Willughby, posthumously and under the editorship of Ray. While this is undoubtedly an important issue, the focus upon it has tended to determine the direction taken by each of the writers. So far as we know, Ray played no part in the creation of the Book of Games, although the text does show the hand of other contributors. Furthermore, its content shows Willughby in pursuit of interests which on the face of it are very different from those featured in their collaborative studies. To understand the intent behind the Book of Games, and the process of its compilation, the focus must be on Willughby himself, not on his role within a partnership. In the present context, therefore, while the work of these modern biographers provides our starting point, the perspective of the study is inevitably different.

The manner in which the evidence and comments of seventeenth-century contemporaries have informed the biographical tradition is significant, for the two principal sources are both authoritative and sympathetic, and have given the basis of a biographical sketch which is surprisingly little altered in the modern accounts. The first is the memoir by Ray himself, who in his

---

4. We are grateful to Michael Hunter for allowing us sight of his revisions to Boulger's article for the *New Dictionary of National Biography*, currently in press.

5. Welch (1972: 71–85; 1977: 33–40); see also her entry in the *Dictionary of Scientific Biography* (Welch 1981).

position as posthumous editor of Willughby's work on birds provided a prefatory essay to the *Ornithologia* in honour of his late patron and friend.[6] Ray's efforts to secure backing for the publication of Willughby's researches ensured that, despite his friend's premature death and lack of any substantial scholarly contribution in print, his personal reputation among contemporaries did not die with him. In his biographical tribute Ray praises Willughby both for his character and his abilities. He describes how he had studied to the injury of his health:

hence it came to pass that he attained very good skill in all parts of learning, and particularly got a deep insight into those Sciences which are most abstruse and impervious to Vulgar Capacities, I mean the most subtil parts of the Mathematicks. Of his skill in Natural Philosophy, chiefly the History of Animals, [Birds, Beasts, Fishes, and Insects,] … it hath not yet been my hap to meet with any man either in *England* or beyond Seas of so general and comprehensive knowledge therein.

(Willughby 1678: A2)

Ray comments how, in his travels in England and Wales and on his subsequent continental trip, Willughby 'did himself accurately describe all the Animals he could find or procure' so successfully 'that not many sorts of Animals described by others escaped his diligence'. He intended to extend his research to North America, but was prevented from doing so by his premature death (Willughby 1678: A2).

The second account, from quite a different perspective, is the description by his daughter Cassandra, who compiled a history of the Willoughby family, bringing the narrative down to her own time.[7] Cassandra apparently began to write her two-volume work some 30 years after her father's death, continuing the task until at least 1721.[8] She had been a child aged two when he died, so it is necessarily a second-hand perspective, but she had the advantage of surviving papers (many now lost) and family memories to add more intimate details to his public reputation, for which she drew largely upon Ray. Her contribution is unique in describing Willughby as he was known within his most immediate family circle, although she is unable to be precise about dates and events, and regrets that Ray did not provide more details in his description. Part of the special value of Cassandra's account lies in the fullness of her picture of the Willoughby family's development and of its marriage alliances in the seventeenth century in particular. She describes a close-knit group. The account of her grandparents (drawn from their letters and other evidence, now lost) and of her own more recent recollections allow

---

6. Willughby (1676: Praefatio); subsequently published in an English edition (1678: Preface).

7. Cassandra Willughby's account survives in two manuscript volumes; NUL Mi LM 26, 27. Selections from the first can be found in Stevenson (1911: 504–10). The second volume, published in full, describes the lives of successive members of the family, including a section about her father (Wood 1958: ch. 7). For convenience the present study cites Wood, with the exception of a few occasions when the original manuscript is quoted to clarify obscurities in the text.

8. The date 1702 is written at the start of the first volume and a passage in the second volume mentions the current year as 1720 (Wood 1958: xi). A reference to the passing of 25 years since the death of her aunt Lettice Wendy (1627–1696) would indicate that the account of her father, which follows this passage, was composed in the early 1720s (Wood 1958: 100).

us to speculate upon the various familial influences upon her father, as well as providing practical details about his domestic life. Other early memoirs, which Cassandra acknowledges and quotes from extensively, such as that in Anthony Wood's *Athenae Oxonienses* (1691), were also indebted to Ray, while including additional details from other sources.

1.1 Family context

The essential details of Willughby's early biography are easily summarized. He was born at the family seat of Middleton, in Warwickshire, on 22 November 1635, the only son of Sir Francis Willoughby (1590–1665) and his wife Cassandra (*c*. 1600–1675). He had two elder sisters; Lettice, who married Sir Thomas Wendy of Haslingfield in Cambridgeshire, and Catherine, who married Clement Winstanley of Braunstone, Leicestershire. Sir Francis and Lady Cassandra were the first of the Willoughbys to make their home at Middleton, for the Willoughbys were primarily a Nottinghamshire family, with their principal seat at Wollaton, a few miles south-west of Nottingham. The family's origins can be traced back to the early thirteenth century, to Ralph Bugge, a Nottingham wool merchant. His acquisition of land in Willoughby on the Wolds led ultimately to the change in the family name to 'de Willoughby', and began a process of property expansion which was successfully continued by his descendants. By marriage alliances and by careful financial and legal management the Willoughbys had by the late sixteenth century built up an extensive estate ranging across more than 20 counties. Middleton and the Warwickshire estates were acquired through marriage into the Freville family in the fifteenth century. The new Wollaton Hall, built for Sir Francis Willoughby (1546–1596) by the architect Robert Smythson (1535–1614) in the 1580s, was an impressive statement of the family's social identity and aspirations. Without male heirs, Sir Francis, dubbed 'The Builder', ensured continuity of his line by arranging the marriage of his daughter Bridget to a distant cousin, Percival Willoughby, of Kent, who was descended from the Willoughby d'Eresby family. It was at Wollaton Hall that Percival Willoughby, grandfather of the naturalist, was knighted by James I in 1603 (Wood 1958: 37).

The family's archival remains include an impressive quantity of evidence, particularly in the form of deeds which chart the pattern of land acquisition. Records about the management or revenue of these lands are more patchy, and a full analysis of the economic base of the Willoughby estate and the family's fluctuating resources in the sixteenth and seventeenth centuries has yet to be undertaken.[9] The family had extensive coal-mining interests in Nottinghamshire, and under the naturalist's great-grandfather Sir Francis

---

9. Smith's studies of the family's coal-mining interests in the Tudor and early Stuart periods demonstrate the impact of their industrial investments and illustrate some of the difficulties of assessing their landed income (Smith 1964; 1989).

Willoughby in the late sixteenth century industrial investment was extended to several other enterprises, including iron ore and woad, the latter used to produce a blue dye for textiles.[10]

The building of Wollaton Hall had, however, been an extravagant enterprise and Sir Francis fell deeply into debt, his difficulties compounded by his grand style of life, by the falling revenues of the Wollaton coal pits, and by unsuccessful entrepreneurial ventures. He left his son-in-law an impoverished estate. Even with the resources of his Kentish patrimony, which was sacrificed to maintain his Midlands inheritance, Sir Percival and his family lived in financial embarrassment.[11] When in 1615 he settled Middleton upon Sir Francis and Lady Cassandra, they found the estate heavily encumbered, but good management enabled them to clear the debts and to establish themselves in comfort.[12] Economy was evidently a major element in the decision not to return to Wollaton and refurbish it after Sir Percival died in 1643, within a year of a serious fire in the hall. Lady Bridget, Sir Percival's widow, joined her son's family at Middleton, and Wollaton was to see only occasional family visits until the naturalist's children, Francis and Cassandra, established themselves there in 1687. After the sudden death of the young Sir Francis in 1688, Wollaton remained the home of Cassandra and the new heir, her brother Thomas, who continued to live there after he was elevated to the peerage as the 1st Lord Middleton in 1712.

1.2 Education and university contacts

Francis Willughby, the naturalist, received his early schooling locally at Sutton Coldfield, where William Hill, a classical scholar of some note, had been master since 1640.[13] Contemporary accounts claim that he showed early promise and that his family encouraged his talents. It was a family in which education was valued, as Cassandra Willoughby observes in writing of the care taken by Sir Percival in the schooling of his children. Francis Willughby's further education followed the pattern of his father and other family members, with attendance both at university and one of the Inns of Court.[14] On 9 September 1652 he was admitted fellow commoner at Trinity College,

---

10. The ironworks and woad-growing entrepreneurial ventures of Sir Francis Willoughby are described in Smith (1961; 1967).

11. A summary of the family fortunes at the turn of the seventeenth century can be found in Smith (1988).

12. Wood (1958: 87–8). Francis Willughby in his will asks for a memorial to be erected in Middleton Church for his parents 'for there care in breeding up of there children and recovering the estate that was utterly ruined in the eye of the world' (NUL Mi 4/149/15).

13. Described by Cassandra Willoughby as 'the most famous schoolmaster of his time', William Hill (1619–1667) graduated MA Oxford 1641. He later became master of St Patrick's School Dublin, and edited many classical texts for school use (Wood 1958: 103; DNB).

14. His father had been educated at Magdalene College, Oxford, and Lincoln's Inn (Foster 1892: iv, 1651).

Cambridge, and graduated BA in 1655–56.[15] His tutor was James Duport (1606–1679), who in 1660 dedicated his *Gnomologia Homeri* to Francis Willughby and three other fellow commoners, all of them holding aristocratic titles or landed estates (Duport 1660: sig. a2–b2).[16] Duport's regard for Willughby is further demonstrated in two Latin poems. The first, written in Willughby's last years, refers back to the enthusiasm with which even as a student he had pursued science and learning; reins to restrain him were more appropriate than spurs to goad him. Duport reminds him that addiction to study is a form of excess and recommends that he look after his health and enjoy his family and his houses at Wollaton and Middleton. In a second poem, written after Willughby's death, Duport recalls how frequently, but without effect, he had urged his favourite student to moderate his reading and take care of his health. Willughby had been, he claims, 'bitten by the snake of learning' (Duport 1676: 315–17, 495).[17]

Apart from such retrospective comments, little is known of Willughby's Cambridge years, though much can be inferred from our knowledge of his associates and from subsequent events. One influence of importance was certainly Isaac Barrow (1614–1680), the renowned mathematical and classical scholar who was then a tutor at Trinity.[18] Willughby's taste for mathematical speculation, so evident in the Book of Games, led to a friendship with Barrow, who in 1655 dedicated his edition of *Euclid's Elements* to Willughby, together with Edward Cecil and John Knatchbull (Barrow 1655: A3). After Willughby had left Cambridge he continued to correspond with Barrow on mathematical matters.[19]

Another of the Trinity tutors was John Ray, himself a former pupil of Duport's.[20] Ray's botanical interests, begun after illness in 1650, occupied him increasingly in the following decade, leading to the publication in 1660 of *Catulogus Plantarum circa Cantabrigiam nascentium*, a work in which he pays tribute to the collaboration of friends, including both Willughby and Peter Courthope, another of Ray's Cambridge associates who became a lifelong friend (Ray 1660: sig. *6). Courthope (1639–1725), a distant relative of Willughby's, was admitted a fellow commoner at Trinity College in 1655 (Venn 1927: i, 405). He left Cambridge without graduation in 1657 on his inheritance of the family estate at Danny, in Sussex (Gunther 1937: 343–5).

---

15. Venn 1927: iv, 423; he may have taken his degree at any time between November 1655 and October 1656: the college records of this date do not give a precise graduation date (personal communication from the College Librarian, D.J. McKitterick, 14 May 1996).

16. The other dedicatees (Edward Cecil, John Knatchebull and Henry Puckering) similarly followed their studies at Trinity College, Cambridge with membership of one of the Inns of Court.

17. We are grateful to Wolfgang de Melo for advice on the interpretation of rhetorical allusions in these texts.

18. Barrow was appointed to the chair of Greek at Cambridge in 1660, and subsequently became the first Lucasian professor of mathematics in 1665, resigning this latter post in favour of his pupil Isaac Newton in 1669.

19. Two letters from Barrow to Willughby, concerning technical mathematical topics and with detailed geometrical diagrams, are printed in Derham (1718: 360, 362–5).

20. Ray graduated BA in 1647–48 and was appointed Greek Lecturer in 1651, Mathematical Lecturer and Tutor in 1653 and Humanities Lecturer in 1655.

Intermittent entries in the college accounts show that he was again in Cambridge from 3 February 1659 to 14 December 1660, and he wrote from Trinity College to Willughby on 17 March 1660 with news of friends and scientific experiments.[21] The six surviving letters from Willughby to Courthope speak not only of their family association but of their common interests; both were men whose family fortunes were linked to land and industry, while they shared a taste for the scientific pursuits of Ray and his circle.[22] Ray's subsequent correspondence with Courthope includes a number of references to Willughby and their joint activities.[23]

Two other men who were in future years to be associated with the work of both Ray and Willughby appeared in Cambridge at this time. In April 1653 a Nathaniel Bacon of Suffolk was admitted pensioner at Trinity; he has been identified as the Nathaniel Bacon who later accompanied Willughby on his tour of the Continent.[24] Two years later, Philip Skippon (1641–1691), son of the more famous general of that name, was admitted as fellow commoner at the college. Skippon, like Courthope, was to be numbered among Willughby's friends, although in his case it is possible that the friendship did not start until they were brought together in 1662 as Ray's travelling companions.[25] Ray's influence in the circle was important from the start. He formed the centre of a group whose scientific investigations were already known to a wider circle of scholars in Oxford and beyond.[26] There can be little doubt that ties were forged during the 1650s at Cambridge which were later to hold these men in sympathy and common intellectual interest.

The years at Cambridge were followed in Willughby's case by study at Gray's Inn, where he was admitted on 21 May 1657 (Foster 1889: 283). The combination of university residence with a period in one of the Inns of Court was a familiar pattern in the education of an heir to a significant landed estate. Peter Courthope, his cousin, was meantime following a similar route, having been admitted a member of the Inner Temple in 1655 (Inner Temple 1877: 356). Gray's Inn was perhaps a natural choice for Francis Willughby of Middleton: other Willughby names from Nottinghamshire and Warwickshire can be found in its registers about this time (Foster 1889: 263, 266, 272).

---

21. Information about residence supplied in personal communication from D.J. McKitterick, 14 May 1996; Derham (1718: 357–8).

22. The letters are in the East Sussex Record Office (ACC 5653/1/1–6); we are grateful to Philip Bye, Senior Archivist, for details about these items, enabling their collation with the extracts published by Gunther (see below, Bibliography A). Courthope's uncle, Walter Burrell of Cuckfield, was 'one of the chief iron-masters of Sussex', and contributed information for the article on iron working appended to Ray's *Collection of English Words* (1674: 129). His brother Thomas Burrell was also associated with Ray's later work (Raven 1950: 52, n. 2).

23. Twenty-one letters from Ray to Courthope survive (East Sussex Record Office DAN 344–64); 17 of these are published in Gunther (1928), and two further ones in Gunther (1937).

24. Venn (1927: i, 65). There were four students of this name at Cambridge between 1648 and 1661, but this has been judged the likeliest candidate (Raven 1950: 131).

25. For an account of Willughby, Courthope and Skippon in their roles as pupils and friends of John Ray see Raven (1950: 50–53). Ray was initially uncertain whether Willughby would find Skippon a congenial companion; see letter to Courthope, in Gunther (1937: 374–5).

26. Raven (1950: 37–8, 54 n. 5), quoting a letter from John Worthington to Samuel Hartlib, and citing Hartlib's report to Robert Boyle of Worthington's news from Cambridge.

Although no details survive to show precisely the dates of his attendance or to give an individual account of the experience of membership, we can assume that it followed the usual pattern.[27] We can also be fairly sure about some important contacts which he may have made here. In at least one case a man who later became a friend of Willughby's and executor of his will may have been encountered for the first time through common membership of the Inn, if that much can be deduced from the presence of Francis Jessop (1638–1691), of Broom Hall, near Sheffield. He became a member on 11 March 1656, a year before Francis Willughby's own admission (Foster 1889: 276, 283). Jessop was at Greenwich in 1658, where he made a drawing of a stranded whale, an illustration which survives with Willughby's collections of natural history illustrations.[28] Nathaniel Bacon, one of the younger sons of Nicholas Bacon of Shrubland, Suffolk, was admitted to Gray's Inn on 15 November 1655. It has been plausibly suggested that this was the previously mentioned Nathaniel Bacon of Trinity College.[29]

Although we cannot with certainty trace Willughby's movements in the late 1650s, we know something of his activities. He stayed on at Cambridge longer than was usual for a fellow commoner, and received his MA in 1659.[30] These years partially overlapped with the Cambridge period of John Wilkins (1614–1672), formerly Warden of Wadham College, Oxford, who was appointed Master of Trinity College, Cambridge, in August 1659 and held office until ousted after the Restoration of 1660. His acquaintance with Willughby, presumably begun at this time, was to become both a collaboration and a lifelong friendship. It may also have been at this time that Willughby first became acquainted with the work of the Cambridge platonist, Henry More (1614–1687). More's significance for Ray is well known.[31] Whether Willughby knew him personally is not recorded, but is perhaps implied in the evidence that Willughby wrote to him in 1670, in connection with the controversial writings of Henry Stubbe (1632–1676), who had singled More out for particular criticism.[32] By 1660 Willughby was

---

27. On the Inns of Court as 'England's Third University' see Baker (1990); for a dated but still useful account see Pearce (1855); the educational experience of the gentry at both university and Inns of Court is reviewed in Heal and Holmes (1994: 261–73).

28. NUL Mi LM 25/16. Jessop became a friend also of Ray's, and was one of those who supplied material for the second edition of Ray's Collection of English Proverbs (1678²: iv). On Jessop, see further Armytage (1952) and Davison (1956).

29. Foster (1889: 275); Venn (1927: i, 65); see also Raven (1950: 131, n. 4).

30. College residence was not required for this degree, but the college accounts indicate his presence, showing him owing money to the buttery between December 1658 and January 1660 (personal communication of D.J. McKitterick). The second edition of Wood's Athenae Oxonienses contains an additional footnote, citing manuscript notes by Revd Thomas Baker (1656–1740) of St John's College: 'He is M^r of Arts also, having continued a longer time in the university than usually fellow-commoners do. But he is lately gone from the university. His father is a Knight in Warwickshire and would have him in the country to settle there, he being his only son' (Wood 1813–20²: ii, 246).

31. More's Antidote against Atheisme (1653) has been identified as the starting point for Ray's Wisdom of God (1691) (Raven 1950: 458–61).

32. The letter is not extant but More mentions it, together with a letter from Joseph Glanvill on the same subject, when writing to Lady Anne Conway on 6 August [1670] (Hutton 1992: 303).

certainly familiar with More's published work; extracts from his writings can be found in Willughby's Commonplace Book, in terms suggesting a sympathy with More's views.[33] Willughby also mentions More by name in the Book of Games (p. 5). Whatever the nature of such wider intellectual contacts, Willughby certainly continued to be occupied during the late 1650s in scientific experiments with Ray; entries in his Commonplace Book recording chemical experiments dated between 28 November 1658 and March 1659 are annotated as being 'by Mr Wray'.[34] His involvement in Ray's botanical researches also developed new areas of interest. On 25 February 1660 Ray wrote to Willughby, now back in residence at Middleton, to ask if he would locate and catalogue botanical specimens in Warwickshire and Nottinghamshire, to be part of his planned county flora (Lankester 1848: 1–3).

The fieldtrip made by Ray and Willughby, probably in August and early September 1660, has been described by Raven as a 'turning point' in the lives of both men, determining the partnership of interests which would follow (Raven 1950: 116). Using the evidence of subsequent journeys and from notes of specimen discoveries, Raven has reconstructed the probable route of this first joint expedition, which took them, he suggests, north through Yorkshire into Cumberland and across to the Isle of Man, returning via the Wyre estuary and south through Lancashire.[35] The primary purpose was to make a study of the natural history of the areas and to collect botanical specimens, but such journeys were bound to be occasions for the observation of all manner of local customs and curiosities. Their variety is most fully recorded for the later continental journey, which includes detailed descriptions of towns visited, cultural differences, and local occupations and institutions as well as antiquarian sights. Curiosity to investigate any unusual report was always liable to interrupt an expedition; on the 1662 trip, for instance, Willughby was diverted from his route to inspect a coin hoard (Lankester 1848: 5–6).

At some point during these years Willughby also made contact with Joseph Glanvill (1636–1680), the Oxford divine, who wrote attacking the dogmatism of scholastic philosophy and in defence of the new empirical science. A more than passing acquaintance seems indicated in the prefatory address to Glanvill's *Lux Orientalis* (1662), which he dedicated, no doubt with an eye to possible patronage, to 'the much Honoured and Ingenious Francis Willoughby Esquire'.[36] Glanvill offers as explanation 'that delight & satisfaction that I have received in discoursing with you on such matters; and knowing that your noble genius is gratified by such kind of speculations'. He adds:

---

33. Records of Willughby's reading include, for example, extracts from More's *Mystery of Godliness* (1660) in notes attached to NUL Mi LM 15/1 p. 124.

34. NUL Mi LM 15/1, especially pp. 404–15, 436–9.

35. For dating of this journey, see Welch (1977: 34), correcting Raven (1950: 116) on the basis of archival evidence.

36. Thanks are due to Mordechai Feingold for drawing our attention to this preface.

I know you love to be dealing in high and genrous *Theories*, even where your self are a dissenter [...] amidst the flowing aboundance of the world's blessings with which you are encircled, you can yet dedicate your selfe to your beloved *contemplations*; and look upon the furniture and accomplishments of the mind, as better riches, than the largest doals of fortune, and the wealth and Revenues of an ample inheritance.

(Glanvill 1662: A3v–A4)

He does not imply that an intellectual curiosity about speculative philosophies was at odds with the empirical study of the natural world but, on the contrary, extols Willughby's capacities in this regard:

To be reviewing the Recesses of Nature, & the beauteous inside of the universe, is a more manly, yea *angelick* felicity, then the highest *gratifications* of the *senses*; an happinesse, that is common to the youthful *Epicure*, with his Hounds and Horses, yea your ends are more August and generous, then to terminate in the private pleasure you take, even in those *Philosophical Researches*; For you are meditating a more general good, in those careful & profound inquiries you are making into *Animals*, & other concerning affairs of nature, which I hope one day the world will be advantag'd by.

(Glanvill 1662: A4v–A5r)

A scholarly interest in the natural world did not constrain Willughby within narrow boundaries, any more than it did his friend John Ray.

These comments help us to interpret the records of Willughby's visit to Oxford University in 1660, when he consulted rare works in the library.[37] Derham, in his *Memorials of John Ray*, claims that Willughby's purpose in studying at Oxford was to read works on natural history, in an attempt to undertake for zoology what Ray was accomplishing for botany (Lankester 1846: 15). While there is no doubting Willughby's interest in zoology, he was in fact pursuing broader interests at this time. Evidence survives in the shape of at least some of the notes he made on his reading at Oxford, complete with their library call marks, in papers found with his Commonplace Book. They show him consulting authors on a wide range of scientific and theological subjects, including some works on astronomy which are referred to in the Book of Games, and related texts on magic and judicial astrology.[38] Although his study touches on what seem to be unconventional interests for a natural historian, it was entirely in line with the pursuits of contemporary scientists. Indeed, as Charles Webster has established, this period saw 'a late outburst of judicial astrology, the continuing flourishing of Paracelsian medicine, undiminished appeal of alchemy and hermeticism, and the full fruition of Cambridge Platonism' (Webster 1982: 10).

When reading at the university library, Willughby would undoubtedly have made the acquaintance of Thomas Hyde (1636–1703), another

---

37. The length of his stay is not known, but he was apparently in residence in September; see his letter to Courthope on 26 September (Gunther 1928: 17–18).

38. For instance, sources used by him, with their Oxford library references, include d'Abana (1550), Cocles (1550) (NUL Mi LM 15/1 p. 243).

Cambridge graduate,[39] who had been appointed under-keeper in 1659 (MacRay 1984: 127). Hyde was a distinguished orientalist whose later publications demonstrate his interest in both astronomy and the history of games: in 1665 he produced an edition of a Persian astronomical treatise (Hyde 1665; Birch 1756–57: i, 412–13); his pioneering work on the origins of the game of chess appeared in 1689, to be incorporated in a larger work on oriental games in 1694. Wood reported that he was planning a further work on the history of playing cards, *Historia Chartiludii: & Dissertatio de Numerorum Notis earundemque Origine & Combinandi Ratione* (Wood 1813–20: i, 525), the proposed title indicating a mathematical approach to the subject intriguingly close to Willughby's own.

1.3 Collaboration with John Ray; travels and widening circles

Willughby's collaborative contacts with Ray clearly affected the direction of his early scientific interests. In 1662 a more sustained partnership was begun, following a profound change in Ray's personal circumstances. The crisis came in August when Ray resigned his college offices, following his refusal to subscribe to the Act of Uniformity.[40] The dilemma had been facing him for some time, and lay in the background during his third fieldtrip, on which he was accompanied by Willughby and Philip Skippon. The expedition, in May–June 1662, took them from Cambridge via Middleton, through Staffordshire into Cheshire and north Wales, then south to Haverfordwest and Tenby.[41] The expedition was a decisive occasion for both men, being the point at which they made a commitment to embark upon a joint plan for the classification of the natural world, with Willughby to concentrate on the animal kingdom, Ray on plants.[42] These plans meant that from this summer onwards they were regularly together, often with Ray in residence at Middleton. The division of labour signalled here has a double significance; not only does it identify their respective responsibilities for the subject areas involved, but it also describes a manner of working which was to characterize their collaboration.

In addition to its significance for Willughby's friendship with Ray, there is persuasive circumstantial evidence that the 1662 trip has a special relevance for the Book of Games. As we shall see, both his description of Stowball and Skippon's account of Hurling are likely to have been made on this occasion,

---

39. Hyde had been a student at Queen's College Cambridge, matriculated 1654, created MA 1659. He migrated to Oxford in 1658 where he became reader of Hebrew at Queen's College (Foster 1892: ii, 783; Wood 1813–20: i, 523).

40. On Ray and the Act of Uniformity see Raven (1950: 58–61) and McMahon (2000).

41. Ray's travel diary concerning this trip is printed in Lankester (1846: 163–205). A different itinerary the previous year had also seen Ray travelling with Skippon, but without Willughby, although Lankester mistakenly includes him in the company (ibid.: 131–63).

42. As subsequently reported by Ray to William Derham (Lankester 1846: 33); Raven discusses the significance of this expedition for the future partnership of Willughby and Ray (Raven 1950: 123).

the latter observed after Ray and Skippon left Willughby in Gloucestershire and continued their journey into Devon and Cornwall.

On the 1662 expedition, Willughby cut short his journey, after falling ill at Malvern (Lankester 1848: 5–6; Gunther 1937: 376). It appears that he responded to this evidence of his vulnerable state of health with a sense of urgency in action, rather than an inclination to conserve his energies. April 1663 found him again in company with Ray and Skippon, and, joined now by Nathaniel Bacon, ready to embark for the Continent. Willughby, who seems to have been the prime mover behind this venture, tried unsuccessfully to persuade Peter Courthope to join them despite his estate responsibilities, arguing that the difficulty of settling affairs to run smoothly in one's absence should not stand in his way: 'that does not move me at all, when I consider that time and youth are not to be bought' (Gunther 1928: 36). Their route took them through Flanders to Germany, Switzerland and Italy, where they spent the winter. In April, after viewing Naples and Vesuvius, the travellers parted; Ray and Skippon set out for Sicily and Malta leaving Willughby and Bacon to continue their tour in Italy.[43] In Rome Willughby collected illustrations of fish, to be added to those from Germany and Switzerland.[44] By 31 August he was on the French–Spanish border and spent the next ten weeks travelling through Spain.

A continental expedition of this kind was not, of course, uncommon for young men of Willughby's background. Many accounts from the seventeenth century describe the experiences of travellers abroad, providing rich detail of the places seen and the people met. Occasion was taken to observe and record not only sights which impressed, but also the varying nature of political, social and economic structures. Activities which were not pursued at home or were conducted there in a different way were of particular interest. Visits were made to famous places of learning, and introductions allowed the travellers to make direct contact with persons of repute or station. Skippon's narrative of their experiences records several such occasions. One of the earliest took place on 29 May 1663: 'We made a visit to monsieur *Hugenius* his house, having a letter of recommendation to his second son *Christianus Hugenius* a learned astronomer and virtuoso, who was at this time in *England*'. The travellers were shown various scientific instruments belonging to Christiaan Huygens (1629–1695), including a pneumatic engine and the telescope with which he made his famous observations concerning Saturn's ring (Skippon 1732: 393). A couple of months later, in Mannheim, they were received by the Prince Palatine, Willughby having brought with him a letter of recommendation from John Wilkins, who had been chaplain to the Prince when in England (Skippon 1732: 432, 440). On 24 July they inspected the Prince Palatine's library in

---

43. The chronology, as Raven indicates, is clear from Skippon's later account, although Derham mistakenly claims that the friends separated at Montpellier (Raven 1950: 134; Skippon 1732: vi, 609; Lankester 1846: 16).

44. For descriptions of these and related collections see Welch (1972: 80–81).

Heidelberg, and were shown his collection of coins. Later, in Rome, after the travellers had separated, Ray and Skippon visited the German Jesuit, Athanasius Kircher, at the Collegium Romanum, where they saw all his works, both printed and manuscript, and various rarities including a supposed perpetual motion machine (Skippon 1732: 672–4).[45] Ray was sceptical about Kircher's scholarship, and later refers to him in a letter to Edward Lhuyd as a 'credulous person' (Gunther 1928: 211). Nevertheless, Willughby in the Book of Games (p. 9) makes a note to enquire whether Kircher's writings include anything relevant to games.

Foreign travel could be as hazardous as it was instructive. The itinerary was, from the start, determined by the state of war then prevailing with France. There was discomfort and personal risk at many stages, particularly with travellers so intrepidly determined to investigate their surroundings. Illness could affect plans: Bacon caught smallpox and Ray suffered an attack of fever in Rome (Ray 1673: 694; Raven 1950: 135 n). Willughby's letter to Ray in 1664, recounting his journey into Spain, gives few details of the difficulties encountered, remarking merely that he had 'escaped very well all along' (Lankester 1848: 7–9). In 1685, when trying to complete his edition of *Historia Piscium*, Ray tells Tancred Robinson about the loss of his notes of natural history observations from their journey through the Netherlands and Germany (Lankester 1848: 166). Details of the scale of this disaster can be gleaned from a letter sent in 1665 by Edward Browne to his father, and mentioning his recent encounter with Ray in Rome:

Mr Wray hath made a collection of plants, fishes, foules, stones and other rarities, which he hath with him; and Mr Skippon, beside a great number he hath sent home, though they had the ill fortune to loos one venture with a servant of their who is now slaue in Tunes.

(Browne 1835–36: i, 86)

Although the loss of such valuable research data was a real catastrophe, other observations, collections and records did survive from the continental tour. It was, despite the setbacks, a successful venture, which greatly extended their experience and brought them reputation and wider contacts.

Ray, Skippon and Willughby all left written narratives of their experiences during all or parts of the period, in Willughby's case, confined to his months in Spain.[46] Even Nathaniel Bacon left evidence of their industry; his sketch at Genoa of a 'Pesce Trombette' was probably not his only contribution to the recorded observations.[47] Ray's principal concern was, of course, with the botanical observations and collections; his inclusion in his travel diary of a

---

45. Perpetual motion machines were currently of interest. Willughby himself, for example, used a page at the end of the Book of Games (p. 384) to draw a diagram of what appears to be such a device.

46. Willughby's account of his travels on his own, after parting from his friends, was published together with Ray's own narrative (Ray 1673: 466–99). A letter from Willughby to Ray shows his particular interest in local industries (Lankester 1848: 7–9). Skippon's account was published posthumously, in Skippon (1732: vi, 359–736).

47. Now with the other illustrations collected by Willughby (NUL Mi LM 25/2). The fish in question is the Scolpax Rondeletii, described in the *Historia Piscium* on pp. 160–61 and illustrated Tab. I 25.

general narrative of the tour was, according to Raven, prompted by a need to give the publication more general appeal by offering descriptions of places visited and their histories and occupations, details recorded at Willughby's request, who for instance asks Ray at one point to 'get the exact government of all the towns' (Raven 1950: 131; Lankester 1848: 9). Evidence has also survived in other ways, as for example in documents which relate to arrangements for the trip.[48]

The most important survivals are those manuscripts which show Willughby and his companions using the opportunity of foreign travel to investigate scientific and philosophical issues. During the winter of 1663–64 the party took advantage of a visit to Padua University to extend their knowledge of medicine and dissection. Willughby matriculated at the university, where a Dr Charles Willoughby was then in residence.[49] The travellers attended anatomy demonstrations by Pietro Marchetti between 10 December 1663 and 2 January 1664; notes of the dissections and lectures, with corrections and annotations in Willughby's hand, survive with his papers.[50] In addition to making their own observations the travellers also purchased engravings and paintings of birds and fishes as well as specimens of dried plants. This was again a joint undertaking. As Ray, in the Preface to his *Observations topographical* points out, their investigations followed agreed lines, each focusing on complementary areas of their common enterprise:

What Birds, Beasts, Fishes and Insects I observed abroad, whether common to us in *England*, or peculiar to other Countries, I have forborn to set down, because the taking notice and describing of them was the particular design and business of that excellent person Mr *Francis Willughby* lately deceased; and he having prepared store of materials for a *History of Animals*, and likewise digested them into a convenient method, that work [...] is intended to be made public.

(Ray 1673: Preface)

Some of these illustrations were indeed used in the posthumous natural history editions by Ray after Willughby's death, and also in his own later publications.[51] In his preface to the *Ornithology* (1678) he provides details of some of the continental sources from which Willughby obtained images of birds.

The hands of Willughby and Skippon are responsible for a bundle of manuscripts which record another type of collaborative work, the sampling of various foreign languages. Already when in Wales in 1662 Willughby had

---

48. Willughby's passport survives, and several letters of introduction (NUL Mi 4/149a/1 and Mi 4/149a/2/1–5).

49. The matriculation certificate is preserved (NUL Mi F 10/6). Whether, or how, Willughby was related to Charles Willoughby, who made his subsequent career in Ireland, is unknown. Charles Willoughby (c. 1630–1694) graduated MD from Padua in 1663 and is recorded as elected to the Royal Society in July 1663 (Birch 1756–57: i, xliv).

50. Willughby's copy of manuscript notes in English describing the anatomy demonstrations includes a reference to the role of 'Dr Willoughby's man' (NUL Mi LM 15/2). Ray's anatomy notes from Padua were posthumously published in *Phil. Trans.* 1706: vol. 25, no. 307, 2283–2303.

51. For further details of the material collected and purchased by Willughby on the Continent see Welch (1972).

collected a sample of Welsh words. On the Continent they continued this in a systematic way. Using a Latin prompt list of some 500 words of core vocabulary, they obtained from informants comparative samples of a variety of European tongues.[52] Examples of Maltese and 'Romauntsh' (Lingua Rhætia) collected by Skippon using the same prompt list were printed in his travel diaries (Skippon 1732: vi, 624–6, 197–9). Such investigations sprang from contemporary preoccupation with the origin and diversity of language, a concern which had many manifestations. Ray's contribution to the study of English dialects is well known,[53] but for Willughby and Skippon, too, the gathering of linguistic data seems to have been an integral part of their observation of both occupational and leisure activities, an aspect which lends a powerful immediacy to their descriptions of the playing of games.[54]

1.4 Willughby and the Royal Society

Willughby was among the earlier members of the Royal Society, which dates its official foundation to 28 November 1660 when a proposal to found 'a college for the promoting of physico-mathematicall experimentall learning' was adopted.[55] John Wilkins, who had chaired the meeting supporting this resolution, proposed Willughby a year later on 20 November 1661 as a candidate for membership. He was admitted on 4 December following, seven months before the date of the Society's first charter on 15 July 1662.[56] The Royal Society and the network of members it offered played an important role throughout the latter part of his life. The first record of his attendance was in October 1662. The continental travels, which began in April 1663, kept him away until January 1665, but absence did not wholly break his contact. At a meeting on 9 March 1664, Wilkins, then Secretary, proposed that the Society write to Willughby and his companions asking that they make a detour to Tenerife to undertake certain astronomical observations.[57] On 30 March the Society nominated Willughby to join a new Committee on Trades, which was established to investigate all activities in industry, manufacture and husbandry that involved processes of scientific interest (Birch 1756–57: i, 407). On 4 January 1665, 'home from his travels', Willughby presented to the

---

52. The samples collected by Willughby are preserved in the family archive at Nottingham University (NUL Mi 4/149a/3). On the methodology of the word lists, see Cram (1990); the Welsh lists are examined in Cram and Awbery (2001). It is worth noting that Ray's trilingual *Dictionariolum* (1675) was based on the same prompt list as used by Willughby for his language samples from abroad.

53. Ray published a collection of English proverbs (1670) and his *Collection of English Words* (1674) has been described as 'the starting point for the study of dialect and folk-speech' (Raven 1950: 271).

54. For Skippon's description of expressions used in the playing of cards in Venice see Appendix 3; Willughby's Book of Games particularly notes any expressions peculiar to the playing of a game.

55. Birch (1756–57: i, 3). On the origins and early membership of the Society see Purver (1967), Webster (1975) and Hunter (1982).

56. He was listed among the 'Original Fellows', under the terms of the Society's second charter of 20 May 1663 (Birch 1756–57: i, xliv, 54, 66).

57. Birch (1756–57: i, 393–4). The request was received in Seville by Willughby, then travelling on his own, and communicated by him to Ray in a letter (Lankester 1848: 7–9).

Society an account of observations of Jupiter made by Giuseppe Campani (*c.* 1620–1695) on 30 July 1664. He was asked to give the Society at its next meeting notice of his other observations and collections made on the Continent.[58] He was not to have a further opportunity to travel widely, and from this point the Royal Society itself, particularly through its Secretary Henry Oldenburg (1615–1677), provided one of the few certain channels which Willughby used to keep informed of scientific developments in the world beyond Middleton.

During 1665, 1666 and 1667 there are indications of a seasonal pattern in Willughby's London visits, which allowed him to attend meetings in May, June or July.[59] From 1668, the year of his marriage, this pattern ceased, but correspondence continued. His last attendance at a meeting was in May 1672, less than two months before his death. During the ten years of his involvement his correspondence with the Society covered a wide range of subjects. Natural history topics were, inevitably, the most frequent; they included observations on wasps, insects, maggots, worms, flies, spiders, the rising of sap in trees and its possible circulation, and references to his extensive experience in the dissection of fish and other creatures. At times Oldenburg helped him in practical ways. Willughby used this channel, for instance, to seek assistance in procuring a thermometer and barometer.[60] Oldenburg was also a source of news about recent publications. On 4 July 1670 Willughby thanks him for accounts of several new books, evidently including the recent attacks by Henry Stubbe on the work of the Royal Society: 'I doubt not but Stubs has now exhausted Himselfe quite of His Venome and may bee as safely dealt with as Redis Viper after sevcrall bitings or Dr Tongues spiders after the combate'.[61] He was concerned that Stubbe should 'bee soundly chastised' (Oldenburg 1965–86: vii, 53–4).

The series of letters show Oldenburg soliciting information on specific subjects, seeking answers to problems, particularly within natural history, and mentioning news of distinguished visitors and topics that are currently interesting members of the Society. So, for example, in July 1669 Oldenburg writes: 'I pray forget not the account of ye practise of Agriculture, of yt countrey, where you are, and the parts adjacent' (Oldenburg 1965–86: vii, 103–4). Several letters from Oldenburg sent jointly to him and John Ray speak warmly of the value of their work. After a particularly welcome communication in January 1671, for instance, the Society asked them to send

58. Birch (1756–57: ii, 3). If a further report was made, it is not recorded.

59. The plague caused an interruption in Society meetings, from 28 June 1665 to 14 March 1666 (Birch 1756–57: ii, 58, 65). See below Section 5 (Chronology) for a listing of Willughby's attendance 1662–72 and related references. Occasions not discussed elsewhere in this account are noted in Birch (1756–57: i, 113–14, 115, 116; ii, 3, 48, 50, 52, 54, 97, 98, 100, 102, 162, 182, 239, 381–2, 392, 414, 418, 422–3, 435, 449, 476, 478, 487, 488, 495; iii, 49).

60. Mentioned in letters of 19 March, 16 April, 3 May 1670 (Oldenburg 1965–86: vi, 578, 635; vii, 3).

61. Henry Stubbe (1632–1676), in *Legends no Histories* and other works, had attacked Thomas Sprat's *History of Royal Society* (1667) and the new philosophy. Oldenburg on 17 May 1670 had sent Willughby an account of observations made by Israel Tongue (1621–1680) concerning a 'duel' between a spider and a toad (Oldenburg 1965–86: vii, 18).

further observations: 'The publication of such things will not only excite but prove a patterne to others, how to Inquire into ye nature of particular Bodyes, wch is ye thing yt will make Philosophy usefull, and therfore valuable' (Oldenburg 1965–86: vii, 409–10). Other letters refer to Willughby's interest in astronomy, which prompted his nomination to a committee concerning astronomical experiments in 1666 (Birch 1756–57: ii, 98). An exchange which linked his interests in natural history with astronomical speculation occurred in 1670 when Oldenburg encouraged him to investigate whether the phases of the moon affected the success of grafting. Willughby responds: 'I must confesse my selfe yet a Haeretick, in deniing that the moone has anie influence upon our selves or the animalls and Vegetables. […] mee thinks the doctors that Have the oversight of Bedlam might sooner discover whither Lunaticks deserve that name or not'.[62]

One other Royal Society venture with which Willughby was formally involved was the investigation of trades. As we have seen, Willughby was nominated to join the committee established on 30 March 1664 to report in this area. The investigation was intended to cover all activities in industry, manufacture and husbandry which involved processes of scientific interest. The establishment of the committee brought into focus an area of concern which had in fact been prominent in the 1650s background to the origins of the Royal Society, involving some of its most prominent members. Papers left by John Evelyn (1620–1706), William Petty (1623–1687) and Robert Boyle (1627–1691) show their development of an agenda for investigation. Despite, or perhaps because of, its ambitious programme, the committee never actually submitted a report and the commitment of its members to the proposed tasks seems to have been uneven.[63] Willughby was doubtless included because of his family background, and its known involvement in coal-mining interests in the Midlands. In fact, there is no record of any formal contribution by Willughby to the enterprise, although the observation of industrial and agricultural processes represented an abiding interest of both Willughby and Ray throughout their lives. The accounts of their travels, the Commonplace Book, and Ray's various published works all bear witness to this.[64] It is possible that Willughby did begin to bring together such accounts in a single manuscript. That at least is the implication of his daughter's later reference to a manuscript in her father's hand which 'describes the mannor

---

62. Letter of 7 June 1670, in response to enquiry of 3 May. The text of Oldenburg's reply on 28 June does not survive (Oldenburg, 1965–86: vii, 3; 29–30, 51).

63. On Evelyn, Petty, Boyle and the early ambitions for 'Histories of Trades' see Petty (1927: i, 203–205), Sieveking (1923: 40–47) and Houghton (1941a: 33–60). Ochs (1985) provides a review of the origins of the programme and its limited achievements; but see also Webster (1975: 425–8). Contributions concerning different industries, mechanical processes, and husbandry sometimes took the form of privately circulated papers; one such work which has only recently been published is John Evelyn's *Elysium Britannicum, or the Royal Gardens* (Evelyn 2000).

64. Willughby's brief comments on enamelling and soldering, for example, can be found in Lankester (1848: 63–4). His Commonplace Book includes many entries of relevance. Ray's contributions in this area, gathered together under the title 'An account of preparing some of our English Metals and Minerals' and including observations on refining silver and gold, working with tin and iron, the preparation of copperas, red-lead and allom and the making of sea salt, were published as an appendix to his *Collection of English Words* (1674).

of doing most sorts of work' (Wood 1958: 105), but this text has not been identified among the surviving manuscripts. The vellum-bound folio volume on the cover of which he wrote the title 'Notes on different Trades. Colliers &c.' does not in fact contain descriptions of industry, but was used by him for the present Book of Games.

Mathematical and mechanical interests, very much a part of the histories of trades agenda, are also evident throughout Willughby's contacts with the Royal Society. They have a particular interest in the light of Willughby's concern in the Book of Games with physical activity and the movement of balls and other objects, propelled with force and sometimes rebounding from walls or stationary bodies. In a letter of 29 May 1669 he sent Oldenburg a set of mathematical observations expressing criticism of the theories of motion proposed by Christopher Wren (1632–1723) and Christiaan Huygens, asking (an unusual request) for these to be presented to the Society as an anonymous communication. His purpose, he claims, is to encourage them to provide the experimental proofs for their proposals, without which, as he demonstrates, it is possible to counter the general rule 'that Bodies properly moved move properly allso after impulse'.[65] The paradox he identifies, 'that there would be an Encrease and Diminution of the Summe of Motion in the World' was presented to the Society by the President, William Brouncker (1620?–1684). Wren, present at the meeting, described the supposed paradox as a corollary which he had in fact anticipated as a truth, and claimed that his theory had been demonstrated by experiment. The members agreed that the anonymous writer should be informed of this, thanked for his 'ingenious reflexions' and asked to let them know of any further relevant experiments of his own. On 21 June 1669 Willughby responded with further comments on the theories of Wren and Huygens, again asking that the authors provide experimental evidence to support their hypothesis, for, as his earlier letter had protested: 'no man ought to thinke his fame strong enough to impose an improbable thing upon this inquisitive world nakedly, without either reasons or Experiments'.[66] The Society on 8 July agreed that Willughby and Ray should be sent the unpublished record of the experiments on motion by Wren and Laurence Rooke.[67] Willughby, in a response of 23 July 1669, welcomed the promise of the experiments, with speculations about possible tests (Oldenburg 1965–86: vi, 150). Given the repeated mention of games in contemporary discussion of mechanics, it is disappointing that Willughby appears to have made no further contributions on the subject in his correspondence with Oldenburg, although the latter again raised the question in January 1670. He has, he says, assumed that Willughby was conducting experiments of motion, 'either to confirme, or invalidate Dr

---

65. Willughby's original letter and Oldenburg's response both survive (Oldenburg 1965–86: v, 571–2, vi 35–6) and are abbreviated in the record of the Society's meeting of 10 June 1669 (Birch 1756–57: i, 381). See further below Section 4.2.

66. Willughby's letter responds to Oldenburg's report on 15 June of the Society's meeting, and another (lost) letter (Oldenburg, 1965–86: vi, 35–6, 63–4; v, 571–2).

67. Birch (1756–57: ii, 392); Oldenburg reports this on 9 July 1669 (Oldenburg 1965–86: vi, 103–4).

Wrens' and Mr Huygens's Theory of that important subject', adding hopefully: 'I persuade my self you will in convenient time communicate to us the result of such tryalls'. Willughby's reply explains that for the present he has deferred work on Wren's theories, as he expects a visit from Wilkins and hopes for his assistance on the subject.[68] In the months to come he lacked opportunity, and complains in June 1670 that 'a great manie troublesome businesses' are preventing him from thorough examination of 'Dr Wrens noble Theorie'. Oldenburg's response to this, on 28 June, concludes the records of their correspondence on the topic.[69] Willughby was indeed under increasing pressure from both official and private commitments, and his opportunity to engage in serious scientific investigation on any subject seems to have been severely curtailed in his final years.

That Wilkins was expected to visit Middleton in 1670 is not a surprise; the bishop used Middleton as a regular staging post on his journeys between London and Chester (Raven 1950: 166). He in his turn entertained Ray and Willughby at Chester; the friends' discovery of a porpoise at Chester in April 1669 was reported to the Royal Society on 9 November 1671 with details of the dissection.[70] The friendship was certainly strengthened by common membership of the Royal Society, but a strong personal tie was also established in the 1660s, confirmed by Willughby's association with the project which became Wilkins's central preoccupation till the end of his life, namely the design of a Philosophical Language.[71] The scheme was published in 1668 as *An Essay toward a Real Character and a Philosophical Language*. It appeared under the auspices of the Royal Society; indeed, after Wilkins's death the Society set up a committee to examine ways in which it might be improved and implemented.[72] Wilkins's purpose was to construct an artificial language from first principles which, among other things, would be an appropriate medium for the new experimental science.[73] Part of this project was the development of a philosophical grammar, which would function in the way that newly developed algebra did. But the central part was a methodical classification of things and concepts, based on the most recent scientific knowledge, which would allow for names and terms to be established on a rational basis.[74]

---

68. Oldenburg writes on 20 January 1670; Willughby replies on 29 January (Oldenburg 1965–86: vi, 437–8, 451–2).

69. Willughby writes on 7 June 1670. The full text of the reply does not survive (Oldenburg 1965–86: vii, 29–30, 51).

70. Gunther (1928: 58–63); Birch (1756–57: ii, 488); *Phil. Trans.* (1671: vol. vi, no. 76, 2274–9). An account of the dissection also appears in the *Historia Piscium* (Willughby 1686: 32).

71. In his biographical sketch of Wilkins, Aubrey says of the Philosophical Language that it 'was his Darling, and nothing troubled him so much when he dyed, as that he had not compleated it' (Aubrey 1898: ii, 302).

72. For a study of what became of the work of this group, see Salmon (1974).

73. On the question of language and Royal Society, see Hüllen (1989); on universal language schemes see Couturat and Leau (1903), Slaughter (1982) and Cram and Maat (2001).

74. The general outline of this system of classification will be familiar to modern readers through its reincarnation in Roget's *Thesaurus* (1852). Peter Mark Roget was Secretary of the Royal Society in the mid-nineteenth century, and based his scheme, as he states in the preface, on that of his seventeenth-century predecessor.

Wilkins enlisted the acknowledged experts in their fields to assist with the classificatory tables for his scheme, and it was to Willughby and Ray that he turned for help with the all-important sections on natural history. It is noteworthy that he singles them out among the very few scholars identified by name in his Epistle to the Reader (others being Seth Ward, Wilkins's first collaborator in the scheme, and William Lloyd, who had compiled the alphabetical dictionary forming the final part of the *Essay*):

Among others, I must not forget to make particular mention of the special assistance I have received in drawing up the Tables of *Animals* from that most Learned and Inquisitive Gentleman, a worthy Member of the *Royal Society*, Mr *Francis Willoughby*, who hath made it his particular business, in his late Travails through the most considerable parts of *Europe*, to inquire after and understand the several species of *Animals*, and by his own Observations is able to advance that part of Learning, and to add many things, to what hath been formerly done, by the most Learned Authors in this kind.

And as for those most difficult Tables of *Plants*, I have received the like assistance, from one of his Companions in Travail, Mr. *John Wray*, Late fellow of *Trinity Colledge in Cambridge*, who besides his other general Knowledge, hath with great success applyed himself to the Cultivating of that part of Learning.

(Wilkins 1668: The Epistle to the Reader)

Willughby was in fact a patron of the project from the early days of its planning. He writes to Peter Courthope in the late 1650s to encourage his involvement: 'I should be glad to heare you were acquainted with O: [*sic*] Wilkins & engaged in the Character Designe, if you bee, you must not faile to carry my very Humble Service' (Gunther 1937: 343). His collaboration became a more active one after his return from the Continent, and after the Great Fire of London in which the plates for the *Essay*, along with Wilkins's manuscripts, were destroyed. On 20 October 1666, Wilkins approaches Willughby:

I must desire your best assistance for the regular enumeration and defining of all the families of plants and animals. I thought to have found great benefit in this kind by Dr Merret's late book,[75] but it hath not answered my expectation; nor do I know any person in this nation who is so well able to assist in such matters as yourself, especially if we could procure Mr Ray's company to join in it.

(Derham 1718: 366)

Willughby and Ray did indeed rise to Wilkins's request for help, and spent most of the following months working on the project, as Ray reports to Martin Lister on 18 June of the following year:

The most part of the winter I spent here in revising and helping to put in order Mr. Willughby's collections of Birds, Fishes, Shells, stones and other fossils, seeds, dried plants, coins etc., in giving what assistance I could to Dr. Wilkins in framing his tables of plants, Quadrupeds, Birds, fishes etc. for the use of the *Universal Character*.

(Gunther 1928: 111)

---

75. I.e. *Pinax rerum naturalium* (1666) by Christopher Merret (1614–1695) FRS, physician, Fellow of the Royal College of Physicians in 1651, expelled for non-attendance 1681 (*DNB*).

Ray found it irksome that Wilkins required the tables to be drawn up according to a structure imposed by the needs of the philosophical language. In a retrospective comment to Lister on 7 May 1669, he complains:

I was constrained in arranging the Tables not to follow the lead of nature, but to accommodate the plants to the author's prescribed system. This demanded that I should divide herbs into three squadrons or kinds as nearly equal as possible; then that I should split up each squadron into nine 'differences' as he called them, that is subordinate kinds, in such wise that the plants ordered under each 'difference' should not exceed a fixed number; finally that I should join pairs of plants together or arrange them in couples.

(Lankester 1848: 41–2; trans. Raven, 1950: 182)

For Ray this seemed to run counter to the inductive approach which he and Willughby employed in the classification of natural history specimens. But whatever his misgivings, he continued to support the enterprise, devoting the winter of 1671–72 to the preparation of a Latin edition of the work, which he is reported to have completed but which does not appear to have survived (Raven 1950: 155). The revised tables which he and Willughby produced for this edition have also been lost; in 1678 Ray particularly commended the tables of insects which Willughby created at this time.[76]

1.5 Marriage, property and official responsibilities

In December 1665 Francis Willughby inherited his father's estate (Wood 1958: 92). That this brought new responsibilities is certain, though initially at least the pattern of his life seems to have been little altered. In June 1667 he again travelled with Ray, this time to the West Country and south in search of further natural history and botanical specimens (Raven 1950: 143–4). Even marriage to Emma Barnard in January 1668 brought little immediate domestic change. His wife was the daughter of a wealthy merchant, Henry Barnard (c. 1640–1680), living now in Shropshire. Since the death of his father Francis Willughby's family had shown increasing concern that he should settle down. The family history later composed by his daughter records correspondence concerning several other proposed matches before the Barnard alliance was made.[77] The couple were to have three children; Francis (1668–1688), Cassandra (1670–1735), and Thomas (1672–1729). The household was an extended one, with Lady Cassandra, Francis's mother, still living with the family and probably managing its domestic affairs. Relations with Francis's older sisters and their families were close. Katherine

---

76. Ray was asked by John Aubrey (1626–1697) for advice about the further improvement of the *Essay* after the deaths of both Wilkins and Willughby. He responded: 'Tables of insects you will scarce meet with better than those Mr. Willughby drew for ye Latin edition of the R[eal] Ch[aracter]' (Gunther 1928: 165). Ray was later to include Willughby's classification of insects in his own *Methodus Insectorum* (Ray 1705).

77. Wood (1958: 108–09). Evidence on the background to the marriage can be found in the marriage articles of 8 January 1668 and the marriage settlement of 29 September 1668 (Mi 1/7/15 and 1/9/1). Barnard was later knighted.

Winstanley and her son James were often resident at Middleton, even before the death of her husband Sir Clement Winstanley. Regular contact was also maintained with Francis's other sister, Lettice Wendy, and her husband Sir Thomas Wendy. Emma's parents, too, appear to have visited frequently.[78]

John Ray, who had joined Willughby at Middleton after his return from the Continent in late 1666, came to be accepted as a member of the household, and, in addition to their scientific research, assisted Willughby in his work on the family's legal archives and other historical papers. Indeed, their most extended area of collaborative study, outside the domain of natural history, was the joint work on the Willoughby family muniments.[79] Ray's place in the family's domestic life was sufficiently established that a household inventory for Middleton specifies 'Mr Ray's Chamber'.[80] Lettice Wendy, in writing to her sister-in-law at Middleton, confirmed Ray's acknowledged role within Willughby's family circle in her occasional references to 'Mr Wray', giving the form of his name which he used until 1670 (Mi Av 143/36, 2,9,10).

To this period presumably belong the patterns of life recorded many years later by Cassandra, as reported by her mother, then a young bride (Wood 1958: 110–11). She describes a daily routine which was dominated by Willughby's scholarly habits: he studied 'very hard' from rising until 11 o'clock, when his mother, Lady Cassandra, had prayers; in the brief period that followed until dinner he would walk, but after his meal would return to his books for the rest of the day, unless there were visitors to entertain. No detail of the 'study' in question is supplied. Although Cassandra does not mention his collection of specimens, we know that there was a 'vivarium' for his animals, and his natural history collections were certainly extensive.[81] Absorbed though he was in his studies, he did not lead the life of a recluse. A sense of public duty and his position within his local community would have prevented that. His daughter mentions his abilities in medicine, and his provision of remedies for the sick and poor in his neighbourhood (Wood 1958: 110). In 1670–71 he served as High Sheriff of Warwickshire,[82] a role which evidently brought some conflict between personal and public conduct. Cassandra records that, 'it being his opinion that a sherif ought not to suffer vagabons to goe about to beg', he commonly avoided sight of the poor people who came to his door looking for food at dinner time, to ensure that there need be no occasion to take official action against them (Wood 1958: 111). In

---

78. Wood 1958: 94–102; correspondence of Lettice Wendy to Emma Willughby provides evidence of close family ties (Mi Av 143/36/1–24, *passim*).

79. Mi LM 13. See below Section 2.1.

80. The inventory (Mi R 322/18) is undated, but its references to the 'Old Lady's Chamber', 'Mrs Barnard's Chamber' and 'Lady Child's Chamber' suggests that it was drawn up in late 1676, after the marriage of Francis's widow to Josiah Child and as she prepared to vacate the house at Middleton.

81. Ray refers to Willughby's 'vivarium' as the observation site for various fungi, including the 'yellow Adders-tongue-Mushrome' (Ray 1690: 10).

82. A bundle containing his acquittance of the Pipe (Mich. 22 C II–Mich 23 C II) survives, together with papers concerning his shrievalty and general points about the office (NUL Mi O 12 and Mi O 10, *passim*). The relevant Court of Session rolls for Warwickshire are not extant, but the indictment books supply dates for his attendance at Quarter Sessions (Ratcliff and Johnson 1941: 232–4).

addition, he could not neglect the obligations of his estates, including those beyond Warwickshire, though his visits to the family estates at Wollaton, Nottinghamshire, also brought opportunities for natural history observation and the collection of specimens.[83]

Family and estate matters were to become especially onerous in his last year of life, and for one particular cause. In February 1671 a distant relative, Sir William Willoughby of Selston, died, leaving to Francis Willughby all his manors of South Muskham and South Carlton in Nottinghamshire. The will was bitterly disputed by Sir William's sister and her husband Sir Beaumont Dixie, and this immediately plunged Willughby, and Ray, into arduous litigation with the executors. The ensuing legal action involved several courts, including the Archdeaconry, the Exchequer, and the Court of Common Pleas. It was indeed not to be finally resolved until well into the eighteenth century, by which time the beneficiary was Thomas Willoughby, Francis's younger son.[84] From February 1671 Francis became responsible for legal preparations to defend the will, although he was already in frail health and apparently vulnerable to feverish attacks.[85] A large quantity of evidence survives, showing his personal involvement in the case. Annotations on copies of legal documents, notes about possible actions, comments on witness evidence, and references to legal precedent all demonstrate his understanding of the legal issues at stake. Even in the case's early days the action generated a huge quantity of correspondence, and must have severely limited Willughby's freedom to pursue his own scientific interests.[86] But much was at stake, and for the sake of his heirs the action was worth the time and effort expended. Although a full analysis of the Willughby fortunes at this point in the seventeenth century has yet to be made, the family does not appear to have been particularly wealthy. Title to Sir William's estates was to consolidate their landed position, and must have contributed to the acceptability of their elevation to the peerage under Francis's son, Thomas.

1.6 The final years

The picture that emerges of Willughby in his final years shows him leading an active life, undertaking the inevitable responsibilities of a family and large

---

83. Ray, writing to Lister in April 1670, describes specimens collected when visiting Wollaton (Lankester 1848: 55–6).

84. The bequest, Dixie's attack, and the immediate impact on the scientific work of Willughby and Ray is described in Ray's letter to Lister, 3 March 1671 (Gunther 1928: 127–8). His daughter Cassandra summarizes the conclusion of the business (Wood 1958: 112–15).

85. Willughby's physical frailty was well known and had caused several alarms for his friends, notably in April 1669 when he and Ray were visiting Bishop Wilkins in Chester (Gunther 1928: 122–3; Wood 1958: 111). Recent illness is mentioned in a letter of Lister to Ray in December 1670 (Lankester 1848: 73).

86. The surviving papers are to be found in bundles within the legal series of the family archive and scattered through other sections. Those worked on by Francis Willughby himself bear evidence of his characteristic methods of study, reminiscent in some respects of the Book of Games; see in particular NUL Mi 2/76/1.

estate, but continuing his interests in scientific investigation both at home
and through his network of contacts. The majority of his friends have already
been mentioned, in particular those dating from his student days at
Cambridge and the years immediately following his graduation. This circle
of like-minded gentlemen-scholars overlapped with that offered by
membership of the Royal Society; by June 1668 Ray, Skippon and Courthope
were all members, all having been proposed – as was Willughby – by John
Wilkins.[87] Francis Jessop (1638–1691), who had met Ray and Skippon on the
Continent,[88] but whose friendship with Willughby is difficult to trace through
the records, was not apparently a member. He did however correspond, and
was often mentioned in the letters of his friend Lister to Oldenburg.[89]

The passing years, and Willughby's extensive natural history
investigations, brought other friendships. It is unfortunate that so few letters
to Willughby now survive in the family archive, since sufficient evidence
remains to show that he was an active correspondent.[90] The Commonplace
Book contains evidence of letters on scientific subjects which suggest that
Willughby systematically kept his correspondence for further reference,
possibly even gathered as a letter book; letters by Jessop and Barrow are both
mentioned, in the context of his notes on woad (NUL Mi LM 15/1 p. 338).
Martin Lister (1638–1712), the physician and zoologist, was also certainly
among his contacts. His work on insects, and particularly on spiders, gave
him a special interest in Willughby's researches. Willughby stayed with him
in Yorkshire, and Lister's correspondence with Ray includes numerous
references to Willughby and to their common scientific interests.[91] Other
correspondents of Willughby, among them his father-in-law Sir Henry
Barnard, record relationships which were primarily personal and social, but
could include reference to natural history phenomena, suggesting approval
and encouragement of Willughby's interests within his most intimate circle.[92]
It was an age of curiosity, speculation and experiment, and it is certain that
there were other acquaintances and visitors with whom Willughby shared his
enthusiasms.

---

87. Birch (1756–57: ii, 172, 203, 293). Courthope was inactive, and ultimately his name was deleted for non-payment of membership dues.

88. Skippon, who routinely notes the names of English visitors encountered in continental cities, records first meeting Jessop and Martin Lister at Montpellier in July 1665 (Skippon 1732: vi, 714).

89. In 1666 his difference in opinion with Wallis on the subject of tides led to a correspondence conducted through the agency of Lister, who sent his letters to Oldenburg, who in turn communicated with Wallis (Jessop 1687; cf. Oldenburg 1965–86: x, 71a; Birch 1756–57: iii, 246; iv, 399). He was known for his mathematical interests and his association with the chemistry work of John and Samuel Fisher, and in 1687 he presented the Society with a copy of his book *Propositiones Hydrostaticæ* (Oldenburg 1965–86: x, 71 n).

90. All letters of a scientific interest were apparently passed to Derham (see below Section 2.1 and Bibliography A, Correspondence). The affectionate letters from his sister Lettice Wendy fortunately escaped this dispersal (Mi Av 143/37/1–3).

91. The visits to Lister are mentioned in correspondence with Oldenburg (Oldenburg 1965–86: viii, 262, 284, 301). Lister's friendship with Ray began in 1665–66, when they met first at Montpellier; after Willughby's death Lister offered Ray a home in York (Raven 1950: 138–40). The Lister–Ray correspondence is published in Gunther (1928: 110–37).

92. Cassandra quotes a letter from her grandfather Barnard in May 1668, giving an account of a strange bird captured in Shropshire (Wood 1958: 111–12).

Willughby's state of health had long been fragile, and suffered its final attack when on 3 June 1672 he 'was seized [...] with a plurisie' (Wood 1958: 115). The extent to which his philosophy, friendships and working relationships were of a piece can most tellingly be seen in his will, dated 24 June 1672, during his last illness. He describes himself in unambiguous if conventional terms: 'a Protestant according to the Doctrine that is delivered in the holy Scriptures utterly detesting and abhorring all the Idolatry, abominable errours and ignorance that is in the Popish Religion'. He names Ray, Skippon and Jessop as his executors, together with his brother-in-law Sir Thomas Wendy and his father-in-law Sir Henry Barnard.[93] Ray is also to receive an annuity of £60, and to undertake special responsibilities in the education of Willughby's sons: 'desiring him to omitt no opportunity of instilling principles of vertue, freedom, and moderation, an eager desire of learning, an abhorrencey of Idleness, intemperance, unchastity and all kind of Debauchery'.[94] Willughby's charitable bequests include provision for the poor at Middleton and Wollaton, with specific reference to child apprentices, the teaching of poor children to write and read, and the annual purchase of Bibles for poor children. Similar provision is made for the communities of South Muskham and South Carlton, within the estates recently inherited from Sir William Willoughby. In years to come the friends had to join together again, to defend their executorship and to represent what they considered Willughby's intentions to have been, in the face of criticism from Willughby's other executor, Sir Henry Barnard, and Sir Josiah Child, the widow's new husband.[95] The circle of friends and interests centred on Willughby at Middleton would not however long survive his death, which came on 3 July 1672 at Middleton.[96] He was buried at the local church, where a memorial giving generous tribute to his abilities was subsequently erected.[97]

---

93. NUL Mi 4/149/5; the will provides in detail for his family and the inheritance of his estate. Sir Thomas Wendy's death in 1673 soon left Barnard, as father of the widow, and the others, as friends of Willughby, more obviously divided in their level of personal involvement.

94. Derham prints Latin 'instructions' from Ray to Francis Willughby's children. Ray's classified vocabulary in Greek, Latin and English, created for the Willughby children, appeared first under the label *Dictionariolum* (1675) but was later re-titled *Nomenclator Classicus* to distinguish it from pirate editions (Cram 1991; Hüllen 1999: 294–9). Derham (1760: 38) also mentions that Ray's wife, Margaret Oakley, whom he married in June 1673, was his assistant and taught young Thomas (later Lord Middleton) his letters and to read English.

95. Numerous papers in the family archive refer to the difficulties between Willughby's chosen executors and Child, difficulties which became acute after the death of Barnard; see in particular NUL Mi L 53–6 and further below, Section 2.1, in connection with access to Willughby's manuscripts.

96. There is little evidence about the links between Ray, Skippon and Jessop after Willughby's death, although sufficient references survive to demonstrate continuing friendship. For Skippon's later links with Ray see Gunther (1928: 148, 287 and 291); Ray is known to have stayed at Francis Jessop's house near Sheffield, and refers to him in letters to Lister (Gunther 1928: 136). In his preface to the *Ornithologia*, Ray pays tribute to the assistance of Skippon and Jessop, and in the preface to the *Historia Piscium* he thanks Skippon for the 'Reutel seu Rotele' fish.

97. His daughter describes his last illness and gives an English summary of his memorial (Wood 1958: 115). The full text is printed in Dugdale (1730: ii, 1053).

Willughby's Manuscripts and the Book of Games

2.1 The manuscripts of Francis Willughby

At the time of Willughby's premature death at the age of 36 he already had some reputation as a scientist within his immediate circle, although wider recognition was limited by his lack of publication. His only known venture into print, apart from his communications in the Royal Society's *Philosophical Transactions*, had been his contribution to the tables of plants and animals which he and Ray prepared for Wilkins's *Essay* (1668). The first reaction of members of the Society, on hearing news of his death, was to enquire about his 'writings and curiosities', to see if they might be acquired for the archives and repository of the Royal Society.[98] Whether Wilkins, who was nominated their representative, did indeed approach Ray on the subject is not recorded; his death on 19 November 1672, within months of his friend, perhaps came too soon to allow any action. Already, however, Ray had anticipated the value of publishing his friend's scientific work. He asked Willughby on his deathbed if he wished this, and although Willughby was modest about the value of his papers he did not forbid their publication.[99] Ray at once set about the task of sorting and editing the material on birds. Willughby's widow agreed to pay for plates for the *Ornithologia* – an expense which she apparently expected to recoup in full.[100] That the work was onerous to Ray is an indication of the incomplete state of Willughby's researches, as well as, increasingly, the difficulty of his position in the Middleton household once his friend and patron was gone.

As a work of science, the *Ornithologia* is well known, but the value of both this publication and Ray's subsequent scientific texts within a biographical study of Francis Willughby is also considerable, in their prefatory remarks and in the frequent incidental references to places and dates of the recorded

---

98. Letter from Oldenburg to Wilkins of 12 July 1672, asking for his assistance, as he was 'so well acquainted with all the philosophical concerns and collections of yt worthy gentleman' (Oldenburg 1965–86: ix, 153).

99. The incident is recounted by Ray in his preface to the *Ornithologia* (1676).

100. Her will of 1674 mentions the profits which might be due from the publication (NUL Mi 1/13/24b).

observations.[101] The *Ornithologia* was printed in 1676 by John Martyn, printer to the Royal Society, on the order of the Society, and Ray was encouraged to translate the Latin text for an English edition. When this was published in 1678 it included sections on Fowling and Falconry as well as other additions.[102] Ray had by this time already published another short text by Willughby, incorporating the notes he had left about his travels through Spain into his own publication in 1673 recording his continental expedition (Ray 1673). Selection of material for this work was influenced both by the need to make the publication appealing to a non-scientific readership and his intention to continue the edition of Willughby's natural history papers and collections. He next turned his attention to the material on fish that Willughby, and his friends, had collected.

A variety of reasons, concerning Ray's circumstances, his access to Willughby's papers, and the financing of the venture, which was ultimately borne largely by the Royal Society, made the preparation and printing of the *Historia Piscium* a protracted affair, and one of considerable interest in the history of seventeenth-century scientific publication.[103] Our interest here is primarily in the fate, then and since, of Willughby's collections and observations. Ray's text for the publication of Willughby's work on fishes was apparently ready for the press about 1678, but remained unpublished in February 1682 when Lister wrote to the Royal Society drawing attention to the 'excellent manuscripts which Mr Willughby had left behind him' and asking for the Society's interest in their publication. He mentioned that the work on fishes had been given by Ray to the London merchant, Josiah Child, who in 1676 had married Emma, Francis Willughby's widow. Child, claimed Lister, now held all the rest of Willughby's papers. He particularly regretted that Willughby's observations on insects would be lost 'without some such powerful intercession and sollicitation as that of the Royal Society'. It was agreed that enquiry should be made about the manuscript on fishes and that Sir John Lowther, a member, should speak to Child about the matter, but some uncertainty must have been felt about the story, for Hooke was also asked to enquire whether Ray had any of the philosophical manuscripts of Francis Willughby (Birch 1756–57: iv, 127). On 5 April 1682 the subject was again discussed, with particular reference to the possible acquisition of Willughby's work on insects. Members were informed by a Mr Hill that the manuscripts had been left in Warwickshire when the family moved after Emma Willughby's marriage, and that 'if Mr Ray should be desired to look them out they might be had for the Society'. Sir John Lowther confirmed the

---

101. For an account of the edition, with particular reference to Ray's key role in supplementing the original material left by Willughby, see Raven (1950: 308–38).

102. Additional sections on Fowling and Falconry were drawn primarily from *The Gentleman's Recreation* (Blome 1686), itself derivative from Turberville (1575). Details of these and other additions are given by Raven (1950: 325).

103. On the publishing history of the *Historium Piscium* see, most recently, Kusukawa (2000) and Kinsley (1999). The survival of Willughby's original materials with Ray's notes as editor and associated papers (Mi LM 25) provides the potential for a particularly interesting study; see Johns (1998: 434 n. 116, 489–90).

willingness of Sir Josiah Child to this arrangement.[104] The offer does not, however, seem to have been taken up and it was still believed by some of Willughby's former friends that Sir Josiah was the obstacle. On 7 June 1683 Francis Aston wrote to Lister that 'Mr Jessop of Broomhal thinks he could be instrumental to get Mr Willoughbys papers about Insects and fishes out of Sir Josiah Childs hands', and suggested that Lister write to Jessop.[105]

Whatever efforts were made, it appears that no further use of Willughby's papers had been possible when early in 1685 the Society, acting through Tancred Robinson, returned to the issue and obtained the text for publication from Ray.[106] That Willughby's papers and specimens were indeed still at Middleton seems borne out both by contemporary inventories and by the later report of Willughby's daughter Cassandra, who in 1689 helped her brother Thomas to remove their father's collections from Middleton to Wollaton. The materials in her description included 'dryed birds, fish, insects, shells, seeds, minerals and plants and other rarities'.[107]

That there may have been problems about access to Middleton Hall in the mid-1680s is not surprising. Even Willughby's own children were increasingly at odds with Child; in 1685 Francis, then only 17, began legal proceedings against his stepfather for waste of the family estate. When he sought to establish a home at Wollaton, Nottinghamshire, Sir Josiah would not allow Francis to remove his father's goods, including his books, from Middleton without a decree in Chancery, an episode subsequently recounted by his sister Cassandra (Wood 1958: 126). In addition, by this stage relations between Ray and Sir Josiah and Lady Child had broken down irretrievably, precluding not only the checking of Willughby material at Middleton but also the possibility that the family might finance the illustrative plates.[108] Ray was no longer tutor to the children and allegations of the neglect of his duties as executor were being pursued at this time. Although he apparently did retain some of Willughby's research papers when he left Warwickshire for Essex, for he refers later to their return to Thomas Willoughby, Ray did not have all he needed; in writing to Tancred Robinson in April 1685, about an uncertainty in his information, he regrets that he does not have Willughby's notes on fishes: 'But it is almost impossible to procure a sight of them' (Lankester 1848:

---

104. Birch (1756–57: iv, 139). The informant was presumably Abraham Hill (1635–1721), Treasurer to the Society.

105. Bodley Library MS Lister 35, f. 101; we are indebted to Mordechai Feingold for this reference.

106. Gunther (1928: 88–98) provides a summary of the Society's involvement in the publication of *Historia Piscium*. See also Birch (1756–57: iv, 371–481, *passim*); Raven (1950: 349–58).

107. Wood (1958: 137). At least two relevant inventories for Middleton Hall exist; one *c*. 1676 and the other December 1687 (NUL Mi R 322/18 and Mi R 318/19). Although primarily concerned with household chattels, they indicate the presence at Middleton as late as 1687 of writings, books and other scientific items.

108. Emma Willughby seems not to have shared her husband's approval of John Ray, but his position at Middleton was not threatened until after the death in 1675 of the dowager, Lady Cassandra, who had supported him. Ray left Middleton, remaining first within Warwickshire and then moving in 1677 to Essex. Emma married Josiah Child in 1676. In 1680 Sir Henry Barnard, the most active of the executors, died, giving Child the opportunity to attempt to remove Ray as trustee. A letter of 1680 about the incident and other correspondence reveals how completely Ray had broken with Francis's widow and her new husband; see in particular NUL Mi E 4/31, Mi L 30/14.

165–6). In July 1685 he mentions in a letter to Lister that no progress has been made towards the printing of the *History of Fishes*, that Mr Child will 'treat with bookseller' about the matter but that Child is 'sordidly covet[ous]' and 'will scarce let his wife part with money to engrave *Hist. of Fishes*'.[109] Ray had more hopes of his former friend's elder son, Francis Willoughby, and suggested to Robinson in March 1685 that he might bear the costs when he should come of age (Lankester 1848: 164). Whether the boy had made the offer or knew of the opportunity is not known. The time was perhaps not a propitious one for either Emma Child or her son to support the venture, but in 1686 the *Historia Piscium* was duly published under the name of Francis Willughby, and with reference to his family in the introduction.

Nothing further was heard of the Society's efforts to procure Willughby's manuscripts, at least some of which remained in the hands of later generations of Willoughbys[110] at Wollaton Hall, Nottinghamshire, which the naturalist's sons Francis and Thomas again made the main family seat. It was apparently in 1689 that Thomas and Cassandra Willoughby finally rescued from Middleton the specimens and collections which their father had assembled, and it may have been about this time that Ray returned to Thomas Willoughby those manuscripts which he had borrowed (Wood 1958: 137). Cassandra describes some of her father's papers in her account of the library, but gives no reference either to the lending of papers to Ray or other individuals or to their return.[111] A considerable quantity of illustrative material on fishes has survived, including plates for the *Historia Piscium*, annotated by Ray and others, but notes and observations, unless immediately associated with an illustration, are not present.

Perhaps the most disappointing among the losses of Willughby's collections is his work on insects, an area of study in which he was clearly acknowledged by contemporaries as active and expert, both as a collector of specimens and an observer in the field.[112] Ray, even as he was engaged on publication of Willughby's work on birds and fishes, recognized this, writing in 1674: 'The History of Insects is that wherein Mr Willughby did chiefly labour and most considerably advance' (Oldenburg 1965–86: xi, 136). It was to Willughby that Philip Skippon in June 1664 had referred the opportunity for acquiring Pietro Castelli's manuscript on insects, and issues concerning entomology figured large in Willughby's correspondence with Oldenburg.[113] Willughby's 'Observations concerning Insects' were at one time in Ray's possession. In a

---

109. Gunther (1928: 136), quoting from Derham's abstract of original correspondence.

110. The naturalist's children reverted to the WILLOUGHBY spelling of the name.

111. Wood (1958: 105). Welch argues that Cassandra and her brother probably worked on their father's collections at Wollaton in the 1690s, i.e. between the publication of the second and third volumes of *Historia Plantarum* (1688 and 1704), as the first two volumes are interleaved with specimens (Welch, 1972: 82).

112. A general discussion in 1684 at the Royal Society, on the subject of the species of warm- and cold-blooded creatures, included the comment that 'the species of insects [are] almost innumerable; Mr. Willughby in one collection having had above 2,000' (Birch 1756–57: iv, 257).

113. Derham (1718: 361). For the pattern and extent of Willughby's correspondence with Oldenburg, discussed above Section 1.4, see further below, Section 5 (Chronology) and Bibliography A.

letter of 19 May 1691 to Waller, then Secretary of the Royal Society, Ray says that he has long since handed these manuscripts over to Willughby's son, Sir Thomas, 'who will I suppose in time take care to publish them' (Gunther 1928: 100). In 1703 Ray sought sight of them, to enable him to conclude the work on insects which had occupied him intermittently since 1690. In April of that year he informed Sloane that he was expecting to receive Willughby's papers on insects from Sir Thomas; he had not had them by July 1703, possibly because of Sir Thomas's illness, but seems to have been in possession of them by August 1704 (Lankester 1848: 416, 430–32, 448–9). Notes for the *Methodus Insectorum* (1705) were apparently revised before publication, following his receipt of the Willughby papers (Raven 1950: 401 n. 9; 388–418). The *Methodus*, a 16-page booklet, included in diagrammatic form Willughby's tables of intransmutable insects (pp. 1–6) and aquatic insects (pp. 11–13). Although these sections are expressly attributed to Willughby and constitute a significant proportion of his work as a whole, the title page bears only Ray's name.

Ray continued immediately with preparations for a larger work, but his death in January 1705 left this unfinished. His widow, now in distressed circumstances, sought Dr Hans Sloane's advice in approaching Sir Thomas Willoughby who agreed to pay to her the annuity which would have been due to her husband at that time. She sent 'the book and papers about insects' which belonged to Sir Thomas to Dr Sloane in November 1706, for transmission on to Wollaton (Raven 1950: 481; Lankester 1848: 476–9). Initially Sloane hoped that Ray's work on insects might be completed by Samuel Dale, the Braintree surgeon and friend of Ray, who undertook much of the practical business in sorting and disposing of Ray's books and manuscripts. But Dale declined the task, although he reported in January 1707 that he had 'already transcribed a great part of Mr Willughby's observations into the Body of the Work', mentioning the need to have Sir Thomas Willoughby's permission for the use of his papers (BL Add MS 4040 f. 297). Over the next five years Ray's papers on insects lay first in the hands of William Derham, who in 1708 sent them to the Royal Society, into Sloane's custody.[114] They were published in 1710, without further amendment or edition under the title *Historia Insectorum*. The relatively undigested state of many of the notes has an incidental advantage for modern historians in occasionally preserving the identification of material from different sources, where Ray might, in due course, have collated and selected his evidence more systematically. The 1705 tables are repeated here, and other observations and contributions by Willughby are extensively acknowledged throughout; notes attributed to 'F.W.' include descriptions of worms, leeches, bugs and fleas.[115]

---

114. For Dale's friendship with Ray and his role at this time, see Raven (1950: 205, 403). Correspondence of Ray, Derham, Dale and others associated with Ray's final work and these posthumous events can be found in the Sloane papers in the British Library, particularly in Add. MSS 4036–4053, *passim*. Ray's letters are edited in Lankester (1848); on their descent and publication history see Gunther (1928: Preface).

115. Willughby was particularly qualified to provide a description of the flea, having purchased a tame one in Venice, which he kept alive by allowing it to feed daily from his hand (Ray 1710: 8).

Despite the references to Willughby in the work, the publication of *Historia Insectorum* in 1710 upset the Willoughby family. They had no prior knowledge of it and took it as 'no better then surreptitious'. On 18 August 1710 Derham sent Sloane an account of his recent meeting with Francis Willughby's widow, Lady Child, and daughter, Cassandra (BL Add MS 4042 f. 164). He reports their response to his suggestion that they supply engravings of Willughby's draughts of insects, which he had seen when they were in Ray's hands, so that they might be incorporated in another edition of the work. They had reservations: 'Sir Tho. Willughby & they also for their parts took it ill, y' Mr Willughby's papers should be published in Mr Ray's name & he carry away y' hon' they thought due to their father'. They explained that Sir Thomas and Dr Man[116] had worked on the material for two years, and a number of plates had already been engraved. They agreed that the family might bear the expense of the plates, provided Sir Thomas approved, but only on condition that the new edition should include Willughby's name on the title page 'so as to do him due honour whose share therein is the greatest'. Sloane's response to this is not recorded; no further edition was published, and, apart from a single sheet bearing specimen illustrations, nothing is known of the fate of Willughby's original draughts of insects, the intended engravings, and the work of Sir Thomas and Dr Man.[117]

Discussion of Willughby's work and the manuscripts he left has inevitably concentrated upon natural history, the area of his most extensive collaboration and the one of most immediate interest after his death. Such a perspective, however, gives a less than full account of his researches and achievements. Indeed, the wish to publish his natural history papers and the later concern to publish his correspondence with Ray both undoubtedly contributed to the disturbance and extensive loss of his manuscript remains. It is uncertain what may or may not have been borrowed by Ray for his various publications and possibly not returned. At a later date Willughby's children definitely supplied William Derham with their father's surviving correspondence. His limited publication of Willughby's letters indicates a very selective use of the correspondence (Derham 1718; Lankester 1848: x). The loss of so many of the principal papers makes it difficult now to see how systematic was Willughby's method of study or how original his contribution. In these circumstances, it is fortunate that his intellectual concerns included areas other than natural history, the evidence for which has in part survived.

One such instance is the extensive research which he undertook together with Ray into earlier generations of the Willoughby family, including their family connections and affiliations and their acquisition of property. The resulting volume, commonly referred to as 'The History of the Willoughby

---

116. Dr Thomas Man of Jesus College, Cambridge, tutor to Thomas Willoughby and a keen naturalist, lived with the family at Wollaton. It is possible that his unexpectedly early death in 1690 interrupted a programme of work on the insects (Wood 1958: 130, 134 138).

117. The surviving illustration (NUL Mi LM 25/213) lies among the drawings and engravings of fish and reptiles.

Family', is entitled 'Memoirs and observations taken out of old minniments videlicet, deeds, fines, accounts, court roles, and all sorts of old writings, which were found the most of them either at Wollaton or Middleton chiefly concerning Pedigrees, Marriages, Titles of land, Purchases and sales, Suits in all courts, of the Familie of the Willughbies' (NUL Mi LM 13). The pages give details of properties held, abstracted from the original deeds, and the pedigrees which linked the Willoughbys to other families. Few of the early family archives escaped their attention. A substantial proportion of deeds and papers in the archive are now endorsed with brief summaries by either Willughby or Ray, the latter responsible for almost one entire section of the volume, which lists the Willoughby deeds from Richard II by county, place and date. The reason for the compilation is not certain, but an association can clearly be made with the contemporary wish of gentry families to establish their ancestry and county positions.[118] When Robert Thoroton's *Antiquities of Nottinghamshire* appeared in 1677, it included a detailed account of the Willoughbys at Wollaton and acknowledged that information had been supplied by Francis Willughby; his executors paid for copies of the engraved plates.[119]

While the results of this particular area of research survive in a clearly identifiable manuscript volume, other works and papers containing observations and speculations certainly existed but cannot now be traced. His daughter Cassandra, in describing papers left by her father, mentions three items which have not been identified and are presumably lost: first, a manuscript 'Upon ye Sherifs office', including 'his opinion of ye Oaths of Allegience & Supremacy'; secondly, a work 'wch shews ye Chances of most Games'; and finally, one which describes 'ye mannor of doing most sorts of Work' (NUL Mi LM 27; Wood 1958: 105). She also refers to 'many other unfinished writings', but does not identify them by title or subject. A significant omission is her lack of reference to Willughby's Commonplace Book, which almost certainly was with his other writings in the library, and is an important source on his work and interests. Cassandra does not record if the manuscripts she lists were entirely in Willughby's own distinctive hand or showed the participation of others. That the Book of Games escaped attention after Willughby's death is not surprising, given how entirely the publication programme concerned the field of natural history and rested on the commitment of Ray who had apparently no involvement in this work. For the same reason, presumably, it escaped the later efforts of Derham to collect materials relevant to Ray's history.

---

118. See Broadway (1999) for a study of the significance of gentry aspirations and identity, and their support for the writing of county histories, an activity running in tandem with the chorographic tradition which the county histories also represented (see below Section 4.1).

119. Thoroton (1677: 220–28); NUL Mi A 102, 13 March 1677.

2.2 The manuscript

The Book of Games is one of a number of volumes, printed and manuscript, which survived in the Library at Wollaton Hall and now form part of the Middleton Collection of family and estate papers housed at the University of Nottingham (NUL Mi LM 14). It can, we suggest, be identified as the 'Book of Plaies' which is listed within the library catalogue of the naturalist's son, Thomas, 1st Lord Middleton (NUL Mi I 17/1). Although the manuscript has never been edited, it was microfilmed during the Second World War before its transfer to Nottingham. The microfilm records the state of the manuscript half a century before the making of this edition, and in a few places has provided readings where physical deterioration has caused loss of text.

The text is written in a folio volume, the approximate overall dimensions being 350 x 220 mm. The binding is of thin limp vellum, quite brittle and with some small tears on the lower edges. The covers, which were loosely attached to the sewn text block with vellum ties, do not have either boards or pastedowns.

The paper text block contains 192 folios and measures 337 x 220 mm. The irregular dimensions of the front cover have left the paper slightly exposed, resulting in physical damage to the first folios. Apart from several additional sections which have been inserted, the paper is uniform, in 16 quires of 12 folios, with the second and fourth quires irregularly gathered in 10 folios and 14 folios. The sections have been sewn onto four leather bands and heavily glued, with the first and last quires additionally supported with a vellum strip, sewn into the structure. Poor quality gold edging has left yellow stains along the paper edges in several sections of the volume. A small section of paper, 105 x 77 mm., has been cut from the top right corner of p. 383.

Following an initial folio, which serves as a flyleaf although it is actually part of the first gather, the paper bears its original pagination, with some errors. Pagination runs: 1–177, 180–93, 196–263, 254–9, 270–89, 280, 281, 291, 290, 292–314, 304, 315–76, 378–9. Several other page numbers have been altered. Modern pencil corrections supply a single sequence of numbers from pages 290 to 382. The incorrect numbers appear to be the result of carelessness, and have no obvious relation to the gathering of the different sections. They occur mainly in the final section of the manuscript, where the pages are blank.

The paper in question bears a watermark consisting of a shield, surmounted by a crown which in turn is surmounted by a small quatrefoil. Within the shield are the initials GT superimposed on each other, and GTRAVERS appears in a flourished label beneath the shield. Briquet records two instances of the G Travers watermark, on paper dated in one case to 1578 and in the other to 1586–90. The former is the specimen most akin to the Willughby manuscript. This paper is identified as French, but the mill location of its manufacture does not appear to be known.[120]

---

120.   Briquet (1968: ii, 497, items 9428, 9429).

A possible late sixteenth-century date for the paper is relevant to an investigation of the Book of Games. It confirms other indications that Willughby used for this work a paper source which was not new. The most convincing proof of this lies in the worm holes in the paper, at least some of which were present when the manuscript was written. For example, on page 19, Willughby writes the words 'wh ole' and 'sup pose' with a space in the appropriate place to avoid the hole in the paper. The imperfect gilding offers a possible explanation for the availability of such a quantity of bound unused paper. The volume may have been prepared for a different purpose, perhaps at the time of the naturalist's great-grandfather, Sir Francis Willoughby 'The Builder', only to be set aside when the staining of the paper became apparent. It is also possible that the paper block, with its solid sewing structure, raised bands and glued back, was intended to have a more robust and protective binding than it ultimately received in its vellum cover. The paper also bears evidence of water stains, both at the spine and along the fore-edge. Willughby's writing covers some of the damp sections, and the ink has been affected in parts, but whether the paper became damp before or after writing is not apparent.

A note in Willughby's hand on the rear cover of the volume (top right-hand corner when inverted) reads 'Notes on different Trades'. The contents of the volume are: an initial folio on which are jotted the names of a large number of games (below, Appendix 1); an index for the volume, listing the games alphabetically within classified groups (p. 1); the main body of the text on games (pp. 3–276); a few notes on popular superstitions, describing occurrences or phenomena that can be used to foretell the future (p. 379); and an illustration (apparently unrelated) of a perpetual motion machine (p. 384). Almost 100 blank pages separate the last of the games descriptions from the few notes on superstitions, suggesting that the latter, which are not noted on the flyleaf or in Willughby's index, are conceptually distinct from the rest of the book.[121] The text is largely in Willughby's autograph, but two other hands can also be identified, that of Philip Skippon (inserts 3, 4, 5, 6), and one which, as discussed in the following section, appears to be that of a child (pp. 90, 220, 229–33, 236, 241, insert 7 and flyleaf).

There are in all seven additions attached to the volume.[122] These were apparently inserted by Willughby himself, since their location is specified in his table of contents:

1   A small notebook, entitled 'Plaies', measuring 140 × 87 mm and containing 15 folios which have been sewn together, attached to p. 3. This

---

121. See Aubrey (1881) for a contemporary collection of folklore and superstitions. Those noted by Willughby fall into the category of 'omens', to use the label found in early folkloric collections (Bourne 1725: 70–75; cf. Brand 1777: 87–101). It is significant that the examples which attracted Willughby's attention concern divination, given his known interest in judicial astrology (see above Section 1.2).

122. At some stage most of the insertions were detached, probably by accident or to allow microfilming in the 1940s. So far as can be detected, no other insertions have been lost.

is in Willughby's hand. Several folios have been removed from the gathering, which seems originally to have been used for another purpose and contains notes not related to the present text.

2   Three loose folios, measuring approximately 145 x 90 mm, attached to p. 13. These describe Stow Ball and are in Willughby's hand.

3   A bifolium, measuring 200 x 145 mm, attached to p. 14. This describes the game of Billiards. It is in the hand of Philip Skippon, with additions by Willughby.

4   A bifolium, measuring approximately 310 x 200 mm, attached to p. 15. This describes the game of Tennis. It is in the hand of Philip Skippon with additions by Willughby.

5   A fragment measuring 110 x 120 mm, cut from paper which bears other writing, attached to f. 2 of the bifolium on Tennis. It adds details to the account and is in the hand of Philip Skippon.

6   A single folio, measuring 210 x 155 mm, attached to p. 155. It describes the game of Hurling and is in the hand of Philip Skippon with some additions by Willughby.

7   A bifolium, measuring 335 x 220 mm and folded both horizontally and vertically, attached to p. 254. It describes the game of Nine Men's Morris and is in the hand of Willughby, with some material in the unidentified juvenile hand.

None of the papers in question is from the same stock as the volume itself. Inserts 1 and 2 look physically alike, though their dimensions differ and they cannot have come from the same gathering of cut pages. Willughby appears to have used small notebooks of this format in his work, and other examples survive.[123] Inserts 3 and 6 bear a similar Three Circles watermark, but differ from Insert 4, which has a very faint mark. Insert 7 is from quite different paper, with a Bunch of Grapes watermark. The possibility has been considered whether these physical characteristics might help to date the inserts more precisely, but as yet no other examples of the paper types in question have been identified and the arguments about the sequence of writings fall back largely upon internal textual evidence and our knowledge of Willughby's biography.

2.3   The composition of the Book of Games

In understanding the composition and structure of the Book of Games, a useful comparison can be made with another of Willughby's surviving manuscripts, the Commonplace Book (NUL Mi LM 15). This is a volume displaying many immediate points of similarity with the Book of Games, both in terms of the presentation of the text and the evidence of layers in its

---

123.   For example, notes from his reading at Oxford in 1660 are on a similar notebook, inserted in the relevant section of his Commonplace Book (NUL Mi LM 15/13 formerly attached to p. 243).

composition. The features are characteristic of familiar commonplacing methods, as adapted and incorporated into seventeenth-century practice. Although the tradition was a medieval one in origin, the method lent itself to the needs of scholars following inductive principles and was particularly well suited to those engaged in classificatory and taxonomic pursuits.[124]

Francis Willughby's Commonplace Book is a folio volume, not unlike the Book of Games in appearance. It has the standard format of such works, with a set of general headings (often, as with Virtue and Vice, in pairs of opposites) written as page headings. These are not in the hand of Willughby; as we do not know when or from what source he acquired the volume we cannot tell whether he took over its use from an earlier owner or whether these headings were prepared for him in the manner of the printed Commonplace Books.[125] In addition to the traditional headings, Willughby also supplied a typical seventeenth-century access to the contents, by means of a separately constructed alphabetical index.

Willughby used the volume for a variety of purposes, and over a period of time ranging from his Cambridge days onwards.[126] He made systematic notes, including regular page references, on works that he was reading, gathering together extracts from different authorities on a single subject. There is a mixture of languages, largely English and Latin with a sprinkling of Greek, with notes typically taken in the language of the source. In some cases, the content concerns Willughby's own speculations or calculations, rather than the work of others. The volume was also used occasionally to record dated scientific observations, such as the series of chemical experiments already mentioned, and an early investigation by Willughby of the rising of sap in trees, subsequently reported to the Royal Society.[127] Other topics dealt with which have particular relevance to a study of Willughby's intellectual concerns in general and the Book of Games in particular include mechanics, as illustrated by the bouncing of a tennis ball (below, Appendix 2), the conduct of trades, such as the production of woad, and the art of decorative paper-cutting. His mathematical speculations about the efficiency of planting trees in a quincuncial figure, subsequently reported to the Royal Society, were first recorded here (NUL Mi LM 15/1, pp. 353–4, Mi LM 15/21; Birch 1756–57: i, 115). Willughby's was not the only hand present; the entries concerning the chemical experiments are largely in another hand, of neither Willughby nor Ray. From the contents one can gain an invaluable picture of

---

124. On the importance of commonplacing in this period, see Bolgar (1954), Lechner (1962), Beal (1987) and Moss (1996).

125. Such volumes were indeed available for purchase; see Foxe's *Pandectae locorum communium* (1572), which offered readers a blank commonplace book, with headings printed at the head of most pages, a brief printed preface and pages prepared for the compilation of an index.

126. Relatively few of the entries are dated, but in many cases the dates of publication of books referred to can provide a *terminus post quem*. An overall date range of 1658 to 1665 has been suggested (Welch 1972: 83).

127. Willughby's first recorded experiments on birch trees at Middleton took place in March 1665, before Ray had returned from the Continent (NUL Mi LM 15, pp. 433–4); later reported in *Phil. Trans.* (1669: vol iv, no. 48, 963–5).

the variety of Willughby's intellectual interests. These include topics with which we do not commonly associate him, such as the question of Anglo-Saxon and Celtic origins of English place names, on which he made extensive notes. This etymological material relates to Willughby's other dialect and linguistic interests, which as we have seen he shared with Ray and Skippon.

With the model of the Commonplace Book in mind, it is easier to understand the composition of the Book of Games. There are many immediate physical indications that here, too, the text was not written sequentially through the book but that, as in a commonplace book, headings were first provided for pages and sections, and that text was then added from time to time. The headings can be related to a confused mass of notes on the flyleaf, naming various games which were, presumably, candidates for inclusion (see Appendix 1 below). The index provided by Willughby at the front of the work groups the games by category and provides page references. For the subsequent descriptions he has with rare exceptions used only the right-hand pages. An exception to the normal pattern is the section on Children's Games, where a different hand has written descriptions of 11 games across five consecutive pages. It is clear from the shades of ink, the handwriting, and the use of space on the page that even on a single page the text was not always written at one sitting, but returned to for additions and further references. The symbols '*Q*' (quaere), '*V*' (vide) and '*X*' or '*X X*' appear at various points, indicating questions to be further investigated, and references to sources or other parts of the work. These and similar symbols are also used by Willughby in the Commonplace Book. The structure of the volume, in short, is that of a classified list, with all the data available to Willughby noted under the relevant heading from the index.

Examination of the contents of the book enable us to hypothesize a little further about its inception. A strong argument can be made that the sections on Stowball, Billiards and Tennis were among the earliest portions written. Each was on separate paper stitched into the first leaves of the codex, rather than within the appropriate categorization of game later in the volume. By contrast, the inserts on Hurling and Nine Men's Morris have been placed in the section to which they belong.

If we are correct in assuming that Stowball was one of the earliest descriptions of a game made by Willughby, we can speculate about a possible date for the development of Willughby's interest in the subject of games. The game of Stowball was geographically restricted to certain parts of Wiltshire, Gloucestershire and Somerset,[128] and it is likely that Willughby's observations would have been made on one of his visits to the West Country, either in 1662 or 1667. This would be consonant with the physical character of the loose notes on which the description of Stowball was written, for such pages provided a handy means for the recording of notes on a journey. In this case the pages, apparently torn from a small notepad, also contain a cancelled observation regarding the absence of sea coal between the Wye and the Usk,

---

128. See the Glossary of Games below.

supporting the suggestion that it dates from the 1662 trip, when Willughby passed through Wales en route to south-western England, and when Ray's record of his itinerary includes a similar comment on the geographical distribution of sea coal.[129] An additional clue that the Stowball description marks the start of Willughby's systematic investigation of games lies in the nature of the description itself, which is markedly less clear than his account of other games, indicating either that he was somewhat hurried at the time, or that he had as yet little practice in making such descriptions.

Ray's record of the 1662 expedition to the west does not mention any occasion when Stowball was observed and makes no explicit reference to local games as an ongoing focus of the travellers' attention, but it gives an insight into the way in which such journeys were conducted. Ray may have been primarily engaged in making a study of the natural world, but this was not narrowly defined and he also notes details of the residents of the country, their activities, and their history. On 5 June near Cardigan, for instance, Ray reports an account of an annual competition between two of the local communities, who each attempt to throw a wooden ball over a bank on the Monday of Whitsun week (Lankester 1846: 173). On 19 June at Bristol 'we took notice of the bowling green, and the plain about it', while on 5 July he records an account of 'hurling-play' from Cornwall (Lankester 1846: 179, 193–4). Such entries support the suggestion that the circumstances of the 1662 trip may have encouraged Willughby to speculate about 'plaies' and to begin his work of description.

If this hypothesis is correct, we have a ready explanation for Philip Skippon's contributions to the work, for Skippon was also on the journey in 1662. The reference to Hurling on the flyleaf of the Book of Games with Skippon's name attached to it suggests that this contribution may have been offered by Skippon when he became aware of Willughby's occupation. Willughby possibly knew of an account made by Skippon in 1662. His description certainly contains structural and verbal echoes of the description of Hurling in Ray's Itinerary (below, Appendix 4) and probably came from the same source and occasion. Skippon's other contributions, on Billiards and Tennis, were also provided on loose sheets which Willughby then attached to his codex in the appropriate section. Skippon, based in London, may have had readier access to these courtly pastimes (particularly in the case of Real Tennis) than did Willughby in Warwickshire. His role in the Book of Games is intriguing, for his own personal interest in the subject can be demonstrated from the following year, when he travelled to Italy with Willughby, Ray and Bacon. Skippon's subsequent account of his experience includes descriptions of the playing of cards, in particular Basset, in Venice and their manufacture in Padua, as well as an account of an ancient game in Venice, known as Gioco d'amore.[130]

---

129. The cancelled comment in Willughby's notes reads: 'No coales between Wie and Uske but all the countrie over else' (p. 14, f. 13/ii^v); Ray records for 14 June 1662 'Coals are dug up on both sides of the two rivers just mentioned [Uske and Wye], but not between them' (Lankester 1846: 178).

130. Skippon (1732: vi, 508–9, 520–21, 533; see Appendix 3 below).

Of even greater significance is another insertion, of a small notepad. Similar in appearance, this was presumably written before the main volume was started, for it was attached to one of the early folios of the volume. Its interest lies in its content: speculations by Willughby about various possible classification of 'Plaies'. The kinds of divisions and categories he suggests show him applying the same techniques of scientific description to games and recreations that he was employing in his natural history work. He lays out the directions such a study could take, and explores some possibilities for creating a taxonomy of games. These notes convey a sense of Willughby's early and speculative definition of his subject. Further notes of the same general type were later added directly to the codex leaves.

We do not know at what date Willughby attached his notes on 'Plaies' and Stowball to the old blank codex in his possession and began adding further material directly into the book, but any speculation on this needs to take into account the title on the outer cover of the volume – 'Notes on different Trades'. As we have suggested, this presumably relates the volume to Willughby's intended contribution to the Royal Society's programme for compiling descriptions of trades, following Willughby's nomination to the relevant committee in March 1664.[131] Based on this knowledge we may suggest that it was 1665 at the earliest that Willughby put the volume to a different purpose, the recording of his descriptions of games.

Some further speculation on the evolution of the text is suggested by examination of its different elements. The description of each game is generally introduced by its title on a new page, or with a line dividing different games within a single category. On occasion a title is given but no text has been supplied. Apart from the loose papers and notes attached to the beginning of the volume, a thematic structure is apparent in the ordering of the entries. The earliest entries would appear to have been the numerological notes on pages 5 to 9, to be discussed below, and the sections on games at Tables and Cards. All of these come towards the first part of the codex, and are united by their heavily mathematical content, indicating the centrality of this aspect of games in Willughby's interests. Subsequent categories which can be identified include: Running, Drawing and Lifting, Leaping, Ball Games, Kit-Cat, Children's Games, Word Games, Throwing Games, Morris Family, Animal Sports and Games of Combat. The categories are generally separated by blank pages to allow for further insertions later. Some sections have very few entries, but the quantity of blank paper left available by Willughby suggests that this should be seen as a sign of the work's incomplete state rather than a conscious restraint or omission.

The heavily annotated flyleaf offers further clues to Willughby's intentions. It bears notes about games which might be included, with their names then crossed out as descriptions were completed. There are grounds for suggesting that the flyleaf was originally blank and that its use represents a middle stage in the enterprise. A number of the names are repeated, making

---

131. See further above, Section 1.4.

it likely that the list was made over a period of time. The codex may simply have lain open on a table during this period, since the haphazard arrangement of names on the flyleaf suggests that Willughby was not sitting in front of the book when he wrote them. The entries were clearly made at different times with different quills and often apparently with haste. Some are difficult to decipher. A number appear to be in the juvenile hand identified elsewhere in the volume. Some of the thematic sections seem to have been first introduced at this stage, such as Drawing and Lifting, and Games of Combat, each of which begins with one of the titles listed on the flyleaf (Drawing Dun and Fistie Cuffs respectively). In other cases, games seem to have been added to existing sections following their identification on the flyleaf. The double-handed games at Tables and Cards, as well as Hannikin Canst Abide It, come into this category. Many of the most familiar contemporary games, which are included in the volume itself, do not appear on the flyleaf. These include Bandy-Ball, Football, Bowls, Blindman's Buff, Call and I Call, Fox and Goose, Horn Billets, Nine Men's Morris, Prison Bars, Quoits, and Stoolball. Their absence supports the suggestion that the notes on the flyleaf represent some form of brainstorming to identify further games to be included once the most obvious ones had been dealt with. Already by this stage the sections on Running Games, Balls, Bowls and Children's Games had apparently received some attention. The table of contents had, possibly, already been constructed; it is worth noting that the games missing from it (particularly examples of Children's Games) are ones listed on the flyleaf.

The contents of the manuscript are not its only significant features: there are also some noteworthy lacunae. Many of the games named on the flyleaf are not included in the text, and there are headings for games without any text, most notably Draughts. Willughby also has a cross-reference to a proposed section on Chess, which was not written, perhaps owing to the vastness of the subject and the substantial body of Chess literature already in circulation.[132] Furthermore, Willughby has made no allowance for dice games other than the games at Tables. This is particularly striking, since one might expect that his interest in probability would have attracted him to a class of games so intensely mathematical. The omission adds weight to the argument that Willughby may have written another text on this subject, possibly the work he occasionally refers to within the Book of Games as the 'Book of Dice'. This may indeed have been the volume described by his daughter as a work 'w[ch] shews y[e] Chances of most Games', which was among her father's manuscripts.

The section on Children's Games presents one of the most intriguing problems in the volume. The hand responsible for these pages and for a few other juvenile games in the volume appears to be the only one to join Willughby in the creation of the codex itself;[133] Skippon's contributions are all

---

132. See the Glossary of Games.

133. The unidentified juvenile hand appears not only in the core section on Children's Games (pp. 229–33) as discussed here but also on pp. 90, 220, 236, 241 and 254/i–ii. These occurrences are flagged in the text below. See Figure 9 for a sample of this hand.

on loose sheet inserts. There are various clues suggesting that the scribe was somebody with imperfect writing skills, and most probably a child. To assist the writer, the pages are ruled, the only pages in the volume to be so treated. In composition and grammar, the passages lack polish and the spelling is unorthodox, in many places simply phonetic. The work has been meticulously corrected by Willughby himself, who not only extended and amended the text but also made alterations to the spelling, grammar and punctuation by overwriting the original text. He altered certain elements consistently, changing the writer's final long 's' for his own preferred form, amending the 'e' graph and substituting 'v' for consonantal 'u'. In some cases the alteration is clearly a matter of style, with Willughby replacing something quite acceptable by his own preferred form. It is a compelling conclusion that in these passages a child has been allowed to make the description, which has then been corrected by Willughby. It would be pleasing to present this as evidence of collaboration between father and son. However, although the young Francis Willoughby had precocious abilities, reading the Bible by the age of five and capable of writing 'very pretty letters to his friends', he was less than four years old when his father died and there is no certainty that these passages had not been written at an earlier date than this (Wood 1958: 118). From Cassandra Willoughby's later family memoir and the family correspondence, particularly from Lettice Wendy to her sister-in-law Emma Willughby, it is clear that there were other children in the family circle: Katherine Winstanley and her son James (born 25 March 1668) were, for instance, frequently resident at Middleton.[134] No candidate is, however, particularly indicated, and it seems probable that the identity of the juvenile writer of the children's games will remain unknown.

---

134. Wood (1958: 100); references to social activities and the visits of friends and relatives to Middleton are scattered through Lady Wendy's correspondence (NUL Mi Av 143/36/1–24).

Early Writings on Games

3.1 Games literature

Willughby's compendium of games is a unique and outstandingly rich source of information on an important domain of human activity, with very little in the way of close parallels elsewhere in the medieval or early modern tradition. Yet if games literature is taken in a broad sense to include all writings that focus on games from a more or less technical perspective, the genre had centuries of history behind it prior to Willughby. The history of European games literature is a massive and largely unexplored topic, and even the bibliographic basis for its study is lacking, but at least a preliminary survey of the antecedents to Willughby's work will be of use here to help understand the text's position in the history of writings on the subject.[135]

The earliest work in the European tradition in any way comparable to Willughby's treatise is certainly the book of games of Alfonso X ('Alfonso the Wise') of Castile, dating to 1283, which describes over two dozen dice games and board games, the latter including Chess, Three, Nine and Twelve Men's Morris, Fox and Goose, the Astronomers' Game, and various games at Tables.[136] The handsome appearance of Alfonso's richly illustrated folio volume, with its precise description of the games, doubtless reflects in part a personal passion for the games themselves, but Alfonso presided over one of the most sophisticated courts of medieval Europe, and as an active patron of the sciences his treatise must also have been motivated by an interest in the intellectual dimension of the games. The classes of games covered in the manuscript supports this interpretation, since all involve strategy, mathematics or geometry, or a combination of the three. On the other hand, the inclusion of Three Men's Morris, which the manuscript implies is principally a game for children, and of details on the manufacture of game components, suggests a desire for a kind of encyclopedic comprehensivity

---

135. For discussions and bibliography on the history of games, old but still useful, see Jessel (1905) and Avedon and Sutton-Smith (1971: 19–54); on early games literature concerning cards, see Parlett (1991: 51–60); for a further discussion of the sources for the study of games, see the introduction to the Glossary of Games.

136. For a facsimile edition, see Alfonso (1913); transcribed with German translation in Alfonso (1941).

within the classes of games included. It is also worth noting that the lavish illustrations of Alfonso's book, while profoundly different in character from Willughby's, do share with Willughby the emphasis on visualization as an integral part in the understanding of a game.

Other medieval games literature is more limited in scope, generally dealing with only a few selected board games. A number of manuscripts contain illustrations of game boards; one early English example, dating to the tenth century, offers an illustration with commentary of the initial board set-up for a game entitled *Alea Evangelii*, a version of the northern European game known in Scandinavia as *hnefatafl*.[137] An Anglo-Latin manuscript of the early fourteenth century describes the board set-up and victory conditions for a dozen games at Tables.[138] The Middle Ages also produced a substantial corpus of 'problem literature', collections of hypothetical board-game situations as set pieces in game strategy. Most of these problems deal with Chess, with some material on games at Tables and games in the Morris family.[139] The first European treatises on Chess also appear in the Middle Ages; a number of such texts were printed in the sixteenth century, and by Willughby's day the genre was well established in English.[140]

Only a few of the other pastimes mentioned by Willughby have a literary history that can be traced to the Middle Ages. Sports with martial associations play a relatively minor role in Willughby's treatise, but are among the oldest forms of European sports literature. Treatises on combat arts can be traced as far back as *c.* 1300, those on equitation to the fifteenth century, and on gymnastics (especially vaulting, which derives from the equestrian accomplishment of leaping into the saddle) to the sixteenth century.[141] Hunting treatises, which overlap with Willughby's reference to coursing, can also be found in the Middle Ages.[142] Collections of riddles existed in pre-Conquest England, with antecedents dating to late Roman times, and conjuring tricks are occasionally found in manuscript compendia of the Middle Ages; the printed tradition in both areas was extensive by Willughby's day.[143]

During the sixteenth century, the topics covered by games literature began to broaden considerably. Not surprisingly, many of the pioneering examples come from Italy. Perhaps the earliest treatise on sports is Antonio Scaino's *Trattado del Giuoco della Palla* (1555), a vigorous account of Football, Tennis,

137. Corpus Christi College, Oxford, MS cxxii, reproduced in Bell (1960: plate 5); see also Murray (1962: 61–2). A late thirteenth-century manuscript includes two illustrations of game-boards, without text, Trinity College Cambridge MS O.2.45 2ᵛ–3ʳ; Murray (1962: 580).

138. BL MS Roy 13.A.xviii, printed inaccurately in Fiske (1905: 161–5). The text also has a section on Chess.

139. There were two major families of games texts, known as *Civis Bononiae* and *Bonus Socius*; Murray (1962: ii. ch. 7); also Murray (1962: 614–24, 643–4, 702–3, 733 and *passim*).

140. Murray (1962: ii. chs 3, 4, 6–8, 11–13); see also 'Chess' in the Glossary of Games.

141. On these topics, see 'Duelling', 'Running and Races', and 'Leaping, Vaulting' in the Glossary of Games.

142. On hunting treatises, see Cummins (1988).

143. On these topics, see 'Riddles' and 'Tricks' in the Glossary of Games.

and Balloon (a game roughly comparable to modern Volleyball); Scaino
describes the games in considerable detail, providing illustrations of
equipment and scale diagrams of the playing areas. The Florentine Giovanni
Maria Bardi in 1580 published a description of his city's variant of Football.
Bartolomeo Ricci (1553–54) and Vincenzo Giustiniani (1626) have left us
works on Pall-Mall.[144]

The sixteenth century also witnessed an expansion of the range of table
games covered in games literature. A large part of Girolamo Cardano's
treatise *De Ludo Aleae* (c. 1526, first published in 1663) consists of a pioneering
study of probability, but the overall focus of the text is on games at dice,
tables and cards, with some material on the nature of gaming, on cheating
and on games in the classical world; Cardano was also the author of a lost
treatise on Chess.[145] A similarly intellectual spirit informed the appearance of
a number of treatises on 'scholarly' games. Claude de Boissière published in
1556 both Latin and French versions of a treatise on the Philosophers' Game,
adapted into English by Ralph Lever in 1563. William Fulke published in
1571 a treatise on the Astronomers' Game (Willughby's 'Ludus
Astronomicus'), and in 1578 a further one on the Geometric Game.

A different kind of technical interest in table games appears in the genre of
'rogue literature' that was also emerging in England at about this time.
Gilbert Walker's *A manifest detection of ... diceplay* (1552) set the tone for a
substantial body of texts and portions of texts centring on the tricks used by
professional cheats.[146] This tradition, in which Willughby shows some
interest, was to be a major contributor to English games literature: one text in
the genre, Charles Cotton's *The Nicker Nicked* (1669), was to form the core of
the most enduring and influential English games treatise of the seventeenth
century.

Another class of games literature dating to the sixteenth century focuses
on verbal games for use in courtly circles. These games, known in France as
jeux d'esprit, were party entertainments involving discourse on courtly and
scholarly themes such as love, the liberal arts and society; they are the
aristocratic cousins to the relatively simple verbal games in Willughby's
treatise. The genre seems to appear earliest in Spain and Italy. One early
example is Luis Milan's *Libro de Motes* (1535); the classic work in this
tradition, Innocentio Ringhieri's *Cento Giuochi Liberali* (1551), was abridged
into French within a few years of its first publication, and its contents were
recycled many times in the seventeenth century.[147]

---

144. Scaino (1984); Bardi (1580); for Ricci and Giustiniani, see Bascetta (1978: ii, 251–350). A French
treatise of 1592 is said to describe the game of Tennis (Forbet 1592); we have been unable to locate
a copy of the treatise, but it may be the same as the section with the same title in La Marinière (1674:
134–46). An Italian manuscript treatise of the sixteenth century, apparently still unedited, offers
descriptions of some sports and parlour games, as well as a list (without details) of other games,
including board games and children's games (Furno 1903).

145. Cardano (1663); Ore (1953); Dummett (1980: 366–70).

146. Kinney (1973); Aydelotte (1913); cf. also Scot (1584: 331–3); Cotton (1930: 1–9); Holme (2001:
iii.xvi.2.47a).

147. Milan (1951); Ringhieri (1551; 1555); cf. Sorel (1657).

Such collections of courtly games emerged during a period that saw a growing number of prescriptive treatises on education and gentlemanly accomplishments, and in the seventeenth century a part of this latter genre began to converge with the tradition of games literature. Baldassare Castiglione's *Il Cortegiano* (1528) touches only briefly on the topic of games, but Sir Thomas Elyot's *The Gouernour* (1531), Roger Ascham's *The Scholemaster* (1570), and James I's *Basilikon Doron* (1599, 1603) have much to say about the proper choice of pastimes.[148] Ascham's *Toxophilus* (1545) and Richard Mulcaster's *Positions for the Training Up of Children* (1581) both emphasize the importance of physical training in a well-rounded programme of education, offering some substantial detail about archery in the case of the former, and about various athletic sports in the latter. The corpus of works in this tradition expands in the seventeenth century. Henry Peacham's *The Compleat Gentleman* (1622) and Richard Brathwait's *The English Gentleman* (1630) both discuss at length the proper repertoire of pastimes for the gentry, with emphasis on sports.[149] Gervase Markham's *Country Contentments* (1615) describes in detail the arts of the horseman and hunter, and also includes brief sections on Archery, Bowls, Tennis and Balloon. Later seventeenth-century versions of the genre offer fairly technical information on various gentlemanly entertainments, again emphasizing hunting and related sports. Examples includes Nicholas Cox, *The Gentleman's Recreation, in Four Parts, viz. Hunting, Hawking, Fowling, Fishing* (1674); Richard Blome, *The Gentlemans Recreation ... The Second Part, Treats of Horsmanship, Hawking, Hunting, Fowling, Fishing, and Agriculture. With a Short Treatise of Cock-Fighting* (1686); and Robert Howlet, *The School of Recreation* (1684), which discusses Billiards, Bowls, Tennis, cockfighting, horse-racing, and archery. A few treatises focus on particular entertainments in the gentlemanly repertoire: to those subjects already mentioned, such as Chess, martial arts, hunting, and equitation, several on cockfighting were added in the seventeenth century.[150]

Where early seventeenth-century writings in the prescriptive tradition had focused heavily on sports, a new generation of games literature made its appearance in mid-century in both England and France, offering substantial repertoires of indoor games for readers looking for social self-improvement. The emergence of this new trend in games literature corresponds very closely with Willughby's lifetime. The genre owes much to the *jeux d'esprit* tradition: it appears to begin with the publication in 1642 of Charles Sorel's *La Maison des Jeux*, a text which includes a long dialogue on games, with emphasis on parlour games, supplemented with a large selection of games taken from Ringhieri. Shortly thereafter Denis La Marinière published anonymously the rules for a card game, *Le Jeu de Piquet*, of which the earliest known edition dates to 1647. The booklet was reprinted in 1652, and in 1654 La Marinière

---

148. Castiglione (1987: 166–7 (ii.31)); Elyot (1531: 62ʳ–74ʳ, 94ᵛ–103ʳ); Ascham (1570: 19ᵛ–20ʳ); James I (1603: 120–27).

149. Peacham (1622: 177–85); Brathwait (1630: 165–231).

150. See the Glossary of Games under 'Cockfighting'.

incorporated it into his *La Maison Académique*, a compendium of diverse games including card games, Tennis, Ticktack, Billiards, and a selection of Ringhieri's *jeux d'esprit*. La Marinière's extremely successful book was reprinted in expanded versions numerous times into the eighteenth century, and its success may in part have prompted Sorel to issue a second part of his own *Maison* under the title of *Les Récréations Galantes* (1671), with a selection of divination games, verbal games and other genteel pastimes.

This outpouring of games literature for a gaming audience had an impact across the Channel, beginning with an English translation of La Marinière's first treatise, *The Royall and Delightful Game of Picquet* (1651). In 1655 the first edition of John Cotgrave's *Wits Interpreter* included a variety of entertainments, such as card tricks, verbal tricks, tricks with paper and string, and mathematical puzzles; the second edition in 1662 added the rules for Picket from La Marinière, as well as rules for Chess and the card games L'Ombre, Gleek, and Cribbage. *The Mysteries of Love & Eloquence*, published anonymously in 1658, described a variety of courtly party-games, including Cross Purposes, Gliphing, and Rhyming ('Crambo').

Cotgrave's rules for card games were themselves cribbed by the most successful of the seventeenth-century English treatises on games, *The Compleat Gamester*, which first appeared anonymously in 1674; in the eighteenth century it was attributed to Charles Cotton. The first part of the text was a reprint of *The Nicker Nicked*, a text on the techniques of cheaters first published in 1669 under the pseudonym Leathermore. The remainder combined the sporting orientation of the treatises on gentlemanly accomplishments with details on fashionable indoor games; topics included riding, archery, cockfighting, Chess, Tables, Billiards, Bowls, dice games and card games. Cotton provides reasonably complete rules for many of the indoor games he describes, but in some cases the rules are omitted or given in a condensed form that presumes prior knowledge on the part of the reader; generally speaking, the rules seem intended chiefly as an aide-memoire, and much of the text is given over to discussing techniques and strategies, and to vivid evocations of the pleasures and perils of gaming.

As with many previous examples of games literature, *The Compleat Gamester* might be termed 'gamester literature', in that it was evidently written by a gamester for a gaming audience. It was very well received: new editions continued to be published well into the eighteenth century, and the text was a major influence on Richard Seymour's *The Court Gamester*, published in numerous editions from 1719 onward. It is this tradition of guidebooks for the aspirant game-player which produced, in 1742, Edmond Hoyle's essay on Whist, the first of Hoyle's detailed studies of games which were eventually to form the base of the most authoritative of all English games texts and the model for subsequent games literature written for a gaming audience.[151]

---

151. It is worth noting that Hoyle's first work on the game of Whist, 1742, included an appendix dealing with the calculation of probabilities; he later published a separate treatise on the subject of the doctrine of chances in 1754.

3.2 Encyclopedic, scholarly and antiquarian writings

Cotton's accounts of various games were further reused in a very different kind of work, Randle Holme's *Academy of Armory*, partially published in 1688.[152] Ostensibly a treatise on heraldry, the *Academy* is in fact an outstandingly ambitious encyclopedia, and it includes several passages on games. Book 3 chapter 5 offers fairly detailed accounts of Billiards, Tennis, Chess and Draughts, and chapter 16 of the same book (unpublished until 1905) has substantial passages on dice games, games at Tables, Chess and other board games, Bowls, Nine-Pins, and card games, as well as a long list of other pastimes and sports, with brief descriptions of a few of them.[153] Although Holme's work draws on *The Compleat Gamester*, his coverage of games goes well beyond Cotton both in breadth and depth. The heraldic emphasis on technical language and precise description manifests itself in Holme as an interest in the technical vocabulary of his subjects, and much of the content of his sections on games deals with the specialized terminology of each. In this respect he has much in common with Willughby, and a resemblance can also be found in other aspects of the text. Like Willughby, Holme's treatment of games has a strong visual component (embodied in the quasi-heraldic images of the games and game equipment he mentions), and combines a fairly detailed account of fashionable pastimes, like cards, Tables, Tennis and Billiards, with a more cursory but still wide-ranging list of other games, including country pastimes and children's games. It may also be significant that one of the most prominent subjects in the *Academy* is the description of trades, a subject which Holme evidently researched in part through interviews with practitioners. Holme's interest in this topic, as well as his methodology and general encyclopedic outlook, connects him intellectually with the work of the Royal Society, and with Willughby's own interests. However, although Willughby's 1662 journey through western England, which seems to have stimulated the games treatise, passed through Chester, where Holme was a moderately important figure, there is no evidence that the two men met.

Games had in fact figured in the European encyclopedic tradition since its reemergence in the twelfth and thirteenth centuries, but the thrust of these early encyclopedias was largely theoretical, and they offered very little detail on games: few are even named, let alone described.[154] The kind of detail found in Holme, or in Willughby, has more in common with the related genre of classified vocabularies whose medieval progenitor can be found in the names and vocabulary relating to games at Tables and ball games included in

---

152. Holme (2001 [1688]). The latter part of Book 3 remained unpublished in Holme's lifetime (Holme 1905). Randle Holme (1627–1699) was, like his father and grandfather, an heraldic painter and professional genealogist, and acted as deputy Garter for Cheshire, Shropshire, Lancashire and North Wales; see *DNB*.

153. Holme (2001: iii.v.8.147–9, iii.xvi.2).

154. See for example Hugh of Saint-Victor (1939: 44 [ii.xxvii]); Trevisa (1975: ii, 1056).

Isidore of Seville's *Etymologies*.[155] These lists often have a dual nature: their immediate function is as tools for language reference and teaching, but they can also be read as rudimentary encyclopedias. A literary analogue appears in chapter 22 of Rabelais's *Gargantua*, which lists some 200 games played by the hero during his youth.[156] Similarly encyclopedic in tone is the extended discussion of games in Robert Burton's *Anatomy of Melancholy* (1621), which under the rubric of considering the usefulness of exercise as an antidote to melancholy offers extensive information on games, their context, and their history.[157]

A further connection between language instruction and games literature can be found in bilingual dialogues from the sixteenth century and later, many of which include scenes of games ranging from schoolyard entertainments to cards and Tennis.[158] Also relevant in this context are the bilingual dictionaries which were published in significant numbers in the seventeenth century. These often draw on classified vocabulary lists, and frequently provide a brief description of individual games, giving them a certain encyclopedic dimension.[159]

The classified vocabulary and language instruction traditions are merged with a visual pedagogical technique in Jan Amos Comenius's *Orbis Sensualium Pictus*. This illustrated polyglot vocabulary for children was initially published in German and Latin in 1658, and was translated into numerous European languages over the following years; the English edition dates to 1659. The *Orbis* includes three scenes of games, each with a description in Latin and the vernacular: a fencing school, a Tennis scene, and a scene of boys' games, which includes Bowls, Nine-Pins, Closh (a relative of Croquet), whipping the top and archery.

Comenius offers a point of contact between the literary tradition and a tradition of games iconography stretching back to the Middle Ages. Depictions of games are found in the margins of numerous medieval manuscripts, some of which, such as the early fourteenth-century Flemish *Roman d'Alexandre* (MS Bodley 264), feature games as prominent recurring motifs.[160] In the sixteenth century, games became a standard element in the repertoire of the emblemists, whose collections of moralizing icons with accompanying epigrams made extensive metaphoric use of games.[161] Closely

155. Isidore of Seville (1985: 299–301 [xviii.60–69]). For other classified vocabularies with sections on games, see Wright and Wülker (1884: i, 737–8, a fifteenth-century list); Pollux (1608: ch 9, a classical work still used as a textbook in the seventeenth century); Golius (1579: ch. 51); Hadrianus Junius (1585: 293–300, 520–22); Frischlin (1600: s. 177); Withals (1602: 260 ff.); Hoole (1657: s. 45); Howell (1660: part 2, s. 28); Du Cange (1678: iii, 1450 ff.).

156. Rabelais (1973: 98–104); English translation by Thomas Urquhart (Rabelais 1653: 93–7).

157. Burton (1990 [1621]: 338–50, [ii.ii.4]).

158. See for example Vives (1970); Florio (1591); Minsheu (1599).

159. See for example Thomas (1587); Cotgrave (1611); Minsheu (1617); Littleton (1678).

160. For a facsimile edition, see James (1933).

161. See for example Paradin (1989: 182, 237); Peacham (1969: 81, 113, 168); Quarles (1643: 40, 88, 104); Visscher (1949: 8, 20, 41, 61, 137, 143, 160, 165); Wither (1634: 16). The books by D'Allemagne (1902; 1903; 1905) are probably the richest single source of early games iconography.

related is the genre of art depicting numerous games either in a single scene or in a suite of images; children's games were a particular favourite, the most famous example being Pieter Bruegel's painting on this theme.[162] Other works in the genre include Pieter van der Borcht's sixteenth-century prints of game-playing apes, the French *Les Trente-Six Figures* (1587), Jacob Cats's *Kinder-Lustspiele* (1657), and Jacques Stella's *Les jeux et plaisirs de l'enfance* (1657).[163]

Comparable to the tradition of encyclopedic writings is the corpus of antiquarian and scholarly studies that address games from an historical or ethnological perspective. A pioneering example is the early sixteenth-century study of ancient games by Celio Calcagnini, used by Cardano for his own treatise on games.[164] Johannes van Meurs in 1622 published a dictionary of classical Greek entertainments, including with it a study by Daniel Souter entitled *Palamedes, sive, de tabula, lusoria, alea, et variis ludis: libri tres*, which examined games from philological, historical, and ethical standpoints.[165] The principal English example in this genre was the monumental *De Historia Shahiludi* (1689), and *De Historia Nerdiludii* (1694) (on Chess and Backgammon respectively) by Thomas Hyde. These works offer an historical and comparative study of various board games and other games, including Draughts, games of the Morris family, ball games and children's games, drawing heavily on Asian as well as European material.

Similar scholarly and antiquarian impulses lie behind the genre of local geographies that occasionally included reference to games. This kind of writing about games has early antecedents: William FitzStephen's twelfth-century account of London enumerates some of the entertainments used there; John Stow's Elizabethan description of London printed FitzStephen's text, with additional historical and contemporary information on Londoners' pastimes.[166] Both of these texts merely list rather than describe the games in question, but Richard Carew's *Survey of Cornwall* (1602) has a substantial description of Hurling and wrestling as practised by the Cornish, and George Owen's description of Pembrokeshire (*c.* 1603) includes a fairly detailed account of the Welsh game of *Cnapan* (akin to Hurling).[167] John Aubrey's natural history of Wiltshire (1685) has a few remarks on Stowball, although the description is limited to the physical apparatus and geographic distribution of the game.[168] Edward Chamberlayne's description of England (1669) includes two lists of games played by the English, one the games of

---

162. Hindman (1981); Vanden Branden (1982).

163. Stella (1969); Cats (1657); *Les Trente-Six Figures* is reproduced *passim* in D'Allemagne (1902, 1903, and 1905). On van der Borcht and Cats, see Hindman (1981: 460–62).

164. 'De Talorum ac Tesserarum at Calculorum Ludis, ex more veterum', printed in Gronovius (1697–1702).

165. Meursius (1622).

166. Robertson (1875–85: iii, 9, 11); Stow (1912: 84–91).

167. See the Glossary of Games under 'Hurling', 'Wrestling'.

168. See the Glossary of Games under 'Stowball'.

'the Nobility and Chief Gentry', the other of 'the Citizens and Peasants'.[169] Chamberlayne is of particular interest because as a Fellow of the Royal Society he offers a point of comparison for understanding the interpretation of games among Willughby's intellectual associates. The following section provides further discussion of the relevance of these contemporary studies to Willughby's own Book of Games.

---

169. Chamberlayne (1669: 45–7). Similar lists of games by the classes who play them can be found in Burton (1621: 342) and Peacham (1641: 31).

4

Approaches to the Book of Games

The period during which Willughby's Book of Games must have been composed, from about 1662 until his death in 1672, coincided with the emergence of the genre of 'gamester literature' typified by Cotton's *Compleat Gamester* (1674) and other works discussed in the previous section. Willughby's Book of Games is like these works in as far as he describes the rules of specific games in sufficient detail to instruct a novice, gives details of the processes of betting,[170] and comments on strategies for victory.[171] Furthermore his allusions to methods of cheating[172] have parallels in Cotton, as well as evoking the related genre of 'rogue literature'. It is apparent from the detail of Willughby's comments that he himself played and enjoyed some of the games in question, and on a few rare occasions he alludes to his own gaming experience at both cards and tables in the first person.[173]

Nevertheless, other aspects of Willughby's text set it apart from the tradition of gamester literature. Its very scope is both different and broader. He includes, for instance, a large number of rural games and pastimes, which in itself extends the interest of the work well beyond that of the kind of readership at which *The Compleat Gamester* aimed. Willughby has a separate section of children's games and elsewhere he describes games played by young boys, including both those demanding physical skill and those involving word games or similar activities associated with methods of learning. Even more unusual is his attention to the 'first things children play with', a list including whistles, rattles, pieces of coral for their gums and 'babies' (i.e. dolls), described from what would appear to be first-hand observation – as indeed it might have been after 1668, when his first child was born. The scope of Willughby's work extends to traditional pastimes, represented particularly in games associated with Christmas (pp. 231ff.). There is a small collection of superstitions at the end of the volume, and references to folkloric knowledge are scattered through his text.

170. See for example pp. 15/ii^r, 21, 33, 59, 71, 73, 79, 83, 150, 151, 155/i, 272.

171. See for example pp. 29, 31, 39, 41, 59, 67, 69, 80, 81, 83, 87, 89, 155, 168, 246, 254/i^r, 254/i^v.

172. See for example pp. 21 ff., 55, 58, 68, 218, 219, 268, 269.

173. See for example pp. 39, 85.

Finding a comprehensive and accurate label for the range of activities covered by Willughby raises interesting definitional problems, not least because there has been semantic restructuring of the English words in question between the seventeenth century and the present. The word 'game' had then a much narrower sense, as a note made by Willughby on his classification scheme makes clear: 'The word game is more properly used for Cards, Tables, Chests &c. and not for games of exercise' (p. 3/ii).[174] The seventeenth-century term most closely corresponding to the relevant sense of the modern English 'game' (as in 'the game of chess') was 'play', as used by Willughby for his booklet entitled 'Plaies'. The catalogue of the Willughby library at Wollaton, dating from the early eighteenth century, lists a volume entitled 'Book of Plaies', which on this basis can be identified as the present text (NUL Mi I 17/1). However, since the usage of 'play' in this sense (as a count noun) is now obsolete, the present editors, to avoid confusion with stage plays, have reworded the title of Willughby's work as the Book of Games.

In order to address more general questions of scope and motivation, the Book of Games needs to be located in a contemporary context which is broader than simply the tradition of gamester literature. The range and structure of the work, as also its manner of assemblage, can only be adequately accounted for in terms of Willughby's other pursuits. His scientific preoccupations, evident in the introductory biographical sketch above, indicate an intellectual curiosity characteristic of his time, and an application of philosophical and empirical thinking equally of his age. He was indeed a seventeenth-century virtuoso with both the inclination and opportunity to indulge his talents, and he applied his training with equal vigour to any subject which caught his attention. The seventeenth-century scientific tradition was not, however, a monolithic one but involves several distinct, and not wholly compatible, philosophical frameworks. To these can be traced both the inspiration and the methodology for Willughby's description of the world of games.

4.1 The Baconian tradition

For those seeking to promote scientific observation and experiment in the seventeenth century, Francis Bacon (1561–1626) served as an important figurehead. Bacon left a powerful legacy in his call for 'histories' of all kinds, intended to be combined into a great natural and experimental history which would serve as the foundation for a 'Great Instauration' of the sciences.[175]

---

174. Willughby's gloss is, of course self-contradictory: the term 'game' is polysemous, being used both in the narrower sense prescribed, and also in a broader generic sense, as in the expression 'games of exercise' itself.

175. 'History' in this context means a systematic account of a set of natural phenomena, without reference to time (OED, sense 5), as distinct from other senses of the term involving either narrative or chronological sequence. On the 'Great Instauration' of the sciences, see Webster (1975).

Histories of this sort aimed to be comprehensive in coverage, and to be based on first-hand observation wherever possible, with second-hand reports being ranked for reliability. Most characteristically, they resulted in taxonomies of knowledge based on categories arrived at by inductive methods. Some of the most enduring achievements of this scientific methodology lay in its application, through the work of Ray, Willughby and their contemporaries, to the natural world. But the scope of the Baconian programme was not limited to natural history. Human activities of all sorts were also to be studied, both for exploration in their own right, and in order to extrapolate whatever local artisan knowledge might be of interest to scientific concerns. Thus in a programmatic scheme published as an appendix to his *Novum Organum Scientiarum*, Bacon outlined a general 'Catalogue of particular histories' calling for investigation.[176] The natural histories are listed in the first three sections, ranging from the heavenly bodies, or astronomical history, to the history of serpents, worms, flies and other insects. In a fourth and final section are grouped together items falling under the rubric of 'histories of man'.[177] These range from human anatomy to a final miscellaneous category including 'common experiments which have not grown into an art'; sandwiched in between we find the full range of human arts, sciences, professions, trades, and structured activities of all sorts. There would be no grounds for excluding the study of games from this agenda, and indeed it is listed as item 123: *Historia Ludorum omnis generis* (History of games of all kinds).[178]

Willughby was personally engaged with the Baconian programme through his association with the Royal Society committee concerned with the description of trades, as well as through his own reading.[179] He was, moreover, actively involved with another seventeenth-century mapping of human knowledge that can itself be seen as a response to Bacon's call. This was Wilkins's philosophical language, for which as we have seen Willughby made a notable contribution in supplying the classification schemes for animals. It is instructive to see how the position of games is demarcated in Wilkins's work, where they are included under the category of 'Motion' (itself a subcategory of 'Action'), which itself falls under the superordinate heading of 'Recreation'. The definition is as follows:

By RECREATION, *Diversion, Pastime, Sport, Exercise*, are meant those several kinds of *Actions* which are used for divertisement or *Exercise*: to which may be annexed the word GAME, *play, Prize*, signifying such kind of *Exercises*, wherein there is an endeavour for *Mastery*.

(Wilkins 1668: 241)

---

176. 'Catalogus historiarum particularum secundum capita', printed at the end of 'Parasceve, ad historiam naturalem et experimentalem' appended to Bacon (1620; reprinted in Bacon 1887–1901: i, 405–10; trans. iv, 265–70).

177. At the very end of the list, Bacon adds histories relating to 'Pure Mathematics', which he says, must also be written, noting however that 'they are rather observations than experiments'.

178. Bacon himself drafted an outline for such a history of 'Play' (Bacon, 1887–1901: vii, 210–11).

179. Notes on various of Bacon's writings are scattered through Willughby's Commonplace Book (NUL Mi LM 15); the Willughby Library Catalogue (NUL Mi I 17/1) lists a copy of the 1623 first edition of his *Collected Works*.

Closer examination reveals striking parallels between Wilkins's taxonomic scheme and Willughby's discussion in the booklet entitled 'Plaies' which is inserted in the Book of Games (pp. 3/ii^r–3/iv^v). Here he analyses games in terms of a similar branching scheme. Both Wilkins and Willughby start with a general dichotomy which divides games into those associated with mind and those associated with body. Each of these categories then subdivides into a trichotomy: thus Wilkins divides games of the mind into those depending on chance only, those depending on a combination of chance and skill, and those depending on skill only, which matches (albeit in a different order) Willughby's three-way division of games into 'those that have nothing of chance' (e.g. Chess), 'those that altogether depend upon fortune' (e.g. Irish, Cross and Pile) and 'those that have art and skill both' (e.g. most games at cards and Tables). A diagrammatic display shows clearly the parallels between the two schemes:

Recreation
 of the mind
  depending on chance only
  depending on chance and skill
  depending on skill only
 of the body
  in respect of the whole [football, bowling, dancing, wrestling etc.]
  in respect of the eye or the ear [including theatre and music]

A. Wilkins's classification

'Plaies' that exercise
 the wit
  those that have nothing of chance
  those that altogether depend on fortune
  those that have both art and skill
 the body [including Tennis, Stowball, etc.]

B. Willughby's classification

Willughby goes on to identify further subcategories of games on the basis of common distinguishing characteristics, employing the same method as used elsewhere in the identification and classification of natural history specimens. He thus groups together: games of pure chance; games of chance and skill; games of pure skill; table games; games of exercise; simple and complex games; games mostly played by children, by women and by men; games for various numbers of players; games using a spherical ball; and so on. Further categories emerge from the structure of the treatise, the groupings either being made explicit in the text itself or in Willughby's own index: games played on the Tables board; card games; running games; games of sheer strength (pulling, lifting, throwing); jumping games; games involving balls and other projectiles; children's games; word games; games based on throwing at targets; board games; and violent games. The games at Tables are further subdivided into games involving half the board and those involving the entire board; his index similarly divides the card games into those in which all the cards are used and those where some cards are left out; and the sections on card games and ball games offer further ideas on the formal classification of these games.[180]

Whatever the taxonomic similarities between Willughby's Book of Games and Wilkins's universal language scheme, however, there is also one fundamental difference. Wilkins's *Essay* expressly omits from detailed consideration things which are 'appropriate to particular *Places* or *Times*', on the grounds that things which are locally or temporally variable are not to be assigned primitive signs in a universal language (Wilkins 1668: 295). On these criteria, there is no place for a more detailed analysis of 'games and plays' in his work, once their general place in the classification scheme has been established. (Similarly excluded were terms for dress, cuisine and other things with a local or ephemeral aspect.) Willughby's more ramified classification of games, with its inclusion of the division of games by country or other limiting identification, must thus be seen as complementary to Wilkins's scheme, rather than simply a part of it.

These distinctive aspects of Willughby's work might arguably link it with another sphere of activity in the seventeenth century which was stimulated by the Baconian philosophy, namely the systematic description of localities, covering not only their physical geography, flora and fauna, but also their human geography. The subject material of such investigations ranged from buildings and antiquities to trades, dialects, customs, superstitions and other characteristic phenomena. Such county histories, as they came to be known, using the term 'history' in its full Baconian sense, are represented early in the century by Carew's *Survey of Cornwall* (1602), to which Willughby refers for an account of Hurling. The work of later seventeenth-century county historians is familiar through the studies of Warwickshire by William Dugdale (1656), Oxfordshire by Robert Plot (1676) and Nottinghamshire by Robert Thoroton (1677).[181]

County histories, and other works of a chorographical nature, are by definition concerned with what is local and specific (in contrast to the non-local concerns of Universal Language), but the methods employed to garner such information were themselves systematized in a manner comparable with the experimental methods being developed in the circles of the Royal Society. Thus Robert Boyle drew up a set of 'General heads for a natural history of a country, small or large' (Boyle 1666a) which was published in *Philosophical Transactions* in the same year as his more specific questionnaire

---

180.   See pp. 57 and 167.

181.   A broad survey of regional studies in the seventeenth century can be found in Mendyk (1989); see especially chapter 8, which deals with the concerns of the Royal Society in these matters.

concerning mines (Boyle 1666b).[182] This would not have escaped Willughby's attention, given the family's mining interests. Robert Hooke composed a similar scheme, published only posthumously (Hooke 1705), which gives fine-grained instructions as to how observations for the compilation of a natural history should be recorded.[183] Nor did these directives remain purely theoretical and programmatic; to gather data for his description of Oxfordshire, Robert Plot had a broadsheet printed for distribution which listed headings under which information was solicited, and Edward Lhuyd likewise circulated a printed questionnaire for his description of Wales.[184]

It is apparent from Willughby's working notes that the Book of Games shares something of the spirit of the chorographical tradition of county histories. In his booklet on 'Plaies', in which he outlines his general classification, he sets out a distinction which focuses specifically on variability with respect to time and place.

Plaies are also either {
Ancient (Quoits &c.)

or modern
}

Proper to several countries {
Europe
America
India
Africa
Asia
}

Elsewhere in the booklet he observes (p. 9): 'In most places there are games proper for the severall seasons of the yeare', and in the codex itself he goes on to make the following notes (p. 3):

Games at set times of the yeare.
Throwing at cocks on Shrove tuesday

These considerations support the hypothesis that Willughby's project may have had its first origins in his observation of the highly localized game of Stowball, which he would have had the opportunity to witness during the journey to the South-West in 1662, with an additional impetus supplied by observations from Ray and Skippon regarding West Country Hurling, gathered after Willughby had returned home. Significantly, as we have seen,

---

182. Although this questionnaire is primarily concerned with geological matters relating to mining, the breadth of coverage is indicated by the 'promiscuous enquiries' at the end, one of which asks: 'Whether Diggers do ever really meet with any subterraneous *Dæmins*; and if they do, in what shape and manner they appear; what they portend; and what they do, &c.' (Boyle 1666b: 343).

183. It is worth noting that Hooke's taxonomic system (1705: 22–6) has a primary divide between natural and artificial histories, the latter ('Artificial and mechanical operations', i.e. histories of trades) including a category of 'vaulters, tumblers, wrestlers etc.'.

184. A reproduction of Plot's broadsheet 'Enquiries' is appended to the facsimile edition of his *Natural History of Oxford-shire* (1972). On Lhuyd's 'Parochial Enquiries', see Emery (1959).

the closest parallels to the present work in the publications of Willughby's circle of friends are to be found in travel writings: Ray's own description of Hurling from the journey to the West Country in 1662, and Skippon's notes on card games and on the making of cards, observed in Italy.[185]

At the same time, it must be observed that, beyond these initial notes, Willughby's Book of Games in fact contains relatively little concerning things which are particular to time and place. Of the normal concerns of the chorographers, only the origins and histories of games receive much attention in the treatise. At the end of the insert on 'Plaies' Willughby has a cursory note referring to Leon Baptista Alberti as a source on the origins of games (p. 13/iii^v), a topic which also figures in his Commonplace Book (NUL Mi LM 15/1, pp. 313, 314). On several occasions he offers speculations as to the ways in which games have changed over time, and how complex games may have been derived from simple ones; these speculations are in many cases based on numerological or etymological considerations (pp. 15/ii^r, 21, 41, 72, 164, 222). In the case of Beast, Willughby offers the information that it is a new game of French origin (p. 81). With these few exceptions, contextual issues mentioned in the 'Plaies' insert are largely lacking from the body of the text. There is surprisingly little reference to the seasonality of specific games, except for Throwing at Cocks (p. 269), Cobnut (p. 219), and 'Christmas Gambols' (p. 231), even though other games in the compendium, such as Stoolball and Football, are known to have had strong seasonal associations. The geographic distribution of games is also largely omitted, even in such cases as Stowball and Hurling where the game is known to have been strictly regional; Skippon alludes to Hurling as sometimes being played by Cornish against Devonshire men, but there is no specific discussion of the matter. The absence of any mention of the regionality of Stowball is particularly striking if it was indeed this aspect of the game that attracted Willughby's attention in the first place.

The social environment of games is an issue mentioned only tangentially in Willughby's discussion, although he was writing during a period which saw the gradual divergence of popular and elite culture, manifested in part through recreational occupations.[186] The omission is of interest, for without doubt Willughby was aware of the distinctions which led to the association of particular games with particular groups of people and might have seen this as a defining attribute in listing games by categories. His friend John Ray made such an allusion in his gloss on the proverb 'All fellows at football'.[187] The subject was discussed by many of Willughby's contemporaries and predecessors: indeed, as has been noted, his Royal Society colleague Edward Chamberlayne adopted a classification of games based on the classes of

---

185. See above Section 2.3 for discussion of the significance of the 1662 trip and Skippon's Italian observation; also below, Appendices 3 and 4.

186. On the divide between popular and elite culture in the seventeenth century, see Burke (1994: 270–86); see also the collection of essays in Reay (1985).

187. 'If gentlemen and persons ingeniously educated will mingle themselves with rusticks in their rude sports, they must look for usage like to or rather coarser than others' (Ray 1670).

people who practised them (Chamberlayne 1669). Many of the games in Willughby's treatise are known to have been associated with specific social constituencies: Football, Prison Bars, Stoolball, Cudgels and Pitching the Bar are all identified in other sources as plebeian or rustic sports, while Tennis, Billiards and horse races were pastimes for the upper classes, and pursued by those aspiring to social acceptance. Willughby, however, mentions social distinctions only in passing; for instance, in remarking that his version of Bowls is considered 'the most gentile play' (p. 244), and in describing the suit of diamonds in a pack of cards as familiarly known to 'the countrie people' as 'picks' (p. 53).

Distinctions of age are represented somewhat better, but by no means systematically. The children's games beginning on p. 217 are identified as such by their heading, but it is not clear at what point this section ends; those up to p. 230 are clearly played by children, but this is not necessarily the case with those on p. 231. In the following pages, Selling of Bargains (p. 235) and Dust Point (p. 236) seem to be juvenile games, while Glyphs (p. 234) and Purposes (p. 237) were not exclusively for children. Other children's games are mentioned elsewhere, with the constituency at most implied by the language of the text or by the fact that the description is in the juvenile hand: examples include Wheehee (p. 90), the pulling games (pp. 157 and 158), Hop Frog (p. 162), and Scotch Hopper (p. 163). Lilman (p. 154) is described as being played by a 'lusty youth'. Only in the case of Father Fitchard (p. 187) does Willughby note that the game is 'used only by boyes'.

The possibility that a game might be played by multiple constituencies is mentioned in the case of Bowls, where Willughby remarks that one must not outbowl women or young people by main strength (p. 243). Otherwise, gender distinctions are largely ignored, except in the general reference in the insert on 'Plaics'. Many of the games in the compendium were in fact played exclusively by men (Hurling, Tennis, Football); some might be played by both sexes together (Stoolball, Barley-Breaks). Although none was exclusively female, some were especially favoured by women: the 'Plaies' insert mentions cards, and the same might be said of Troll Madam. Particularly significant is Willughby's lack of comment in the case of Barley-Breaks, which, to judge by other sources, was normally played by mixed-sex couples – the running, grabbing, and changing of partners providing a proverbially famed opportunity for rustic flirtation. Not surprisingly, there seems to be a gender bias in the choice of games, at least those of children: the juvenile games described are the characteristically competitive and hierarchizing games which later folkloric studies found to be especially associated with boys; there is very little of the mimetic games associated with girls (such as 'Ghost' and 'Mouse and the Cobbler' in Gomme 1894–98), and the reader should bear in mind that the games culture of girls is probably under-represented in the text.

4.2 Mathematical and scientific aspects

It has been argued by Charles Webster that the county histories which were produced by fellows of the Royal Society draw attention to the presence within the Society of an influential group 'relatively out of touch and indeed out of sympathy with the mechanical philosophy in its various forms', the works being more relevant to the museum of dead objects that Ashmole founded than the world of experimental science in either its pure or applied forms (Webster 1982: 59–60). Given this divide, Willughby's sympathies must be seen as lying not with the county historians, but with the experimental scientists, and it is to this aspect of his thought that we now turn.

Although Willughby is today primarily remembered for his work on natural history, for contemporaries he was as highly regarded as a mathematician as a naturalist; Ray's posthumous tribute to his friend gave special reference to Willughby's understanding of 'the most subtil parts of the Mathematicks'. As we have seen, he had been trained at Cambridge by Isaac Barrow, and the two corresponded on mathematical issues after Willughby left the university. Most compelling, perhaps, is the evidence of his correspondence with Oldenburg, in his capacity as secretary of the Royal Society, which includes regular discussion of mathematical topics as well as those relating to natural history.[188] The Book of Games needs to be read in the light of these concerns. Scattered throughout the text are observations which demonstrate the mathematician, observing, testing and speculating about the games in question and their origin and meaning.

These concerns are set out in a programmatic way at the start of the volume in the booklet on 'Plaies'. Here (with explicit cross-reference to the relevant section on cards), Willughby attempts to provide an explanation for the mathematical patterns of games by reference to ancient astronomical lore.[189] Thus he observes that:

The cards beeing divided according to the lunar months, the number of the solar months & daies in each month are brought in in the reckonings of severall games. 12 in Trumpe, Gleeke &c, 31 in One & Thirtie, Loadum, Cribbidge.

(Book of Games, p. 6/p. 52)

Willughby returns to this notion repeatedly throughout the text, positing that astronomical reference is involved in the manner of scoring in Tennis (p. 15/ii), Hannikin (p. 60), Ruff and Trump (p. 71), Ging (p. 88) and Bowls (p. 246). His speculation concerning the significance of sexagesimal reckoning in this connection is spelled out in more detail:[190]

---

188. See above, Section 1.4, and the tabulation of Willughby's correspondence in the Bibliography below.

189. The initial observations are explicitly drawn from notes on his reading (surviving in his Commonplace Book, NUL Mi LM 15), the works referred to being Cardano's *Commentary on Ptolemy's On the Signs of Astronomy* (1555), and More's *Mystery of Godliness* (1660).

190. John Wallis has a related but different view of the use of sexagesimal fractions for the measurement of angles and units of time, concluding that it is done 'principally in compliance with Ptolemy's Tables; and a kind of tenaciousness of old Customs, rather than any necessity or even convenience of so doing' (Wallis 1685: 30).

The numbers 7, 5, 15, 16, 12, 32, 30 are most used in games because they are most used in astronomicall accounts, in numbering the parts of time &c. 7 is the number of the planets; 15 is ½ of the degrees in a signe; 16, ½ + 1; 12 is the number of the signes; 30, of the degrees in a signe; 31, of the degrees + 1; 5, of the lesser planets. 16 & 31 are more used then 15 & 30. One would expect 8 and 13 should bee used as wel as 12 and 7. But the reason for 16 & 31 is that the sun is supposed to have gone thorough ½ of a signe when hee is entred into the 16ᵗʰ degree & the whole signe when hee is entred into the 31.

(Book of Games, p. 9)

The assumption on which these observations are based, and which would have been shared by many of Willughby's contemporaries, was that games which were of an ancient origin could have retained a numerical structure that was the product of astronomical knowledge of that time. This knowledge may have since become submerged but might be retrievable by rational analysis of the games themselves.[191]

A second and more strikingly contemporary aspect of mathematics evident in the Book of Games lies in entries which show Willughby's interest in the calculation of odds in dice and card games. Indeed, modern probability theory has its origins in this period of the seventeenth century (Todhunter 1865; David 1962). It emerges partly from analyses of mortality rates (e.g. Graunt 1662), and partly on the basis of works dealing with games of chance such as Christiaan Huygens's *De Ratiociniis in Ludo Aleae*, itself drawing on earlier works such as Cardano's *De Ludo Aleae*.[192] Among others who at this period called for a systematic study of games in connection with the doctrine of chances was Leibniz:

Il seroit bon que celuy qui voudroit traiter cette matiere, pour-suivit l'examen de jeux de hazard; et generalement je souhaiterois qu'un habile Mathematicien voulût faire un ample ouvrage bien circonstancié et bien raisonné sur toute sorte de jeux, ce qui seroit de grand usage pour perfectionner l'art d'inventer, l'esprit humain paroissant mieux dans les jeux que dans les matieres les plus serieuses.

(Leibniz 1882: v, 448)[193]

There is evidence from Willughby's text that his interest in games was heavily motivated by mathematical considerations of this sort. However, what observations he has to make about the calculation of odds are not extensive,

---

191. A similar sort of assumption was currently made concerning proverbs, which, even though passed down in a folk tradition, might represent submerged philosophical knowledge from an ancient source. On the social history of proverbs at this period, see Davies (1975) and Obelkevich (1987).

192. Cardano's work was composed in the mid-sixteenth century, but first printed in the *Opera Omnia* (1663: i, 262–76). The treatise by Huygens was first published in 1657 as an appendix to a work by Fransiscus à Schooten; it appeared as a separate work in English translation in 1692. Shortly after the turn of the century, important tracts were produced in both areas by another member of the Royal Society, de Moivre (1711, 1718 and 1725).

193. 'Anyone wanting to deal with this question would do well to pursue the investigation of games of chance. In general, I wish that some able mathematician were interested in producing a detailed study of all kinds of games, carefully reasoned and with full particulars. This would be of great value in improving the art of invention, since the human mind appears to better advantage in games than in the most serious pursuits' (Leibniz 1981: 466). Leibniz expresses the same idea on other occasions (see Leibniz 1882: iii, 620, 621, 667; iv, 570).

and are largely limited to the section on cards. One reason for this may well be the absence from Willughby's text of a section dealing with games involving dice alone (setting aside the extensive section on board games using dice), a lacuna which might be explained, as we have suggested above, by the hypothesis that the 'Book of Dice' to which he refers on several occasions was a compilation of his own that has not survived. But whatever the work referred to, Willughby's note at the outset of his card section, 'All the demonstrations of dice may bee applied to cards' (p. 50), indicates that the mathematical apparatus he was deploying involved a systematic body of proofs.

Closely associated with these references to probability are Willughby's more general observations on the mathematical properties of the games he is describing. In the working notes in the booklet on 'Plaies', one of the questions that he poses for investigation is: 'How games may bee altered, varied and what may bee added to them' (p. 3). This preoccupation adds a speculative dimension to the fundamentally observational tone of the work, and this is sustained throughout. Thus, for example, in his discussion of games at Tables, he adds the note: 'Games may bee invented with 3 or 4 tables as wel as with 1 or 2' (p. 21) and similar notes occur in his discussion of One-and-Thirty Bon Ace (p. 60), and Laugh and Lie Down (p. 62). In his notes on Noddy and Cribbage, he poses the question why a sequence of cards should not follow a geometrical progression rather than a simple arithmetical one (p. 66). Indeed, after his discussion of Cribbage he appends a whole variant of the game of his own invention and speculates whether any of the other possible mathematical progressions might be here employed (p. 69).[194] It is apparent from these notes that their primary purpose is not the invention of games as such, but rather the attainment of a mathematical understanding of how the games work. As Willughby himself says: 'A game is fully understood when it can bee fitted for any number of plaiers' (p. 58), and likewise only when each of its mathematical parameters has been examined. In the same manner, the presentation of the Puzzle of the Ship in the Book of Games is complemented by a note in the Commonplace Book, speculating how the problem can be generalized to all possible cases.[195]

A third area of scientific interest relating to the Book of Games concerns the mathematical investigation of motion, percussion and other aspects of mechanics. Willughby's preoccupation with the theory of motion is well attested. As we have seen, his doubts about the theories proposed by Wren and Huygens led him to submit a paper of his own on the subject for the consideration of members of the Royal Society, asking Oldenburg to present this as an anonymous contribution.[196] This prompted an exchange of letters

---

194. 'Q: Whither any of the ten other proportions of Pappus should be brought in' (p. 69).

195. 'Q: How this may bee done in any number, when the number of those that are to be saved is more or lesse then the other number' (NUL Mi LM 15/1 p. 360).

196. See above, Section 1.4. Willughby's paper was registered; it is in Latin and, although anonymous, is in his own distinctive hand (Royal Society Classified Papers III (i), no. 54). The broader mathematical context of this episode, with details of the background to the theories of Huygens and Wren, is summarized in Hall (1966–67: 24–38), who also provides a translation of part of the text of Willughby's paper.

with Oldenburg between May 1669 and June 1670. On 23 July 1669 Willughby wrote to suggest ways in which Wren's theories on motion might be empirically tested: 'either with pendulums knocking one another, bullets shot out of one Barrel into another, whether they should Find other Bullets at rest, or boules upon planes' (Oldenburg 1965–86: vi, 150). He hoped, with Oldenburg's encouragement, to undertake further experiments himself on 'Dr Wrens noble theorie', in which he expected also to involve John Wilkins. The conclusion of the correspondence without further mention of any such experiments appears to close the subject, but there is evidence that he did indeed consider experiments, and that he saw in games a natural laboratory.

In the account of Tennis supplied for the Book of Games by Philip Skippon there are observations about particular strokes of the racket, 'brickwalling' and 'cutting of a ball', which affect the way the ball rebounds from a wall or floor (p. 15/i$^\text{r}$). These phenomena were evidently a matter for debate and correspondence, since an additional loose sheet in Skippon's hand records some further observations which he has received from a Mr Hoogan,[197] giving a more elaborate definition of one of the strokes in question:

Cutting of a Ball is when with a swift motion of a racket the ball is made to glide from on side of the rackett to the other, so that when 'tis off the rackett this wirling of it makes it in its progressive motion turne upon its owne axis, & consequently when it meetes with any opposition of the ground or wall it lyes almost still & rebounds but a very little …

(Book of Games, p. 15/iii)

and offering further diagrams which illustrate two different effects. Willughby's own thoughts on the topic are recorded not in the Book of Games itself but in an entry in his Commonplace Book (below, Appendix 2). This rehearses the facts concerning the verticity of a ball about its own centre (i.e. 'spin') and the way this can cause a ball to rebound 'contrarie to the rules of reflection'. He illustrates the angles of contact by means of a diagram similar to those in Skippon's text. The passage concludes with a programmatic statement (reminiscent of the comments in his letter to Oldenburg of 23 July 1669) about the sorts of experiments which might be conducted to investigate the matter systematically:

Experiments should bee made with round Boules thrown hard against a wall, *X X*. with tennis balls reflected at all angles and an exact calculation made of the difference of the angles. *X X* and whither a ball strooke with a contrarie verticity would not rebound as other balls but with a bigger angle *X* & would have a contrarie effect. *X X*

(NUL Mi LM 15/1, p. 350)

Other speculative aspects of mechanics are alluded to in the Book of Games, but take the form of tangential queries in the context of otherwise factual

---

197. This may be Christiaan Huygens, whose treatise on percussion, 'De motu corporum ex percussione', was compiled around 1659 (published posthumously 1703), but it has not been possible to confirm the identification.

descriptions of games. Thus, in discussing the way in which the 'cat' can be positioned so as to rebound differently when struck by a staff in the game of Kit-Cat, Willughby speculates:

Q: Whither it bee not the same reason that makes a flint breake & a bullet flat sooner upon a soft place as a bed &c.

(Book of Games, p. 174)

adding the note 'V: Cartesses French Letters', a reference to the French edition of Descartes *Correspondence* (Descartes 1657–67), where there is a discussion of such matters.[198] Other scattered observations relating to motion can be found in the descriptions of Copsole (p. 157), Pitching the Bar (p. 161), the Running Jump (p. 168) and 'posting' balls (p. 174).

4.3 Religious and moral aspects

In a century marked by extremes of religious fervour and social unrest, the activities which fall under the headings of leisure and recreation themselves roused conflicting passions about moral perceptions and legal controls. Furthermore, the definition of recreation was itself coming into question as a result of social and political processes which were to effect radical changes in distinctions between work and leisure during the transition from pre-industrial to industrial society.[199] Behind the violence and variety of contemporary opinions concerning the propriety or impropriety of individual pastimes – in particular those involving gambling – new opinions about the very nature of 'play' and 'games' were being formed and articulated. Thus in a discussion of gambling, Charles Morton argues that while it is quite lawful to use money to procure recreation (i.e. to meet incidental costs), it is never lawful to play with the intent and purpose of procuring money (i.e. to gamble); his conclusion is based on the argument that: 'it Destroys the necessary distinction between Work and Play' (Morton 1684: 32).

The intense legal and moral preoccupation with games, though deeply concerned with contemporary religious beliefs, had in fact a long history going back to classical antiquity and a literature with which seventeenth-century commentators were well familiar.[200] There were different strands to this concern, but some common elements can be identified. Moral questions came inevitably to the fore in discussions of recreations which involved betting and which might be conducted in contexts leading to drunkenness or debauchery; as the proverb had it: 'What the Gaming-House leaves, the Tap-

---

198. Letter from Descartes to Mersenne, 25 December 1639 (Descartes 1996: ii, 631).

199. On the categories of work and leisure in the sixteenth and seventeenth centuries, see Thomas (1964), and other contributors to the same collection of essays.

200. Contemporary surveys of earlier literature on play and gaming, including classical and patristic authors, can be found, for example, in Taylor (1660: book iv, ch. 1), and Morton (1684).

House, Tavern and Whore-House receives' (cited by Morton 1684: 47). Considerations of a more political and social nature prompted efforts to control behaviour and limit occasions of public disturbance, which might, for instance arise through community engagements such as Football. At the same time, moral, social and political justifications could also provide explicit support for physical games and other recreations. Defence of the realm was a justification for physical sport going back to the Middle Ages: practice at the longbow provided a trained force which could be called upon in military necessity.

The special circumstances of the seventeenth century inevitably brought changes in attitudes towards recreational activities. The period's civil and political upheavals were fuelled by religious convictions which ranged from mild reformism to the excesses of Ranters and other sectaries (Hill 1972). Opinions within particular groupings were far from uniform, and shifted over time and through the experience of civil war. Those who addressed the issue of sports and games did not speak with a single voice, and apparently common voices sometimes reflected different motivations. The result could be considerable fluctuations in what was considered appropriate, proper and lawful. The pattern is familiar in the cycles of fashion and prohibition suffered by the English stage in the seventeenth century.[201] Any form of recreation might be subject to a similar range of attitudes.

Conflicting views about the correct observance of the Sabbath gave rise to some of the most explicit statements about games and leisure. Perhaps the most controversial came from the crown itself. In James I's Declaration on Sports in 1618 the king, feeling the necessity to 'rebuke some Puritanes and precise people', overrode local prohibitions against Sabbath game-playing. While barring games or similar activities during the time of divine service, the Declaration made a practical case for Sunday sports:

when shal the common people haue leaue to exercise, if not vpon the Sundayes and Holydayes, seeing they must apply their labour, and winne their liuing in all working dayes?

(Govett 1890: Appendix)[202]

Such arguments did not convince those Puritans who observed the Sabbath strictly, and believed that all forms of recreation on the Lord's Day were sinful. In fact, the use of Sundays for leisure activities was, to some degree, inevitable. Records of local practice are sparse. The church courts were concerned primarily with absence from divine service; evidence that games

---

201. On the stage in the Interregnum period see Butler (1984); for discussion of Puritan gentry attitudes to recreation and the theatre see Cliffe (1984: ch. 7) and Heal and Holmes (1994: ch. 8). Useful surveys of contemporary recreational activities can be found in Sieveking (1917), Manning (1923), McIntosh (1963) and Rühl (1984). The social history of leisure more generally is examined in Brailsford (1969), and in popularizing earlier works such as Hole (1949) and Wymer (1949).

202. The Declaration remained controversial; James issued a defence of it in 1624 and Charles I published his own version in 1633. For further background on its reception and Puritan attitudes towards sports on the Sabbath see Hill (1964: 169, 197, 200–205).

occasioned such absence is surprisingly rare.[203] The Commonwealth period saw increased focus on the Sabbatarian issue, and extended the prohibition to the playing of games on the monthly fast days instituted by Parliament (Firth and Rait 1911: i, 81). Monthly days of rest and recreation were however established to replace the traditional holy days (Firth and Rait 1911: i, 954, 985). Recreational activities as such were by no means prohibited, although strongly discouraged by some. George Fox for instance reports: 'And we told them when they went to their sports and games and plays and the like that they had better serve God than spend their time so vainly' (Fox 1998: 234). The restoration of the crown, and the libertine court of Charles II, posed a greater challenge to moderate opinion, with the clear demonstration of excess polarizing attitudes for and against the merits of card playing, gambling and other courtly pursuits.

Of the theological arguments which were marshalled against games, some of the most complex and interesting concerned games of chance, typified by games involving randomizers such as dice and cards. These were, of course, precisely the types of game which particularly engaged Willughby's attention as a mathematician. One strain of religious thinking saw games of chance as unlawful, not because of any immoral behaviour associated with them, but in themselves. From a theological point of view games of pure chance were seen as making an improper use of the lot, which Morton defined as 'A casual event purposely applied to the decision of some doubt or question' (Morton 1684: 10). As a way of deciding weighty matters, the drawing of lots was considered a quite proper procedure, on the assumption that the outcome of the roll of a die is determined by God, as an instance of special providence (as distinct from general providence); under this view 'The Lot is an ordinance of God, appointed for special ends and purposes'.[204] However, its use for 'vain and unnecessary ends', as in gaming, is sacrilegious, and on these grounds intrinsically unlawful.[205] The theological arguments can become convolute. Daneau (1586: F4) points out that a game of pure chance, if unlawful on that basis, ceases to be so if a player cheats and thereby controls it, though the act of cheating of course renders the game unlawful on independent grounds.

Although games of chance were to be condemned on these grounds by many writers in the sixteenth and seventeenth centuries, the position was not

---

203. Records of the Nottingham Archdeaconry court, for example, reveal few instances of presentment by church wardens on such grounds; it is not clear if the explanation lies in a genuine absence of the offence, a relatively permissive attitude in local parishes, or other factors. The occasional presentments – generally from early in the century – usually concern playing at cards: e.g. NUL AN/PB 295/4/78 (1613); 302/121,142 (1621); 339/13/11 (1629). We are indebted to Narita Pike for alerting us to these sources.

204. Such usage was deemed to be sanctioned by appeal to scriptural authority, with reference, for instance, to the choice of Saul as king (1 Samuel 10: 21), the selection of Matthias as the successor to Judas (Acts 1: 23–36) and the division of Christ's garments (Matthew 27: 35–7; Mark 15: 22–4; Luke 23: 35; John 19: 23–4).

205. Perkins (1608: 105–6). An objection based on similar grounds was made by the sectaries against the non-serious use of oaths, in that they constitute a frivolous invocation of the special presence of God (Morton 1684: 13–14).

without its challengers. One of the earliest and most influential of these was Thomas Gataker, who argued that the rolling of a die in a game of pure chance involved only a 'common' providence, and that no 'special' providence is thereby invoked (Gataker 1619; 1623).[206] It followed that there was nothing inherently sacred about lusorious lots as such, and thus nothing intrinsically unlawful in their use. As Morton was later to sum up Gataker's position, it is 'the too common abuse, and not the bare use of a lusory lot that is blameable' (Morton 1684: 13). This debate between those who accepted Gataker's arguments and his opponents was a live one throughout the century.[207] The speculations surrounding this controversy, which served to establish a theologically respectable view that the fall of a dice is determined purely by chance, opened the way for the development of modern probability theory in the latter half of the century.[208]

There were indeed arguments which went one step beyond seeing sports and pastimes as activities to be tolerated and proposed their active encouragement in some circumstances. Recreation as physick had been argued for earlier in the century by Robert Burton, who in looking at the phenomenon of the melancholic man provides a detailed discussion of games and recreations and their proper application in 'putting off melancholy'.[209] This is echoed by Jeremy Taylor and other writers, sometimes extolling the virtues of particular games. In 1680 an anonymous minister offered the same opinion in a broadsheet on Chess. 'This I premise, that I think Recreation to be in it self Lawful, yea that like Physick it is to some persons, and in some cases very needfull: Also that this Game of Chesse is not only Lawful, but it may be the most ingenious and delightful that ever was invented.'[210] Even in this context however excess and abuse might creep in. The writer goes on to demonstrate that even that most acceptable of intellectual challenges could give rise to inappropriate 'abuse' in the form of addiction and obsession. He explains his reasons for 'disusing and declining' the game of Chess. It is, for one thing, a time waster. 'It hath had with me a fascinating property', namely that 'when I have begun, I have not had the power to give over [...]. When I have done with it, it hath not done with me.' Clearly seventeenth-century doctors and clergy were aware of the effect of games and gaming on health and of the possibility of addiction, even in the case of Chess, revered as the most civilized and civilizing of games.

---

206. Gataker's treatise was an explicit response to a work by John Northbrooke (1579). He was in turn challenged by James Balmford (1623), who reasserted that 'we are not to tempt the Almightie with vaine desire of manifestation of his speciall providence' (Balmford 1623: 102). Gataker replied in (1623) with a further defence of his arguments.

207. Morton, who was himself against the Gataker position, provides a list of other critics (1684: 21). Mainstream theologians such as Jeremy Taylor, in defending the lawfulness of such games, demonstrate an acceptance, implicit or explicit, of Gataker's approach (Taylor 1660). Earlier tracts invoked in this debate include Daneau (1586) and Fenner (1590).

208. On the early history of probability theory, see Todhunter (1865), David (1962) and Coumet (1970); for more specific discussion of the theological issues involved, see Bellhouse (1988).

209. Burton (1990 [1621]: ii, 67–97).

210. *A Leter from a Minister to his Friend concerning the Games of Chesse* (Anon. 1680).

Assertions of the moral and religious acceptability of playing games can be found in other contemporary sources. Taylor, perhaps the best known of the Protestant casuists, addresses this issue in his *Rule of Conscience* (1660). Here he examines the ethical issues of games and recreations in two sections. In the first, Taylor rehearses the arguments put forward by theologians against the playing of games, and concludes that it is nevertheless lawful. In the second he goes on to consider the need for specific rules to ensure that occasions of recreation do not become ones of excess and abuse, and that the dangers which can be attendant on games are avoided, mentioning specifically the evils of swearing, drunkenness, the squandering of money required for family necessities, and the associated temptation to sins of the flesh. Some games were clearly perceived to be more open to abuse than others. The context in which they were played, in alehouses or inns or locations where other pleasures might be wrongfully indulged, could make the players vulnerable, while some games – those for instance involving dice and gambling – were in themselves intrinsically more dangerous.

A similar position on the lawfulness of games was adopted by John Tillotson, one of the most celebrated preachers of the period, and a reluctant Archbishop of Canterbury in later life.[211] In a sermon on the education of children, Tillotson writes:[212]

I have likewise known some Parents that have strictly forbidden their Children the use of some sorts of *Recreations* and *Games* under the notion of heinous Sins, upon a mistake that because there was in them a mixture of *Fortune* and *Skill* they were therefore unlawful; a reason which I think hath no weight and force in it, tho I do not deny but human Laws may for very prudent reasons either restrain or forbid the use of these *Games*, because of the boundless expence both of *Money* and *Time* which is many times occasioned by them.

(Tillotson 1694: 196–7)

These words can be taken as indicating the broad balance of mainstream opinion in the post-Restoration period; a tolerant attitude towards legitimate recreation in general, coexisting with pockets of stricter and more austere opprobrium.

Willughby's Book of Games provides no explicit statement of his views, moral or otherwise, on these controversial issues, but the absence of any argumentation and the very nature of his undertaking is itself significant. The closest Willughby comes to a general comment on the ethics of play is in his section on cards: 'If the abuse bee no Argument against the use, there can nothing bee said against Cards, the first Invention beeing verie Ingenious & of Excellent use to Exercise the wits, to Instruct & not to debauch the youth'

---

211. John Tillotson (1630–1694; *DNB*) was a close friend of John Wilkins and a patron of John Ray (Raven 1950: 274, 431). He was elected a fellow of the Royal Society in 1672.

212. This paragraph follows one in which Tillotson distances himself from Ministers who, after it became fashionable for children to wear their hair below the ears 'did in every *Sermon* either find or make an occasion with great severity to reprove the great Sin of *long Hair*' (Tillotson 1694: 195–6).

(p. 52). Willughby is here citing a Latin legal maxim the very invocation of which would have been sufficient to situate him in contemporary controversies concerning the lawfulness of games. 'Abuse is no argument against use' might almost be seen as the rallying cry of those treatises which sought to defend the lawfulness of games. Although Willughby gives us no more than this and has left us no other statement on ethics, other close friends within his circle did publish in these areas. An unambiguous expression of this was offered by Ray in *A Persuasive to a Holy Life*, using words which echo verbatim those from an earlier publication by Wilkins.[213] In Chapter 8 'Of Pleasure' Ray argues for the rightness of enjoying in moderation the things which God has made pleasurable. He refers specifically to games:

As for those things which we call by the name of *Sports* and *Diversions*, Religion doth likewise admit of a moderate use of these: And what is beyond such a use doth rather tire men, than recreate them: It being as much the property of such things to weary a man, when he is once sufficiently refreshed by them, as it is to refresh him when he is wearied by other things.

(Ray 1700: 71)

These are sentiments to which the writer of the Book of Games would certainly have subscribed.

---

213. Quoting from Wilkins *Of the Principles and Duties of Natural Religion*, published posthumously in 1675.

5

Chronology of Willughby's Life

22 November 1635	Birth of Francis Willughby at Middleton, Warwickshire.
	Educated at Sutton Coldfield School where William Hill was Master.
1653	Enters Trinity College, Cambridge, under the tutorship of James Duport who had formerly been tutor to John Ray.
1655–56	Graduates BA, Trinity College, Cambridge.
21 May 1657	Admitted to Gray's Inn.
1659	Graduates MA, Trinity College, Cambridge.
Late 1650s	Notes on joint chemistry experiments with John Ray, dated between 29 November 1658 and March 1659, recorded in his Commonplace Book.
25 February 1660	Ray asks Willughby for assistance with data from Warwickshire and Nottinghamshire for a catalogue of British plants.
1660	Visits Oxford to consult works in the University library.
1660	Ray in his *Catalogus Plantarum circa Cantabrigiam* alludes to help received from Willughby and to his success in the study of insects.
August 1660	Accompanies Ray on a first trip north through Yorkshire, then into Cumberland across to Isle of Man returning to the Wyre estuary, Pilling Moss and Garstang and south through Lancashire.
1660	James Duport dedicates his *Gnomologia Homeri* to Willughby and three others.
1661	Ray's second botanical expedition, accompanied by Philip Skippon, but not by Willughby (*pace* Lankester 1846: 131).
20 November 1661	Wilkins at the Royal Society reads letter from Willughby concerning insects. Proposes Willughby for membership.

4 December 1661	Admitted to the Royal Society.
26 March 1662	Barrow writes to Willughby in response to his observations on mathematical questions.
8 May–16 June 1662	Accompanies Ray and Skippon on journey from Cambridge through Wales, collecting samples of Welsh words as well as botanical specimens and other observations. Parts company with them in Gloucestershire, where he inspects a hoard of Roman coins near Dursley.
1 October 1662	Willughby, apparently at his first meeting of the Royal Society, conducts experiment concerning snake's eggs.
8, 15 October 1662	Attends meetings of the Royal Society; demonstrates the mathematical efficiency of planting trees in a quincuncial figure; produces a whiting's head to demonstrate movable skin over eyes, following discussion of snakes.
10 April 1663	Passport issued from Whitehall in favour of Francis Willughby and Nathaniel Bacon with two servants.
18 April 1663	Embarks on Continental journey with Ray, accompanied by Philip Skippon and Nathaniel Bacon. War with France dictates that they travel via Flanders, and thence through Germany, Switzerland, Italy, Sicily and Malta.
29 May 1663	Visit in The Hague to the home of Christiaan Huygens, currently in England; is shown his pneumatic engine and telescope.
22 July 1663	Received by the Prince Palatine in Mannheim.
Winter 1663–64	Attends anatomy lectures at Padua.
12 January 1664	Receives certificate of matriculation in University of Padua. While in Padua acquires volume of specimens of dried plants.
9 March 1664	Wilkins proposes that Willughby and his companions be asked to make a detour to Teneriffe to make certain experiments on behalf of the Royal Society, for which directions and the necessary instruments are to be dispatched.
30 March 1664	List of various committees of the Royal Society includes Francis Willughby on the Committee for Histories of Trades.
April 1664	Willughby and Bacon travel on separately from Ray and Skippon, who remain in Naples. Willughby later visits Rome, collecting fish illustrations.
31 August–mid-November 1664	Willughby journeys through Spain.
Early 1665	Returns home, possibly on hearing news of his

	father's failing health. His fellow travellers remain on the Continent until April 1666.
4 January 1665	Attends meeting of Royal Society: produces account of astronomical observations on the Continent.
Late March 1665	Experiments on the rising of sap in birch trees at Middleton.
May–June 1665	Attends various meetings of the Royal Society: present at experiment concerning the breeding of mites in eggs; seeks advice on instruments for conveying smoke to destroy mites; offers specimens of egg affected by lime; testifies to Wilkins's account of an experiment involving dissection of a dog.
5 October 1665	Barrow replies to correspondence from Willughby on mathematical questions, including motion.
7 December 1665	Death of Sir Francis Willoughby, his father.
June–July 1666	Present at several meetings of the Royal Society: provides specimens of Bononian stone; nominated with others to act in support of Hooke's astronomical observations; among those contributing observations on solar eclipse; proposes experiment on water newts following observations on salamanders; proposes enquiry about specimen of 'stone' cut from a womb.
20 October 1666	Wilkins writes to ask Willughby's assistance in enumerating and defining plants and animals for his 'Real Character and Philosophical Language'.
Winter 1666	At Middleton with Ray, arranging his natural history collections and working on Wilkins's project.
28 March 1667	Wilkins presents to the repository of the Royal Society specimens of a substance taken by Willughby from a shellfish.
27 June 1667	Present at meeting of the Royal Society: provides observations on coal seams, in connection with discussion of tin ore and mineral deposits.
25 June–13 September 1667	Tours south-west England with Ray, travelling through Worcester, Gloucester, Cornwall, Dorset, Hampshire, and collecting natural history specimens. Material since lost included a list of Cornish words.
11 January 1668	Named among those from whom Wilkins is to solicit support in connection with a new building for the Royal Society's college.
January 1668	Marries Emma Barnard, second daughter and coheiress of Mr (later Sir) Thomas Barnard. Establishes household at Middleton Hall.

1668	Wilkins in the Preface to his *Essay towards a Real Character* acknowledges a debt to Willughby for his work on animals, and to Ray for his on plants.
13 September 1668	Birth of first son, Francis.
1668–71	References to Willughby's health in his daughter's later account mention violent fevers; for relief he drinks the waters at Astrop Wells, and visits Sir Job Charlton's at Ludford near Ludlow to drink the Cleehill waters.
September 1668–March 1669	At Middleton, with Ray a regular visitor. Activities include further experiments with motion of sap in trees.
April 1669	Willughby falls seriously ill while visiting Wilkins at Chester. Witnesses the dissection of a porpoise at Chester with Ray and Wilkins.
29 May 1669	Writes to Oldenburg, enclosing report of experiments made with Ray on the motion of sap in trees; letter read at meeting of the Royal Society on 10 June 1669.
21 June 1669	Writes to Oldenburg with further thoughts on the circulation of sap and its relation to theories of motion. Following discussion by the Royal Society on 8 July 1669 he is asked to continue his investigations and is sent a paper describing experiments by Wren and Rooke.
23 July 1669	Continues correspondence with Oldenburg about experiments concerning motion and a natural history enquiry.
20 January 1670	Oldenburg writes to Willughby on the suggestion of Wilkins to seek his opinion on specimen of worms found wrapped in leaves.
29 January 1670	Writes to Oldenburg, with box of insect specimens: replies to enquiry concerning worms wrapped in leaves; reports his observations of spiders in September 1669; mentions expectation of having Wilkins's company and assistance in experiments on 'the noble theory of motion'. Letter reported to Royal Society meeting on 10 February 1670.
17 February 1670	Oldenburg sends specimens to Willughby for opinion.
12 March 1670	Willughby writes from Middleton to Oldenburg about circulation of sap in trees; requests thermometers and barometers.
19 March 1670	Oldenburg replies to Willughby, apparently including an account of Tonge's work on spiders.
16 April 1670	Willughby at Middleton sends notes to Oldenburg

	containing observations on sycamore trees, black poplar and the walnut, together with his thoughts on dwarf oaks and stellar fish.
23 April 1670	Birth of daughter, Cassandra.
28 April 1670	At Wollaton with Ray, who writes to Lister.
5 May 1670	Meeting of Royal Society directs that a specimen of a worm wrapped in leaves be sent to Willughby; Oldenburg sends specimens and other enquiries on 17 May.
7 June 1670	Writes from Middleton to Oldenburg, mentioning recent return from London and responding to questions about effect of the moon on living creatures and the vegetable world and other points.
29 June 1670	Again at Wollaton with Ray, who writes to Lister about botanical specimens and reports Willughby's comments on spiders.
4 July 1670	Writes from Middleton to Oldenburg, correcting a mistake in the *Philosophical Transactions* account of their report on sap in trees.
19 July 1670	Writes from Middleton to Oldenburg, confirming meaning of Lister's report on sap in trees.
19 August 1670	Writes to Oldenburg from Astrop, Northamptonshire, home of his Leigh relatives, with account of his investigation of bees in rose leaf cartridges. Letter reported to meeting of the Royal Society on 27 October 1670.
2 September 1670	Writes to Oldenburg from Middleton with further progress of his study with Ray of bees hatching from maggots in rose leaf cartridges. Letter and specimen rose leaves reported to meeting of the Royal Society on 27 October 1670.
1670–71	Holds office of sheriff of Warwickshire.
22 December 1670	Letter from Lister to Ray refers to Willughby's general poor health and recent recovery from attack of illness.
13 January 1671	Willughby and Ray both write letters to Oldenburg from Middleton; their accounts of the hatching of bees and of acid spirits in ants were presented to the Royal Society on 19 January; Oldenburg replies to Willughby on 21 January with details of their reception.
10 February 1671	Death of Sir William Willoughby of Selston. Will in Willughby's favour prompts protracted litigation by other claimants.
Spring 1671	Ray at Middleton, suffering from jaundice.
16 March 1671	Writes from Middleton to Oldenburg; gives account

	of further trials on movement of sap in trees. Letter reported to meeting of the Royal Society on 27 April 1671.
21 April 1671	Writes to Oldenburg from Middleton; corrects report of 16 March 1671 and adds further comments on relative capacities of different trees for transmitting water. Letter reported to meeting of the Royal Society on 27 April 1671.
13 May 1671	Oldenburg sends Willughby a specimen of a twig with insect eggs attached, as directed by the Society on 30 March.
10 July 1671	Writes to Oldenburg from Middleton with account of the hatching of bees collected previously in rose leaf cartridges at Astrop, Northamptonshire.
24 August 1671	Writes to Oldenburg from Middleton with observations made with Ray on the life cycle of the sort of wasps called *vespæ ichneumones*. Letter reported to meeting of the Royal Society on 2 November 1671.
Mid-September 1671	Willughby makes one of apparently two brief meetings to Lister in York.
18 November 1671	Willughby and Ray both in London.
23 November 1671	Royal Society requests that Ray (present at the meeting) and Willughby experiment to test report of maggots grown large through special method of feeding.
Late 1671	Considers a journey to America, but is prevented by ill health.
9 April 1672	Birth of second son Thomas.
8 May 1672	Willughby at meeting of the Royal Society comments on Lister's observations of hair worms and promises to send dissection details of fishes, birds and mammals in which he had found worms.
3 June 1672	Willughby falls seriously ill.
24 June 1672	Makes his will.
3 July 1672	Death of Francis Willughby at Middleton Hall, followed by burial in Middleton church.

Figures

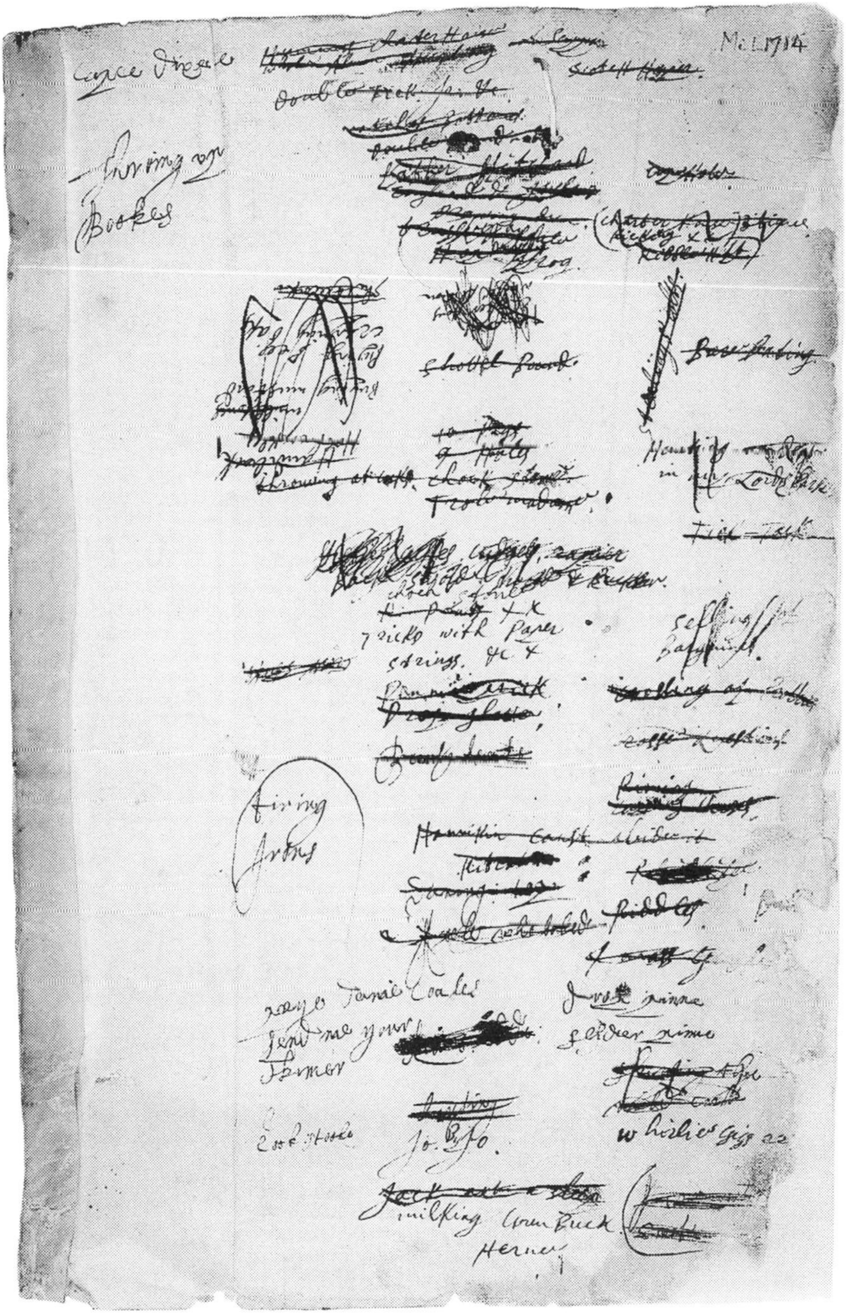

Figure 1   Flyleaf
of the Book of
Games; see
Appendix 1.
NUL Mi LM 14
flyleaf

Figure 2
Description of the
board used for
Tables.
NUL Mi LM 14
p. 19

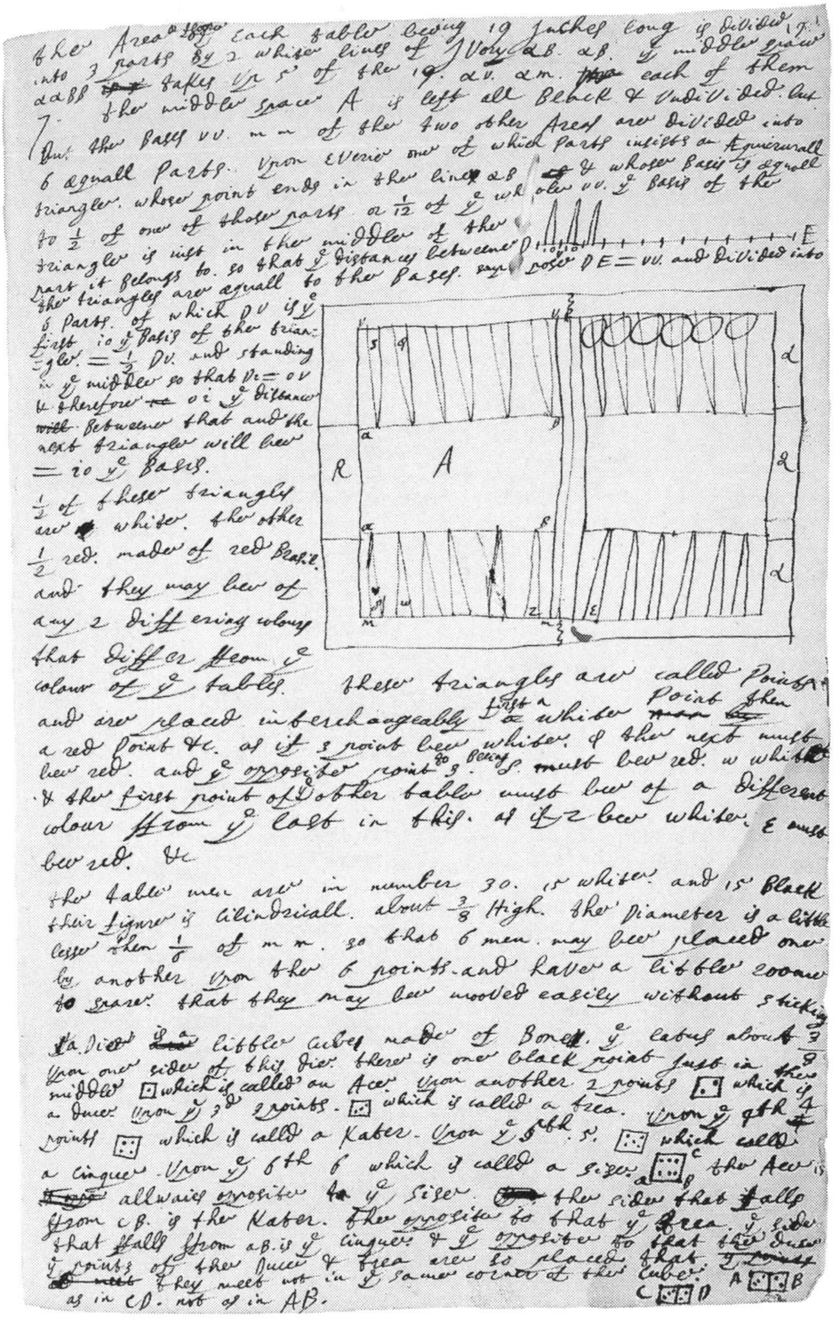

[Handwritten manuscript page with diagram of a tables (backgammon) board. The text describes the construction of the board, the triangles (points), the table-men, and the dice.]

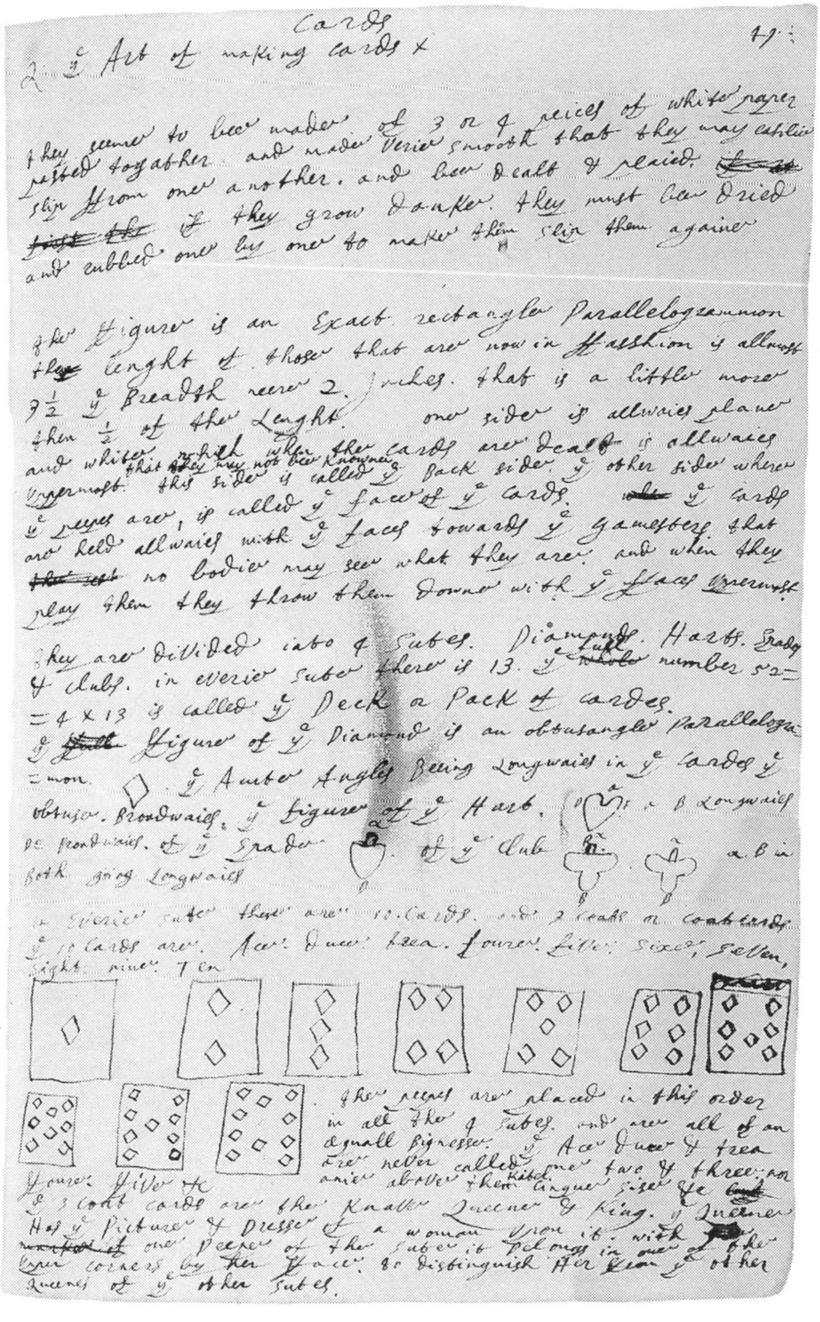
Cards
2. ye Art of making cards x 49:

They seeme to bee made of 3 or 4 peices of white paper pasted togather and made verie smooth that they may easilie slip from one another. and bee dealt & peiced. if they grow danker they must bee dried and rubbed one by one to make them slip them againe

The figure is an Exact rectangle Parallelogrammon the lenght of those that are now in ffasshion is allmost 3½ ye Breadth neere 2 inches. that is a little more then ½ of the Lenght. one side is allwaies plaine and white which when the cards are dealt is allwaies Uppermost. that they may not bee knowne this side is called ye back side. ye other side where ye peices are, is called ye face of ye cards. ye cards are held allwaies with ye faces towards ye gamesters that no bodie may see what they are. and when they play them they throw them downe with ye ffaces uppermost.

They are divided into 4 sutes. Diamonds. Harts. Spades & clubs. in everie sute there is 13. ye number 52 = 4 x 13 is called ye Deck or Pack of cardes.
ye figure of ye Diamond is an obtusangle Parallelogrammon. ye Acute Angles being Longwaies in ye cardes ye obtuse. Broadwaies. ye figure of ye Hart. a b Longwaies de broadwaies. of ye Spade. of ye club. a b in both going Longwaies

in Everie sute there are 10 cards. and 3 coate or coatecards. ye 10 cards are. Ace. Duce. trea. foure. five. sixe, seven, eight. nine. Ten

The peices are placed in this order in all the 4 sutes. and are all of an equall bignesse. ye Ace Duce & trea are never called one two & three, nor anie above them [illegible] &c
foure five &c
ye 3 coat cards are the Knave Queene & King. ye Queene has ye Picture & dresse of a woman upon it. with one peece of the sute it belongs in one of the upper corners by her face. to distinguish her from ye other Queenes of ye other sutes.

Figure 3
Description of playing cards.
NUL Mi LM 14
p. 49

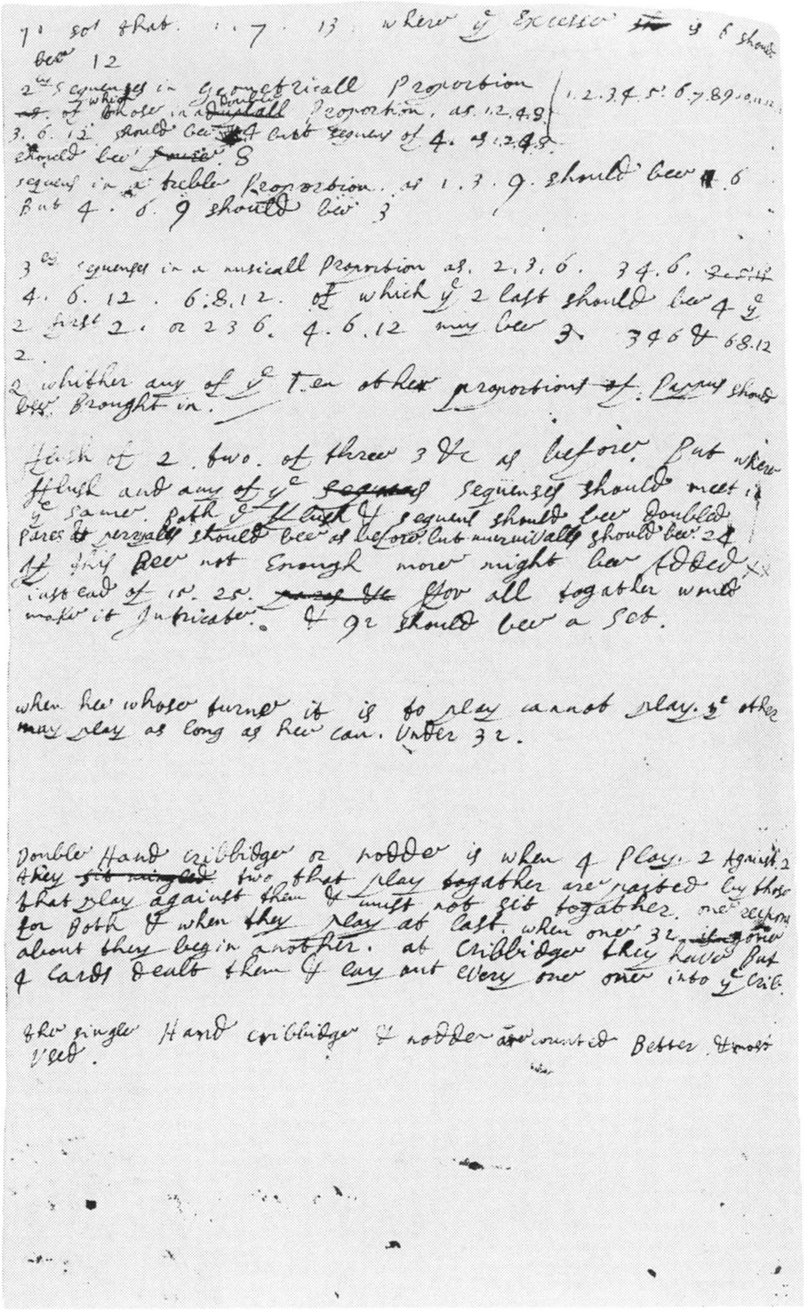

7ly so that . 1 . 7 . 13 . where ye Excesse is 6 should bee 12

2ly sequences in Geometricall Proportion | 1.2.3.4.5.6.7.8.9.10.11.12
which of those in a Duplicall Proportion, as 1.2.4.8.
3.6.12 should bee 4 but sequence of 4. as 1.2.4.8.
should bee 8
sequences in a treble Proportion as 1.3.9. should bee 6
but 4.6.9 should bee 3

3ly sequences in a musicall Proportion as. 2.3.6. 3.4.6. 2.6.12
4.6.12. 6.8.12. of which ye 2 last should bee 4 ye
2 first 2. or 2 3 6. 4.6.12 may bee 3. 3 4 6 & 6 8 12
2.

Whither any of ye ten other proportions of Pappus should
bee brought in.

flush of 2 two. of three 3 &c as before. but where
flush and any of ye sequences should meet in
ye same. both ye flush & sequence should bee doubled.
Pares & pervalls should bee as before but murnivalls should bee 24
If this bee not enough more might bee added
least end of 10. 20. for all togather would
make it intricate. & 92 should bee a set.

when hee whose turne it is to play cannot play. ye other
may play as long as hee can. Under 32.

Double Hand cribbidge or nodde is when 4 play 2 against 2
they two that play togather are parted by those
that play against them & must not sit togather. one reckons
for both & when they play at last. when once 32 is gone
about they begin another. at Cribbidge they have but
4 cards dealt them & lay out every one one into ye Crib.

The single Hand cribbidge & nodde are counted better & most
used.

Figure 4 Part of Willughby's description of Cribbage, with details of his own variant of the game. NUL Mi LM 14 p. 70

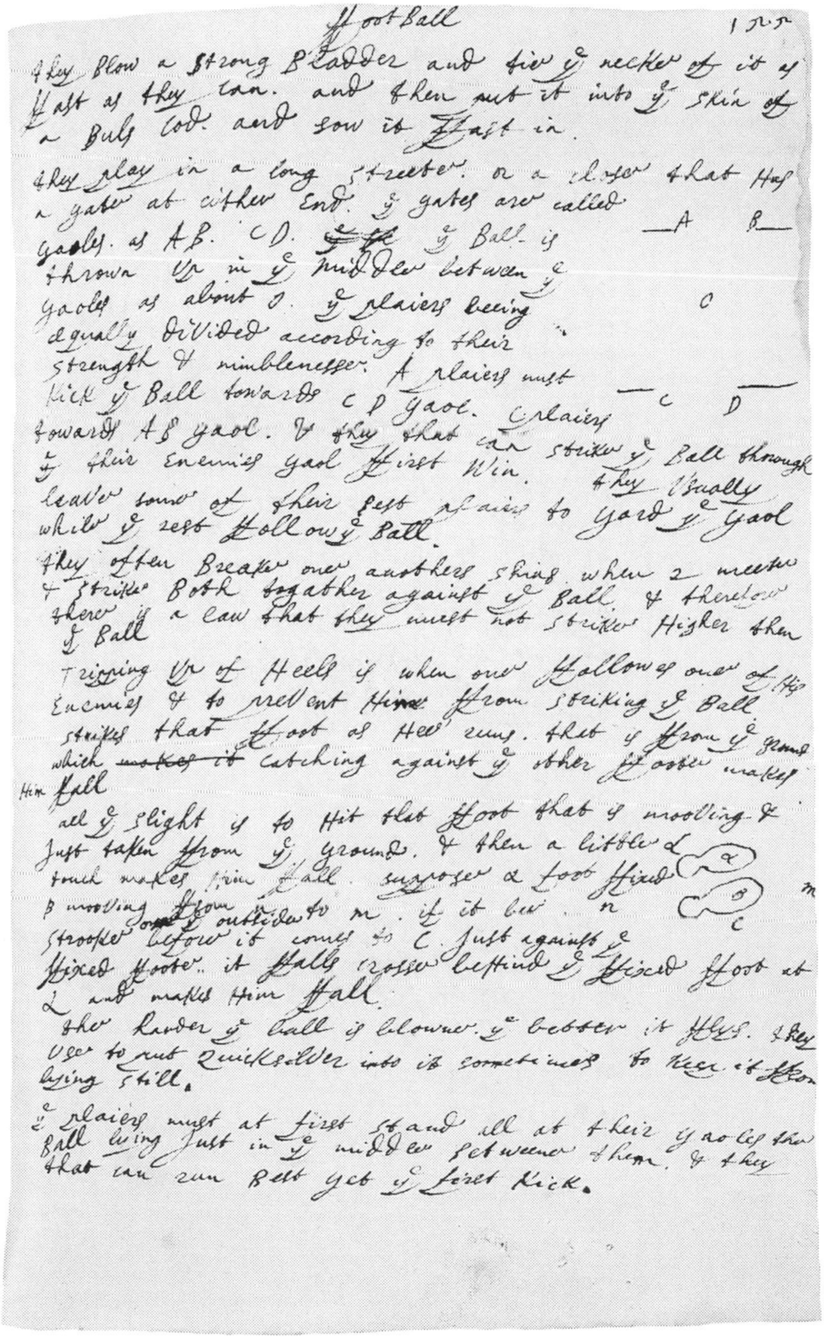

ffoot Ball

They Blow a strong Bladder and tie ye necke of it as ffast as they can. and then put it into ye skin of a Bulls Cod. and sow it ffast in.

They play in a long streete. or a closer that Has a gate at either End. ye gates are called goales. as A B. C D. ye Ball is thrown vp in ye middles between ye goales as about O. ye plaiers beeing equally divided according to their strength & nimblenesse. A plaiers must kick ye Ball towards C D Gaol. Grlaiers towards A B gaol. & they that can strike ye Ball through their Enemies gaol ffirst win. They usually leave some at their gate whiles ye rest Hollow ye Ball as strive to yard ye Gaol

They often Breake one anothers shins when 2 meete & strike Both together against ye Ball. & therefore there is a law that they must not strike Higher then ye Ball

Tripping vp of Heels is when one Hollowes one of his Enemies & to prevent Him ffrom striking ye Ball strikes that ffoot as Hee runs. that if ffrom ye ground which makes it catching against ye other ffoote makes Him fall.

all ye slight is to Hit that ffoot that is mooling & Just taken ffrom ye ground. & then a little touch makes him fall. suppose a foot ffixed B mooling ffrom outside to m. if it bee strooke belowe it comes to C Just against ye ffixed ffoote. it ffalls crosse behind ye ffixed ffoot at L and makes Him fall.

ye Harder ye Ball is blowne. ye better it fflyes. they vse to put Quicksilver into it sometimes to keep it ffrom lying still.

ye plaiers must at first stand all at their gaoles then Ball lying Just in ye middle between them. & they that can run Best get ye ffirst kick.

Figure 5
Description of
Football.
NUL Mi LM 14
p. 155

Figure 6
Description of
Hurling in the
hand of Philip
Skippon, with
notes by
Willughby.
NUL Mi LM 14
p. 155/i [r]

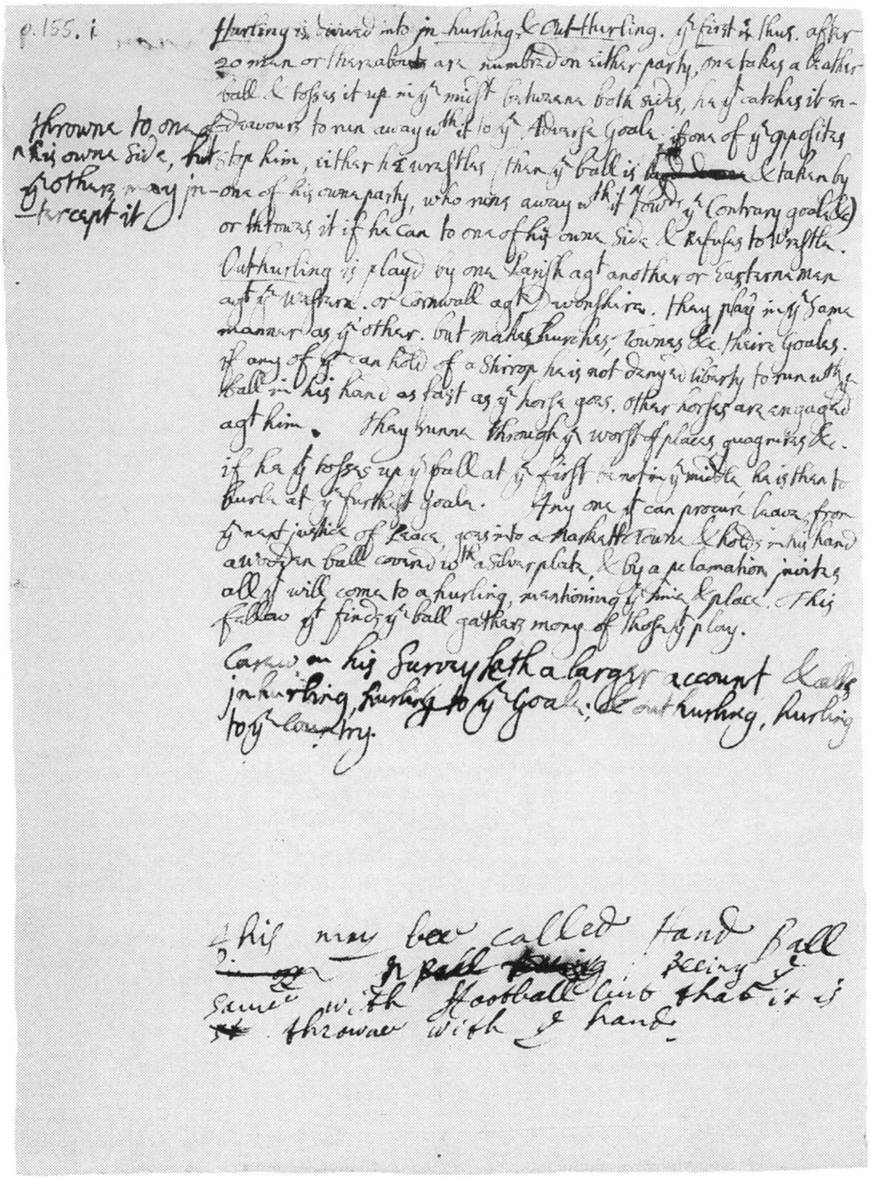

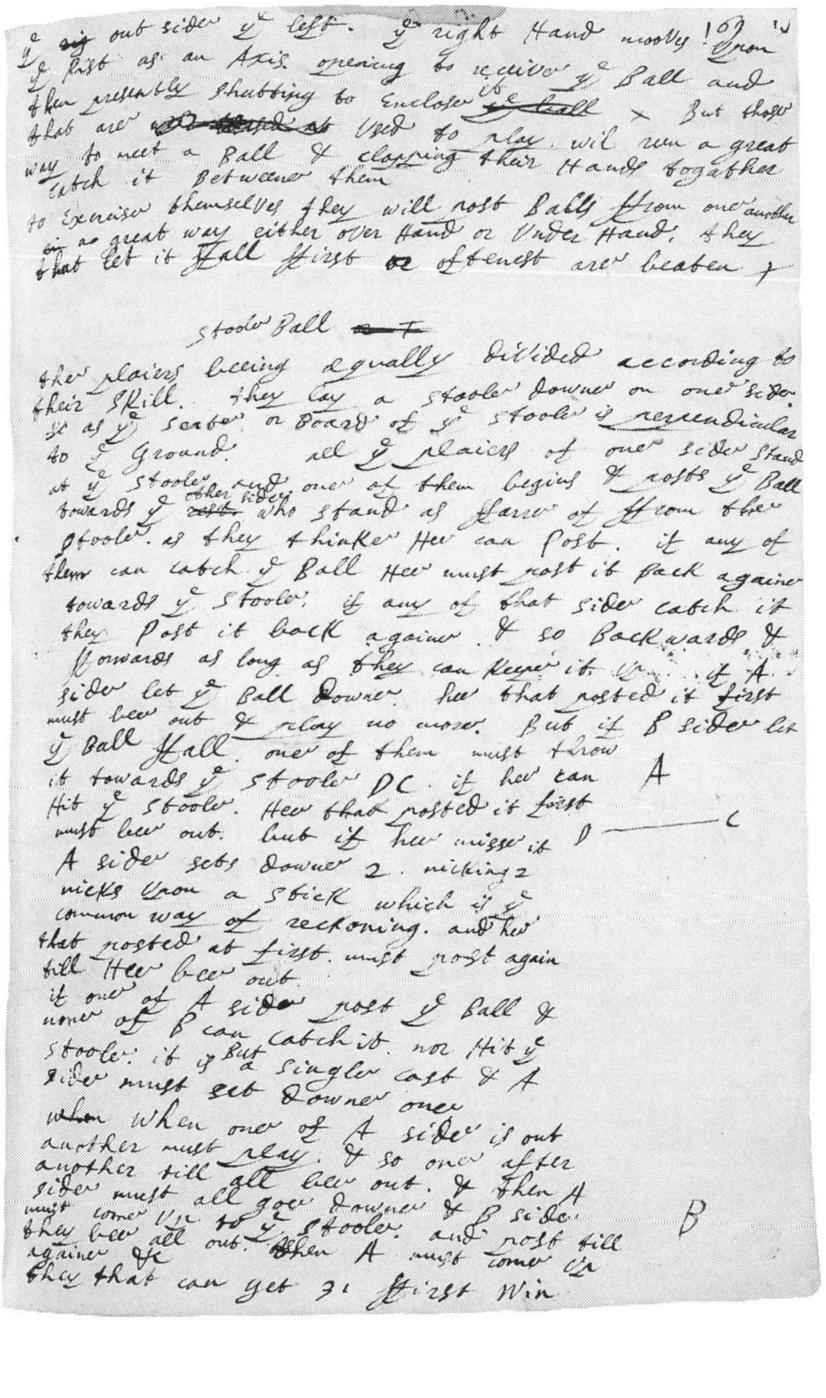

e out sider yᵉ left. yᵉ right Hand mostly 109 vpon
yᵉ fist as an Axis opening to receive yᵉ Ball and
then presently shutting to Enclose the ball × But those
that are vsed to play wil run a great
way to meet a Ball & clapping their Hands togather
Catch it betwene them
to Exercise themselves they will rost Balls from one another
in as great way either over Hand or vnder Hand, they
that let it fall first or oftenest arᵉ beaten ~

Stooleᵉ Ball

theᵉ plaiers beeing æqually divided according to
their skill. they lay a stooleᵉ downeᵉ on oneᵉ sideᵉ
yᵉ as yᵉ scaber or board of yᵉ stooleᵉ is perpendiculaᵉ
to yᵉ Ground. all yᵉ plaiers of oneᵉ sideᵉ stand
at yᵉ stooleᵉ and oneᵉ of them begins & rosts yᵉ Ball
towards yᵉ otheᵉ sidey who stand as farᵉ of from theᵉ
stooleᵉ as they thinkᵉ Heᵉ can post. if any of
them can catch yᵉ Ball Heᵉ must rost it back againᵉ
towards yᵉ stooleᵉ. if any of that sideᵉ catch it
they post it back againᵉ. & so Backwards &
fowards as long as they can keepe it. if A
sideᵉ let yᵉ Ball downeᵉ heᵉ that rosted it first
must bee out & play no moreᵉ. But if B sideᵉ let
yᵉ Ball fall. one of them must throw
it towards yᵉ stooleᵉ DC. if heᵉ can
Hit yᵉ stooleᵉ. Heᵉ that rosted it first
must bee out. but if heᵉ misse it
A sideᵉ sets downeᵉ 2. nicking 2
nicks vpon a stick which is yᵉ
common way of reckoning. and heᵉ
that rosted at first must rost again
till Heᵉ bee out
if one of A sideᵉ rost yᵉ Ball &
noneᵉ of B can catch it. nor Hit yᵉ
stooleᵉ: it if But a singleᵉ cast & A
sideᵉ must set downeᵉ oneᵉ
when when one of A sideᵉ is out
another must play. & so one after
another till all bee out. & then A
sideᵉ must all goeᵉ downeᵉ & B sideᵉ
must comᵉ vp to yᵉ stooleᵉ. and rost till
they bee all out. then A must comᵉ vp
againᵉ &c
they that can get 31 first win

Figure 7
Description of
Stoolball.
NUL Mi LM 14
p. 169

Figure 8
Description of children's games and playthings.
NUL Mi LM 14
p. 217

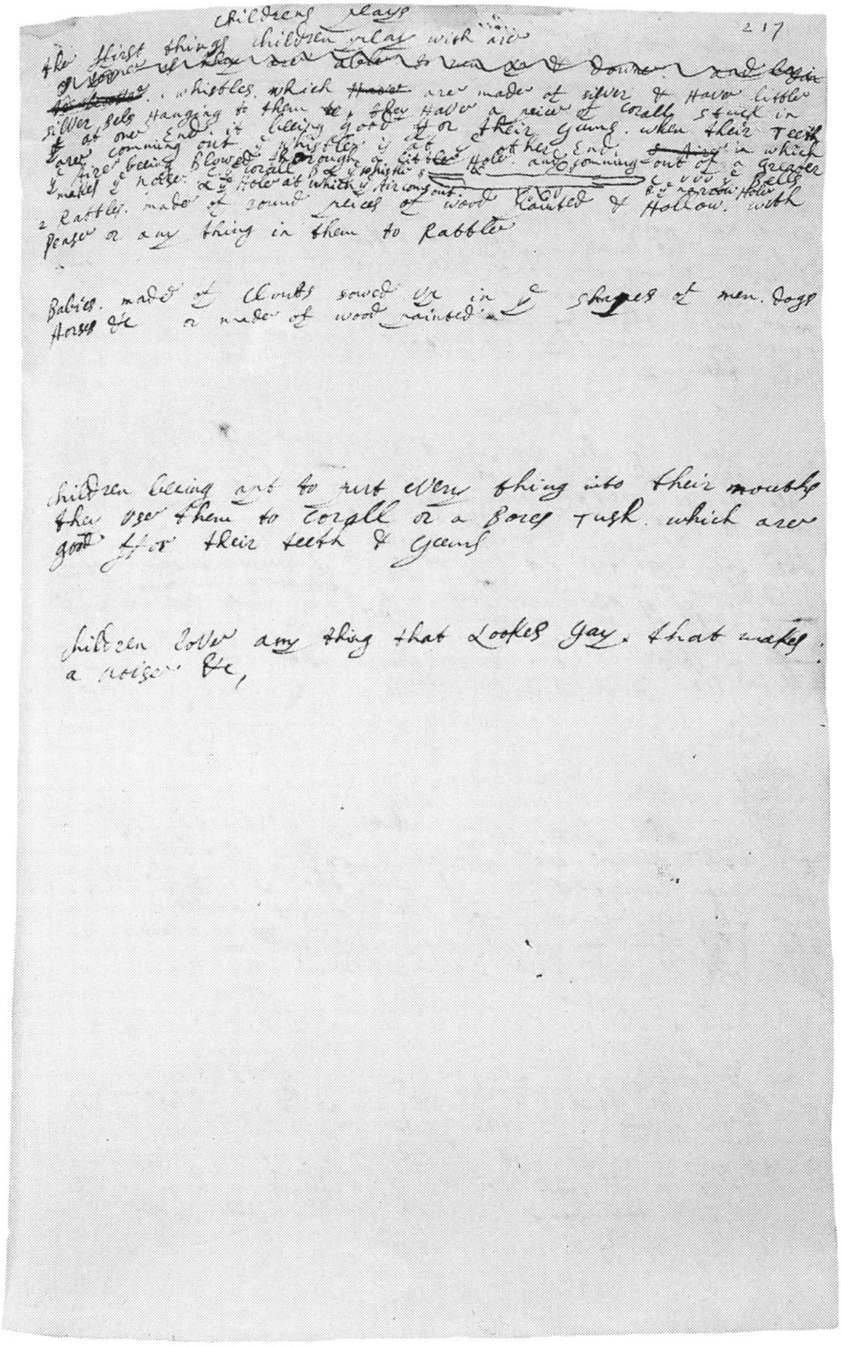
Childrens playes 217

rattles. made of round peices of wood turned & hollow. with pease or any thing in them to rattle

Babies. made of clouts sowed &c in the shapes of men. dogs Horses &c or made of wood painted

children beeing apt to put every thing into their mouths they use them to corall or a bores tusk. which are good ffor their teeth & gums

children love any thing that Lookes gay. that makes a noise &c,

fire and no smoke   233

they play 8: 7 standing in the points of a triangle 3: at one angle
and two and two at the other two they stand just behind on another
where euer there is three it is called fire the eight, that is
left out followes the first, the hindermost of the three stil
running the neuer angle and standing before the two that were
there then the hindermost of that angle runs the next if
he that is without the triangle can him that changes places
with a stick that he carries in his hand, he goeth to one of the
angles, and he that is taken runs about without

C euing bigger E. then D before H &c   DEC   F G
H followes then round and striues to
touch C D or G as they run from   A
one corner to another. Hee that is touch. B
must run about & then H goes to one C   H
& the corners

they follow ye motion of ye sun as they run
ye sum number 7 = to ye number of the planets

Jack art asleepe

two stand by a forme one of one side and one of another with bootes in
their hands the third Vaults ouer and they strike at him saying Jack art
asleepe if thou beest flo water them. If he offens to go ouer and
Vaults
not and either of them strike at him he that struck must lay
downe in his place and be struck at with the bootes as before.

Figure 10
Description of
Nine Men's
Morris.
NUL Mi LM 14
p. 254/i ^r

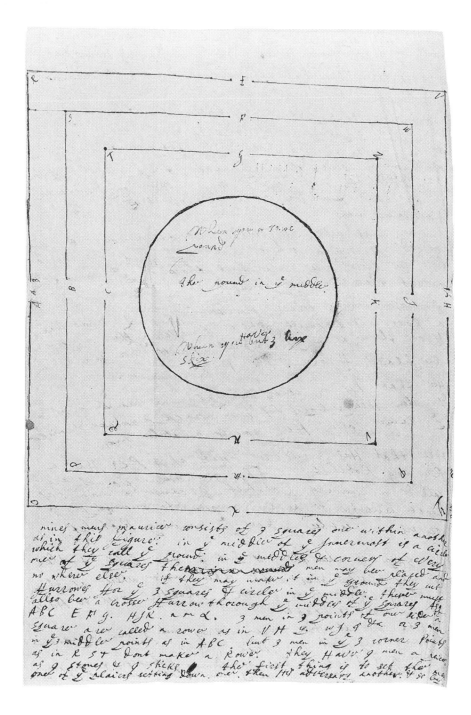

Francis Willughby's
Book of Games

Willughby's Index lists the games alphabetically in four columns, grouping some within classified categories; page references are to those of the manuscript. This index does not give a full list of the headings in the text, children's games being notably under-represented. For a full index, see the Glossary of Games at the end of the volume.

3. *Running*] followed by cancellation *Leaping &c.*

4. *Crosse*] MS *Crosses*.

5. *Board*] word is not completed; ink appears to have run out.

6. *23*] the number 3 is supplied from the 1940s microfilm.

7. *101*] supplied from the 1940s microfilm.

8. *249*] supplied from the 1940s microfilm.

9. *Tricks ... 229*] supplied in part from the 1940s microfilm.

1. The volume was mispaginated. The text for Bull Baiting actually appears on p. 269; Cock Fighting appears on p. 268.

2. *Trumpe, Trumpe and Ruffe*] altered from *Ruffe*.

Willughby's general remarks about games, under the heading 'Plaies', are written in a small notebook attached to the folio volume immediately following his index. It is clear that this notebook was originally used for other purposes; the following text on the booklet's first page has been cancelled by two parallel lines.

2 *blank*; 3/i^r   Tetragonismus nondum inventus est quanquam inveniri posse certum est. Marini in data Euc: 6[10]

Vli[ss]is Aldrovandi
Ornithologia   20 li: in 3 foliis
De insectis   7 li: 1 fo
De crustaceis   4 li: [postmortem][11] editi[12]

Gesneri liber quartus
de Aquatilibus cum
Paralip[omena][13]

Worsly:
Wignal:[14]

---

10. 'The tetragonism [i.e. the method of squaring the circle] has not yet been discovered, although it is certain that it could be.' The observation comes from the commentary on Euclid's *Data* by the fifth-century mathematician Marinus of Flavia Neapolis (Marinus 1625: 6). Willughby has noted down the same quotation in the Commonplace Book (NUL Mi LM 15/1, p. 341).

11. *postmortem*] word only partially legible.

12. The publications of Ulisse Aldrovandi were used extensively by Willughby and Ray in their work on natural history. The three titles listed here, *Ornithologiæ* (1610), *De animalibus insectis* (1602) and *De reliquis animalibus exsanguibus libri quatuor, post mortem eius editi* (1606), appear in the Middleton Library Catalogue (NUL Mi I 17/1, shelf numbers C38, C39 and C8 respectively). The collective work is listed in the *Wollaton Hall Sale Catalogue*, 1925, Item 148.

13. The reference here is to Book 4 of Conrad Gesner's *Historia animalium*, entitled *De piscium & aquatilium animantium natura* (1604), which in later editions carries mention of the appended 'paralipomena' on the title page. The work is listed in the *Wollaton Hall Sale Catalogue*, 1925, Item 368.

14. Neither *Worsly* nor *Wignal* has been identified.

Plaies

3/i[v] *blank*; 3/ii[r]

Plaies may bee divided either into

> those that exercise the bodie, as Tennis, Stowball &c., or
>
> those that exercise the wit as Chests, Tables, Cards &c.

> Those that have nothing of chance, as Chest &c.;
>
> those that altogather depend upon fortune,
> as Inne & In, Crosse & Pile, One & Thirtie;[15]
> or those that have art & skill both, as[16] most games at Cards & Tables.

The word Game is most properly used for Cards, Tables, /Chests &c., & not for games of exercise.   3/ii[v]

Plaies are allso either

> auntiant, Quoits &[c.],[17]
>
> or modern.

Proper to severall countries, as:

> Europe
> America
> India
> Africa
> Asia   X X

The countries where plaies have bene invented & the persons that invented them. The time when they first begun to bee generally used.

Q: Wither there bee not something of chance in all games whatsoever, as in Chest it selfe, Boules &c.   3/iii[r]

Plaies either

> more simple & easie, in which but one instrument is used:
>   as Boules, Quoits.
> Compound & intricate: Chests, Ludus Astronomicus &c.

---

15. *One & Thirtie*] interlineated.

16. *as*] followed by cancellation *Card*s.

17. *Quoits &*] interlineated.

Used most[18]

> by children: Put-pin, Cherrie-stone.
> By women: Cards.
> By men: Tennis.

Plaies

3/iii[v]
> where onely two can plaie: Cribbidge, Tables, Chests.[19]
> Where a fixed number: as 3 at Gleeke. 4, 6 &c.
> Where as manie as will: /Stowball &c.

A great manie plaies for exercise use a sphærula or ball: Hurling, Stoole Ball, Stow-Ball, Boules.

The etymologie of the names of plaies.[20]

Amongst the exercises may bee reckoned Running, Wrestling, Shooting &c.

---

18. *most*] replaces cancellation *onely*.

19. *Cribbidge, Tables, Chests*] interlineated.

20. Queries and comments concerning the etymology of names are scattered throughout the work; see pp. 53, 55, 57, 61, 66, 72, 149, 162, 164, 177, 221.

[*The Puzzle of the Ship*]

Placing the cards or table men that everie tenth of the white or black may bee taken. *V:* p. 360, De Geometria &c.[21]

How to place them that everie eight may bee taken, everie sixt, &c.; that black & white may bee taken by turnes &c.

Whatever[22] the number of white or black man bee to [bee] taken or spared, place them at first as it happens, and then count to the 5th, if every fifth bee to bee taken, to the 6th, if every 6th, &c., and if it bee of the contrary colour, change it and put that in the place of another and another in the place of that, putting those that are right placed in a row above the former, that you bent confounded and mistake the places, & so count round till you have placed all the men of one sort right and then fill the interstices[23] with the other sort. As if the number of both bee 20, 12 white & 8 black, everie fifth man is to bee taken, and I would place them so, that all the white should bee taken before[24] any of the black. Let **o** stand for black, **a** for white, and place them as it happens:

3/iv^r

3/iv^v

In this example whereever there was an **a** in the fifth place twas remooved into the upper line, whereever there was an **o** it was /carried to another place where there was an **a**, and the **a** brought thither and placed in the upper line. In the same manner if there were 3 or 4 severall sorts to bee picked out one after another, as black, white, red, &c., they might bee placed at randome at first, and then remooved into their true places, so as all the white should bee taken first, then the red, then the black &c. Or they might be placed so as to bee taken by turnes, first a white man, then a red man, &c.; or that 1 white should bee taken for one black, or in any other proportion that should bee required.

3/v^r

---

21. The reference here is to p. 360 of Willughby's Commonplace Book (NUL Mi LM 15/1) where, in the section on geometry and related matters, he has made notes on this puzzle. The heading here has been supplied by the editors, using the name by which the puzzle has become commonly known (see 'Puzzle of the Ship' in the Glossary of Games). See also the section on Tricks at Cards below (p. 101), where Willughby indicates how suits of cards can be similarly arranged.

22. *Whatever*] follows cancelled line at top of page *cf the V: p. Præcedentem X X* (that is, 'cf. the mark "*V:*" on the preceding page').

23. *interstices*] MS *instertices*.

24. *before*] followed by cancellation *everie a one*.

3/v^v There can bee but 1 way to place them, for if one black should bee put in the place of a white man it must come to bee taken instead of a white man and the order would bee confounded. *X X X X X*

If they should then bee set in a circle there could bee but one way, but if in a streight line there might bee severall waies, as in the last example the line might bee begun at the end of every five, as **a o o a a** &c., or **o a a o a** which is the third five.[25] *X X*

3/vi^r Suppose the sum given bee 40, 20 white, 20 black, everie fifth to bee taken; divide 40 by five: ⁴⁰⁄₅ *X X*

3 Games at set times of the yeare.
Throwing at Cocks on Shrovetuesday. *X*

How games may bee altered, varied, and what may bee added to them.[26]
Playes where they are blinded. Hock Kocles, Blindmanbuffe, &c.

4 *blank*; 5 *V:* Cardani comment: in Ptol: de Astro: Indiciis P: 128.[27]

Ubi ex sententia Haly 2 assignantur causæ quare zodiacus et annus in 12 dividitur partes.

1. Quia toti lunæ & solis sunt coniunctiones.[28]

2. Quia 4 anni tempora principium medium finem habent, at 3 x 4 = 12.

Harum prior rationi consentanea et proculdubio vera.[29]

From this the number 12 came in request, the 12 great gods &c. nothing but the 12 monthes, the sun beeing accounted the onely deity.

V: Dr Mores Mysterie of Religion.[30]

---

25. *If they should … the third five.*] three intersecting crossed lines on the page may indicate the cancellation of this passage.

26. Willughby notes later that: 'A game is fully understood when it can bee fitted for any number of players' (p. 58). He makes further speculations about variants in connection with Ticktack (p. 31), Laugh and Lie Down (p. 63), Cribbage (p. 69), Trump (p. 72) and Gleek (p. 77).

27. The reference is to Cardano's treatise on judicial astrology (1555: ch. 9, 36–7), in the section 'De anni temporibus, & quatuor angulorum natura'. A copy of this work is listed in the Middleton Library Catalogue (NUL Mi I 17/1, shelfmark S1).

28. *toti … coniunctiones*] altered from *toties Luna soli coniungitur.*

29. 'Where, according to Haly, two reasons are given as to why the zodiac and the year are divided into 12 parts. 1. Because that is the number of the conjunctions of the moon and the sun. 2. Because the four seasons of the year each have a beginning, middle and end, and 3 x 4 = 12. Of which reasons the former is by common assent and without doubt the true one' (cf. Cardano 1555: 128). Haly, the eleventh-century Arabic astronomer Ali ibn Abî al-Rijal, was author of a noted work on judicial astronomy.

30. The reference is to Henry More, *Explanation of the Grand Mystery of Godliness* (1660); see the section on astrology in book vii, ch. xv. Willughby's notes made while reading this work are preserved in his Commonplace Book (NUL Mi LM 15/1, pp. 124, 338).

Because the yeare was divided into 12 monthes, therefore allso they divided the day & night into 12 houres, at first the whole time betweene sun rising & sun setting into 12 æquall parts, as allso the time between sun setting & sun rising, so that onely in the æquinoctiall the night houres were æquall to the day houres. Nor were the houres of any day æquall to the houres of the præcedent or following day. This way of unæquall houres beeing at last found troublesome & inconvenient they divided the whole day & night, that is the time in which the sun leaving the meridian returns again unto it, into 24 æquinoctiall houres.

There are 7 daies in a weeke because there are so manie planets, the houres beeing divided among the planets. Every day was calld by that planets name to whose lot the first houre fel, as giving the first houre of Saturday to Saturne because hee mooves in the highest sphære, the next to Jupiter &c. The 25th houre or the first of the following day falls to the sun & therefore that day is called Sunday. The 49th or the first of the third day to the moone & therefore is calld Dies Lunæ &c. Now the reason that never 2 planets happen to light upon the same day is because that for the last houre of everie day you must adde 3 to 21, that is 3 to 3 sevens, or 3 whole circles, or for the first houre of the following day you must adde 4. Therefore if you begin at Saturn, the fourth from Saturne will bee the second daies planet, the fourth from the sun the third daies, the 4th from the moone the 4th daies &c. Now because 7 is not measured by 3, everie day must necessarily have a severall planet till you have gone thorough them all.

The first division of time beeing into yeares[31] from the suns motion, the next into months from the moon, the third into weekes, why should the weekes have any more then 5 daies,[32] there being but 5 planets left. The reason is because 28, the number of the daies of a lunar month, is measured by 7 but not by 5.[33]

All in this side belongs to p: 52.[34]   6

Q: How the Ægiptian months consisting of 30 daies were divided, whither   7
into weekes at all.[35] **XX**

The 2 great planets having gotten the yeares & monthes, that the lesser should not thinke themselves wronged the daies are allotted to them, & the sun & moone are brought in againe because else the months could not bee æquallie divided. And seeing there could bee no reason fetched from the motion of the planets to determine them to particular daies, why should they

---

31. *yeares*] follows cancellation *monthes*.

32. *daies*] followed by cancellation *the reason is the reason is 28 is measured by.*

33. *measured by … not by 5*] altered from *divisible by 5 but not by seven.*

34. The notes on cards on this page have been moved, as Willughby directs, to p. 52 below.

35. The Egyptian calendar consisted of 12 equal months of 30 days each (Ionides 1939: 169; Bomhard and Yoyett 1999: xii).

not rather have observed the order of the spheares, and have allotted the first day to Saturne, the second to Jupiter, the third to Mars & so on, then this astrologicall conceit. Or why should they not have divided every month into 7 weekes, by putting the 4 S[a]turdaies togather, & the foure Sundaies &c., so as the first weeke should have bene Saturns weeke, the 4 daies of it the first, 2^d, 3^d & 4th Saturday &c.

The reason why a circle was divided into 360 degrees is beecause there are neere so manie daies in a yeere. It was not divided into just 365 or 366, because then it could not have bene divided[36] into quadrants, sextants &c. without fractions.

The generall rule is that wherever any number is indifferent there is something in nature that determines men to one number more then another. Therefore the numbers of the next page beeing the usuall & naturall divisions of time are used allso in games. For when a number is to bee chosen a man will necessarily fall upon some number that hee has bene used to allreadie rather then a new one.

De Septenario A: Gellius 94, 95. Septentriones, septimo signo bruma et Æstas.[37]

8 blank; 9   The numbers 7, 5,[38] 15, 16, 12, 31, 30 are most used in games because they are most used in astronomicall accounts, in numbering the parts of time &c. 7 is the number of the planets; 15 is $\frac{1}{2}$ of the degrees in a signe; 16, $\frac{1}{2}$ + 1; 12 is the number of the signes; 30, of the degrees in a signe; 31, of the degrees + 1; 5, of the lesser planets. 16 & 31 are more used then 15 & 30. One would expect 8 and 13 should bee used as wel as 12 and 7. But the reason for 16 & 31 is that the sun is supposed to have gone thorough $\frac{1}{2}$ of a signe[39] when hee[40] is entred into the 16th degree & the whole signe when hee[41] is entred into the 31.

15 & 31 are used but 11 & 21 never.

---

36. *was not divided … bene divided*] partly interlineated, replacing cancellation *could bee divided into just 364 or 366, because then.*

37. Aulus Gellius, *Attic Nights*, iii. x. 4: 'Ac necque ipse zodiacus septenario numero caret; nam in septimo signo fit solstitium a bruma, in septima bruma a solstitio, in septimo aequinoctium ab aequinoctio (*And the zodiac itself is not uninfluenced by the number seven; the summer solstice occurs in the seventh sign from the winter solstice, and the winter solstice in the seventh after the summer, and one equinox in the seventh sign after the other*)' (Gellius 1984: i, 268).

38. 5] added beneath the line.

39. *signe*] replaces cancellation *degree*.

40. *hee*] altered from *it*.

41. *hee*] altered from *it*.

In most places there are games proper for the severall seasons of the yeare.[42]

Q: Whither there [bee] any thing about games in Kircher.[43]

---

42. Willughby makes scattered references to seasonal games, cf. pp. 2, 219, 269.

43. The polymath Athanasius Kircher was the author of a number of works on numerology and on Oriental antiquities which Willughby may here have had in mind; Skippon and Ray visited him in Rome in 1663 (Skippon 1732: 672–4).

Stow Ball[44]

Willughby's description of Stowball is on three small loose sheets attached to page 13.

The ball is either made of a knob of elme or of leather hard wrought up togather, the staves they strike with they call Stow Ball staves, which are strong short staffes a little bigger & longer then those they strike Kit-cats with. They hold the ball in one hand, & throw it up & then strike it with both hands, putting the hand that held the ball quickly upon the staffe. There are two pins at a convenient distance fastened into the ground; one of them they call the Lay Pin, the other the Boot Pin. They play 2, 3 or 4 of a side but seldome above 4. They begin at the Lay Pin and strike downwards towards

13/i^v   the Boot Pin, the other side standing against them /& striking the ball back again, if they can hit it either at first or at the rebound.[45] They must strike the ball on the[46] right side of the Boot Pin and so come up again to the Lay Pin, the other side still striking it back again if they can hit it. If they chance to strike the ball on the wrong side the Boot Pin they must come back again halfe way. When they are gotten about allmost at the Lay Pin, one of those that are to strike the ball up stands behind those that are to strike it back

13/ii^r   again & stops it as neere the Lay Pin as hee can. A lay is counted / as much as a man can reach with his Stow Ball[47] staffe, setting his foot where the ball was stopped. There is allwaies one more lay allowed then there are players, as if there bee 3 plaiers there is 4 layes allowed; and if the ball bee stopped without the compasse of 4 laies it stands for nothing but they must strike it againe. When one side has gotten the ball round & within the compasse of the laies then the other side is to strike the ball round in the same manner, & they that can get it within the layes with fewest strokes win. Every lay is reckoned

13/ii^v   as a stroke, as if /one get the ball about with 14 blowes within 2 layes it is reckoned as 16 blowes, and if the other side cant get it about with fewer blowes & layes, they loose.

A Boot, quasi, About Pin, from striking the ball about it.

If they dont strike the ball fairly amongst those that stand to stop it, they cry, Anew, Anew, and are to strike it again. But that blow is not reckoned.[48]

---

44. *Stow Ball*] follows cancellation *Stow*.

45. *the rebound*] replaces cancellation *a bound*.

46. *the*] followed by cancellation *side*.

47. *ball*] interlineated.

48. *reckoned*] followed by cancellation *No coales between Wie and Uske but all the countrie over else*. For argument that this reference dates Willughby's observations to his itinerary of June 1662 see above, Introduction, Section 2.3.

There is one more lay allowed then there are plaiers, for him to stand in that stops the ball, a lay beeing as much roome as a man takes up when hee stands to strike. α is the Lay Pin, ω the Boot Pin.

13/iii^r

They must strike it downe by **B** and bring it up by **C** side. If there bee 3 plaiers the space betweene α **B** may bee allowed for one lay or for roome for one to stand in, between **B C** & **C D** for 2 more, and then **D E**, the 4th lay, is left for him that stops it. They dont allwaies stand in this order but sometimes all between α & ω and sometimes halfe on one side & ¹⁄₂ on the other as they expect.

V: Leon. Baptista Alberti, p. 295.[49]

13/iii^v

[*Q:*] Who were the first inventors of plaies.

---

49. See Leone Baptista Alberti's *Architettura* (1565, book viii, ch. vii), 'Gli Arcadii si dice che furono, i primi che trouassero i giucchi (*The Arcadians are said to be the first who invented games*)'. There was a copy of Alberti's work in the Middleton Library Catalogue (NUL Mi I 17/1, shelfmark A/D 23); notes on its contents are scattered throughout the Commonplace Book (NUL Mi LM 15/1).

14 *blank*; 14/i^r

[Biliards]

The description of Billiards, with the exception of a few notes added by Willughby, is in the hand of Philip Skippon. It is written on a folded sheet of paper which has been attached to page 14.

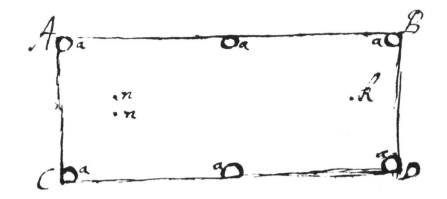

The Biliard table **A B C D** is a long square covered with a greene cloth. **a a a a a a** are the boxes, hazards or holes the balls fall in, one at each corner & one in the middle of each side. A ledge is raised round the table on the edges of the outside about 2 or 3 inches high, lined with greene cloth & stuft with tow, that the balls may the better reflect. The Biliard staves are made of brasell wood, in number two; about a yard long, bended and squared. One end is thick & tipt with ivory about an inch square, the other end is thinner & narrower, that it may (if need be) come the easier betweene the ledge & the ball.

k is a naile whereon the King is placed, made of ivory, & is like a Chesseman. The Porte is like a gate shapt into an arch at **n n** (which are 2 nailes heads wheron they place this porch) made of ivory or heavy wood; the passage thorough is for the ivory balls which are 2 in number & are about an inch diameter a peece, marked with severall distinctions, that they may bee known asunder.[50]

The players are but two; he that plays first, standing at the end wher the King stands, carryes his ball as farre as he can reach with his staffe & then strikes it with his Biliard staffe (if he can) behinde the Porte, but if his ball touch that end ledge, its a losse. The other player may also lay his ball as farre as he can reach & has liberty to strike it against the end ledge, but if he touches his adversaryes ball, it is a losse to himselfe. Yet if he layes his ball no further then the King, he may strike his opposites (if he can) into any one of the boxes & then it is made his adversaryes losse. After this A[51] that played

---

50. *that they may bee known asunder*] added by Willughby.

51. *A*] A is repeated in the margin, perhaps to aid clarity as text is smudged.

first (if there be no losse before) endeavoures to strike B's ball into a box, which is a losse to B; or else strives to passe thorough Porte. Then B either aimes at A to strike it into a box or else endeavours to passe first thorow the Port. When B is thorough he makes what hast he can to touch the King & then B getts a game. If B throwes downe the King it is B's losse. All this while A /   14/iv
followes him & endeavours to strike B into a box or else make B throwe downe the King, which is B's losse. B likewise uses the same endeavours to strike A into a box or make A throw downe the King.

If they passe the Porte forward, they must passe backward for the wrong passage. (Another sort of play is to passe thorough the Porte forward & backward. Then they must both proceed just from the King.)

Every losse is reckoned a game, & 5 or 7 games &c. makes a sett. If a ball be toucht more then once with a Biliard staffe it is a losse. In some places if a player layes his hand on the table, it is a losse. He may rest it on the ledge.

If a ball be toucht with his hand it is a losse.

The ball which is strucke over the table, it is his losse that struck it. **X**

If the King be toucht by the ball before the passage thorow the Port, it is a losse.

If the Port or Bridge falls, it is his losse that strucke it downe.

The arch after the first stroke is not to be toucht.

If in hazarding or holing both the balls goe in, it is his losse that strucke.

If you passe backward thorow the Porte twice & your adversary not once, touching the King, it is a double game, but may be prevented by the adversary at any time yeelding a single game.

Text reverts to Willughby's hand.

Q: Whither 4 losses should not make a game & 4 games a set as in Tennis. This seemes to bee compounded of Tennis & Boules.

Q: Whither the holes should be within the ledge or without it.   14/iir

15 *blank*; 15/iʳ

[Tennis]

The text on Tennis is in the hand of Philip Skippon, with a few additional notes by Willughby. It is written on a folded sheet of paper attached to the blank page 15, and endorsed by Willughby on page 15/iiᵛ with the identification 'A verie exact and punctuall description of Tennis by Phi. Scippon Esquire'.

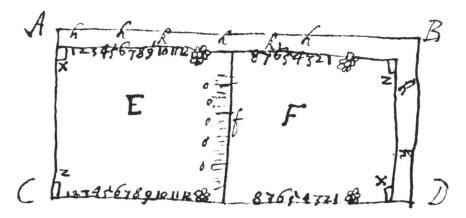

The Tennis court is a long & square place, paved with freestone. The breadth is usually the 3^d part of the length.[52] **A B C D** the Tennis court walls, **h h h h h** the Penthouse, so termed because made sloping, of boards; it is somewhat about a mans heigth from the pavement to the eaves, where at the corners **x x** the upper hazards begin. **z z** are the lower hazards levell to the pavement. Both the upper & the lower are diametrically opposite. **f** is a rope or line that goes crosse the middle of breadth, which is fastened on one side to the gallery **k k**, about breast high, & on the other side to the wall **C D**, the same heighth. **o o o o o** are strings that hang from the rope towards the ground. The use of them is to know[53] whether a ball be struck underline. If it be the strings hinder its motion. The walls of the court are playsterd smooth & blackt over. From the eaves of the penthouse to the pavement is a wall, excepting the gallery **k k** which is under the penthouse. Here the lookers on stand to see the gamesters play. Tennis courts differ in many circumstances, some are covered & some are longer & higher then others &c. The upper hazarde at the end **B D** in some places has a grate & is called a <u>grill</u>, the other at **A C** is of wood & is called the <u>board</u>. In the Pickadilly[54] at London the upper hazard reaches from the eaves of the penthouse to the pavement & is about a foot broad. Ordinarily the hazards are about 3 feet square, some more, some lesse. Many sorts[55] of play, but these following are most common.

---

52. For records of the dimensions of tennis courts at this period, see Marshall (1878: 79–80).

53. *know*] follows cancellation *stop*.

54. See Glossary of Games under 'Tennis'.

55. *sorts*] MS *sports*. Reading uncertain as *p* of *sports* is either smudged or cancelled.

The ordinary gamesters play or tosse halfe dozens. They are either 4 or 2. Each keepes a hazard. They play crosse from lower to lower hazard, or from upper to upper, & endeavour to strike the ball into one anothers hazard, which is a losse to him that can't stop it. If one takes a ball in his hand & strikes it to his opposite with his rackett it is called <u>Service</u>. If a ball be struck under line & it runs to the adverse end & rises at the <u>Nick</u> (which is an obtuse angle to the pavement & the end wall that the ball may rise the better after this manner.

g is the pavement, **m m** the end walls, **i i** the nicks, **c c c c** the ball running along the pavement & rising at the nick **i**, where with a rackett it is strucke over the court & made alofte, which is called Smothering a Ball).[56] If the ball comes under line & not so farr as the end, then they meet it with their racket & bandy it over the court or rake it into the opposite hazard.

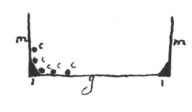

They play also at Running Hazards which is the same, with only they forbeare bandying & smothering but hitt hazards & if a ball comes under line into the hazard its a losse to him that strucke it. He that loses the first two balls payes 3^d (in some places 4^d or 6^d) & then they begin againe.

<u>Brickwalling</u> of a ball is thus: the ball **s s s**, struck against the side wall **c b** at **r**, falls on the pavement at **x** & rebounds up (according to true reflexion) to the end wall **a b** at the point **z**.

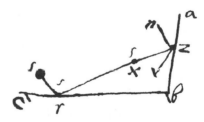

Here the ball moves not according to true reflexion to **n**, but quite contrary to **v**.

If a ball in its progressive motion turnes upon its owne axis it is called <u>Cutting of Ball</u> which is thus: a ball struck at **r** falls on the pavement **a g** at **s**. It reflects to the end wall **h g** at **l** where the ball moves not (as when it is commonly struck) in an arch to **t** but downwards to **i**.

Quære further of these 2 last motions.[57]

---

56. *the Nick (which … Ball)*] sentence is not continued after the bracketed text and diagram concludes.

57. See Appendix 2 for related notes by Willughby on the effects of spin on the rebounding of tennis balls.

15/iᵛ   The ball is made of taylors shreds beaten by a hammer & shaped in a wooden mould. Then its hard tyed about with packthread. After this they sow white cotton about it or kersy.

The rackett is after this fashion: **a b c d e** the hoope & handle of wood. The strings that run the length are biggest & are called the <u>maine strings</u>, those that goe crosse, the <u>crosse strings</u>. They are the same with violl strings & are stretcht to a strong stiffnesse. The handle is usually covered] with whitleather.

The gamesters (2 or 4), agreed to <u>play a sett</u> upon equall termes, throw up a racket for the end **A C** (see the first diagram of the Tennis court) which if gained is an advantage. They aske whether they'll have Knotts or Flatts which is like Crosse or Pile. He that serves, strikes the ball upon the penthouse. It must fall beyond the rose at the end **B D**. If he misses 3 times together it is a losse & the adverse reckons fifteene towards the game & calls 15 Love;⁵⁸ if he misses 3 times againe or the adverse hitts his hazard, or if the adverse returnes the ball & the other strikes it over the court or under line, he reckons 15 more & calls Thirty Love⁵⁹ & if he makes another losse any of the aforesaid wayes, the adverse reckons ten more & calls Fowrty Love.⁶⁰ The next losse he counts <u>Game</u>. Fowre of these make a Sett. When each of the gamsters have gott a stroke, which is by the adverse his losing one, they reckon 15 All & so if the adverse getts the next stroke he reckons 30 for the others 15, who (if he that is 15 getts the next stroke) reckons 30 & calls it <u>Dewce</u>. Whoever getts the next calls <u>Vauntage</u>. If the adverse getts a stroke before the other is game, then the other is brought backe from vauntage & both reckon dewce againe.

A <u>long rest</u> is when the ball is kept up a good while by the gamsters, who are not allowed to strike it after the 2ᵈ bound. Now if a gamster neglects to take a ball at the 2ᵈ bound it is counted a <u>chase</u>. When there is 2 of these chases made (which may be both of one side or one on each side) then they <u>turne line</u>, i.e. exchange ends & play for them. The manner is thus. Suppose E serves a ball which is taken by F & struck back againe over line to the person E. If E neglects to take this ball & letts it bound twice, where it bounded the 2ᵈ time, there is counted the chase (as right against the figures **1 2 3 4** &c.). Now when another chase is thus likewise made, E goes on the other side of the line, i.e. to the end **B D**, & F serves to E who returnes the ball if he can to F. Now if F takes not the ball, & at the 2ᵈ bound it light better then the chase

---

58. *& calls 15 Love*] interlineated.

59. *Love*] interlineated.

60. *Love*] interlineated.

they played for (which was made before they turned line), E wins the stroke & reckons 15 onward to his game. If the ball lights worse at the 2ᵈ bound then the chase they play for, E loses the stroke & F counts / fifteene[61] towards his game. A chase is counted better or worse as it is nearer or further from the end of the court, a chase at the figure **1** being esteemed the best of all the figures, but the best of chases is at the nick on the serving end **A C** & the rose on the hazard side, i.e. the end **B D**. If he that is on the hazard side takes not the ball & it rebounds at the 2ᵈ bound beyond the rose, it is accounted his losse & the other reckons a stroke. If either of the gamster[s] take a ball before it comes to the ground it is termed Vollee (i.e. flying). Those are the best strokes that come swift & very close to the line, so they be over it. The designe of each gamster being to strike such strockes as the adverse party cannot take.

15/iiʳ

If any controversy arise about reckoning &c. the court keeper is to determine it, or, if he cannot, the company that looke on in the gallery. 6ᵈ (12ᵈ in some courts) is paid for every sett. Sometimes odds are given, & commonly a <u>Biske</u> is allowed, which is one stroke that may be had when the party (allowed it) pleases, as if he be fowrty he may take it to make him game &c. It is but once in the whole sett.

E	F
15 Love &c.	15 All
30	Dewce
Vauntage	Dewce
Dewce	Vauntage &c.
Vauntage	
Game	

Text reverts to Willughby's hand.

4 Games a Sett

A game consisting of 4 losses, a set of 4 games it is as if 16 were up.

Q: Why they reckon 15, 30, 40 &c. and not one, 2, 3.

Why they reckon by games & not 4, 8, &c.

Whither they reckon 45 or 50 a game. If they reckon 45 as it is most likely, bating 5 from ten as they bated it before from 15, then 4 games = 45 x 4 = 180, ¹/₂ of the degrees of a circle, and 8 games, that is as manie as both sides should get, are = 360, the degrees of a circle or the dayes in 12 Ægiptian monthes.[62]

---

61. *fifteene*] MS repeats last word of previous page *counts fifteene*.

62. See note 35 above.

It is very likely Tennis is much altered from what it was at the first invention and a great deale lost out of it.

Q: Whither at first 45 losses did not make a game, which beeing to tædious they afterwards altered to 4 though they kept the same numbers.

15/ii^v If the numbers on both sides on the wall[63] bee no more then 12 they repræsent the 12 signes. *X X*

And if there should bee but 3 losses in a game, then in a set there would bee the same number 12 to. It seemes that there should be but 3 losses in a game. Because else it would be reckoned 60. *X X*

> *The following notes, in Skippon's hand, are written on a further small fragment of paper, attached to the main description.*

15/iii^r Since my last to you I received from Mr Hoogan[64] some illustrations of particular circumstances in Tennis. 2 of the most considerable I shall mention, viz. <u>Making for a Sett</u> is thus: when each of the gamsters the former wayes have gott 3 games, because they will not venture all they play for upon one game, they usually make for it either two games or first come at two, he that getts the last game having it in his power to make which he pleases. First Come At 2 is when each has got a game they play the next for the sett; Two For It is when either of them can gett 2 before the other getts one.

<u>Cutting of a Ball</u> is when with a swift motion of a racket the ball is made to glide from on side of the rackett to the other, so that when 'tis off the rackett this wirling of it makes it in its progressive motion turne upon its owne axis, & consequently when it meetes with any opposition of the ground or wall it lyes almost still & rebounds but a very little, so that whereas a ball in its ordinary bound[65] from the wall suppose describes a large circular; thus:

The ball **b** falls upon the pavement **p p** & rebounds up to **c**, describing in its descent to **a** a large circular line: whereas a ball that is cutt rebounds only thus:

---

63. *on the wall*] interlineated.

64. The Mr Hoogan referred to has not been firmly identified. It might possibly be Christian Huygens, whose home, in his absence, Skippon and Willughby visited on their continental tour in 1663, and who was a corresponding member of the Royal Society. As the author of *De motu ex percussione* (written around 1659, published posthumously in 1703), Huygens was himself centrally interested in these issues. See also above, Introduction, Section 1.4 and 4.2.

65. *bound*] replaces cancellation *motion*.

p p the pavement, **b** the ball rebounds to **c** & in its descent describes a very small circle as falling extreame quick by the rule of motion, an extraordinary quick motion if meeting with a great hindrance or opposition ceases its motion.[66]

---

66. *in its descent*] two sets of crossed lines appear to cancel the rest of the passage, but the extent of the cancellation is not clear.

16 *blank*; 17   *Text reverts to Willughby's hand.*

Tables

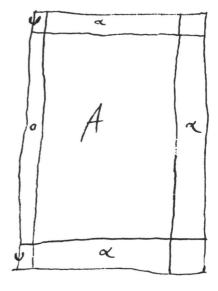

A table is of an oblong figure about 22 inches long, 13 broad, allmost 2 thick. In this there is a hollow or cavitie on either side, on the inner side for Tables, on the outer for Chests. That for Tables is $1\frac{1}{4}$ deep, for Chests $\frac{1}{4}$, so that the floore to play upon is $\frac{1}{2}$ thick. The ledge that goes about this cavitie is of the ends and out side $1\frac{1}{2}$[67] broad, on the inside where it is joined to another neere[68] $\frac{3}{4}$ or a little lesse then[69] halfe so much, so that the lenght of the hollow to play in is 19 long, the breadth $10\frac{3}{4}$.

A is the area or floore upon which they play, which is lower then the sides **α α α o** on the Chest side or outside $\frac{1}{4}$ of an inch, on the inside or Tableside $1\frac{1}{4}$. The sides **α α α o**, rising perpendicularly from the floore **A**, keepe the dice from flying out and the table men from slipping of, but on the Chest side where they use no dice the ledges not bee so high. **α α α** ledges are $1\frac{1}{2}$ broad, but **o** ledge scarce halfe so much.

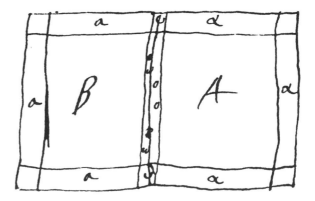

At **u u** to **o** ledge there is another table fastened with hinges, just of the same bignesse with the former, so that beeing folded upon the former, **α α α ω** fall just upon **α α α o**, and in the hollow or box which these 2 make beeing shut are the Table men kept. When the tables are open, **o** ledge joined to **ω** makes the ledge in the middle allmost aequall to **a a a α α α**, the side ledges. But on the

---

67. $\frac{1}{2}$] altered from $\frac{1}{4}$.

68. *neere*] interlineated.

69. *a little lesse then*] interlineated.

opposite for Chests there is no ledge in the middle, either table making but half a Chestboard, and because the area **D E** is not a perfect square, the Chestboard dos not begin just at the ledges but at a little distance from **a α** so that the area taken for the Chest board may bee a square.

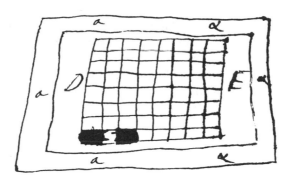

This is the measure of the best tables that are now in fashion, but they may bee bigger or lesse, or of any proportion that one shall fansie or desire.

The tables are made of black ebonie. Halfe the little squares for Chests of ivorie or bone.

The Chest play is described p:

> *Despite the indication of intent, Willughby does not include a section on Chess either here or elsewhere in the volume.*

The area or floore[70] of each table beeing 19 inches long is divided into 3 parts by 2 white lines of ivory **α β, α β**. The middle space **α α β β** takes up 5 of the 19, **α v, α m**, each of them 7. The middle space **A** is left all black & undivided but the bases **v v, m m** of the two other areas are divided into 6 æquall parts, upon everie one of which parts insists an æquicrurall triangle, whose point ends in the line **α β**, & whose basis is æqual to $1/2$ of one of those parts, or $1/12$ of the whole **v v**.

18 *blank*; 19

The basis of the triangle is just in the middle of the part it belongs to, so that the distances betweene the triangles are æquall to the bases.

Suppose **D E** = **v v** and divided into 6 parts, of which **D v** is the first. **i o** the basis of the triangle = $1/2$ **D v** and standing in the middle so that **D i** = **o v** & therefore **o i**, the distance betweene that and the next triangle, will bee = **i o**, the basis.

D ⟋⟍⟋⟍ ⊢⊢⊢⊢⊢⊢⊢⊢ E

---

70.   *or floore*] interlineated.

¹/₂ of these triangles are white, the other ¹/₂ red, made of red brasil, and they may bee of any 2 differing colours that differ from the colour of the tables. These triangles are called Points and are placed interchangeably, first a white point,[71] then a red point &c., as if **s** point bee white, **Q** the next must bee red, and the opposite point to **s** beeing **δ** must bee red, **w** white, and the first point of the other table must bee of a different colour from the last in this, as if **z** bee white, **ε** must be red, &c.

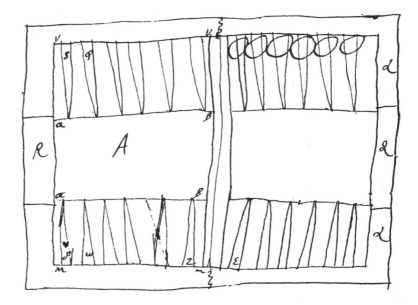

The table men are in number 30, 15 white and 15 black. Their figure is cilindrical about ³/₈ high. The diameter is a little lesse then ¹/₆ of **m m**, so that 6 men may bee placed one by another upon the 6 points, and have a little roome to spare, that they may bee mooved easily without sticking.

A Die is a little cube made of bone, the latus about ³/₈. Upon one side of this die there is one black point just in the middle ⊡ which is called an Ace. Upon another, 2 points ⊡ which is a Duce. Upon the 3ᵈ, 3 points ⊡ which is called a Trea. Upon the 4ᵗʰ, ⊡ 4 points which is called a Kater. Upon the 5ᵗʰ, ⊡ 5 which calld a Cinque. Upon the 6ᵗʰ ⊡ 6 which is calld a Sise. The Ace is allwaies opposite to the Sise. The side that falls from **C B** is the Kater; the opposite to that, the Trea. The side that falls from **a B** is the Cinque, & the opposite to that, the Duce. The points of the Duce & Trea are so placed that they meet not in the same corner of the cube, as in **C D**, ⊏⊡ⴴ not as in **A B** ⨍⊡β .

20 *blank*; 21   *Q:* Whither at first they had any more then one table & one die. *X X X* Dublets &c. needing but one. *X*

71. *first a white point then*] altered from *a white man by*.

The 30 daies in a month or the 30 degrees in a signe determined the number of the table men to bee 30 & the number of the signes or monthes[72] determined the points to bee 12. 30 x 12, the points of one table, or 15 x 24, the points of a pare of tables, = 360, the degrees of a circle or the daies of a yeare that consists[73] of 12 months each having 30 dayes.

The motion of the table men round[74] thorough the points repræsents the motion of the sun thorough the signes of zodiack. It is therefore likely that tables were at first round, but that beeing found inconvenient for the placing of the men they afterwards came to this oblong figure.

The gamesters stand allwaies one on one side the tables & the other on the other.

The gamesters lay the mony they play for upon the ledge at **L L**, and if one stake belong æqually to them both, as if in a shilling either of them have 6 pence, they lay it in the middle at **Q**.

In all games the first thing is to throw for the dice. Each gamester, taking a die, throws it in one of the tables, and hee that throws the biggest cast[75] has the dice and begins the game. When hee has thrown once, then his antagonist throws & so by turns as long as the game lasts.

The cast is that side of the die that lies uppermost when it rests.

They may begin from either side, as either from **Q** or **R**, but the rule is allwaies to play towards the light as if the windores of the chamber they play in bee towards **Q** side, they begin from **R**, if towards **R** from **Q**.

Cogging of Dice is when by sleight of hand or anie trick, the cast they would have is throwne, there beeing foul play whenever the casts of the dice depend not purely upon fortune. *V:* the Booke of Dice.[76]

To prevent cogging they throw the dice out of a little long boxe.

---

72. *or monthes*] interlineated.

73. *consists*] MS *consits*.

74. *round*] interlineated.

75. *cast*] follows cancellation *die*.

76. This reference could in principle be to treatises on chance by either Cardano (1663) or Huygens (1657). Alternatively, the reference may be to a lost work by Willughby himself, identified by his daughter Cassandra as one 'which shews the chances of most games' (Wood 1958: 105). The 'Booke of Dice' is referred to again on p. 88 below.

WAIES OF CHEATING

1. Playing with severall pare of false dice, which the opposite plaier dos not discover. Dice are false when one side is heavier then the other, the die allwaies resting on the heaviest side.
2. Wetting a side of the die, with spittle, sweat, earwaxe &c. which makes it rest on that side.
3. Slurring, which is a trick to make the die slide & not tumble over.
4. Throwing the dice just one upon another; the undermost will never change the side it is thrown upon.
5. [*No text supplied.*]

22   There is never a game in which they use but one die though in Dublets they use but one table. **X X**

Games may bee invented with 3 or 4 tables as wel as with 1 or 2.

In all games at Tables you must play just as you throw either 2 men or one man at lenght for both casts, but onely at Dublets you must never play a man at lenght, as if your casts bee a trea and a duce you cannot play a cinque for them.

There must never bee more then one man mooved for one cast, as if you throw a sise you cannot play 2 treas or a kater & a duce instead of it, but must moove one man 6 points.

In all games the men at first are set in the tables, and are plaid about quite round till they are plaid of (as in Ticktack they are all placed in the first point, in Irish in the 6th, 8th 12th, 24th &c.), and are never plaied into the tables from without.

They allwais throw for the dice at first but afterwards hee that wins the game has the dice, and begins the next.

At all games, all that is throwne must bee plaied if it bee possible.

They use hexaedricall dies rather then 4edricall &c.

1. Because it is probable[77] cubes were invented first.
2. Because the sides of 2 cubes are = 12. **X X**

23   The games of Tables may bee divided into those that use but one table & those that use them both.

Those that use but one table are:

---

77. *it is probable*] altered from *they were.*

[Dublets]

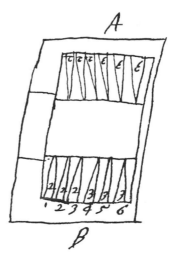

1. Dublets, in which the 15 black & white men are placed at either end, as if A gamester have the white men hee places them all at **A** end, & B places all the black men at **B**. They are placed according to the figures in the points, as 2 in the first, 2[d] & 3[d] points & 3 in the 4th, 5th & 6th points, which makes up the whole number 15 and in the same manner at **A** end. They are set at first one upon another, as 2 one upon another in the 3 first points & 3 one upon another in the 3 last points.

The[78] first thing is to play down the men, as if B gamester have the dice & throw a sise & a cinque, hee puts one man downe from the 6th point & another from the 5th point. Then A throwes and puts downe 2 men according as his cast is.

The putting downe of men is the setting of them one before another, as if in **B C** point there stand 2 men one upon[79] another, when one is put downe they stand as in **D n** point, so that in the 3 first points there is one man to bee put down, & in the 3 last 2 from every point. If one or both[80] of the casts happen to light upon a point where they are all put down allreadie they stand[81] for nothing.

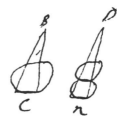

When the[82] men are all plaid downe, then they play them of, as if the[83] casts bee a sise & a trea one must bee plaid from the 6th point & another from the 3[d] point, and hee that can play of all his men first wins the game.

There must none of the men bee plaid of till everie one of them bee plaid downe. This playing of of men they call Bearing, and if when they are come to bearing, the casts they throw light upon points[84] where all the men are borne they stand for nothing. Whenever they throw dublets, that is 2 duces, or 2 cinques, or any other, they play downe or bare as manie men as there are

---

78. *The*] follows cancellation *After they have thrown for the dice.*

79. *upon*] altered from *before.*

80. *or both*] interlineated.

81. *they stand*] MS *it stands.*

82. *the*] MS *they.*

83. *the*] MS *they.*

84. *points*] follows cancellation *men.*

peeps in the dublet, as if they throw 2 sises, they play down or bare 12, if they throw 2 duces, they play downe or bare 4 &c. Nor doe they observe the points, but play them from any points where they think good, & from this *24 blank; 25* manner of playing dublets / the game is called Dublets.

If a game bee plaid & there happen no dublets in it, the summe of all the casts that serve to play downe the men & bare them is = 93, that is 3 x 31, or $\frac{1}{4}$ of a yeare that has 12 monthes, and every month 31 daies. And the summe of all the casts that serve to play of the men at both ends is = $\frac{1}{2}$ of such a yeare. But if 3 men bee placed upon the 3^d, 4th & 5th points, the summe of both will bee æquall to 6 monthes of 30 daies.

93 is one lesse then $\frac{1}{2}$ of 187, the summe of all the casts that serve to play about the men at Irish, but is 3 more then $\frac{1}{4}$ of 360, the summe of the casts that play about the men at Ticktack. *X X*

This is the most childish game at Tables in which there is nothing but chance & scarce anie skill.

Q: Whither those that throw dublets should have the dice againe. *X X*

Ticktack

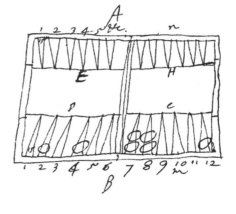

The name Ticktack comes from touching & playing, it beeing the law of this game that the man that is touched must bee plaied.

All the 15 men at first are set upon the first point, from which they play them round thorough both the tables, A gamester from 1 till they come round by 12, 11, &c. and are at last borne of over 1 point on B side. And in the same manner B gamester plays round from 1 till hee bares his men over 1 in A point.

Taking a Point is when you can play 2 men upon the same point, as if you throw[85] 2 sises at first you may play them both upon the 7th point, and take that point. Or if you have one man upon the 2d & another upon the 4th point, and throw 6 & 4, you may take the 8th point.

Binding a Man is when you have one man upon a point and play another upon it, as if you have a single man upon the 2d & 4th points and throw an ace & a trea[86] you may bind those 2 men. Or if you have one man upon the 12th point & throw eleven, that is a Sise & a Cinque, you may bind that man from home at lenght.

Binding at Lenght, or Playing at Lenght, is when you play but one man for both your casts, as mooving[87] one man 11 points, instead of mooving 2, one 6 & another 5 points, when you throw a sise & a cinque.

Playing at Home, or Playing in his owne Tables, is when B gamester plays his men in his owne side, or A gamester on A side. But most properly 1 point is called Home & playing your men from thence Playing them from Home, all the men beginning their journie & circuit from that point.

They may play as manie men as they will upon a point but it is counted bungling to play more then 3 or 4, nor doe they ever doe it but to avoid a greater inconvenience.

---

85. *throw*] followed by cancellation *12*.

86. *trea*] altered from *kater*.

87. *mooving*] altered from *playin*.

You may play upon any point that has no men upon it or that has your own men or but one of your antagonists. But if there bee 2 or more of his men, you cannot play upon them nor can you play one man at lenght, if the point you are to passe thorough bee taken by your antagonist, as if you throw[88] 2 sises, you cannot play one man at lenght if the 6th point from the point you play from bee taken before by the contrarie gamester. Nor can you play sise-cinque at lenght / if the 5th & 6th point bee taken before. But if but one of those bee taken, as the 6th point, you may play it first as a cinque, & from thence as a sise, or if the 5th bee taken you must play it first as a sise & then as a cinque. But wherever points are taken by your own men, they doe not hinder you.

28 *blank*; 29

A Blot is when one man is upon a point, and within 12 or fewer points of some of your opposites men.

A Blot of a Die is when one man is upon a point & within 6 or fewer points of some of your adversaries.

Hitting a Blot is when you can play upon that point where your adversary has but one man, as if A[89] throw eleven, and one of Bees men bee eleven points of, A[90] may hit that blot.

THE SEVERALL WAYES OF WINNING A SINGLE OR DOUBLE GAME AT TICKTACK

1. Whoever can hit a blot first wins the game.[91] This happening oftenest is but a single game, all the rest are double games. *X X X* Except the 5 of which I am doubtfull of. *X*

2. Taking all the points in any one end of either table, as all the points in **A E**, **n H**, **D B**, or **c m** end, wins a double game, or as much more as they play for. The taking all the points in **B D** end by B[92] or **A E** end by A[93] is called Tootes. This happens the oftenest of any of this kind of double games and when they throw very little casts as 2 aces, duce ace &c., they alwaies plaie for Tootes. The antagonist to prevent Tootes plais his men as fast on forwards as hee can, to bee within reach of hitting blots which hee that plaies for Tootes makes in his tables. There being but 15 men in all,[94] that is as many as will take all the points & but 3 to spare. If you chance to throw a sise or two, which carries your men out of that end of the tables, you must give over Tootes & plot some

---

88. *throw*] followed by cancellation *12*.

89. *A*] altered from *you*.

90. *A*] altered from *hee*.

91. *1. Whoever … game*] Replaces uncertain cancellation *1. Whoever was hit he that can hit him first a blot* (unclear text) *first wins the game*.

92. *end by B*] interlineated.

93. *by A*] interlineated.

94. *all*] followed by cancellation *if you chance to throw a sise*.

other game. Of these the 6 points in **n H** are seldomest [taken] by B or the 6 points in **c m** by A.

3. Rovers which is when you can get a single man in the 12th & 13th point from home. It wins a double game if you have no more men out, but if there bee other men out it stands for nothing.

4. It is a double game when you[95] can take the 12th & 13th points or the first & 24th or last point, that is when you can leave 2 men or more in the first point and get 2 more quite round into the last.

The keeping of 2 men in the first point is calld Keeping your Sweethart, and when you are forced to play away all or all but one it is Breaking or Loosing your Sweethart. They strive to keepe this sweethart as long as they can to hinder the antagonist from getting[96] a double game and in hopes to get one themselves by having the first & 24th points.   *30 blank; 31*

5. The fifth and last way is when you can get about all your men and beare them of the tables, over the 24th point. Hee that can beare them all first wins a double game.[97] This very rarely happens, it beeing allmost a thousand to one that the game is won or lost first some of the other waies.

There beeing 4 variations of the second way & 2 of the 4th, all the games are in number 9. But Tootes & Rovers beeing excluded, there remaines 7. Tootes and Rovers are never plaied unlesse the gamesters both [agree] to make them at first.

They endeavour to prevent their antagonists winning a double game, by setting blots on purpose to give him a single game, by taking one of the 6 points in the 2d way or one of the two points in the 4th way, by playing as forward & getting as neere him as they can, to bee readie to hit blots.

Q: Why the taking the 7th & 18th points, or the 6th & 19th should not win double games, as wel as the taking of the first & 24th, or the 12th & 13th. Unlesse the reason bee that they would not have more then 7 games.

The art of playing consists in getting as manie points as you can togather, in getting as soone as you can into the 12th or 13th point, in placing your men so that they bee readie to take more points,

---

95. *you*] followed by cancellation *get the 12th & 13th points with 2 more.*

96. *getting*] followed by cancellation *the 4th doub.*

97. *game*] followed by cancelled phrase … *Irish*; first element obscured by cancel strokes.

in venturing the hitting of a blot, so it bee not a blot of a die, to take one of the double game points, and if you cannot bind a blot to play your men so that you may bind it next time &c.

The dice in Ticktack is a great advantage and counted as good as 7::6.[98] The æquallest play were to throw for the dice everie game[99] for else hee that wins one game will goe neere to win 3 or 4 before the other recovers the dice.

32 blank; 33 Whenever A gamester has wun either a double or single game & oversees it, B wins as much as A should have done, as if A gamester bee in reach of a blot & oversees it, and B catch him, B wins a single game, or if A could have wun a double game, & oversee it, & B catch him, B wins the double game. This is calld, Why Not, because when A[100] has plaied or touched a wrong man B[101] saies, And Why Not Here.

Vie Ticktack is when one has as hee thinks the advantage & is likely to win, hee saies to the other, I Vie. If hee thinks there bee no hopes of it hee yeilds the game. But if hee have a mind to venture longer and not yeild, hee saies, I See It. This doubles whatever they play for. If the game bee not wun the next throw, it may be vied againe, and then what they plaied for at first is trebled. If it bee vied againe, the stake is quadrupled, &c., there beeing as many stakes to bee plaied for as there have bene vies beside the stake at first, as if there has bene 4 vies & they play for 6 pence the stake will bee ½ a crowne. They use either to stake as often as they vie or reckon the[102] vies with counters. A double game doubles the stake & all the vies. *X X*

Of all the double games next Toots & Rovers, that which is wun by getting the 12th & 13th points oftenest happens.

Whatever double games should bee made by getting 2 opposite points, it must bee the same summe of casts reckoning from the first that must win them, as twice twelve and twice eleven = 46 gets the 12th & 13th point from home. For the 2 next points, that is the 11th & 14th, twice ten & twice 13 = 46 gets them, that is the same summe as before, & so for any other opposite points till you come to the first & 24th, which having kept your mistris whole, twice 23 = 46 wins. The reason of this is because that as manie points as you goe forward from the 13th in your opposites tables, so manie points you come back in your owne from the 12th, which makes the summe the same.

---

98. The sign of proportion '::' was in standard use in contemporary arithmetic textbooks (e.g. Kersey's Appendix to Wingate 1671).

99. *game*] altered from *time*.

100. *A*] altered from *B*.

101. *B*] altered from *A*.

102. *the*] MS *they*.

The summe beeing the same to take any two of the opposite points they only chose the first & last pare for the double games, and left all the middle. 46 is one halfe + 1 of 90, the quadrant of the circle or ($\frac{1}{8}$ of 360) + 1. The sum for Rovers is 23, more by $\frac{1}{2}$ then $\frac{1}{16}$ of 360.

46 x 8 = 368, 4 more then 364   34
46 x 2 = 92, 1 more then 91, that is one more then $\frac{1}{4}$ of the daies of a yeare.
The summe for the first sixe or for Tootes = 30
for the second sixe[103] = 102
for the third sixe = 174
for the last sixe = 246

It is not reckoned a game to get all the points with single men, because it is impossible but some of them should first bee taken.

They name the casts as they are set downe here, allwaies naming the biggest   35
first. Besides which they have allso these ridiculous names & phrases for them, which sound a little like the names of the casts or rime to them.[104]

2 Aces: Maumsay, Amsace, Ambling Annice, Mice, from their littlenesse.
Duce Ace.
Trea Ace: Trash & Trumperie.
Kater Ace.
Cinque Ace: Sing Alse & Ile Whistle.
Sise Ace.
2 Duces: Two Twoes, Two Tups.
Trea Duce: Traduce mee Not.
Kater Duce.
Cinque Duce.
Sise Duce.
2 Treas: 2 Taylors.
Kater Trea: Cats are Gray.
Cinque Trea: Some Fought Some Run Away.
Instead of Sise Trea, Sixe & 3.
2 Foures: 2 Katers.
Cinque Kater.
Instead of Sise Kater, 6 & Foure.
2 Fives (2 Cinques not so often): 2 Fives, 2 Theives[105] besides the Caster.
Sise Cinque, or Eleven: A Living a Dog would not Have It.
2 Sixes or Twelve: The Yard, from their lenght.[106]

---

103. *sixe*] followed by cancellation *174*.

104. *They name … rime to them*] squeezed into space at top of page. See Glossary of Games under 'Dice'.

105. *Theives*] altered from *Theefes*.

106. *lenght*] followed on next line by cancellation *sixe & foure in*.

They say Twelve instead of 2 Sixes because no 2 other casts besides 2 sixes make 12. They never say Sise Trea, or Sise Foure, Sixe and Three & Sixe and Foure[107] sounding better.

All the rest according to this table & never otherwise, as never Foure Twoe instead of Kater Duce.

They never say 2 Ones, nor 2 Threes, but 2 Aces, & 2 Treas. But 2 Twoes, 2 Foures, 2 Fives, as often as 2 Duces, 2 Katers, 2 Cinques. They never say 2 Sises, but 2 Sixes or Twelve.

---

107. *Foure*] MS *found.*

Irish

In Irish, the men are placed at first as in this scheme, that is, A places 5 of his men in the 6th point, 3 in the 8th, 5 in the 13th, and 2 in the 24th, which make up 15. A places his men in the opposite pointes, as 2 in the first of Bees, which is the 24th of As, &c.

They play the men just as they doe in Ticktack, only this is the difference, that in Ticktack they play their men from home & bare them of from their antagonists tables, as B playes from 1 & bares them of from the 24th point in As tables, & A plaies from his first point & bares them of from the 24th point, that is the first point in Bees tables. But in Irish they bring their men home & bare[108] them of in their own tables, as B

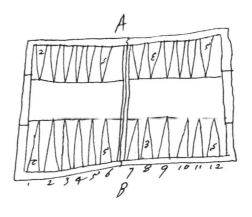

brings his 2 men from the 24th point, his 5 from the 13th, his 3 from the 8th & his 5 from the 6th &[109] brings them still homewards towards 1 point, thorough 13, 12, 11, 10 &c., till hee can bare them of from his own tables over 1 point.

If a blot bee hot in Irish,[110] the game is not lost, but the man that is hot must bee put to enter.

Taking[111] a Point upon a Mans Head is when B can take a point where there is a single man of As.

Nipping a Man is when you hit a blot with a single man & then play him on forwards, not setting him downe upon the point where the blot was hot, as if A have a man in 10 point, B another in 12 point, if B[112] throw Kater Duce hee may nip As man with a duce & then play his owne man still forward to 6 point.

Bees man that is taken must enter, that is must bee plaid as if hee were quite out of the tables over the first point of As. If B throw an ace hee must enter

---

108. *bare*] altered from *play*.

109. *&*] followed by cancellation *bares*.

110. *Irish*] altered from *Tables*.

111. *Taking*] follows uncertain cancellation *Entering is when a man is taken, he oft bene taken*.

112. *B*] altered from *A*.

his[113] man in As first point, if a duce in As second point, &c. But hee cannot enter upon a point where A has 2 men. But if A have one man in a point & B enter upon him and hit him, As must bee entered into Bee tables. If B have a man or men to enter, all the rest of his men must stand still till those are entered. Nor can either of them stirre their men as long as they have any to enter.

38 *blank*; 39   Binding up the Tables is when B or A have taken all their first six points.

If B have his tables bound up and A have a man or men to enter, the tables must bee Opened or Broken, for if B should keepe his tables bound up it were impossible for A to enter. Breaking or opening is the remooving all the men from a point but one, as if there bee 3 upon a point, 2 must bee remooved; if 4, 3; if 2, one &c. Those men that are thus remooved must bee entered again as if they had bene taken, as B must enter his men that were remooved thorough As tables. But if A have never a man to enter, B may bind up his tables & keepe them bound. When the tables are bound up & men to enter, they both throw the dice, & hee which throwes the biggest casts chuses which point hee will have broken or opened, as if one throw ten & another eleven, hee that throwes eleven chuses the point.

They that can bare all their men first win the game. But none of the men must bee begun to bee borne till they are all brought home into the first 6 points, as Bees men[114] must bee all in the points 1, 2, 3, 4, 5, 6, before any of them can bee borne.

A Fore Game is when the[115] men are plaied about & borne of without having bene taken & put to entring and hee has the better of a fore game that has his men forwardest & neerest home.

A Latter Game is when they see themselves behind & that they are past all hopes of winning a foregame they set blots a purpose that they may bee taken & put to entring, for so getting a point or two in their enemies tables, and making up their own tables as wel as they can, if hee blot (as it is likely hee will before hee bare all) and bee hot, the game may bee recovered. It is possible for A[116] to recover a game when B has borne all his men but one. I once wun such a game, but I dont expect ever to see it againe.

It is a proverb, An Irish man is never dead till his head bee cut of[117] (the Irish

---

113. *his*] altered from *a*.

114. *Bees men*] follows cancellation *As men*.

115. *the*] MS *they*.

116. *for A*] interlineated.

117. This proverb is not in Tilley's comprehensive listing of seventeenth-century proverbs (Tilley 1950), but there is an apt allusion to it in John Webster's *White Devil* (Act iv, Scene 1): 'Like the wild Irish I'le nere thinke thee dead, / Till I can play at footeball with they head' (Webster 1937: 123).

having a custome to cut of the heads of all those they have killed), nor a game at Irish wun till the last man bee borne.

A Foregame is the surer to trust to, but there is more art in playing a Lattergame.

If you say (Bee your Leave) at Irish or Ticktack, you may touch a man & not play it, otherwise the man that is touched must bee plaied at both.   40 *blank*; 41

The cunning consists in contriving to get as manie points as you can togather to stop your antagonists men, and cheifly in the first 6 points, to keepe him from entring.

The best points thereabouts are the 4th, 5th, 6th, 7th.

If B bee to breake, it is most commonly best to breake in the ace point, that so though A enter, hee may yet bee kept from running away by the other points that A has taken in his way. But if it fall to As lot to chuse a point to bee broken Bees tables, hee most commonly chuses the 5th or 6th, that so beeing entred hee may bee freer to get away.

The best casts at first are sises, which take the 7th point from the 13th, or the 18th from the 24th,[118] sise ace which takes the same from the 13th & 8th, trea ace which takes the 5th from the 8th & 6th, eleven which saves a man from the 24th lodging him on the 13th, &c.

Loosing of Men is when some of yours are imprisoned in your antagonists tables, you are forced to play most of the rest upon 1st, 2^{d} or 3^{d} points, for so not having men enough to bind up the tables, though you should hit a blot it would do you no good, your adversary having free roome to enter & get away againe. Saving a Man is the bringing him safe out of his enemies quarters.

Q: Whither the Irish invented this game.

It is 48 that brings the 2 furthest men home and bares them; 24, or ½ 48, that bares the 3 men in the 8th point; 30 that bares the 5 in the 6th point; & 65 that bares the 5 in the 13th point. The summe of all these is = 167, wanting one of 168, the number of the daies in 6 months of 28 daies.

But had they bene placed 5 in the 6th as before, 2 in the 8th, 2 in the 13th, 4 in the 15th, and 2 in the 24th as before, the summe would have bene just 180 = ½ 360, = ½ the summe in Ticktack, or to ½ the summe if they were all plaied from the 24th point. But this makes the game to tedious & not so good for taking of points at first.

---

118. *or the 18th … 24th*] interlineated.

42 *blank;* 43

Back Gammon

Back Gammon, in the placing, playing, baring the men, binding up & opening the tables &c., differs nothing from Irish.

The onely difference is that dublets must bee plaied double, as if you throw 2 treas you must play 4 traies; if 2 cinques, 4 cinques, &c.

In Irish there can but a single game bee wun, but in Backgammon if you throw dublets the last cast of the game, or if you bare all your men before your antagonist have brought all his home into the last six points, you win a double game. And if you throw dublets at last & bare all your men to, before your antagonist get home, you win a treble game or 3 times as much as is plaid for.

Double hand Ticktack, Irish or Backgammon is, when 4 play, 2 on[119] either side, and this is all one as when there is but one on a side if they should throw 4 dice at a time. They both throw the dice one after another & hee that has the best skill plaies them.

They that have the dice throw but one of them the first time, but afterwards allwaies 2 of a side throw & then the other two.

The double hand of any of these is duller and wors then the single hand.

Of all games at Tables, Irish is counted the best.

---

119. *2 on*] altered from *one against anot.*

Long Laurence

A Long Laurence is a long parrallelopipedon, one of whose sides has nothing cut upon it and is called Blanke, the opposite side has severall crosse lines & crosses & is called Soope All. One of the other sides has 2 crosse lines, & the opposite to it one.

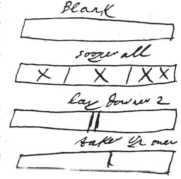

Everie one of the plaiers stakes one at first, and then they throw the Long Laurence by turnes as a die. If a Blanke bee throwne they neither take up nor lay downe any. If Soope All, they take up all. If the side that has | | upon it, they lay downe 2. If the side that has |, they take up one. And as often as all are taken up they all stake againe.

A tetraedricall die would serve better for this game, with the same marks upon the 4 sides.

Cards

Q: The art of making cards. **X**

They seeme to bee made of 3 or 4 peices of white paper pasted togather and made verie smooth that they may easilie slip from one another, and bee dealt & plaied. If they grow danke, they must bee dried and rubbed one by one to make them slip[120] againe.

The figure is an exact rectangle parallelogrammon. The lenght of those that are now in fasshion is allmost 3 ½, the breadth neere 2 inches, that is a little more then ½ of the lenght. One side is allwaies plane and white, which when the cards are dealt is allwaies uppermost, that they may not bee knowne. This side is called the back side. The other side where the peepes are is called the face of the cards. The cards are held allwaies with the faces towards the gamesters, that no bodie may see what they are, and when they play them they throw them downe with the faces uppermost.

They are divided into 4 sutes, Diamonds, Harts, Spades & Clubs. In everie sute there is 13. The full number 52 = 4 x 13 is called the Deck or Pack of cardes.

The figure of the Diamond is an obtusangle parallelogrammon ◇ the acute angles beeing longwaies in the cardes, the obtuse broaduaies. The figure of the Hart '♡ **a β** longwaies **D E** broadwaies. Of the Spade, ♠ of the Club, ♣ **α β** in both going longwaies.

In everie sute there are 10 cards, and 3 Coats or Coatcards. The 10 cards are ace, duce, trea, foure, five, sixe, seven, eight, nine, ten.

The peeps are placed in this order in all the 4 sutes, and are all of an æquall bignesse. The ace, duce & trea are never called one, two & three, nor anie above them kater, cinque, sise &c. but foure, five &c.

The 3 coat cards are the Knave, Queene & King. The Queene has the picture & dresse of a woman upon it, with[121] one peepe of the sute it belongs in one of the upper corners by her face, to distinguish her from the other Queenes of the other sutes.

All the demonstrations of dice may bee applied to cards. **X X**   50

Q: How often one may expect a murnivall in Gleeke, or the probability of any other chance in other games.

The Knaves & Kings have pictures of men upon them, & to distinguish the   51
suites they have a peepe of the sute they belong to in one of the upper corners as the Queenes had. The Knave is knowne from the King by beeing yonger & slenderer, and having his legs from his knees downwards without any covering over them. The King has a broader, older and more majesticall face, and has allwaies a gown & other habiliments[122] reaching quite downe to the bottome of the card, and most commonly covering his legs.

The Hart, Spade & Diamond have the figures of harts &c., the true spade beeing that which is pointed at the bottome, ♉ which enters the ground easier, & not that which is most in use now, with a broad bottome. ♤

Q: Whither they were wont formerly to have such iron knobs ♣ at the ends of their clubbs.

The valor or powre of the cards is according to the number of their peepes or names, a duce winning an ace, a trea a duce &c. to ten, & in Ruffes &c. are reckoned according to the number of theire peepes.[123] Of the 3 coat cards the King is the best, next the Queene & then the Knave. But in some games the ace is made the best as in Gleeke, Beast, &c.[124] The Knave wins all the rest from ten downwards. But when they are reckoned in Ruffes &c. none of them stand for more then ten.

The 13th card is called the King from having the greatest powr & winning all the rest. The next to him is the Queene, the third the Knave, that is the cheife councelour or servant.

---

121. *with*] followed by cancellation *the marke of.*

122. *habiliments*] followed by cancellation *covering his legs.*

123. *& in Ruffes ... peepes*] interlineated.

124. *&c.*] followed by cancellation *in Gleeke the valore.*

The 52 cards in a deck are æquall to the number of the weekes in a yeare. The 4 sutes represent the 4 seasons of the yeare. The 13 cards in everie suite, the 13 lunar months[125] or the 13 weekes in everie season. And if the Knave, Queen & King bee reckoned[126] eleven, twelve, thirteen, the summe of all the peepes = 364, the number of the daies in 52 weekes, or of a yeare that consists of 13 lunar months, for the peepes in each sute are

$$= \frac{13 \times 13 + 1}{2} = 13 \times 7, = \text{to the number of the weekes in a quarter.}$$

The number of a mans fingers determining numbers in arithmetick to a decimall progression, so that all numbers were but tens or the parts of ten so manie times repeated, and ten beeing allwaies counted the most perfect number, they were loth to have any more then ten peepes upon a carde. Nor are the King,[127] Queen & Knave reckoned at more then ten in any games I have ever hard of, though perhaps at first they were reckoned 11, 12, 13,[128] and might afterwards bee brought down to tens because of the difficultie of reckoning, whereas now there beeing so manie tens, that is 4 in everie sute, the other lesser cards joined with tens are easily reckoned. And yet in Gleeke the King & Queen when they are honnours are reckoned the King 3 & the Queen 2, because the true valor should bee 3 & 2 more then they are now reckoned, & therefore the gleekes of Knave, Queen, King are 1, 2, 3.

V: Gleeke p. 77, Loadum [p.] 83

52 If the Coats did not stand for 11, 12, 13, they could not bee sequens, as they are reckoned in Gleeke, Cribbidge &c., nor would a nine, ten, Knave bee sequens, but nine, ten, ten.

The usual way of reckoning with counters is to lay them all in a line just before them.

All that are in the lines αβ, αβ stand for unites, those above at **C C** stand for tens, those below at **D D** for fives. So the summe of those in the first example is = 18, in the second to 31.

---

125. *months*] followed by cancellation *in a yeare.*

126. *reckoned*] followed by cancellation *ten.*

127. *are the King*] altered from *is the King though hee win the.*

128. Note that these are the values of the Knave, Queen, and King in Willughby's 'New Cribbage or Noddy' (p. 69).

They left reckoning the King, Queen & Knave 11, 12, 13:

1. Because they were more troublesome to count,
2. Because they could not so easily make 31 with them.

Cards cut in long triangles & dipt in melted brimstone make the best matches.

Playing Boobie is when 2 or more make a private compact to favour one another & cozen and make a boobie of the rest.

Giving to the Boxe at cards is allowing the Butler or him that finds the cards some of the winnings, as the odde counter of those that are bidden for the stock. *X X X*

In all games at cards hee that wins the trick begins to play next.

V: p. 6[129]

The cards beeing divided according to the lunar months, the number of the solar months & daies in each month are brought in in the reckonings[130] of severall games. 12 in Trumpe, Gleeke &c.; 31 in One & Thirtie, Loadum, Cribbidge.

If the abuse bee no argument against the use, there can nothing bee said against cards, the first invention beeing verie ingenious & of excellent use to exercise the wits, to instruct & not to debauch the youth.

In those games where dealing is an advantage to the dealer as Gleeke &c., if dealing bee lost hee must not deale againe, but it must goe to the next to deale. But where it is an advantage to loose dealing, the dealer must deale againe till hee can deal without loosing. *X*

Loosing of Dealing is when more or lesse are dealt to the plaiers then the game requires.

The name Cards comes from Charta, of which they are made. 53

Q: Why they are called Sutes. *X X*

---

129. *V: p. 6*] at this point refers back to the instruction on p. 6 *All in this side belongs to p: 52*, signalling the insertion on p. 52 of the text which follows: *The cards beeing divided … debauch the youth.*

130. *reckonings*] follows cancellation *daies.*

Q: Whither the 4 suites have any[131] thing in them besides their number to signifie the seasons. One may fancie Spades to bee the spring from digging & preparing the ground, Harts summer from the heat, Clubs autumme from the cudgel play & other exercises in use then, but there is no reason why Diamonds should bee winter. **X X**

The colours black[132] & red may bee for the 2 halfes of the yeare divided either by the æquinoctiall or solstitiall points. Let the Harts then repræsent the time between the æquinoxe & the summer solstice, the Diamonds the time in which the sun is going back from the solstice to the autumnall æquinoxe, or the riches of autumne, the red colour of both fire or the heate of summer. The black colour of the other two, the long nights, or the dismallnesse of winter, of which Clubs should bee the time between the autumnall æquinoxe & the winter solstice, Spades the time between the winter solstice & vernall æquinoxe. Or supposing the yeare divided by the solstitiall points, the red should bee the time in which the daies are lenghtening, the black the time in which the nights lenghten. But then it would bee harder to give a reason for the 2 sutes in either halfe. Diamonds is reckoned the least of all the suites but that may [bee] because the figure is lesse then the figures of the other three.

Diamonds is the gentile name. The countrie people call them Picks, from the points of the Diamond.

In all games the first thing is to lift for dealing which is something like throwing for dice. The whole deck standing all one upon another, everie one of the plaiers lifts up as manie of the cards as hee thinks good, leaving, to bee sure, enough for the rest, & everie one looking upon the face of the card that is undermost, they that have the least card deal. And if two happen to lift both the same, & the cards they lift bee lesser then any of the rest, they must lift againe. But the Ace of Diamonds is counted the least of all the cards & hee that lifts that must deal & not lift again though others should lift aces. Dealing the cards is the giving of everie gamester as manie as hee is to have by the lawes of the game.

54 blank; 55   The gamesters sit round a table, and holding the cards with their faces towards them, throw them downe upon the table as they play them. The dealer is allwaies youngest[133] [&] deales himselfe the cards last, & is to play last. Hee that has the cards dealt first to him is the eldest & begins to play. Hee that sits next him plaies the second & so round in a circle till it comes to the dealer. They deal by turnes. Hee that sits next to the dealer and is eldest now must deale the next dealing. This circle of dealing & playing may goe either from the right hand or the left, but the generall custome is to goe round

---

131. *any]* followed by cancellation *relation to.*

132. *black]* altered from *white.*

133. *youngest]* followed by cancellation *& plaies last.*

from the left hand. And the reason is because hee that sits next on the left hand of the dealer has his right[134] hand readie to receive the cards from him.

In all games the elder has the advantage of the younger, as if the Ruffes bee æquall the Ruffe of the eldest wins. If 2 or more can show up, the eldest of them onely wins &c.

In manie games after all the gamesters have had all their cards dealt them, the uppermost of the remaining cards is turned with his face upwards & is called Trumpe.[135] The sute of which the trump is, is the best sute for that dealing & wins anie of the other suites, and all the cards of it are called Trumps.

In most games they must Follow Suite, that is play one of the same suite if they have it. Not playing one of the same suite[136] is called Renouncing, & whoever is catcht renouncing falsly must forfeit as much as is plaid for & deserves to bee turned out of all companies for a wrangler & foule plaier.

A Trick has as manie cards as there are gamesters, everie one playing down a card. Hee that plays the best card wins the trick, takes it up & layes it by him & must begin to play next as if hee were eldest. Hee that cant follow sute may play a trump if hee will, and then unlesse another play a greater trump hee wins the trick, whatever cards there bee in it. The biggest card allwaies or the trump wins the trick. But if anie other cards bee plaied that are neither of the suite nor trumps they signifie nothing.

Trump is derived from the French word Tromper, for when a man thinks to win a trick, a trump comes and deceives him.

Two of the same valor of differing suites are called a Pare, as 2 sixes a Pare of Sixes, 2 Knaves a Pare of Knaves, &c. Three are called a Pare Royall, or Perryall, or in some games a Gleeke. Foure are called a Double Perryall, & in some games a Murnivall.[137]   *56 blank; 57*

Q: Whence the words Murnivall & Gleeke are derived.

In all games where gleekes, pares, murnivalls are worth any thing, the gleeke is treble of the pare, as if the pare bee two, the gleeke is sixe, and the murnivall is double of the gleeke, is = 12. The reason is because 3 may be varied into 3 pares, as if the 3 cards bee A B C, the 3 pares are AB, AC, BC, & 4 may bee varied into 6 pares, as A B C D into AB, AC, BC, AD, DB, DC.

---

134. *right*] altered from *cards readie*.

135. *trumpe*] followed by cancelled interlineation *The cards of those suites are called Trumpe*.

136. *suite*] followed by cancellation *if they have it*.

137. *Murnivall*] follows cancellation *mourni*.

Therefore a gleeke is as much as 3 pare, a murnivall as much as 6 pare. But were a murnivall reckoned as having so manie gleekes in it, it would bee = 24, that is to 4 gleekes. For in everie 4 there are 4 treble variations or 4 gleekes, as in A B C D, ABC, BCD, DAB, DAC. But there is no game that I know of in which a murnivall is reckoned 24.

Games at cards may be divided into those:

> where they use all the cards: One & Thirty, Laugh & Ly Downe, Loadum, &c., Cribbidge.
> where some of the cards are put out: Gleeke, Beast
> where the ace is put out: Ging.
> where a fixed number plaies: Gleeke, Cribbidge.
> where any number: Loadum, Post & Pare.
> where there is no trumps nor distinction of suites:[138] Laugh and Ly Downe, Put.

58   A game is fully understood when it can bee fitted for any number of plaiers.

Shuffling the Cards is mingling and dispersing them, one among another, holding some in one hand & some in the other.

The dealer is to shuffle the cards, and when hee has shuffled them, hee sets them by him that dealt last before, who is to cut them to the dealer. Cutting is dividing the cards about the middle, and setting them in 2 heapes. The dealer takes them up, putting that heape that was lowermost before, uppermost.

The use of cutting is to hinder the dealer from setting the cards. Setting the Cards is when hee that shuffles mingles the cards so that when hee deales those may fall to his share that are the best for the game they play at.

The full number of cards that every gamester is to have are called a Hand, from beeing held in the hand. Good cards a Good Hand, bad cards a Bad Hand, &c.

The cards soone grow foule, and may bee knowne by spots on the back sides, and therefore the best gamesters chang them often & take fresh.

59   They usually play with counters made of brasse, silver, bone, &c., a dozen of counters standing for a shilling, 20 shillings &c., and when they have done playing, they pay one another according to the number of the counters they have lost & wun.

---

138. *nor distinction of suites*] interlineated.

The cards that remaine when the rest are dealt are called the Stock, in Gleek & other games.

A blank space, followed by a line across the page, separates this text from the title of the next game.

One and Thirtie

The first & most simple game of cards is One and Thirtie, in which the dealer deals 3 cards a peice to everie gamester, taking them from the top of the deck, and askes the eldest first if hee will stick or if hee will have it. If hee say hee will stick, hee leaves him & askes the next & so round to himselfe but if hee say hee will have it, hee draws one from the bottome of the deck & gives it him. If hee say hee will have another hee gives him another &c. When they have all had as manie cards as they will, those that are more then 31, reckoning the coates tens & the rest according to their peepes, are said to bee out & loose. If they all happen to bee out, the dealer wins without more adoe. Of those that are in, hee that is neerest 31 wins a single game of all the rest, and if there bee two that are æquall, the eldest wins. Just one and thirtie is called Hitter, & whoever is hitter showes his cards[139] & wins a double game of all the rest.

All the art is to know when to stick. At 27, 28, 29 or 30 one may stick. But it is better to venture beeing out then to stick under 27, especially if there bee manie plaiers.

The elder may stick at a wors game then the younger or dealer.

60   **One and Thirtie Bon Ace** is when the uppermost of the three that everie gamester has is turned with the face uppermost. Hee that has the best card turned up[140] wins a counter of all the rest. An ace wins any card, and the Ace of Harts is called Bon Ace and wins any ace. After this is done they stick or draw cards as before.

Drawing is asking the dealer for a card or telling him you wil have it.

Hitter is most commonly reckoned but as a single game.

X X But there is as much reason 31 should be reckoned double here, as in Nodde, Cribbidge &c. *X X*

---

139. *cards*] follows cancellation *game.*

140. *turned up*] interlineated.

Hannikin Canst Abide It

Everie one has a single card dealt him. The dealer askes the eldest, Hannikin Canst Abide it. If his card bee a 6, 5[141] or under, hee saies hee can. The dealer then draws him one from the bottome of the deck as in One and Thirtie. 15 is hitter. They commonly stick at 7, 8, or 9 in this, as at 27, 28 & 29 in 31.

This game plainly showes that they had respect[142] to the degrees of a signe,[143] for else they would have made 21 or 11 hitter.

---

141. *a 6, 5*] follows cancellation *a 5*.

142. *respect*] altered from *relation*.

143. *the degrees of a signe*] follows cancellation *the signes*.

61   **Laugh & Ly Downe**

At Laugh & Ly Downe they play with all the cards.

The number of gamesters is 5.

Everie one stakes 2 at first, as 2 counters, 2 sixpences &c., and the dealer stakes 3. The dealer is to keepe all the stakes till the end of the dealing.

Everie one has 8 cards dealt him one by one, the dealer going 8 times round, that the cards may bee the better divided.

8 x 5 beeing = 40 & 52 − 40 = 12, there remains 12 after the cards are dealt, which 12 are spread upon the table with their faces upwards among the plaiers, amongst which if there bee any murnivalls as 4 sixes &c., the dealer takes them up & laies them by him. The eldest, if hee have the fellow of any of those that lie upon the table, plaies it & takes them both up & laies them by him, as if hee have a sixe in his hand, and there bee a sixe upon the table, hee takes it up & laies it with his owne sixe by him or if there bee 3 sixes upon the table hee laies them all 4 by him. In the same manner the next to the eldest &c., till it come round to the dealer & eldest againe. Hee that cant fellow anie of those that ly upon the table must lay downe all his owne cards, and the rest must play and take them up still as at first as long as they can. From this laying downe of cards, & the rests laughing at him that lays them downe, comes the name Laugh & Ly Downe. When they have all plaied as long as they can, and laid downe all their cards one after another, if there bee anie cards left, as most commonly there is, the dealer must have them.[144] They then all count their cards, and they that have 8 cards, that is as manie as they had at first, neither win nor loose. Those that have more or lesse, for every 2 cards loose or win one, as if they have 6 cards they loose one, if 10 they win one, & are to pay what they loose to the dealer or[145] receive what they win from him.

Whoever takes up the last trick reckons 6 for it.

62   No bodie must play twice togather, that is when all the rest of the gamesters have laid downe their cards & can play no longer, hee that takes up the last trick must take up no more, though hee could, but all the cards hee has in his hand and all that ly upon the table must bee the dealers.

If you have a peryall in your hand & the 4th lys upon the table, it is best not to take it up as long as you have any other play, it beeing sure not to bee taken from you, the whole cunning of the play consisting in keeping as manie

---

144. *them*] followed by cancellation *whoever takes up.*

145. *to the dealer or*] altered from *& likewise.*

plaies before hand as you can, and holding out from laying down your cards as long as you can.

If you have a pare in your hand & there ly the other pare that are the fellowes upon the table, as if you have 2 sixes & there bee 2 more sixes upon the table, they are sure cards & cant bee taken from you, or if their ly a pare upon the table, and you have a third[146] in your hand, you are sure of one of the pare.

But if you have a pare in your hand, and there ly but one more upon the table, it is best to plaie[147] one of your pare as soon as you can, it beeing likliest to bee taken from you. The next to bee plaied is when you have a single card in your hand & there ly another single one fellow to it on the table.

Whoever has a murnivall in his hand may lay them downe.

If one have a pare in his hand, and hee see the fellow to them plaid & taken up from the table, hee may lay them downe as if hee had wun a trick.

Whoever has a perryall in his hand may lay downe a pare of them.

Whatever is overseen is his that can catch it first, as if the dealer oversee to take up a murnivall. If there bee a perryall upon the table, and but one of them taken up, the other pare is his that can catch it. If one forget to lay down a pare in his hand, when the other pare is plaied and it bee discovered when hee lays down his cards, it is his that can get it &c.

If the game bee plaied nimbly manie of these oversights will happen, which makes the sport.

One[148] winning as manie tricks allwaies as another or others loose makes the account even for the tricks. There beeing 12 cards remaining of the deck which are worth 6, & the last trick reckoned 6, that is 5 more then an ordinary trick, 5 + 6 = 11, is = to the eleven counters that were staked at first, which makes the whole account even.

The game may bee made for 4 if 10 cards bee dealt apiece and if the last trick bee reckoned 4. For everie one staking 2 & the dealer 3 at first, the summe is = 9. The 12 cards left in the deck valued 6 & the last trick valued 3 more then ordinary makes the summe 9. So the account will bee even.

In the same manner this game may bee fitted for any number of gamesters,   63

---

146. *third*] follows cancellation *singl.*

147. *plaie*] altered from *he plaied first.*

148. *One*] follows cancellation *There beeing 5 Gamesters, the.*

either by altering the value of the last trick, altering the stakes, dealing more or fewer cards, &c.

There is no other game at cards that is any thing a kin to this.

The best hand at this game is to have the fewest pares, for then there will bee most variety for playing.

Nodde

At Nodde they play with all the cards. They have 3 cards dealt them one by one, and then the uppermost of the deck is turned with the face up. 31 is up, to make up which they reckon a pare, 2; a perryall, 6; a double perryall, 12; everie fifteene, 2 (as a five and a ten, a sixe and a nine, a 7 & an eight, a trea, foure & eight, &c.). In some places they reckon every twentiefive, 2 (as 2 tens and a five, 3 eights & an ace, &c.); a sequens of 3, two; a sequens of foure, foure; a sequens of five, 5 &c. (a sequens is 3 cards in arithmeticall progression, as Knave, Queen & King; seven, eight, & nine &c.); flush of 3, three; flush of 4, foure; flush of 5, five &c. Flush of 3 is three of the same sute, flush of 4, foure of the same suite &c.; Nodde,[149] turned up, 2; in ones hand, 1. Nodde is the Knave, which if it bee of the same suite that is turned up is reckoned but 1, but when it is turned up is 2.

You may make all the games you can, with those 3 in your hand, and that which is turned up, as if you have 3 nines in your hand & a sixe is turned up, you may reckon 12, for a perryall, 6, & for 3 fifteenes, 6. If you have 2 eights in your hand & a seven turned up, sixe, for 2 fifteenes & a pare. If you have 2 sevens and an eight in your hand, & a seven or an eight bee turned up, you must reckon 12. If you have 3 fives in your hand & a five bee turned up, you must reckon 20, for a double perryall, 12, & for 4 fifteenes, 8, there beeing 4 severall 3 fives in 4 fives & everie 3 fives making fifteen. If you have a trea, duce & ace in your hand & an ace bee turned up, 6; for a pare, 2, & for 2 sequenses, 4; & so for flushes &c.

They must reckon all their games without showing their cards, & set them downe either with counters or upon a board.

A sequens of fowre is 4, because it containes 2 sequenses of three, as 1 2 3 4 has 1 2 3 & 2 3 4. But by the same reason a sequens of 5 should be 6, a sequens of sixe, 8, for 1 2 3 4 5 6 has 4 sequences, 1 2 3, 3 4 5, 2 3 4, 4 5 6. X   66

Q: Why other sequences are not reckoned where the excesse is more then 1, as 2 4 6, 3 6 9 &c.

Why sequences in geometricall proportion are not reckoned, as 2 4 8, 1 2 4, 1 3 9.

But so manie things would make the game to intricate.

---

149. *Nodde*] followed by cancellation *Knave*.

All the games reckoned are in number 7: Pares

Sequences

Flushes

Fifteen

Noddes

Twentiefives

Thirtie One.

Q: Why 31 should not bee reckoned in ones hand as wel as when it is plaied.

Q: The derivation of Nodde & Cribbidge.

67 **A B C D** is a Noddie Board, in which there is a double row of holes on either side, **α β m** and **m δ v**. From **α** to **m** there is just 31 holes, **m** beeing the one and thirtieth, as likewise 31 from **v** to **m**. One gamester begins with a peg from **α**, and remooves his peg still as manie holes forward as hee has games, & when hee is gotten up to **β**, hee comes downe again towards **m**.

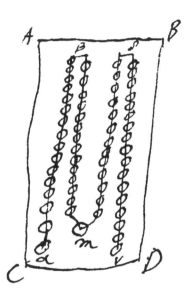

In the same manner his antagonist goes about with his peg from **v**, and hee that can get into the great hole at **m** first wins the game. They usually have 2 pegs, still leaving one fixed as they moove the other forwards, & mooving allwaies the hindermost peg, they count from the formost.[150]

When they have reckoned & set downe all their games they begin to play, the eldest laying downe a card with the face upwards, and the dealer playing one of his cards to it, & making if hee can any of the forementioned games, as a pare, fifteene, &c. Then the eldest plays another card, and so by turnes as long as they can play under 31. If either of them can make just 31, they set downe 2 for it. But if one make 28, 29 &c., and the other cant play under 31, hee is to set downe but one for it. This is called the Latter Game.

They deale by turns, the elder reckoning & setting down first. Nodde Knave that is turned up is allwaies the dealers, and hee may reckon & set down that before the other reckons his, so that if the dealer want but two of 31 and turne up Nodde, hee is up & wins, though his antagonist could make up to, Nodde

---

150. *They usually … count from the formost*] apparently added later, squeezed into gap before following text.

having the advantage to bee reckoned before any thing else. But else though both could make up the elder must win of the younger or dealer.

In playing the cards there can but one fifteene bee reckoned, nor in single hand Nodde or Cribbidge. They can play to 31 but once, the other cards that would serve to begin another 31 beeing not reckoned. All the art is in playing the cards so that your antagonist may make as few games as is possible & your selfe as manie, as if you bee eldest and begin, avoid playing a five, for then your antagonist is likely to make fifteene by playing a ten &c. The skill is allso in / guessing at what cards your antagonist has by what hee reckons, 68 & playing accordingly. When the cards come all to bee plaied & showed, you must bee carefull to observe that your antagonist has set downe faire & not reckoned more then hee has.

A game at Nodde & Cribbidge is called a Set.

Q: Why 31 is not reckoned in ones hand as wel as in play.

The distinction of suites in Cribbidge & Nodde is not regarded.

69   **Cribbidge**

Cribbidge has fifteenes, pares & all the other games that Nodde has. It differs from Nodde, in that the gamesters have 5 cards a peice dealt them one by one. Of these 5 cards they must lay out 2 a peice before they turne up the card that is the uppermost of the deck: the 4 cards thus laid out are called the Crib, and allwaies belong to the dealer, who after they have reckoned & plaied their 3 cards as in Nodde, makes as manie games as hee can out of those 4 cards and the card that is turned up. And because the Crib at first would bee to great an advantage for the dealer, the other gamester sets downe 3 the first dealing in lieu thereof, but has nothing for it afterwards, they dealing & taking the Crib by turnes.

The Crib usually affords as manie or more games then all they get besides & therefore the set is 61, wanting[151] but one of [as] much more as the set at Nodde.   X

If one gets 61 before the other gets 45, it is called a Lurch and reckoned a double game.

There is more cunning in this then in Nodde, which consists most in laying out cards in the Crib, so that you may get most when it is your Crib & your antagonist fewest when it is his. A five is a good card for your own Crib, but a dangerous card when it [is] his.

                    A New Cribbidge or Nodde

One might invent another Cribbidge in which these should be the games.

Sequens of 3, two; of 4, foure; of 5, sixe; &c., for the reason p. 66.[152] This where the excesse should bee but one. But where the excesse should be 2, all these games should be doubled, as 4 6 8 sequens of 3 should bee foure; sequens of 4, eight &c. Where the excesse should bee 3 the games should bee trebled, as 3 6 9 should be eight; where the excesse should be 4, quadrupled; where 5, quintupled &c. The reason is, because the first sequens would happen twice as often as the second, 3 times as often as the third, &c. In this Cribbidge, the 70   King, Queen, Knave should be reckoned 11 12 13 / so that 1 7 13, where the excess is 6, should be 12.[153]

---

151. *wanting*] altered from *or*.

152. The cross-reference is to the discussion of sequences on page 66 of the Book of Games, above.

153. To assist with his reckoning here and in the following paragraphs, Willughby has jotted a line of numbers in the margin, as illustrated below.

2^ly sequenses in geometricall proportion of which those in a double[154] proportion, as 1 2 4 8, 3 6 12 should bee 4, but sequens of 4, as 1 2 4 8 should bee 8.[155]

Sequens in a treble proportion, as 1 3 9, should bee 6.[156] But 4 6 9 should bee 3.

[1. 2. 3. 4. 5. 6. 7. 8 9 10. 11 12. 13

3^ly sequenses in a musicall proportion, as 2 3 6, 3 4 6,[157] 4 6 12, 6 8 12, of which the 2 last should be 4, the 2 first 2. Or 2 3 6, 4 6 12 may bee 3; 3 4 6 & 6 8 12, 2.

Q: Whither any of the ten other proportions of Pappus should be brought in.[158]

Flush of 2, two; of three, 3 &c., as before. But where flush and any of the sequenses should meet in the same, both the flush & sequens should be doubled.

Pares & perryalls should bee as before, but murnivalls should bee 24. If this bee not enough, more might bee added. X X

Instead of 15, 25.[159] For all togather would make it intricate, & 91 should bee a set.

When hee whose turne it is to play cannot play, the other may play as long as hee can, under 31.

[Double Hand Cribbidge]

Double Hand Cribbidge or Nodde is when 4 play, 2 against 2. The[160] two that play togather are parted by those that play against them & must not sit togather. One reckons for both & when they play at last, when one 31 is gone about they begin another. At Cribbidge they have but 4 cards dealt them & lay out every one one into the Crib.

The Single Hand Cribbidge & Nodde are counted better & most used.

---

154. *double*] altered from *duplall*.

155. *8*] altered from *foure*.

156. *6*] altered from *4*.

157. *6*] followed by cancellation *3 5 15*.

158. The fourth-century mathematician Pappus of Alexandria was a primary source for knowledge of Greek mathematics. A copy of his *Mathematical Collections* is listed in the Middleton Library Catalogue (NUL Mi I 17/1, shelfmark A.32). On the ten mathematical progressions, see Pappus (1588: 123) (the edition listed in the *Wollaton Hall Sale Catalogue*, 1925); for a contemporary discussion, see Wallis (1685: ch. xix, 'Of Proportion').

159. *25*] followed by cancellation *pares &c.*

160. *The*] altered from *They sit mingled*.

71   **Ruffe & Trump**

At Ruffe they play with all the cards. The number is 4, 2 against 2, sitting mingled as at Double Hand Cribbidge. They have 12 cards a peice dealt them by 4 at a time. The uppermost of the 4 remaining is turned up for trump, and all the cards of that sute are trumps for that dealing, and win any other suit. Hee that has the most of a suite wins the ruffe, and sets downe 12 for it, everie bodie speaking & telling the most they have for the ruffe.

Everie one having 12 cards a peice, there will remain 4 cards of the deck, which are called the Head. If the Ace of Trumps bee amongst those 4 cards, the dealer must have them or else whoever has the ace. But the ruffe must bee dispatched first. In reckoning for the ruffe, if the suite bee trumps the card that is turned up may bee reckoned with them. Taking in the head is called Rubbing, and whoever has the Ace of Trumps rubs those 4 cards. Instead of those 4 cards they lay out 4 of the worst cards they have, chusing them out of all the whole 16, both of the dozen they had before & the 4 they tooke in. The ruffe must bee wun & set downe before the cards are taken in & put out, but it must not bee seen till after because it would bee a disadvantage for him that has it to have his cards seene before hee that rubs has laid out. As soon as the ruffe is showed and prooved to be as manie as hee said it was, they begin to play, the eldest leading about any card, the second playing another of the same suite & so round till all 4 have plaied. Hee that has the biggest card in the trick takes it up & laies it by him. The ace[161] is the best card, the next the King, then the Queen and so according to the number of their peeps. Whoever has none of the suit may play a trumpe. The trump wins the trick, if no bodie else plaies a bigger trumpe. When they have plaied all their cards, they count the tricks they have wun & as many as they have above 12 they set downe, as if one have 20 hee sets downe 8 &c.

A set at Ruffe & Trumpe is as manie as they make up, which is most commonly 4 dozen & 4, & they that with ruffes & the cards they win can make up 4 dozen & 4 first win the set. They may play the set for a shilling, 5^s, or as much as they will. **X X**

This is called Double Hand Ruffe where the 2 partners reckon their ruffes & cards togather, & all the skill is to play the cards so that they may help one another. All as both of them win above 2 dozen they set downe.[162] Single Hand Ruffe differs nothing but that they all reckon & play for themselves.

72   They make 4 x 12 + 4 a set because there is /so manie cards in the deck or so manie weekes in the yeare.

---

161. *ace*] followed by cancellation *wins any*.

162. *All as both ... set downe*] inserted later, squeezed into space on page.

They may allso play 3 or 2 at Ruffe & Trumpe. But if 3 play 3 x 12 + 4 is up. If 2, 2 x 12 + 12. Hee that rubs takes the 4 uppermost cards of those that are left in the deck, & they play just as they did in 4 Hand Ruffe. But if 3 have 16 cards apeice or 2, 24, they may make 4 x 12 + 4 up as before.

Q: Whither there bee a game called Trump, differing nothing from this but that the ruffe is left out.

Trumpe seemes to have beene one of[163] the first games from which Ruffe & Trumpe, Gleeke, & most others were afterwards invented, by adding ruffes, gleekes &c.

If the 4 cards repræsent the 4 seasons, it is not improbable but that at first that suit that belonged to the present season was the best or the trompe suit for all that quarter as Harts for the summer quarter, &c. But afterwards they altered it & turned up a new trumpe everie dealing, there beeing more sport in variety.

There is more cunning in playing a Double Hand Ruffe, where 2 are partners, then where they all play on their owne heads.

If they chance to have more then makes up the set they must not reckon the overplus towards the next, but begin all again from nothing.

The ace in reckoning for the ruffe is 11. *Q:* Whence the word Ruffe is derived. Whosoevers ruffe is in trumps may show it at first for it can bee no disadvantage to him.

---

163. *one of*] interlineated.

73   **Gleeke**

Gleeke is counted one of the best games at cards. The number that play is three, who have each 12 cards dealt them by 4 at a time as in Ruffe. The duces & treas beeing put out, the number of cards is 44. 44 − 3 x 12 = 8, so that there remains 8 after the 3 gamesters have had their dozen a peice. These 8 are called the Stock, and the uppermost is turned up for trump as in Ruffe. They reckon with counters of which 12 stand for a shilling, 5^s, 20^s, or as much as they make it.

The first thing after dealing is to Buy the Stock. The eldest must bid 12 and take it, if neither of the other 2 wil bid more. The card that was turned up trump must not bee taken but must ly to show what is trumps all that dealing. (But having first laid out 7 of the worst of his cards, hee that has the stock must take the other 7.) The next to the eldest, if hee have a mind to venture for the stock, may bid 13 or as much as hee will, the third 14, the eldest againe 15, &c., or if one give over bidding the other 2 may outbid one another as long as they will. And hee that bids most & gets the stock must divide what hee gave betweene the other two. If it bee an odde number, hee that bid last must have the odde one, as if 19 were bid, hee that bid last must have 10, the other 9.

The eldest that is forced to take the stock against his will is said to bee taken, when hee layes out better cards then hee takes in.

Hoisting the Stock is bidding for the stock and raising the prise without an intent to have it, the other 2 beleeving the good cards are in the stock, which are in his hand that hoists.

The next thing is to Vie the Ruffe. The eldest may vie it first if hee will, but if hee passe it, the next, and if hee passe it to, then it comes to the dealer to passe or vie. If they all passe it, then it is doubled for the next dealing. If any vie it, and no bodie see it, hee that vies has 2 a peice of the others. If either of them thinkes hee has a better ruffe hee may see it. Then they both show their ruffes & hee that has the biggest wins 4 of the other.[164] Seeing & Revying is when hee that thinkes hee has the better ruffe not onely sees the other but revies it to, and then unlesse hee that vied it first see it againe, it is not showed. A ruffe seene and revied & not seene again is 4; if it bee seene 6; if it bee revied again the second time & not seene 6; if seene 8; & so 2 more still for everie time it has bene revied or seene.   **X**

74 *blank*; 75   In reckoning for the ruffe, the coates are tens, the ace is eleven. If there bee 2 æquall ruffes, the eldest wins.

---

164. *other*] follows cancellation *ruffe*.

A murnivall of aces wins any ruffe.

When the ruffe is passed, all the vies &c. are double the next dealing.

Those that have the worst ruffe usually revie to see if they can outdare him that vied it & keepe him from seeing it.

When a ruffe is vied, revied &c., between two, the third is not concerned & is to pay no more then his two to him that wins. But if hee will, hee may vie & revie about with them, & when the second sees it he must aske the third[165] if hee will see it to. When hee has refused[166] or seene it then the second may revie or goe no further, & after him the 3ᵈ if hee had seene it before.

After the ruffe, gleekes & murnivalls are reckoned. A gleeke of Knaves is one, of Queenes 2, of Kings 3, of aces 4. The murnivalls of these are double, as for aces, 8 &c. Gleekes may be reckoned with the card that is turned up, as if one have 2 Queens and a 3ᵈ bee turned up, it is a gleeke of Queenes.[167]

A gleeke or murnivall must bee paied by both the others to him that has it, as hee that has a murnivall of aces must have 16, 8 of each.

Whoever has Tyde, that is the 4 of trumpes, must have 2 a peice of the rest, this beeing to comfort him because it is the worst trumpe. Tyde may be either showed at first or when they play it.

No pares at all nor no other gleekes or murnivalls besides these are reckoned.

When the stock, ruffe & gleekes are dispatched, they play their cards as in ruffe and win as manie tricks as they can, the eldest beginning and afterwards allwaies hee that wins the trick begins the next. While they are playing they observe one another & cheifly him that bought the stock, if hee have all the gleekes he called for, for manie times hee that buies[168] the stock is fain to lay out one or more of a gleek that hee may keepe in better cards, and if hee call for them & bee afterwards catchd, hee must pay back double. The finding which card of a gleeke is missing & asking for it is called Challenging & hee that challenges may looke among the 7 cardes that were laid out for the stock to see if the carde hee / challenges bee among them. But those 7 cards must not bee looke[d] on till the dealing bee ended.

76 blank; 77

Hee that buies the stock must bee sure to bee looked to, that hee lay out all his 7 cards before hee take in the stock.

---

165. *third*] interlineation, replacing cancellation *other*.

166. *When he has refused*] altered from *If he refused then*.

167. *Gleekes may be … of Queenes*] in lighter ink and apparently added later, squeezed into space on page.

168. *buies*] follows cancellation *laies out*.

The honnours at Gleeke are the Knave, Queen, King & Ace of Trumps of which the Knave is called Tom & is reckoned 9, the Queen & King 3 a peice. The Ace is called Tib & is reckoned 15. At the end of the game they count their cards & reckon their honnours, & as manie as their honnours & cards will make above 22 they win, & they loose as manie as they want of 22. If they reckon right the winnings & loosings will allwaies come even and agree. For 3 x 22 (that is all their loosings) is = 66. All the honnours togather are = 30, 3 dozen of cards 36. Therefore all the winnings are = 66 are = to the loosings & the account will bee even.

The second plaier is bound to ten whatever is plaied if he can, or else to play the biggest card hee has, as if hee have neither the ace, King, Queen, Knave or ten of the suite that is plaied, hee must play the biggest hee has.

If the trump that is turned up proove an honnour, it belongs to the dealer, to be reckoned, but not taken in.

The gleekes of the Knaves, Queens & Kings are = to as much as they exceed ten if they were reckoned 11, 12, 13[169] in a continuall progression.

Tib is as much as if there was a 14 card added to the ace. The ace in a Ruffe is 11, that is ten added to the ace.

Q: Why Tom should bee 9.

If Tom were reckoned 8, Tib 14, & the treas put in, 4 might play at Gleeke, everie one having 10 cards dealt them, and reckoning 17 at last to save themselves. 4 x 17 = 68, all the honnours, 28, all the cards 40, 40 + 28 = 68, & so the account will bee even. But because 7 would bee to manie to lay out for the stock out of ten, they might have liberty to lay out a card or two after they had taken in the stock.

In the same manner the loosings & winnings might be divided for any company.

---

169. Note that these are the values of the King, Queen, and Knave respectively (cf. p. 51).

Beast, or Le Beste

The number that play at Best is usually 4. They put out the duces, treas, 4ˢ, 5ˢ, & sixes to lessen the deck. But that is nothing to the game, & if they will they may play with all of them. They play with counters, 6 pences or shillings, &c., every one staking two & the dealer 3. These counters are put in a heape togather in the middle of the table amongst the gamesters & are called the Beast, which must bee bated & wun by the gamesters.

Every one has 5 cards a peice dealt them at twice, by 3 & 2 at a time, and then the trump is turned up. If none of them thinke they can win 3 tricks, or the 2 first tricks, the cards beeing plaied as at Ruffe, they all say, I Passe, one after another, & the cards are put up againe without playing. The next deales the cards again & addes one more to the Beast, and so every one that dealea must still stake one, the rest not staking againe but as it comes to their turne to deal, till the Beast[170] bee wun. The counter that the dealer stakes must ly out of the heape or Beast before the dealer, that they may still know who dealt & whose turne it is next. But when the dealing is past it is put into the Beast & the next dealer lays his one counter before him. If any thinks hee has a game good enough, hee saies, I Play. The eldest then leads a card as at Ruffe, and if hee that said hee plaied can win 3 or more tricks, or can win the 2 first so none of the rest get all the other 3, hee wins the Beast & they all stake againe. But if any of the other 3 can get 3 tricks, or if they can get the 2 first, & hee that plaied cant get the other 3, hee is beasted, that is hee must double the Beast & lay downe as many counters as there are in it allreadie.

By the 2 first are meant not the 2 first tricks of the five, but the 2 first tricks that are wun by one hand.

The Beast comes thus to bee doubled over & over a great manie times, sometimes before it bee wun, though most commonly it is wun at first. X

If any of the other 3 gamesters thinks hee has as good a game as hee that plaies, hee saies, I Counter. If the counterer wins 3 tricks or the first 2, hee takes up the Beast & the player lays downe as manie. But if neither of them can win 3 or the 2 first, they are both beasted, & staking either of them as manie as there is in the Beast allreadie, the Beast is trebled.

Winning of 3 tricks allwaies certainly wins.

Winning of the 2 first tricks wins if no one of the rest gets 3. Hee that gets 3, or the 2 first, is said to Beast[171] him that plaies. But hee has nothing to doe with the Beast unlesse hee countred.

---

170. *Beast*] altered from *Best*.

171. *Beast*] altered from *Best*.

Whoever renounces when hee could have followed suite must be beasted as a punishment.

The ace wins any card as at Gleeke.

A Demonstration is when one has 3 sure cards, as the Ace, King & Queene of Trumps,[172] hee need not play but show his cards & take up the Beast.

When the counterer wins or when hee that plaies is beasted they must stake one a peice & the dealer 2.

No one that has once passed can play that dealing (but hee may counter if another play) unlesse hee have a demonstration, & then hee may passe, to see if hee can entrap another, & though hee have passed he may show his demonstration & take the Beast. If another plays, hee counters & presently shows his demonstration.

The cunning is in judging when to play & when to pass, in allwaies playing against him that plaies for the common good, for as long as the Beast is not wun everie one has hopes of it, in timely throwing away cards when one has the opportunity of renouncing, for fear of doing mischeif at last with them, as when the plaier has got the first 2 tricks and another 2. If your card wins the trick at last you helpe the plaier & save him from beeing beasted.

It is a good rule to contrive allwaies that the eldest[173] next to the plaier may have the trick, for there beeing 2 to play after him, though hee win the trick, there is hopes one of the 2 may recover it again.

The best place to play in is the eldest or youngest.   **X X**

Sometimes they play gleekes to mend the game.

The dealer may if hee will take in the card hee turnes up. But it must bee before hee has looked on his cards and then hee is bound to play whither hee will or not, and when hee has seene his cards, hee lays out the worst instead of that hee tooke in. The ace is seldome refused.

81   It is a law at Beast that the counterer must bee favoured & helped against the player.

When the plaier is like to bee beasted, hee will play against the counterer to bee revenged on him, & if hee can will make another beast them both, that the counterer may suffer as wel as himselfe.

---

172. *Trumps*] follows cancellation *cards*.

173. *eldest*] interlineated.

This game was a late invention & brought out of France.

There uses to bee a great deal of wrangling at this game, for not helping the counterer, for playing boobie & favouring the player, for not throwing away dangerous cards, for telling your game, showing your cards, giving advice, &c.

Prime at Beast is when one has of everie sute in his hand, which is the worst game one can have, for it is impossible to have more then 2 trumps, and the cards may [be] picked out ones hand & the Beast lost before a trick bee wun. *X X*

If 5 should play at Beast, there should bee 6 cards a peice dealt; if 6, 7 &c., & allwaies the number of cards should bee one more then the number of gamesters, that it should bee impossible but for some of them to win 2 tricks. When so manie play there must not so manie cards bee put out of the deck.

But the best Beast is with 4 tricks & 5 cards.

Loosing Lodum

At Loosing Loadum they use all the cards. They may play as manie as will and have as manie cards as the whole deck will afford them, so as there bee allwaies some left and allwaies when some are out the[174] rest have more cards dealt them.

The Loaders are, every ace = 11, everie ten = 10, everie Knave = 1, everie Queen = 2, everie King = 3, and all the rest of the cards signifie nothing.

The King, Queen & Knave beeing reckoned at Loadum as the gleekes of them at Gleeke.

Everie one of the gamesters stakes as much at first as they play for. The stakes are kept all togather for him that wins them at last.

When the cards are dealt round, they play as at Ruffe without turning up trumpe. But as soone as ever anie one renounces & plaies a card of a different sute they looke what is trumpe, and turne it downe again that it may bee forgotten & mistaken afterwards.

Everie one of the gamesters has 3 counters at first, and as soone as any one is out hee puts away one of his counters, when hee is out againe another &c., till hee has lost them all three, & then hee must goe his waies, having lost all his share in the stakes.

Beeing Out is when one has as manie loaders in the tricks hee has wun as will make 31 or more. But if no bodie has 31, then hee that has[175] the most is out.

Beeing out or loosing at Loadum beeing the same as winning at 31.

All the cunning is in avoiding winning tricks; when one has the Ace of Trumps or dangerous cards, to get shut of them as cheap as one can, as to watch to trump a trick with the Ace of Trumps that has but a few loaders in it; to get shut of all loading cards &c.

Hee that renounces falsly must loose all his counters & bee quite put out.

This is the onely game in which the good cards loose.

Challenging at Loadum is when one has gotten 31 in a trick & suspects another to have bene 31 before him, hee challenges him to show his trick. If

---

174. *the*] MS *they*.
175. *has*] MS *hast*.

one challenge another that is not out, hee must bee out himselfe for his labour. One may challenge any that they suspect to bee out whither they bee out themselves or not.

Swallowing at Loadum is when there is a trump in the trick & hee / that takes   84
the trick dos not heed it, but swallows the trick that should have bene wun by the trump.

Hee that stays in longest till all the rest bee out wins all the stakes.

A King, ace or dangerous card is said to bee garded when hee that has it, has a duce, trea, or some little card besides, for if a trick come about that has loaders in it, hee may play his little card, and avoid winning it.

When one has a card that is not garded hee may change it for another if hee can get any bodie to change with him. Hee need not tel what it is, but if it bee a coate when hee askes to change, hee must say, A Coate for a Coate; if a ten or an ace hee must say, A Card for a Card. They allwaies barre the sute so that if the card or coat prove to bee of the same suite they must change it back againe to him that gave it. Else hee that[176] should change a ten, if hee should get an ace for it of the same suite,[177] would be wors then hee was before, or hee that should change a Knave if hee should get a King of the same suit.

They may make once out for all the stakes, or twice, or as manie times as they will.

Winning Loadum   85

I never saw any play at Winning Loadum, but suppose it onely contrary to Loosing, as that the plaiers at first have no counters given them, but whoever can win as manie tricks as have 31 in them, reckoning onely the loaders, has one counter given him, & they that can get[178] 31, or the most under 31, 3 times first, win all the stakes.

Loaders beeing desired as much in this as they were avoided in the other.

---

176. *that*] MS *that hee.*
177. *the same suite*] interlineated.
178. *get*] follows cancellation *win.*

86 *blank*; 87

Ging or Seven Cards

They put out the aces & all the cards to the sevens, onely 4 plaing. 6 cards beeing put out of everie suite there remaines but 28, which must bee dealt out all, 7 a peice to each plaier.

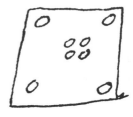

In the middle amongst the plaiers lys a trencher upon which everie one of the 4 plaiers layes 2 counters, one in each corner and one in the middle. Those in the middle are called the Pee. There are 7 waies of winning.[179] The first is when one has the most of a sute, as 38, 29 &c., hee and whoever has the most next him take up either of them one of the corner counters, and the other 2 stake againe. The 2[d] is when one has the most of 2 suits, hee takes up 3 of the corner counters & the other 3 stake againe. The 5 other waies win the Pee & all the counters, & everie one stakes 2 againe. The first & best of these is 7 cards, that is 7 cards of a suite. From this the game it selfe is sometimes called 7 Cards. The 2[d] is 4 sevens, the 3rd, 37, which is called Ging, & from this the game it selfe is called Ging. The 4th, Gentlemen, when one has all coat cards in his hand. The 5th, Bare Shoulders, when one has never a coate in his hand. Bare Shoulders is the worst of these, & is wun by any of the rest, as if one have Bare Shoulders, and another Gentlemen, hee that has the Gentlemen wins, the rest as they are reckoned, there beeing 2 that win Ging, & 2 that loose it.

Of all these games Ging happens the oftenest. But there must bee but just 37 of a suite, for if there bee more[180] it wins but one if it bee the most of a sute. *X X*

The eldest must bee præferred before the youngest. If dealing bee lost, hee that lost it must deale again till hee can deale without loosing, because else it would bee an advantage to loose dealing & they would bee sure to loose dealing a purpose.

There is no skill at all but remembring all the severall waies of winning & counting the cards.

The coats are tens, the rest according to their peeps.

88 There are as manie cards left as days in a month. Each gamester has as manie as daies in a weeke. 37 is = to the daies of a solar month + the daies of the weeke.

---

179. *There are 7 waies of winning*] replaces cancellation *the first is when one.*

180. *more*] followed by cancellation *or lesse.*

364 − 84, the number of the peeps put out, is = 280[181] = 40 weekes.
84 = 12 weekes.

There is no other game in which the ace is put out. **X X**

Q: The severall proportions of the probabilities[182] in which one may expect any of the 5 games that win the Pee & all. 7 Cards is the unlikeliest of all, Ging the likeliest and may bee expected.

V: Booke of Dice p. 77.[183]
To find out how often one may expect 7 Cards find out by the Booke of Dice p. 77 &c. How manie septempllall variations there is in 28, and in so manie dealings you may expect them once.

Find out how many septemplall [variations] there is with 4 sevens in them & so manie times in anie number = all the 7 variations you may expect them, & in the same manner find out how many there is with never a Gentleman & never a Bare Shoulder, & allso how manie there is with[184] a Ging in them. **X X**

There cannot a Ging bee made for any other number without some of the cards bee left remaining, as if there should six play, 6 x 7 = 42, but to make the cards[185] of everie sute æquall there should bee 44. 8 x 7 = 56,[186] more than there is in the deck, but should a card be added to each suite 8 might play, & then the most of 4 sutes should win 7; of 3, 5; of 2, 3; of one, one.

The number must bee even that there may bee as manie to stake as there are counters wun.

---

181. *280*] altered from *284*.

182. *probabilities*] MS *probabities*.

183. The fact that this page citation cannot be identified in the published editions of the treatises on chance by Cardano (1663) or Huygens (1657) is consistent with the hypothesis that the reference is to a lost work by Willughby himself; cf. the earlier mention of the 'Booke of Dice' on p. 21 above.

184. *with*] followed by cancellation *never*.

185. *cards*] follows cancellation *tricks*.

186. *56*] altered from *57*.

89   **Put**

They play with all the cards at Put, of which the trea is best & wins any, the next the duce, then the ace. Afterwards the King, Queen, & so in their order.

They never play above 2 and have 3 cards a peice. There is no trump or distinction of suites, the best card winning whatever the suite bee.

Usually 5 or 7 is up. The eldest leading a carde, the other plaies another to it, and which of them has the best card takes up the trick. If there bee 2 cards æquall, as 2 tens, 2 Knaves, &c., it is called Tie and neither of them takes it up.

Whoever wins 3 or 2 tricks reckons one towards the game. Therefore when 2 tricks are wun by one hand they throw up the cards and begin a new dealing.

Trick, Trick & Tye is when either of them have wun a trick & the 3^d is tye. Then neither of them is to set on any thing.

Whoever thinks hee has a sure game knocks his hand upon the table & cryes, Put. If the other wont see him the cards are throwne up & hee sets downe one, but if the other say, I See It, the cards are plaied as before, and whoever wins 2 or 3 tricks wins the whole game, how manie soever are up.

Most games are wun by putting & seeing, and seldome any come to bee up by setting downe the single ones that are wun by tricks without putting.

This putting is like vying at Gleeke, & whoever can outdare the other must needs win.

If one bee neere up & the other puts, that is none towards the game. It is better yeilding one then venturing the whole game upon it.

If hee that is allmost up puts, it is better to see him then to give him one, for beeing hee is likely to win however one need not feare putting it to the hazard. But it is best for him that has allmost got the set never to put, & for him that has none to put. **X X** [187]

90   They may put, if they will, after one trick is plaied or after 2 tricks when either of them have got one.

Any number may play at this game, though it bee not usuall, & then if they all put & see, hee that wins wins of them all, or of as manie as have put &

---

187. Several incomplete phrases, partially cancelled, finish the page: *The art is in daring bravely. Sometimes with an ill game.* Beneath this is the further cancellation *in putting as of.*

seene, the rest not playing. But it is better for them, if they were any before those that putted beginning again from nothing. **X X**

When manie play at Put, there must allwaies bee one more cards dealt to everie one then there are players, as at Beast, that one at least of the plaiers may bee sure to win 2 tricks, & as manie as win 1 or more tricks set down one.

[Whehee]

The text of Whehee is in the manuscript's unidentified juvenile hand (see Introduction, Section 2.3).

Whehee: Att Whehee every one hath 3 cards dealt him[188] all-to-gather. Whoever[189] hath all his 3 cards of the same suite is said to be Whehee, and the eldest that is Whehee wins. If none of them has Whehee dealt him, then they change cards, the eldest changing a card with the second, the second with the third, the third with the fourth[190] and so round, till it coms to the dealers turne to chang with the eldest. If nobody bee Whehee when they have changed round, then they may chang one with another with out any order, and if they cannot make themselves Whehee, throw up the cards and deale againe. As many may play as the decke will hould out for.

Text reverts to Willughby's hand.

---

188. *him*] altered by Willughby from *them*.

189. *Whoever*] altered by Willughby from *who:ever*.

190. *fourth*] altered by Willughby from *forth*.

Tricks at Cards

V: p. 3. All the 4 sutes may bee mingled in that order, that counting to every tenth man, as they ly with their faces upwards, first one whole sute may bee taken out, then another whole sute &c.[191]

The 4 sutes may bee called French, Spanish, Italian & English, and so placed that first the French, then the Italian, then the Spaniards should be taken & all the English spared.

They divide the cards[192] with diagonall lines. On one side of the diagonall are half the peepes of the card, on the other side halfe of any fantasticall picture, as halfe a cock, halfe a foole, &c.[193] Everie perryall is so divided; the fourth, as the 4th ten, the 4th seven &c., is intire, as a whole ten, a whole seven &c. Besides these they have a fifth card which has the whole picture upon it, as the whole picture of a cock &c. They take the 3 divided cards and the whole card, and placing the whole card uppermost, they hide still B side of the other 3, so that they all appear to bee whole tens. Then laying by the whole ten they place the whole cock uppermost, and cover

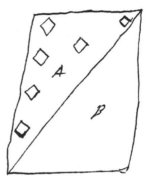

A side of the other 3, so that they all appeare to bee cocks. The back sides of these cards are plane as in other cards. Those that have the slight of it will presently change them from cocks to tens.   **X**

The following forty-six pages are blank.

---

191. This is a variant of the problem described by Willughby on pp. 3/iii^v–3/iv^r above; see Glossary of Games under 'Puzzle of the Ship'.

192. *the cards*] altered from *all the cards of a pack*.

193. *&c.*] followed by cancellation *3 cards*.

148   **Barly Breakes**

They play 6, 2 at **A B**, 2 at **E F**, and 2 in the middle at **C D**.

A B and **E F** stand with their faces one to
another. All the 3 pare hold one another
by the hands, and when the word Barly
Breake is given, **A B** and **E F** break, **B** & **F**
running out towards **n**, **A E** towards **O**. **C**
D run after any of them and endeavour to
catch them. If **A E** can meete one another,
before **C D** catch them, they are safe. But
if **C D** catch either **A** or **E**, **A E** must go in
the middle next time.

O

A   *E*

B   *C D*   *H¹*

n

The middle where **C D** stood is called Hel.
If **A E** and **B F** can meete one another &
not bee catched,[194] **C D** must goe into Hel againe. If **C** catch **A**, it signifies
nothing unlesse **D** bee at the catching of him to, and if **E** get to **A** that is taken
& held by **C** before **D** get to them, **A** is releeved. But if **D** get to them before
E, **A E** must goe into Hel, it beeing all one whither one or both the pare bee
taken. **C D** allwaies aime at one which they both follow. The other 2 seeing
themselves not aimed at walke faire & softly & meete one another.

The paires that are opposite **A E**, **B F** stand togather at the ends next time
unlesse one of them bee taken, so that the fellowes change everie time.

Sometimes there is a barre or post about **O** & **n**,[195] about which they must run.

Another way of playing is when onely two, as **A** & **E**, run,[196] **A** striving to get
to **E F** side, & **E** to **A B** side. More then 6 may play at this, beeing æquallie
divided on both sides, besides the 2 in the middle. They run by turnes, as if
E get safe to **B** side, hee goes to the last place, & **B** is to run next.

149   *Q:* Whence Barly Breakes is derived.

Diing in Hell is to bee left in Hel when they give over.

When they part they cry, Barly, on one side &, Breakes, of the other.

---

194. *& not bee catched*] interlineated.

195. *& n*] interlineated.

196. *run*] follows cancellation *play*.

Chest, Tables, Cards, &c. they play for mony, but at most of the following, as   150
Shittlecock,[197] Prison Barres &c., onely for exercise and victory.

A blank space, followed by a line across the page, separates this text from the title of the next game.

---

197.   *as Shittlecock*] interlineated.

[Running 3 Times thorough the Charter House]

Running 3 Times thorough the Charter House is a common punishment among schooleboys for not playing faire &c.   X

All the boyes sit in 2 rowes one against another, upon the ground, betweene which rowes hee that is to bee punished must run 3 times, the boyes of both sides kicking at him as hee goes thorough. If hee fall by the way hee must goe back & run againe, & whoever kicks him when hee is downe must run thorough the Charter House himselfe. They use to put of their shooes for feare of breaking his legs that runs thorough.

Running[198]

Running of Races is when 2 or more run for a prise or wager which they agree upon, the standers by betting on his side they thinke will win. They run often naked or in their shirts, & if it bee for a great wager they use to exercise themselves & run the ground over before in their cloths, &[199] sometimes carrie waits of lead &c., that they may bee the lighter & nimbler when they run for the wager. They set out togather at a signe given, & hee that can first take a hand kerchier of from a post or out of a mans hand that holds it wins.

In the same manner they run Horse Races, breathing their horses often over the ground before. Those that ride the horses when they run are called Jockeys. If one of the Jockeys bee heavier, the other must carrie as much weight as will make them even.

They diet the race horses with bread made with anniseads, liquorish, &c. amongst the floure.

X X

---

198. *Running*] followed by cancellation *Leaping &c*. The next line contains two words, which have been crossed out and are partly indecipherable, beginning *It*.

199. *&*] altered from *or*.

Prison Barres

The barres or posts they run from are **A C**, **B D**. All those that are of a side, stand by one barre, as **A C**, those of the other side by **B D**. The Prison for the **B** plaiers is a good distance of, about **n**, the Prison for **A** plaiers at **m**. A plaiers stand all with their faces towards **B** plaiers, holding one another by the hands, the worst runner most commonly holding one hand upon the barre & the next with the other hand, the 3[d] holds the 2[d] with one hand & the 4th with the other, &c. The outermost of **A** plaiers runs out from his fellowes towards **E**, the outermost from **B** following him, & so one after another as manie as they will. Whoever of **B** plaiers can overtake and touch one of **A** plaiers, hee brings him to the Prison at **m**, & so as manie of **A** prisoners as are taken must bee brought to **m**, where they must all hold by one another from the Prison as they did from the barre. The Prison is a post, corner of a house, &c.

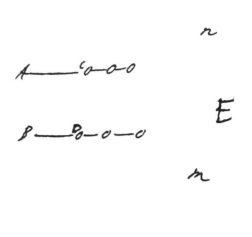

If one of **A** bee taken & another of **B**, they may bee exchanged one for another if they can agree. Whoever touched his barre last or him or they that touched it, may take one of his enemies if hee can catch him. They use to run a step or two & then back againe, a manie times before they run out, & hee that gets the last touch of the barre, or of him or they that touch[200] it chases the other.

Releiving of Prisoners is when one of **A** barre can get to **m** Prison and touch the prisoners without beeing taken. Hee then brings them all home to their own barre. They that can take all their enemies win, or they that can take their enemies barre, that is get to it when they are all away.

Running out from the barres they call Leading Out. They should lead out by turnes, first one of one side & then one of the other.

They that have taken a prisoner cannot bee taken themselves, nor can they take any more then one till they have taken barre againe.

---

200. *or they that touch*] *or they* interlineated; *touch* altered from *touched*.

[Lilman]

Lilman is when onely one lusty youth keeps one barre, & all the rest run a good way from him, and cry, Lil, Lil and All his Men, are not Worth a Buttered Hen, or, Lil, Lil Come Out of thy Den.   X   The Lil Man when they call to him, must come out, & run after them, they striving to get to his barre. Those as get to the barre are safe, but those as the Lil Man takes, hee spits & claps his hands over their heads, and they must bee his men & help him to catch afterwards. When they are all taken but one, hee that is left must bee Lill Man next time. When the Lil Man has taken 3 or 4, they agree among themselves who they shall spare to bee Lilman next time who if hee have no mind to bee Lilman runs in their way of purpose & hinders them from taking the rest to force them to take him.

V: Tick, p. 222

155   **Football**

They blow a strong bladder and tie the neck of it as fast as they can, and then put it into the skin of a buls cod and sow it fast in.

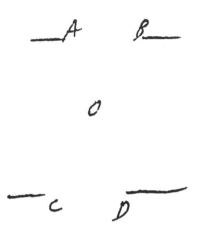

They play in a longe streete, or a close that has a gate at either end. The gates are called Gaols, as **A B**, **C D**. The ball is thrown up in the middle between the gaols, as about **O**, the plaiers beeing æqually divided according to their strength and nimblenesse. **A** plaiers must kick the ball towards **C D** gaol, **C** plaiers towards **A B** gaol, and they that can strike the ball thorough their enemies gaol first win. They usually leave some of their best plaiers to gard the gaol while the rest follow the ball.

They often breake one anothers shins when two meete and strike both togather against the ball, & therefore there is a law that they must not strike higher then the ball.

Tripping Up of Heels is when one followes one of his enemies & to prevent him from striking the ball strikes that foot as hee runs, that is from the ground, which catching against the other foote makes him fall.

All the slight is to hit that foot that is mooving and just taken from the ground, & then a little touch makes him fall. Suppose α foot fixed, β mooving from **n** to **m**.

If it bee strooke on the outside before it comes to **C**, just against the fixed foote, it falls crosse behind the fixed foot at **L** and makes him fall.

The harder the ball is blowne, the better it flys. They use to put quicksilver into it sometimes to keep it from lying still.

The plaiers must at first stand all at their gaols, the ball lying just in the middle betweene them, & they that can run best get the first kick.

[Hurling]   155/i[r]

The following text on Hurling, on a loose leaf insertion, is in the hand of
Philip Skippon with changes and additions, as indicated, by Willughby.
Willughby identifies it on the verso with the description 'Hurling by
Mr Scippon'.

Hurling is divided into In-Hurling & Out-Hurling. The first is thus. After 20
men or thereabouts are numbered on either party, one takes a leather ball &
tosses it up in the midst betweene both sides. He that catches it endeavours
to run away with it to the adverse goale. If one of the opposites stop him,
either he wrestles (then the ball is throwne to one on his owne side, but the
others may intercept it,[201] & taken by one of his owne party, who runs away
with it towards the contrary goale &c.) or throwes it if he can to one of his
owne side & refuses to wrestle.

Outhurling is playd by one parish against another, or Easterne men against
the Westerne, or Cornwall against Devonshire. They play in the same manner
as the other, but make churches, townes &c. theire goales. If any of them can
hold of a stirrop he is not denyed liberty to run with the ball in his hand as
fast as the horse goes. Other horses are engaged against him. They runne
through the worst of places, quagmires &c. If he that tosses up the ball at the
first be not in the middle, he is then to hurle at the furthest goale. Any one
that can procure leave from the next Justice of Peace, goes into a markett
towne & holds in his hand a wooden ball covered with a silver plate, & by a
proclamation invites all that will come to a Hurling, mentioning the time &
place. This fellow that finds the ball gathers mony of those that play.

Text reverts to Willughby's hand.

Carew in his Survey hath a larger account & calls Inhurling, Hurling to the
Goale; & Outhurling, Hurling to the Country.[202]

This may bee called Hand Ball beeing the same with Football but that it is
throwne with the hand.

---

201. *throwne to … intercept it*] altered by Willughby from *layd downe*.

202. See the description of Hurling by Richard Carew in his *Survey of Cornwall* (1602: 73[v]–75[v]).

Drawing, Lifting &c.

Drawing Dun Out of the Mire is when one boy sits behinde a deske or post, and holds as fast as hee can by it with his legs, and with his hands by the next boy, about his middle. The second boy holds the 3ᵈ about the middle, the 3ᵈ the fourth by the middle &c., as manie as there is. Then they draw forwards all as hard as they can, & whoever breaks his holdt must run 3 times thorough the Charter-House or if the Dun bee Drawne Out hee must thorough the Charter House.

England and Ireland is when all the boyes are æquallie divided according to their strenght, a high way in a feild or a board within doore going between them, over which they are to strive to pul one another. 2 boyes most commonly catch hold one of another, & all the rest hang upon them & draw of both sides.

If an Englishman draw an Irishman over the path, hee must bee of his side and help the Englishmen to draw. *X X X* So that when one is taken, that side that takes him grows stronger.

This might as wel bee called France & Spaine &c. *X X*

Copshole, or **Copsole**, is when 2 boyes sitting downe upon the ground set the soles of their shooes one against another, & holding a stick in their hands pull as hard as they can. *X* They must allwaies hold their hands togather just over their toes. The stick is held crosse. Hee that has the inner holdt²⁰³ has the best, holding his between the others.²⁰⁴ Those as have short legs wil bee sure to pull up those that have longer, the lenght of their legs making them stoop forwards, which looses their strenght. The lenght of their legs **E B** makes the bodie bend downwards from **A B** perpendicular to **C B**, in which posture beeing to pul towards **D**, much of their strenght is lost in bearing up the bodie, which the more it declines from the perpendicular **A B**, requires more strenght to support it from falling. But when it is once past the perpendicular **A B**, as in **D B**, the weight of the bodie addes to the strenght. *X X* They must hold their knees strait & turne their feet outwards to pull better.²⁰⁵

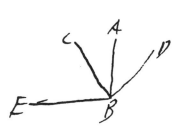

---

203. *holdt*] followed by cancellation *holding his others hand*.

204. As indicated by the symbol *X*, the text *They must allwaies hold … between the others* has been inserted here from above the paragraph.

205. *They must … pull better*] added later, squeezed into space at end of paragraph.

Kibble Heft *X* is when one boy lies down upon the ground with his face upwards & puts both his legs betweene another boyes legs that stands upright, close up to his groine, his toes just comming out at his breech behind. The boy that stands then leans backwards, & lifts him up that lyes along. The boy that stands must bee sure to hold the other boys legs hard between his, & hee that is to bee lifted up must bee sure not to bend a jot / in his hams, for if hee bend never so little it is impossible hee should be lifted   158 up. When hee is lifted up a good way, hee claps his hands upon the boys head that lifts him, & then hee lets his legs goe. He that is lifted up must keepe his bodie in a streight line as much as hee can.

They try their strenght in lifting great weights, throwing great stones &c.   159 *blank*; 160 backwards over their heads &c.

Pitching the Barre. They sometimes pitch with a great long barre of iron called a Crow of Iron, or with a heavie barre of wood, setting one end of it which is pointed upon the right foot & holding the other end in the right hand. They draw the right foot as farre back as they can, that they may pitch with the greater force.[206] They pitch it out so that it turns in flying and lights upon the point, which should bee the heavier end. They let goe their hand, when the foot that pitches comes just before the other.

Pitching of the Arme is when they hold the barre about the middle, with one hand over their shoulders, & pitch it as farre as they can. They pitch great stones in the same manner.

Pitching of the Shoulder, or Throwing of the Shoulder, is when they lay the barre upon the shoulder & hold one end of it with both hands. They pull downe their hands, bring it of their shoulder, & give it a thrust forward.

---

206. *force*] followed by cancellation *then striking the*.

161   **Leaping**

Standing Jumpe is when they stand still and, holding both their legs togather, jumpe as farre as they can.

Running Jumpe is when they run before they leape, which putting the bodie into motion makes them leape further. This running is called Taking of Beere.

When they stand they may jumpe 2 or 3 jumps togather. But when they run, they can never jumpe but one jumpe, not beeing able to rise againe.

They allwaies rise from their toes & fall upon their heeles, thrusting their legs before their bodies when they strive to leape furthest.

They hold sometimes a great stone in either hand when they leap standing jumps. If they leape but one jumpe they throw the stones to the ground behinde them just as they fall. If they jumpe 2 or 3 jumpes, they throw the stones behind them the last jumpe.

The stones thrust them forwards, as if they should thrust themselves from a wall or post.

Halfe Almond is first a hop, then a stride, then a leape one after another, first hopping with one leg, then striding with the other, & then leaping with both.

Whole Almond is first a hop, then a stride, then a hop and another stride & a jumpe at last, wanting but a jumpe of beeing just double of Halfe Almond.

When they practise to leap up in hight, they lay a wand betweene 2 stooles loose, that if they dont leap high enough & hit it, it may easily fly away & not throw them downe.

The ground[207] they leap on must have a little descent.

Inch Pinch is when 2 or more leap one against another, the first leaping a little way, the next a little out leaping him, then the first out leaps him again &c., till they are come to the furthest they can leap. Hee that leaps into the holes the other made, or leaps short, or overleaps them above an inch must bee pinched. **X X**

162   **Vaulting** is laying one hand upon a rale, gate &c., and then just as they rise they clap the other hand upon it and throw themselves over.

---

207. *The*] MS *They*.

The slight is to draw themselves up with the left hand & bare the bodie with the right hand, which they clap on last as they vault over.

A man may easily vault over a place as high as his armc holes.

When they vault over broad places, as tables &c., they lay the left hand upon the hither side, & then clap the right hand about the middle or towards the further side. They vault into the saddle laying their hands upon the horses neck, and over one or 2 horses into the second or third saddle.

The legs and bodie when they are at highest must bee kept in a line parallel to the horizon.

To practice vaulting they have a rale that may bee raised higher with pegs as they wil when they [bee] more expert.

Hop Frog is when all the boys stand one before another, stooping & resting with their right hands upon their knees, a prettie distance asunder so as they may take beere betweene everie one. One of them then goes behind all the rest, and having taken his beere, lays both his hands upon the shoulders of the first, and leaps over his head parting his legs as hee goes over on either side his head. In the same manner hee leaps over all, and then stoops himselfe downe before them all, and the hindermost leaps over them all as hee did, and so all one after another. If any fall downe or dos not stoope faire, or if hee that leaps dos not leap faire, they must run thorough the Charter House. **X X**

Q: If this bee the same with Trusse a Feale. **X X**

Q: When[ce] the words, Beere, Almond[208] are derived.

Leaping with a Staffe[209] is when they hold it at one end as **A**, and fixing the other end in the ground at **B**, standing at **D** they raise themselves up with the staffe **A B** and goe from **D** to **C**,[210] the staffe rising to a perpendicular site & then falling againe. They leap over ditches &c. in this manner.

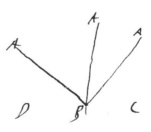

Some have the art when the staffe is perpendicular, to remoove it 2 or 3 times before it falls, keeping it still perpendicular & their bodies hanging at **A**. **X X**

---

208. Long gap on line at this point suggests that other terms were to be added to the enquiry.

209. *Staffe*] follows cancellation *Stick*.

210. *C*] altered from *E*.

163   **Scotch Hopper**

They play with a peice of tile or a little flat peice of lead, upon a boarded floore, or anie area divided into oblong figures like boards.

They stand upon the first board **A**, & lay the tile upon the second board **B**, and then hop upon everie board from **A** to **M** and back againe to **B**, upon which the tile lyes at **α**, and hopping upon **v** betweene the tile and the last chinke betweene **B** and **C**, the next hop from **B** to **A** they strike the tile before them. Then they lay the tile upon the next board **C**, and hopping upon everie board to **M** & then back againe, they strike the tile before them as they come home, as before, in the same manner upon every board as long as they can reach. When they can reach no further, they must throw the tile upon the boards till they come to **M**, and then twice upon **M**, and upon everie board till they come back againe to **B**.

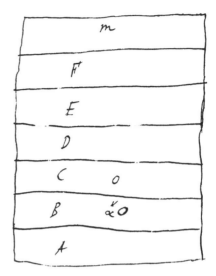

They play usuallie but one against one, but they may play as manie as will, and then they must all play by turnes, first one of one side & then another of the other side &c.

Whoever hops twice upon the same board, skips a board, hops upon a chinke, touches the ground with the other foote, or throws the tile upon a wrong board, or upon a chinke, or dos not hop quite to **M** and back againe, or dos not bring the tile home with him as hee comes back, is out, & his adversary must play till hee bee out, & then the first plays againe, beginning from that board where hee was out before, as if hee were out at **F** board, hee must begin from that board when hee comes to play againe.

They that can get all the boards backward & forward to **A** again win.

If they dont strike the tile quite home to **A** the first blow they may strike it againe, so they dont hop twice upon a board, nor hop backwards againe. But if the tile rest over a chinke they must bee out.

164   The right game is after they have gotten all the boards to **B**, forwards & backwards, to throw the tile upon **M**, and hop 3 times backward &

forward, & then the 3^d time they bring the tile home with them & the game is wun.

If they stand upon the first chinke before they are aware when they are going to throw, they must bee out.

The peice of tile or lead is called [*no text supplied*].   **X   X**

Q: Whither this game bee much used in Scotland.   **X**

They throw Crosse & Pile or draw cuts who shall begin.   **X   X**

165–6 *blank*; 167   **Ball**

They strike balls either with their hands, as in Stoole Ball[211]
with Staves: Stow Ball, 13[212]
with Rackets: Tennis, 15[213]
with [*no text supplied*]: Pelmel[214]
with their feete: Foot Ball, 155[215]
with [*no text supplied*]: Billiards.

The ball is either tossed up in the aire: Football, Stowball, Stoole Ball; or
trulled upon the ground, where it allwaies turnes about its center, as in
Boules, Pelmel, Biliards.

The balls are made of shreds of cloth rapped hard about a bullet, and then
sowed about with overcast titch. But the great balls for rebounding & tossing
have no bullets in them.

X   X   Tossing of Balls is when they strike a ball against the ground, and still,
as it rebounds from the ground, they pat it downe againe[216] with the palmes
of their hands. They[217] make it rebound so from one to another, or else one
strives to keepe it up as long as hee can alone, never letting it rise above a
yard from the ground before hee strikes it downe againe.

168   **I Call and I Call** is when there is a great many plaiers, & one of them throws
a ball hard against a wall, or upon the roofe of a house, & as hee throws it
calls one of his fellows to catch it, who if hee catch it, throws it up againe and
calls another &c. But if hee misse catching it, hee runs & takes it up from the
ground, all the rest of the plaiers running away as fast as they can from him.
Hee must stand just where hee tooke up the ball, and throw it at any of the
plaiers hee is likely to hit. If hee throw and misse them all, hee must bee one
himselfe, but if hee hit, hee that hee hits must bee one. Whoever comes to bee
5 or 7 first, according as they make up, must bee Pillored, that is hee must
stand just against the wall with his face towards it, so that hee cannot see the
rest of the plaiers behind him, & post the ball over his head amongst them at
randome. If the ball bee catched, hee that catches it must make him that is
pillored hold his hand spread against the wall, & standing just by him, throw
the ball as hard as hee can against his hand. But if the ball bee not catched one

---

211. Followed by blank space, possibly for the addition of other games.
212. Reference to Stowball text above, p. 13.
213. Reference to Tennis text, above, p. 15. This reference is followed by a blank space, as if further
      games were to be added.
214. Followed by a blank space, as if further games were to be added.
215. Reference to Football text, above, p. 155.
216. *aguine*] followed by cancelled *they strive*.
217. *They*] followed by cancellation *tosse it so*.

of them must stand where it lights & throw at that distance at his hand. Hee that is pillored must post & bee struck at 3 times.   *X*

Posting a Ball is throwing it up with one hand and striking it with the other. Posting Over Hand is when the hand that strikes it is brought over the shoulder. Posting Under Hand is when the hand that strikes it is brought from the knees.

Those that have the right slight will strike a ball much stronger and further over hand then under hand. A ball struck over hand flys more level, under hand more upwards, and then it falls allmost perpendicular downwards, which makes it easier to bee caught.

A ball will fly furthest if it bee struck about the middle of the fingers. To keepe the little hard balls with bullets in them from hurting their hands, they double their gloves, drawing them back again over their fingers.

They hold their hands to catch a ball so as the fingers of the right[218] hand fall just upon the thumb of the left, and enclose the ball between the palmes, the rist of the right hand beeing fixed upon / the out side the left. The right hand   169
mooves upon the rist as an axis, opening to receive the ball and then presently shutting to enclose it.

X   But those that are used to play, wil run a great way to meet a ball, & clapping their hands togather catch it betweene them.

To exercise themselves they will post balls from one another a great way, either over hand or under hand. They that let it fall first or oftenest are beaten.   *X*

---

218.   *the right*] altered from *one.*

Stoole Ball[219]

The plaiers beeing æqually divided according to their skill, they lay a stoole downe on one side, so as the seate or board of the stoole is perpendicular to the ground. All the plaiers of one side stand at the stoole and one of them begins & posts the ball towards the other side, who stand as farre of from the stoole, as they thinke hee can post. If any of them can catch the ball hee must post it back againe towards the stoole. If any of that side catch it they post it back againe, & so backwards & forwards as long as they can keepe it up. If **A** side let the ball downe, hee that posted it first must bee out & play no more. But if **B** side let the ball fall, one of them must throw it towards the stoole **D C**.

A

D ——— *C*

If hee can hit the stoole, hee that posted it first must be out, but if hee misse it **A** side sets downe 2, nicking 2 nicks upon a stick, which is the common way of reckoning, and hee that posted at first must post again till hee bee out.

If one of **A** side post the ball & none of **B** can catch it, nor hit the stoole, it is but a single cast & **A** side must set downe one. When one of **A** side is out, another must play, & so one after another till all bee out, & then **A** side must all goe downe & **B** side must come up to the stoole, and post till they bee all out. Then **A** side must come up againe &c.

B

They that can get 31 first win.

170   The ground should descend a little from **A**, the stoole, to **B** where the opposite side stands.

Instead of a stoole they have sometimes a great stone at **D** and another at **C**, and if **B** side can throw the ball between the stones, one of **A** must bee out. *X X*

The weaker side usually has the stoole at first.

D C is sometimes called a Tut & the game Tutball.

If a ball bee not posted faire they must post it againe.

---

219. *Stoole Ball*] followed by cancellation *or T[utball].*

Bandie Ball

The Bandie Ball staves they strike the ball with are crooked at one end like Baseting[220] sticks.

They hold them by one end at **A** and strike the ball with the crooked end **B** **C**. All the plaiers beeing æqually divided they stand at two gaoles, as in Football, the ball lying just in the middle. At a signe given, they both run from the gaoles to get the first blow, & they that can strike the ball thorough their adversaries gaole first win. The best place to hit the ball is just at the bending **B**.

---

220.   *Baseting*] altered from *Basetting*, follows cancellation *Basti*.

171–2 *blank*; 173   **Kit Cat**

The Kit Cats are made of little cilinders of wood
sharpened at either end as in the figures **A A A**.

Box or ewe are counted the best woods.

The French Kitcats are onely sloped downe of one side
and not sharpened round. The contrarie sides must be
sloped that however[221] it lights, one of the tips may ly faire to bee struck.

The sharp ends α α A A are called Tips.

The staves they strike with are about ½ or ¾ of a yard
long, & are of a bignesse proportionable to the
strenght of the hand that uses them.

They tread down one of the tips of the Cat as **A**, so that it may stick a little in
the ground, and then striking the other tip **α**, the Cat rises[222] up from the
ground & before it falls again they strike at it as hard as they can with the
Dog, and if they hit it full, strike it a 60[223] yards or further.

20 score is usually up, but they may make as manie or as few as they will.

Each plaier is to have 3 tips, which must bee reckoned, whither they hit the tip
or not, or whither the Cat rise or not, or whither they[224] hit it or not. When one
has had 3 tips, then the other is to have 3 tips, & so by turnes. If the Cat rise
and bee struck the first Tip, where-ever it lights, they tip againe, & so till they
have had all theire 3 tips. The lenght of the Doggstaffe is reckoned one & as
manie Dogstaffe lenghts as they strike it at 3 tips, so manie they set downe or
reckon. They that get 20 score first of this manner win. They most commonly
guesse without taking the paines to measure every time, unlesse when a game
is neere up, or when they cant both agree what they should allow.   **X**

They reckon by tens, as 10, 20, 30 &c., and never regard the odde ones.

They chuse a place to play in where the grasse is low that the Cat may rise
after the first blow againe. They begin both from one place & come to the
same place back again after everie 3 tips.[225] They chuse ground where there is
a little descent to strike the Cat down hill.

---

221. *however*] altered from *wherever*.
222. *rises*] follows cancellation *flys*.
223. *60*] altered from *100*.
224. *they*] MS *the*.
225. *tips*] follows cancellation *trick*.

The sticking a little in the ground at one end makes it rise better, the   174
impression of the blow staying longer upon the tip.

Q: Whither it bee not the same reason that makes a flint breake & a bullet flat
sooner upon a soft place as a bed &c.   *V:* Cartesses French Letters.[226]

The Cat flys upwards rebounding from the ground[227] & being turned upon
the tip that is struck as the center makes it goe forwards.
X X X X X

If a stick bee laid loose shelving of of a table & bee struck very hard,   *Q:*
whither it will fly higher then the superficies of the table. *X   X*

Short Kitcats of the figure of 2 cones with their bases clapt togather are called
[*no text supplied*].[228]

They lay them loose upon the ground and strike
them just upon the middle at **α** to make them rise.

Buzes[229] are cilindricall Cats ▭ used onely for Horn Billets, beeing lesse
dangerous if they should hit their faces.

---

226. Letter from Descartes to Mersenne, 25 December 1639: 'Mais il y a, outre cela, diuerses choses à
considerer en la percussion, comme la durée du coup, qui fait qu'on rendra vne bale de plomb plus
plate en la frapant d'vn marteau sur vn coussin que sur vn enclume (*But there are, beyond this, a
variety of things to consider in the matter of percussion, such as the duration of the blow, which is why one
will make a lead ball flatter by striking it with a hammer against a cushion than an anvil*)' (Descartes, 1996;
Correspondence ii, p. 631). There were contemporary editions of the correspondence of Descartes
in French (1657–67) as well as in Latin (1668).

227. *The Cat ... ground*] altered from *Why the Cat should fly upwards partly rebounding from the ground and
partly.*

228. *called*] followed by the words *Buz Buzzes*, both of which are crossed out without alternative
suggestion.

229. *Buzes*] altered from *Buzzes.*

175   **Hornebillets**

Hornebillets is when they make 2 round holes in the ground, 7 or 8 yards asunder, or further or neerrer as they think good. They play 2 of a side, and have one Cat & a pare of Dogstaffes betweene them. They throw Crosse & Pile for the Doggstaffes at first, & they that get them, keepe the holes, standing either of them at his hole.

The[230] other 2 that play against them stand by them, & pitch the Cat from one hole to another, still striving to throw it in. Whenever the Cat is thrown into either of the holes, they are out & their adversaries take the Doggs, & they must throw the Cat. Those that have the Dogs strive to hit the Cat everie time it is throwne, & if they hit it they run as fast as they can from one hole to another, still putting their Dogstaffs into the holes as they come to them, as **B** runs to **A** hole, & patting his Dog in it, comes back againe to **B**, & so to **A**, counting one for everie time they change holes. In the meane time one of the other 2 runs as fast as hee can for the Cat, & if he bring it & put it into one of the holes, while they are running betweene & both from their holes, they must bee out. Therefore they watch him, & when they see him allmost come with his Cat, give over running & stay at their holes. If a Dog touch a Cat & dos not strike it farre from the hole they are bound to change holes once at least, & if the Cat bee put in before they have changed them, they must bee out. They must strike at the Cat everie time it is throwne, & if they misse it presently clap their Dog into their hole, and if hee that stands by bee nimble enough to put the Cat into the hole before his Dog has bene in they must bee out.

A

O

O
B

63 is up, and for the 3 last they must run both to a hole & strike their Dogs crosse over it which is called Knacking of Dogstaffs.

If 6 play they must have 3 holes if 8, 4 &c., and the Cat must bee throwne round from one hole to another.

Drudge Cat is when onely 2 play one against another, either having his hole. Hee that throws the Cat must fetch it & throw it againe, & from this continuall running & fetching it is called Drudge Cat. Hee that runs must allwaies come back to his hole or else hee must bee out. But when 4[231] or more play, it is no matter which hole they rest at.

X

---

230. *The*] MS *They.*

231. *when 4*] altered from *where 4 play.*

Shittle Cock

176 *blank*; 177

Q: Whither it have not its name from a weavers shuttle from the swiftnesse in flying. **X**

It is made of a round cilindricall peice of corke, the bottome of which **B** is round, the top in which the feathers are stuck, **A**, plane.

The feathers are[232] cut in this figure **C E D**.

At the bottome, the piles are stript quite from the scape, the end **D** beeing thrust into the corke. The extreame end of the feather **C** is allwaies cut of. They stick sometimes 4 & sometimes 6 into a corke, at æquall distances with the bending side of the scapes outwards.

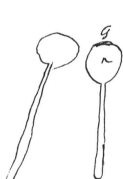

The Battledore is made of a thin hard peice of board cut in this figure.

They hold the end **H** in their hand, and strike the shittle cock with the broad round end **n**. The Shittle Cock allwaies flys with the cork forwards, and beeing struck with the battledore presently turnes about, as the pile of an arrow when it has done ascending & begins to descend. They strike it up into the aire and meete it as it coms downe and strike it up againe keeping it up in the aire as long as they can.

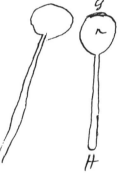

When 2 or more play they strike the Shittlecock from one to another, & keep it up as long as they can. They that misse a blow & let it fall first are beaten. They strike either upper hand or under hand with the Battledores, as they doe a ball with their hands.

178–9

Pages 178–9 not present; numbers omitted in original pagination of MS.

---

232. *are*] followed by cancellation *made of.*

180 *blank*; 181

Shooting

The Bow **A E B** is made of ewe, brasil.

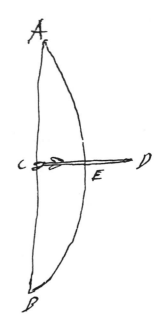

Father Fitchard

They play with little short sticks a little bigger & about the lenght of arrowes, very sharp at one end and sometimes bearded with iron.[233] These they call Fitchards.

The first darts or strikes his Fitchard into the ground as hard as hee can. The next aimes to strike his Fitchard so that the point of it may bee under the point of the first Fitchard.

If there is but 2 plaiers they make 2 round little holes, & in the middle betweene these holes they strike in their Fitchards.

A prettie distance of they have a Prison or Barre which is a wall or post &c.

Hee that struck in the last Fitchard, if it bee just under the other Fitchard so that hee can lift it up without thrusting it any farther into the ground, hee that has his Fitchard lifted up must run to the barre and back againe, & in the meane time the other is digging earth as fast as hee can out of his adversaries hole & filling his owne hole with it. But hee must bee sure to give over before the other comes, for if hee catch him at it then hee must run & the other fills & takes the earth he had gotten.[234]

If one Fitchard bee not neere enough the other to lift it up, the first draws out his Fitchard & strikes it at the others, & so they draw & strike it into the ground til one gets under another.

If one thinks his Fitchard bee under the others & try to lift it up but cannot, then hee must run to the barre & the other digs with his Fitchard out of his adversaries hole & fills his owne.

When one has filld up his hole quite, the other comes to him on his hands & toes, & saies, Pray Father Fitchard, Give mee some Dibbing to Dib Up my Oven. The other lays earth on his back, & hee creeps away with it to fill his hole. If hee loose any by the waie hee must carry it in his mouth.

When there is more then 2, there must allwaies bee as manie holes as plaiers, & when one runs all the rest dig at his hole that runs, & fill their owne. If one misse sticking his fitchard into the ground hee must run.   X

Knack Fitchard is to knack one Fitchard against another as they strike them

---

233. *iron*] followed by cancellation *They usually pl[ay]*.

234. *gotten*] followed by words beginning a new sentence, which has been crossed out: *When one has quite filled up his hole*.

into the ground. Hee that dos not knack must run, & hee that his Fitchard struck downe.

This is a simple play & used onely by boyes. *X X*

Children's Plays[235]

The first things children play with are:[236]

1. Whistles, which are made of silver & have little silver bels hanging to them. They have a peice of corall stuck in at one end, it beeing good for their gums, when their teeth are comming out. The whistle is at the other end, in which the aire beeing blowed thorough a little hole, and comming out of a greater makes the noise.

    C the corall, β α the whistle, α the hole at which the air coms out, v v v the bells, β the narrow hole.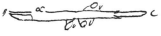

2. Rattles, made of round peices of wood, painted & hollow, with pease or any thing in them to rattle.

[3.] Babies, made of clouts sowed up in the shapes of men, dogs, horses &c., or made of wood painted.

Children beeing apt to put every thing into their mouths, they use them to corall or a bores tush, which are good for their teeth & gums.

Children love anything that lookes gay, that makes a noise &c.

[Put Pin]

218

When they begin to bee able to run up and downe, they play at Put Pin, thrusting 2 pins towards one another till they can thrust them a crosse. Hee that thrusts them a crosse first wins & takes them up both. They must put or thrust by turnes, one beeing to have but one put at a time.

Heads and Points is when one hides 2 pins in his hand clutched. If both the heads lie one way, they are called Heads, if contrary ways, Points.

Hee asks the other, Heads or Points. If hee answer right hee must have them. If wrong, as Heads when they are Points, Points when they are Heads, hee must give him that held them 2.

---

235. Willughby's index has 'The First Games that Children Learn'.

236. *The first … are*] written above cancelled phrase *As soon as they are able to run up & downe and begin to have.*

Even & Odde is when one hides any number of pins, cherrie-stones &c., and askes the other, Even or Odde. If hee guesse right, as even when they are even, odde when they are odde, hee must have them. If wrong, hee must loose as many.

Another way of playing at Even & Odde is when if they name Odde, they must take out any odde number & then count the remainder, or if they name Even he must take out any even number.[237] If the remainder bee as hee guesses hee wins, otherwise hee looses as many.[238] Whoever hides even will bee sure to loose, odde will bee sure [to] win, for even wanting odde will bee odde, wanting even, even; but odde wanting odde will bee even, wanting even, odde.

Upper or Nether, Chuse you Whither is when they hold both their hands one above another clutched, & in one of them, pins, cherrie-stones &c. If hee that guesses names the hand[239] they are in, hee wins them, or else looses as manie. They often cheat one another by letting them fall out of one hand into another.

Crosse & Pile. They throw up a shilling, 6 pence &c. The side that has the crosse upon it & the English armes they call Crosse, the other side that has the Kings face, Pile. One throws it up into the aire, the other guesses, Crosse or Pile, before it comes downe. If it falls with that side uppermost that is named, hee wins, if of the other side, looses.

219

[Cob Castle]

They lay 3 nuts or cherrie stones close togather in a triangle, and another in the middle upon them. This they call a Cob-Castle, and setting it a prettie distance of, they throw a nut at it. If hee that throws a nut, or boules a little bullet at it, can knock it downe, hee wins the 4 nuts that made the Cobcastle. But if hee misses, the other that ownes the Cobcastle has as manie nuts as are thrown.

Cobnut. At the time of yeare when nuts begin to grow hard, they make a little hole thorough the middle of a nut, and put a string thorough it tying a knot at one end, to keepe it from slipping out. They hold the nut[240]

---

237. *if they ... even number*] MS *any even number hee must take out even.*

238. *looses as many*] altered from *lays down as many.*

239. *hand*] follows cancellation *right.*

240. *nut*] followed by cancellation *hard.*

betweene 2 fingers, and pulling the string hard with the other hand, they strike at another nut that lys upon the crowne of a hat, and try which nut will break first. Hee that makes the challenge saies, Hobblete[241] Cut, Lay Downe your Nut, Job Jee[242] before Mee.

A nut is said to bee the Cobber of so manie that it breakes, as the Cobber of 5, the Cobber of 10 &c. They use the tatching ends that shooemakers have, to put thorough their nuts, and sometimes pick out the kernels, and put pitch within them which makes them hold longer. But this is foule.

Cherrie Pit. Either of the plaiers lay downe so manie cherrie stones, which   220
one of them pitches at a little hole in the ground. As manie as hee can pitch into the hole are his that pitches, all that are out of the hole, the other must have.

Hide & Seeke. One stands[243] at a gaole or barre, hoodwinke, & is to count aloud so manie, as 100, 40 &c., all the while the rest hide themselves. When hee has done counting hee saies, A Dish Full of Pins to Prick my Shins, a Loafe of Bread to Breake my Head, Bo Peep I Come. If they get all to the barre, hee winkes againe, but if hee catch one, hee that is catched must wink.

King Heywoods Park

> *No further text supplied under this heading, which is in the unidentified juvenile hand (see Introduction, Section 2.3).*

Hunting a Deere in My Lords Parke is when they all hold one another by the hands in a circle, their faces looking all towards the center. One that is left out, runs round about the outside of the circle, and gives some one of them a little tap, or lets fall a glove behind him or any other marke they agree upon. Hee that is thus touched, must bee let out of the circle, and must run after the other that touched him, who leads him about the circle and crosse it, running under their armes backwards & forwards &c. Hee that is touched & followes must run just after him under the same armes, & if hee mistake & dont follow him right, hee must bee imprisoned in the circle or Parke, but if hee run right & catch him hee followes, hee must bee put into the Parke. The other that is not imprisoned, runs about & chuses out another to follow him &c., till the circle comes to bee so streight that it wont hold all the prisoners. Then they all tumble downe & cry, More Sacks to the Mill. **X X X X**

They strive to run quickly as soone as they are touched, that they may follow

---

241. This was apparently pronounced 'Hobble-tee'; see Glossary of Games under 'Cobnut'.

242. *Jee*] follows cancellation *Jees*.

243. *One stands*] altered from *They stand all*.

him as leads them right. If hee that is out of the circle can run about the circle before hee that was touched begins to follow him, hee that was touched must bee imprisoned.

221   **Blind Mans Buffe. Blind Buck a Davie**

One of the biggest must bee hoodwinked, with a cloth or something tied before his eyes. All the rest have fantasticall names given them, as Buzzard &c., and run about him, clapping their hands. Hee runs after them, and whoever hee catches, if hee can tel his new name, must bee hoodwinked, but if hee call him by a wrong name, hee must bee hoodwinked still himselfe.

They must play in a roome where all the chaires, stooles &c. are set away, for feare of breaking his shins that is blinded.

Hummers are flat round peices of boards, made of trenchers &c. & cut full of nicks like **A B**. This is tied with a string **E C** to the end of a long pole **C**. They hold the other end of the pole **D** in their hands, and whirling about the trencher or peice[244] of board **A B**, it makes a humming loud noise in the aire.

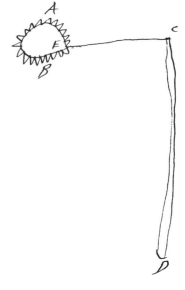

Handie Back, or **Hockcockles**, is when one stoopes downe & lays[245] his head in anothers lap, that hoodwinks him, and his hand spread upon his breech, which one of the rest strikes with the palme of his hand as hard as hee can. If hee can tel who struck him, hee is free & hee that struck must ly downe. But if hee mistake & name a wrong person, hee must ly downe againe, & so till hee guesses right. **X   X**

Q: What Hock signifies; Hockcockles, Hockback &c. **X   X**

222   **Tick.**[246] One boy touches another and cries, Tick. Hee that is touched runs after the other that touched him, to tick him againe, and then runs from him as soone as hee has touched him. Hee that is ticked, & cannot tick againe, is beaten.

---

244. *peice*] follows cancellation *narrow*.

245. *& lays*] altered from *with his hand before his eyes laying*.

246. See 'Lilman', p. 154, and the cross-reference given there.

This is one of the first & most simple of the running sports, from which Prison Barres &c. seeme to bee derived.

Q: Whither to tick bee an old word for to touch.

Top. The top is a cone or rather a conoide of this figure:

The top or apex of which **α α α** is inverted & set perpendicularly upon the ground, & giving the basis or broad end **D C** a twirle with their fingers it gets a verticity & makes it  run upon the ground. They carry a stick in their hands with a peice of a cord or whiteleather tied to[247] the end of it, & with this they follow the top & whip it, to keepe it up as long as they can. At **α** is a brasse naile driven in, to keepe the top from wearing.

They must play upon smooth boards, as ice &c.

Gigs are little tops made of the tips of hornes.

Whirlie Gigs   223

No text supplied under this title.

---

247. *tied to*] altered from *at*.

224–8 *blank*; 229

Tricks to Abuse & Hurt One Another

The text on pp. 229–233 is for the most part in the manuscript's unidentified juvenile hand, corrected by Willughby (see Introduction, Section 2.3) who also supplies the heading.

Buying of Mustard. A lays a trencher loose upon his hand clutched.[248] B askes what he has there. A saies, Mustard, Will you Buy Any. B, Is it good. A, Lick and Tast. Then B makes as if hee would taste and suddenly knatches up the trencher and strives[249] to hit his hand with it. If hee misse, then A must strike at Bs hand in the same manner, but if hee hit, then B must strike at As hand againe &c.[250]

Cropping[251] **of Oakes**. They sit upon a narrow forme with their legs crosse under them like taylours. One[252] houldes his hand spred before his eare with the palm outwards and another strikes at it with his hand open and sitting in the same posture. If A can strike B from the forme he has Cropt an[253] Oake but if B can sit still and endure the blow he must strike at A and so by turns till one be cropt.

He that can knock downe most is the best Cropper.[254]

Buying of Bees. 3 standing in a row togather, the middlemost sets his hat betwixt his legs with the hollow[255] upwards, and asketh his felloues if they will buy[256] any bees, stooping downe and putting[257] his hands[258] in his hatt, then holding his hands in his mouth makes a humming[259] noyse like bees and suddenly strikes att the ears of his fellowes[260] and[261] then stoops againe towards his hatt. His fellows must both strike at him but they must not strike at him before he hath strucken[262] nor after he hath gotten his hands in his hatt againe. His[263] hatt is called his Hive.

---

248. *Buying of … clutched*] in Willughby's hand.

249. *strives*] followed by cancellation *at his hand*.

250. *to hit his hand … As hand againe &c.*] in Willughby's hand.

251. *Cropping*] altered by Willughby from *Croping*.

252. *One*] altered by Willughby from *Wun*.

253. *an*] altered by Willughby from *a*.

254. *Cropper*] altered by Willughby from *Croper*.

255. *hollow*] altered by Willughby from *holow*.

256. *buy*] altered by Willughby from *by*.

257. *putting*] altered by Willughby from *puting*.

258. *hands*] altered by Willughby from *hand*.

259. *humming*] altered by Willughby from *huming*.

260. *fellowes*] altered by Willughby from *felowes*.

261. *and*] followed by cancellation *both strike at him*.

262. *strucken*] altered by Willughby from *struken*.

263. *His*] replaces following cancellation *It*.

Selling of Mill Stones[264]

A greatte many boyes sitt with theire[265] breeches upon[266] the ground, the tallest first, the next betwixt his legs &c., according to their severall heights, the lowest in the last place. One calles all these boyes Millstones and sels them to another who to try them whither[267] they be good or not holdes[268] a trencher hard upon the head of the first and drawes[269] it over all their heads. Their heads being like staires, one higher then another,[270] the trencher raps upon them. When they have tride the Millstones, by the trenchers sounding upon their heads, they must bee bought & drawn away. The least is drawn away first. Hee between whose legs hee sits, holding him fast by the eares, & so all the rest by turnes, beeing still held by the eares by those that sit behind them.[271]

[Robin Alive]

One of the boyes holds a stick in his hand that is a little fired at one end and swinging it about in the aire saies, Robin Alive and Alives[272] Like to Be, If it Dies in your Hand your Back shall be Saddeled[273] and Bridled and Sent to the Kings Hall with a Huf, Puf and All. Or sometimes he saies, Your Back shall be Saddeled and a Pack Put upon[274] It. Then he gives it is next fellow who[275] repeating the same words gives it the third &c., till it hath gone thorow them all and about again till the fire goe[276] out. He[277] in whose hand the fire doth go out in must be saddled, that is, must stoop down and lay his head in one of his fellows lapps, who hoodwinks him as in Hockcockles. Another holds any thing as cusshions, chairs,[278] tongs &c., asking him, What Hould I over You. If he guesse right, he is free and another fire stick must be carried about as before but if he guesse fallse and can not tell what is held over him it must be

---

264. *Selling of Mill Stones*] title added by Willughby.

265. *theire*] altered by Willughby from *their*.

266. *upon*] followed by cancellation *one before*.

267. *whither*] altered by Willughby from *wither*, already replacing the cancelled forms *weth* and *wheder they*.

268. *holdes*] altered by Willughby from *holde*.

269. *drawes*] altered by Willughby from *drawe*.

270. *one higher then another*] interlineated by Willughby.

271. *by the trenchers … sit behind them*] added by Willughby.

272. *Alives*] altered by Willughby from *Alifes*.

273. *saddeled*] altered by Willughby from *sadeled*.

274. *upon*] altered by Willughby from *upont*.

275. *who*] altered by Willughby from *with*.

276. *goe*] altered by Willughby from *go*.

277. A bracket before *He* indicates the start of a parenthesis, but no bracket is present to show where it was intended to conclude.

278. *chairs*] interlineated above cancellation *chirs*.

laid upon his back and something else must be held over him till he doe guesse right. When they lay things upon his back they use to say, Ly Their Till More Comes,[279] or, Ly There Tongs Till the Fire Shovel[280] Comes, or, Ly There Stoole Till the Chair Comes.

They must only bring such things as are in the chamber allready.

231   These and those which[281] follow are[282] called Christmas Gambolls.[283]

[*Bum to Busse*][284]

Two stoope downe[285] bearing them selves up on theire hands and knees so as their backs are parallel to[286] the horizon; the head[287] of one must be towards the feete of the other. Another holds up his fellow about the middle, his face hanging bettwixt his thighs[288] and his legs reaching up beyond his head.[289] He sits downe upon one of the former and bending his back downwards over his fellow that he sits upon. He that was held up sets his legs to the ground and nimbly lifts up his fellow so that his feete that were on the ground before are now in the aire. This trick is easiest done when he that is sat upon lies with his[290] back as high as he can and his fellow as low. They ly downe by turns, first one pare and then the other.

A Foole Who Bobed Thee. One blinds his fellow hoolding 2 of[291] his fingers upon his eyes. Another gives him a boxe of the eare and askes[292] him, A Foole, Who Bobd Thee. If hee guesse right, he that boxed must be blinded, but if hee[293] mistake he must be blinded againe &c. He that blinds him most commonly[294] strikes him himself making him beleeve he blinds him[295] with

---

279. *comes*] altered by Willughby from *coms*.

280. *shovel*] altered by Willughby from *shavel*.

281. *which*] altered by Willughby from *wich*.

282. *are*] altered by Willughby from *may be*.

283. *Christmas Gambolls*] altered by Willughby from *Chrismas Gambose*.

284. Title editorially supplied; see Glossary of Games under this heading.

285. *Two stoope downe*] altered by Willughby from *too li downe*.

286. *to*] altered from *too*.

287. *head*] altered by Willughby from *hed*.

288. *thighs*] altered by Willughby from *thies*.

289. *head*] altered by Willughby from *hed*.

290. *his*] altered by Willughby from *is*.

291. *2 of*] altered by Willughby from *both*.

292. *askes*] altered by Willughby from *axes*.

293. *if hee*] interlineated by Willughby.

294. *commonly*] altered by Willughby from *comonly*.

295. *blinds him*] altered by Willughby from *strikes*.

both hands when he blindes him with two fingers of the same hand. This is like Hockockles but that he that is[296] blinded stands up right.

Shooing the Wild Colt

They lay a pole upon two stooles ar formes that are a prettie way asunder. Upon the middle of this pole, a man must sit with his leges acrosse under him. Upon the two[297] corners of the stooles before him there must be 2[298] trenchers shelving over and likewise upon the two[299] corners of the stoole[300] behind[301] him. In his hand he holdes a stich just long enough to reach the trenchers. If he can knock downe the trenchers with his stich on one side he hath Shoowed the Colt on that side. Then, lifting his stick over the pole is Bridcling of him, knocking thc trcnchers downe of that side is Shooing him of that side. Lifting the stick over the pole behind him is Putting on the Crupper, putting the stick twice[302] under him and taking it with the other hand is Girting[303] of him. Before he can doe all this the Colte will throw him severall[304] times unlesse he have the right art.

Where there is greate Christmasses kept they have[305] lawes or orders hanging[306] up in the hall. Who ever reads these orders with his hat on his head shall be horssed;[307] who ever stands with his back to the fire when there is meat rosting shall be horst.

Horsing, which is the ordinary punnishment,[308] is to be carried[309] a stradling upon a pole between 2 men about the parlour and hall.[310] If the butler be not ready to make them drink at the buttry doore,[311] he must be horst to.

---

296. *that is*] altered by Willughby from *this*.

297. *two*] altered by Willughby from *too*.

298. *2*] altered by Willughby from *too*.

299. *two*] altered by Willughby from *too*.

300. *stoole*] altered by Willughby from *trencher*.

301. *behind*] altered by Willughby from *behing*.

302. *twice*] altered by Willughby from *2*.

303. *Girting*] altered by Willughby from *Girthing*.

304. *severall*] altered by Willughby from *sevrall*.

305. *have*] inserted by Willughby.

306. *hanging*] altered from *hang*.

307. *horssed*] altered by Willughby from *horst*.

308. *punnishment*] altered by Willughby from *pnishment*.

309. *carried*] altered by Willughby from *carred*.

310. *hall*] interlineated by Willughby.

311. *at the buttry doore*] interlineated by Willughby.

233   **Fire and No Smoke**

They play 8, 7 standing in the points of a triangell, 3 at one angle and two and two at the other two. They stand just behind on another. Where ever there is three it is called Fire. The eight that is left out folloues the Fire, the hindermost of the three stil running to[312] the next angle and standing before the two that were there.[313] Then the hindermost of that angle runs to[314] the next &c. If he that is without the triangle can touch[315] him that changes places with a stick that hee carries[316] in his hand, he goeth to one of the angels, and he that is taken runs about with out.

C runs before E, then D before F &c. H followes them round, and strives to touch C, D or G as they run from one corner to another. Hee that is touched must run about & then H goes to one of the corners. They follow the motion of the sun as they run. The number 7 = to the number of the planets.[317]

D E C   *F G*

A
B
C
        H

                        Jack[318] Art Asleepe

Two stand by a forme, one of one side and one of another with boots in their hands. The third vaults[319] over and they strike at him saing, Jack, Art Asleepe, If Thou Beest,[320] Ile Waken Thee. If he proffers[321] to go over and doth not and either of them strike at him, he that struck must vault[322] in his place and be struck at with the bootes as before.

Text reverts to Willughby's hand.

---

312. *to*] altered by Willughby from *two*.

313. *there*] altered by Willughby from *their*.

314. *to*] altered by Willughby from *two*.

315. *touch*] altered by Willughby from *hit*.

316. *carries*] altered by Willughby from *carrieth*.

317. *C runs before E … number of the planets*] passage and diagram inserted in Willughby's hand.

318. *Jack*] follows cancellation *Jhack*.

319. *vaults*] altered by Willughby from *vallts*.

320. *beest*] altered by Willughby from *beist*.

321. *proffers*] altered by Willughby from *poffers*, uncertain abbreviation mark seems to be present above the *p* of *poffers*.

322. *vault*] altered by Willughby from *ly downe*.

Gliffes   234

are a great manie words to bee said in a breath without mistaking:

> Dick Drunke Drinke in a Dish. Wheres the Dish Dick Drunke Drinke in.
> Three Blew Beanes in a Blew Bladder. Rattle, Bladder, Rattle.

Must be said so manie times in a breath.

> Tobacco Hic will make you wel if you bee sick.
> Tobacco Hic if you bee wel will make you sick.

> My Ladie has as no Ladie has. My Ladie has a new shaven fat Ruffe.
> Cuttie, Put, Cut Put.

Gliffes, quasi Griphi.[323]

> *A blank space, followed by a line across the page, separates this text from*
> *the next title.*

---

323. See Glossary of Games under 'Gliffs'.

Drolery or for Exercising the Wit & Making Sport

Selling of Bargaines. Riddles. Purposes &[c.]   **X   X**

235   **Selling of Bargaines**

is when one askes the other a question who answers him simply and pertinently, thinking hee meant honnestly. The first replys againe & catching hold of his answer Sels him a Bargaine. A wishes hee had as manie dogs as there are starres. B asks what hee would doe with them. A replys, Hold up their Teales while you Kisse their Arses.

   A: Which is the best huswife, that scrapes her cheese, pares it or wipes it with a wisp.
   B: That wipes it with a wisp.
   A: Her arse you must kisse.

When B[324] can sel A another bargaine, A saies, A Bargaine Bought & a Bargaine Sold, a Turd in your Mouth a Twelmonth Old.

When B prevents A & gets his bargaine before him, A saies, You say my Word, you may Eat a Dogs Turd.

They strive to sel one another most bargaines as they doe in capping verses who shall capt his antagonist.

   A askes B if hee can say, A Long Pole over a Gutter.
   If B repeat the words, A saies, A Short Turd to your Supper.

All bargaines are either obscene or nastie.

   A bids B repeat Oxe Ball so manie times in a breath.
   B repeating fast saies, Ballox.   **X**

   Such another: In Clap, beeing repeated fast, Clap In.

---

324.   *B*] altered from *A*.

Dust Point   236

The heading and text of Dust Point is in the manuscript's unidentified juvenile hand, corrected by Willughby (see Introduction, Section 2.3).

They make 2 heaps of dust a pretty[325] way asunder, in which they hide points; one for every one that plays, and standing at one of the heaps they throw stones by turns at the other. He that can hit the heape, and uncover any of the points, draws it out and[326] takes it and if he uncover 2 or three or more he must have them all, but if he uncover any with drawing those out they must be covered againe. When they hitt the dust they run to[327] it and kneeling downe looke if they can see any part of a point uncovered. They chuse stones[328] of an æquall bignesse.

Text reverts to Willughby's hand.

---

325. *pretty*] altered from *petty*.

326. *and*] followed by cancelled *hath it for his pains.*

327. *to*] altered by Willughby from *two.*

328. *stones*] altered by Willughby from *stoness.*

237   **Purposes**

A B C D E F &c. sitting round about a fire or table, A askes B a question softly
in his eare. B answers it softly in Cs eare, C in Ds &c., till it come about round
to A againe. When it has gone round they all tel aloud what they[329] were
asked. The sport is that those that are furthest of, as E F, a great manie
questions having passed before it comes to them and not knowing any thing
but the last question, must needs answer very absurdly and impertinently,
guessing manie times at a subiect quite contrarie. A greater number makes
the best sport.

    A: What weather is it.
    B: Fair.
    C: That I love wel.
    D: I love fish better.
    E: If one could catch them.
    F: Theile get away with their broken legs & wings.
    G: You must shoote wel.
    H: The buts are pulled downe.

In this there is 3 absurd answers, of D, F, H.

                            Crosse Purposes

is when everie one askes a question & answers another, as B askes C one &
answers A another softly in his eare. When they are gone round, B puts Cs
answer to As question saying, the question that was asked was &c., the
answer was &c. Now C answering to Bs & not to As quæstion makes the
sport.

    A: Whither is the sea or land bigger.
    B answers to A, the Sea, & askes C what a clock it is.
    C answers B, Nine a Clock.
    Then at last B saies aloud, The quæstion that was asked mee, was Whither
    the sea or land [is] bigger. The answer was, Nine a Clock &c.

---

329.   *they*] followed by cancelled word fragment *an[swered]*.

Riddles

Who was that that was born before his father, begotten before his mother &
had the maidenhead of his grandmother.

Abel,[330] the first that was buried.

Whats that that was but a fortnight old when Adam was no more, & was but
a month old when Adam was fourescore.

The moone.

Theefes came to my house and rapd mee all in woe, my house leapt out of
windore & left mee with my foe.

Fish catched[331] in nets.

Whats that that God never sees, the King seldome sees & I see it everie day.

One better then himselfe.

In the tree it grew, in the root it run,
The smith that smote, the maid that spun,
The goose that beareth of her leg bone,
The bee that bore it in her hive.

An arrow.

Item deriditum all clothed in greene,
The King hee may eat it & so may the Queene.

A pescod.

Who was that that never was of Gods making.

A cuckold.

Black sat upon white & made white black.

A flea.

V: Joh. Heidelffii, Sphinx Philosophica[332] & other books of riddles.

---

330. *Abel*] replaces cancellation *Abel Cain*.

331. *catched*] MS *catced*.

332. See Heidfeld's *Sphynx Philosophica* (1601: section 26 'De Gryphis Grammaticis').

239   **Capping of Verses**

A begins any verse, as: In nova fert animus mutatas dicere formas. B is to say another that begins with the same letter As verse ended with, which was S. B: Si mea cum vestris valuissent vota Pelasgi.[333]

Then A must repeat a verse that begins with an I, and so by turns. No verse must be repeated twice, nor must they have a verse but is out of the old poets. Hee that has repeated a verse and can decline Captus, Capta, Captum &c. thorough all the cases before his fellow can answer him has gotten the victory.

They strive for verses that end in X, Y, & those letters that have but a few verses.

From Captus comes Capping.

                              Riming

A: Able. B: Stable. A: Fable. B: Cable, &c.
Hee that cant[334] find out a word to rime is beaten.

Mr Booker was put to rime to Porringer, who presently answered, The King had a Daughter & hee Gave the Prince of Orange her.[335]

---

333. These are lines 1.1 and 13.128 from Ovid's *Metamorphoses*.

334. *cant*] followed by cancellation *rime*.

335. The Mr Booker mentioned here has not been identified. Mary, daughter of Charles I, had been married to William, Prince of Orange, in 1641.

240

The upper part of page 240 is blank, as verso pages of this manuscript commonly are. On the lower third of the page, separated by a line, Willughby has entered some general notes on Quoits, Bowls and related games, a category of games described more fully from the following page.

In Quoits, Boules &c. a Toucher is sometimes reckoned a double cast or 2. **X**

The best plaiers are reserved to play last.

A boule, quoit &c. is called a Cast, a boule[336] or quoit that is neere the Jack, a Good Cast &c. **X**

The [*No further text supplied.*]

A fixed marke is called a Mistris in manie games. Where there is 2, they stand   241
at one and play to the other & so backwards & forwards.

A mooveable marke is called a Jack, **X X** Jack beeing a common name for boys sent of errands,[337] and is allwaies lesser, as a little boule, a little quoit &c., which is lead or throwne from place to place. **X**

They that are neerest the Jack or Mistris win one for everie boule or quoit they have before their adversarys. Where there is an æquall distance or where both sides touch, it lys dead, that is neither side must set downe any. They play either all of their own heads, or are æqually divided into 2 sides. When they play all of their owne heads, they must all play one quoit or boule one after another, & then the other, but when they play of 2 sides, one pare of the gamesters that are æqually matched play both their boules first, & then another pare &c.

---

336. *boule*] follows cancellation *good*.

337. *Jack ... errands*] inserted here as indicated in the MS, from its initial location, marked by *X*, at the end of the paragraph.

Quoits

The quoits are either flat peices of lead, horseshooes, round peices of tiles, &c.

Everie one of the plaiers has 2 quoits, which they throw at a Mistris or a Jack, throwing them so that they may fall upon the flat side and not upon an edge, holding them in their hands and throwing them parallel to the horizon, and sometimes giving them a verticity about their centers. They strive to throw them rather short of the Mistris then beyond it, that they may shovel up to it.

5 or 7 usually is up.

Pennie Prick[338]

The title and text of Penny Prick is in the manuscript's unidentified juvenile hand, with corrections by Willughby (see Introduction, section 2.3).

They thrust a peg into the ground perpendicularly, leaving about 3 inches out of the ground, and upon the top of the peg they lay a pennie, and then standing a pretty way of, they pitch their knifes att the peg. He that is neerest the peg wins the cast. Whoever can strike the pennie[339] of the peg wins 2,[340] and if he gett the cast to,[341] 3. One or more may strike of the pennie and another win the cast.

Text reverts to Willughby's hand.

5 or 7 is up.

---

338. *Pennie Prick*] altered by Willughby from two previous incomplete titles *Pennie,* and *Pen.*

339. *pennie*] altered from *pnnie.*

340. 2] altered by Willughby from *too.*

341. *to*] altered by Willughby from *too.*

242 *blank*; 243
Boules

Boules are either sphæricall or cilindricall.

Biassed boules are those that have one side bigger
then the other, or heavier with having lead put in. If
the Mistris bee at **A**, they boule towards **B**, setting the
bias side towards **A**, which will bring about the boule
to **A**.

Giving Ground is when one of the same side guesses how much ground his
fellows boule that is to play requires, & sets his foot where hee would have
him play, as at **B** if the boule require so much.

Hee that plaies between the Mistris & the true ground is said to Boule
Narrow as at **m**.

Hee that boules without his ground, as at **n**, is said to Boule Wide.

Hee Hits his Ground that boules just where his fellows foot stood.

Knocking is when one of the adverse parties boules lys very neere the Mistris,
& hee that plaies boules as hard as hee can at it to knock it away.

The boules must bee made of hard firme wood, as brasil &c. and turned very
smooth.

The Trig is a key or flat peice of iron, which is thrown downe for all the
plaiers to stand upon. They set the right foot upon the Trig and, setting the
left foot a step forwards, deliver the boule with the right hand, as evenly and
smoothly as they can, and guesse to give it no more motion then will serve to
carrie it to the Jack. The boule runs forwards continually turning upon its
owne axis, contrary to the motion of a Shovel Board peice which slides upon
a smooth table. The boule should touch the ground as soone as it leaves the
hand, for if it bee thrown forward it will not run so true.

They throw Crosse & Pile for the Jack at first, and afterwards that side that
wins the cast allwais has the Jack, who lead it at the best distance & upon the
best ground for their own boules. But they must never goe above a stride of
from the place the Jack lay before.

244   They play either upon bouling greenes, which must bee kept very smooth
with being often rouled and / the grasse mowed close to the ground, or upon
very smooth allies of gravel.

A Lurch is when one side gets none before the other is up. They must pay 3ᵈ a peice to the Keeper of the greene. Or when one side gets all their casts togather, the other side is lurched,³⁴² though they had gotten some before. This is called the Back Lurch, the other the Fore Lurch.

5 or 7 is usually up.³⁴³

A Rub is any thing in the greene or alley that stops the boules. They cry Rub when it goes to fast, Few when not fast enough.

If there bee any women or young plaiers, they must not bee outbouled. That is, the Jack must not bee lead further then they can play.   X X

The boules for heavinesse & bignesse must bee fitted for the hand that uses them.

The Keeper of the greene has allwaies a reed readie to measure casts. If the reed α β touch the boule & the Jack so as it just stands, that is, is supported by them and dos not fall to the ground, and if it cannot bee made to stand between the others boule & the Jack, hee must loose the cast.

This is counted the most gentile play & is more generally used then any other in England.

342. *lurched*] follows cancellation *up*.

343. *up*] MS *lurched*; cf. earlier correction from *up* to *lurched*.

245   **Ten Pegs or 9 Pegs.   Skittle Pins**

The pegs are made of wood, bone &c., and
sometimes they make the bones in the legs of
beeves serve instead of pegs, standing upon the
broad ends.

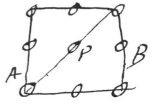

8 of these pegs are allwaies of an æquall bignesse
and lenght, & set about a square at an æquall
distance, 3 of a side as in **A B**. In the middle of
the square at **P** stands a peg 2 or 3 inches longer
than the rest, which is called the Ten Peg.

Suppose the standing place at **A**, in the middle betweene the pegs and **A**
there is a little peg lesse then all the rest called the 5 Peg, or the Five Madg.[344]

The whole number of pegs standing togather is called
the Ruck.

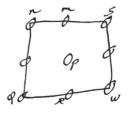

They play with a good heavie boule, and standing at
a convenient distance, as at **A**, boule at the ruck. If
they strike the Five Peg downe by the way they
reckon five, and one a peice for as manie as they strike
downe of the ruck, unlesse they happen to strike
downe the Ten Peg single, and then they reckon ten. If
the boule rest so neere the ruck that they can reach out
the Ten Peg with their hand, so as neither of their feet
bee neerer the ruck then the boule, they set downe ten.
But if it happens that they strike downe another as
they take it out, they must reckon but 2. If the boule ly
without their reach of the ruck, they throw it at the
ruck and get as many as they can, or else, if they bee
expert enough, throw the boule onely at the Ten Peg,
the end of it standing higher then all the rest, & if they
can strike it out so as not to strike downe any of the
rest, they set downe ten, else but as many as they
strike downe, or nothing, if they throw over the ruck
& hit downe none, which often happens.

246   The greatest art is in striking out the Ten Peg for if
they hit it forceably at top with the boule thrown
flatwaies or parallel to the horizon and against a gap,
as **n m**, supposing hee that throws stands at **x**, it flys thorough the gap and

---

344. *Madg*] altered from *Mag*.

strikes downe none of the rest. Hee that throws allwaies falls downe and delivers his boule when hee is allmost at the ground. The reason is because hee directs the boule truer, beeing his own lenght neerer the ruck.

They boule with as much force as will carry the boule to the ruck & a little further, that it may not bee stopt to much if it should hit downe the Madg by the way, and that it may come with strenght enough to strike downe some of the ruck.

If they get none neither with bouling nor afterwards throwing, they must set down none.

They as get to 31 first win. But if one of the plaiers want but a few of beeing up & get more then hee wants, as as manie as makes him 32 or more, hee must goe back again to 16. But [he] must play againe before his adversary to try to get 15.

When they throw the boule against the ruck to get as manie as they can, they throw flatwaies or parallel but not edgwaies and against a corner, as **w**, that the boule first glancing against the side of **w** peg, & striking that downe, that may strike with falling the middlemost & that the outemost of that row,[345] the boule then strikes down **R**, & going into the middle of the ruck strikes down the 10 Peg and some of the further side.

A good plaier will get 6 or 7.

5 = to the number of fingers in one hand, 10 to the number in both, 31 = to the degrees of a signe + 1, 16 to ½ of the degrees + 1.

The pegs are turned broader & a little hollow at the bottome, that they may stand better.

They play sometimes with little bone pegs & a little bone boule upon the boards within doores.

The most that is possible to bee gotten at one bouling is 25, the 5 Madg by the way, then the Ten Peg in running thorough the ruck, which is a rare chance, then the Ten Peg againe if it ly within reach or if they knock it out, so that it is impossible to get 31 at once.

The art is, besides the knocking out the ten, to boule so as to hit the rucke and ly by it, to get but just so manie as they need. 3 are easily gotten standing in a rowe. 2, the ten & one that stands under him. 4, as **A B C D**, the 3 in a rowe & one in the furthermost rowe. 247

---

345. *the middlemost ... that row*] altered from *all of that row*.

Those that are out & goe back againe to 16 may[346] get up if they can hit the Madg by the way & ly within reach of a ten.

They set their pegs usually in path waies &c.

They play sometimes 3 or 4 on a side.

The pegs must still bee set up againe as they are thrown downe fairly & in their right places.

Sometimes they play onely who shall strike downe most at 1, 2 or 3 throwes, standing at a corner of the ruck, & sometimes they play without a 5 Madg.

The ordinary figure of pegs, but they may bee turned into any fashion.

Trole Madame or Nine Holes

248 *blank*; 249

To play at Nine Holes they have a board with 9 square holes like **A B**. Over the holes **o o o** &c. are painted figures in this order, or any other, **X X** but the biggest **9**, **8** &c. should bee of the outsides. The board must bee set perpendicular and crosse an entry or some narrow place. The boule they play with is flat and a little lesse then the holes, that it may goe thorough easily. They stand a prettie distance of and boule at the board. If the boule hit against a blank **n m** and rebound back againe, they reckon nothing, but if it goe thorough one of the holes, they reckon as manie as the figure that is written over it. They that get most at 3 throwes win.

All the art is in bouling steadily, for if the boule shake and waddle as it goes, it will bee lesse likely to hit thorough a hole.

Shovel Board

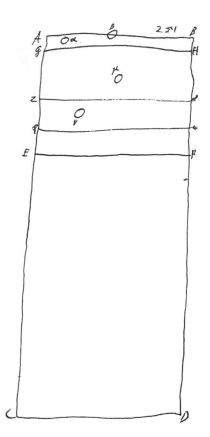

The Shovel Board must bee a very smooth table, best if it bee made of one board. But if it bee made of 2 or 3 boards, they must bee all of the lenght of the table, and not peiced. The Shovel Board peices are either shillings, halfecrownes or round brasse or silver peices made of purpose, very smooth of one side, and with a little edge rising quite round of the other side. The longer the table is the better.

At the further end of the table **A B** is a little boxe made to thrust on or draw of. The use of it is to receive the peices when they are throwne quite of of the table, to keepe them from falling to the ground.

The breadth of the boxe **n m s t** is just æquall to the breadth of the table. Upon the 3 sides **nm, ns, st** are fastened perpendicularly little boards. The side **mt** joines to the bottome of the table, & is supported by 2 pegs **zq, vx**, or little boards.

Under the table are nailed 2 little boards such as **α β**, into the holes of which, **n**, enter the pegs that support the box.

The Shovel Board peice, beeing throwne quite of of the table, is kept in the boxe by the side **n s**.

Towards the further end of the table, is a crosse line **E F** and within little more then the breadth of the peice another **G H**.

The plaiers stand at **C D** end, and have everie one 2 peices which they hold round with all their fingers and thumbe, allmost close to the table & parallel exactly to the horizon, and they deliver them as smoothly as they can, that they may glide along the table. They play by turnes as at Boules, first one delivering a peice & then his opposite another. The peice that is neerest the end wins, as **μ** peice wins of **v**. If a peice bee short of **E F** line it is called a Hog & signifies nothing. A peice resting between **E F**, **G H** is reckoned one, unlesse it bee wun by anothers getting before it.

A peice between **G H** & **A B**, the end of the table, is called a Duce & reckoned two, as **α** peice, **β** peice, hanging over the table & not falling into the boxe is called a Trea & reckoned 3. A trea is also called a Looker from looking over.[347] One duce may win another, but all treas are alike. If one side have 2 treas, they reckon 6, but if one side have one trea & the other side another, it lys dead, as when there is 2 casts of an æquall distance from the end.   252

5 or 7 is usually up.

If a trea bee readie to drop downe into the boxe it is lawfull to thrust him a little farther upon the table.   **X**

To know a trea from a duce that dos but just hang over the end of the table, they draw a shilling or any plane close to the end **A B** & perpendicularly. If the peice stirre when the plane passes by it is a trea. But if it stirre not it is a duce.

Betweene the lines **E F**, **G H** are severall crosse parallel lines to know which peice is formost, & to direct them in measuring.

When one side has gotten a trea, duce or good cast, the other side aimes at it & strives to knock it of.

---

347. *A trea ... looking over*] added later, squeezed into space between text.

253   **Span Counter**

They first lay a counter or any other marke a little distance from a wall, and then holding a counter, 6 pence &c., in their hands, as they doe a shovel board peice, throw it with the flat side against the wall, that it may rebound and fall neere the marke. Hee that has plaid a counter, if it light further then a span, hee must let it ly, and then his fellow must play, and all the counters that are further of then a span must ly still. But hee that can first play a counter within a spans lenght wins them all.

[Nine Mens Maurice]

Willughby's description of Nine Men's Morris is on a large folded sheet, numbered 254/i-ii, which has been attached to page 254. The three phrases of text within the illustration appear to be in the unidentified juvenile hand (see Introduction, Section 2.3); the word 'have' is supplied by Willughby.

Nine Mens Maurice consists of 3 squares one within another as in this figure.[348]

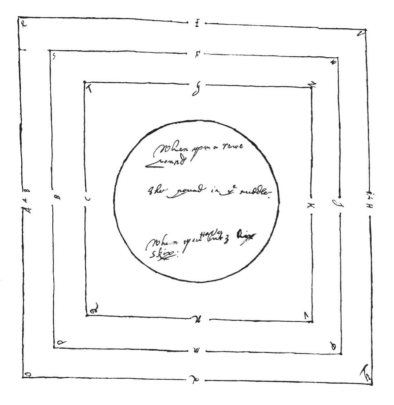

In the middle of the innermost is a circle which they call the Pound. In the middles & corners of every one of the squares the[349] men may be placed and no where else. If they may make it in the ground they cut furrowes for the 3 squares & circle in the middle. There must allso bee a crosse furrow thorough the middles of the squares, as **A B C, E F G, H J K, l n m**.[350] 3 men in 3 points

---

348. The text in the centre of the diagram reads: '*The pound in the middle*'. Above this is the instruction: '*When upon a rowe pound*' (i.e. when you make a row of three, you may pound one of your opponent's pieces), and below: '*When you have but 3 hip skip*', ('hip skip' being explained in the text).

349. *the*] altered from *there is a round*.

350. *l m n*] MS *n m l*.

of one side of a square are called a Rowe, as in **V H Y, W J φ** &c., or 3 men in the 3 middle points, as in **A B C**. But 3 men in the 3 corner points, as in **R S T**, dont make a rowe. They have 9 men a peice, as 9 stones & 9 sticks. The first thing is to set the men, one of the plaiers setting down one, then his adversary another, & so by / turnes till they have placed all their men, placing them still in the middle & corner points **V H Y**. Hee that gets a row in placing his men takes up one of his adversaries men where hee will & puts it into the pound[351] in the circle.

254/iᵛ

When they have placed all their men they Rim, that is remove or play their men, from **B** to **C**, or **Q** to **C**, never removing but to the next point at a time, as from the corner of the square to the middle, from the middle of one square to the middle of the next &c., & hee that gets a rowe pounds one of his adversaries men.

A man must never bee taken out of a rowe to bee pounded as long as there bee any out of rowes, but if there bee none but those in the rowes then one of them may bee pounded.

The reason why 3 corner points, as **O P Q**, dont make a rowe, is because there is never a furrow going from them as in the middle points, nor can a man bee plaied from **O** to **P** &c.

Hee that has a rowe may play a man out of it & when hee plays his man back againe & makes the same rowe hee pounds another man.

Hee that has 3 middle points, as **A B C**, has a Running Rotchet. The 3 middle points are called a Running Rotchet, because a man has most liberty to play or run to one of the 3 corners on either side the running rotchet.

Hip Skip is when there is but 3 men left, & then one may skip over with them anie where, as from **R** to **P**, from **G** to **V** &c. Whoever comes to have but 2 men is beaten.

If both are at Hip Skip, having but 3 men a peice, the game may last a great while.

254/iiᵛ

The cunning is to get & keep a running rotchet, to take up those of your adversarys men that are neerest to / make rowes, to contrive to get 5 points so as to make a rowe every remove, as hee that has **A B C G Z**, having a row at **A B C** & pounding the man that is likliest to get a rowe or to hinder him most, may play next time from **C** to **T** & get **T G Z** row, & pound another man. Then hee may play the next remoove from **T** to **C** and get **A B C** againe

---

351. *pound*] follows cancellation *ground*.

&c., and so backwards and forwards in those 2 rowes till hee has pounded all his men.

Q: If it bee possible to recover a game when your antagonist has 5 such points.

3 Mens Maurice is a square divided with crosse diameters & lines downe from the middle points **A B C D. E**, where all meet in the center, is called the Pee. They play with 3 men a peice and set them first one & then another by turnes, as in 9 Mens Maurice. When they have set all their men they play them, as in 9 Mens Maurice, never remooving further then to the next point, as from **F** to **A**, **B** or **E**. From the Pee **E** they may remoove to any of the points round.

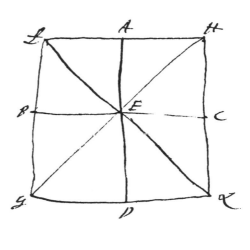

They that get a rowe first as **F A H**, **A E D** &c. win the game. Hee that gets the Pee has the best, and therefore hee that sets first allwaies gets the Pee with his first man.

> *The text on p. 254/ii^v is in the unidentified juvenile hand (see Introduction, Section 2.3).*

First of all sette round, first one and then the other, and if you make a rowwe in setting them pinne[352] but not out of the rooe, and when you have sett all then you rimme, and as you gette your roose still you pound, and if you gette your running ratchit it is grait odds you are beaten. When I have but 3, I am at Hip Skip, and when I have but 2, I am beaten.   254/ii^v

> *Text reverts to Willughby's hand.*

3 Mens Maurice, 9 Mens Maurice, Fox & Goose, Draughts, & Chesse seeme   255
all to have relation one to another. The most simple of these is 3 Mens Maurice.

---

352. *pinne*] word obscure in text.

256   **[Fox and Goose]**

The table for Fox and Goose is made of 5 squares divided all with diagonall
& crosse lines from the middle points, as the square for 3 Mens Maurice, and
placed 3 in a row crossewaies, as in the 2 figures of the next page.[353]

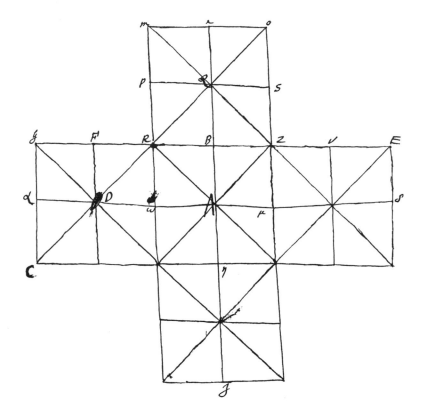

They have 15 men of an æquall biggnesse, like the pawnes at Chest, called
Geese, and one a great deal bigger then the rest, called the Fox.

Of the 2 plaiers that play one against another one has the Foxe, the other the
Geese. The Fox is allwaies placed at first upon the middle point **A**. The 15
Geese are placed all upon one side, in the points **m n o, P Q S, α G F R B Z
V E δ**.

The Geese & Fox moove as the men in 3 Mens Maurice, never further then to
the next point at a time, as from **α** to **C**, from **R** to **ω** &c. The Geese must
moove from the side they are placed on to the opposite, as from **m n o** & all
that side towards **J**, but must not moove back again, as from **B** to **Q** &c.

---

353. In the MS two diagrams appear on the facing page; the first and smaller one appears to be an early
     trial of the one reproduced here, lacking all but one of the alphabetic symbols.

But the Fox may move any way, so hee doe not move further then to one of the next points as from **A** to ω, **n**, **B** &c. Hee that has the Geese must strive to pen up the Foxe, so that hee may have never a remoove, as if hee that has the Geese has the 2 next points quite round the Fox, hee has pend up the Foxe and wun the game.

The Fox is to take as manie Geese as hee can. Whenever there is a Goose in the next point, not garded, hee may hop over him & take him up, as if the Foxe bee in **A**, a Goose at μ, the Foxe may hop over him to the middle point of the next square & take him up. The Foxe may hop over 2[354] or 3 if they stand ungarded before him, as if the Fox bee in **D** point, hee hop over ω & take him & then μ and take him. If the Fox can take all the Geese hee wins the game. If the Fox have gotten 2 or 3 men it is impossible to pen him up. But hee that has the Geese has much the better and will bee sure to pen up the Foxe if hee bee carefull of his men at first.

They make holes sometimes in all the points and instead of pawnes stick pegs in the holes.   *257 figure;* 258

354. 2] altered from 3.

259   **Draughts**

No text supplied.

[Cock Fighting]

260–7 *blank*; 268

Pages 264–8 incorrectly paginated as 254–8 in MS.

When one cock has beaten another hee claps his wings & crows over him.

A breed from an old cock & an old hen will hold their heads high & are called Rampers. These dont carry good heeles; i.e., dont kill. They thrust up their necks & strive to out top one another.

Young cocks & young hens breed cocks that carry their heads low, & fight low but dont carry good heeles.

The best breed is from an old hen & a young cock or from a young hen & an old cock.

They cut of the combs, wattles, tailes and feathers about the necks of fighting cocks.

When both the cocks are blind, there goes 2 men into the pits which they call Setters & set the cocks one against another. The cocks when they feele one another will strike againe, then the Setters let them goe. If one of them peck the other 10 times togather & hee dos not peck again hee is beaten. But if hee peck once they begin & count againe. Twitching them by the feathers of the rump will make them peck againe but that is foule play.

The Setters are officers that chuse the cocks of severall shires or townes & æquallie match them one against another. These are called[355] Battle Cocks. Game Cocks are great cocks kept in bags, called allso Shake Bags. They are kept in bags, and brought into the pit, one bag against another, without beeing compared. 4 Battles & 3 Games are when 4 pare of Battle Cocks[356] fight, & 3 pare of Gamecocks.

When both are æqually beaten & wounded they draw stakes.

Incorrectly paginated p. 259 in MS.

269

---

355. *called*] followed by cancellation *Game Cocks.*

356. *4 pare of Battle Cocks*] follows cancellation *Pare of 4 Battle Cocks.*

Bul Bating, Cock Fighting &c.,
Throwing at Cocks, & Other Sports
Where Animalls Kill One Another

Everie Shrovetuesday in the afternoone, the sport is to Throw at Cocks. The cock is tied by the leg with a string a yard or 2 long, the other end beeing tied to a peg fastened in the ground. The staves they throw with are like dog staves a yard long. They stand 12, 14, 16, 18 &c. yards of. Hee that ownes the cock lets any bodie have 3 throwes for a penny. If hee can knock downe the cock, and run and take him up before hee rises againe, hee wins the cock. But if hee that ownes him can make him stand, lifting him up 3 times and setting him down againe before the other comes, hee saves his cock and the other throwes at him againe. The cock must not bee lifted up to try to make him stand above 3 times. If hee that throwes can win the cock the 3 first throws, hee must pay 2[d], else but a penny for 3 throwes. A cock that is used to bee thrown at will grow cunning & avoid the blow.

Cocks Pits are round theaters with benches going about in circles or ovalls, growing lesse and narrower still towards the bottome.

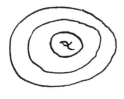

At the bottome α is the place for the cocks to fight in. The cocks peck with their beakes & strike with their spurres, rising up & falling backwards sometimes as they strike with their spurres forwards. The cock that runs away and crys first, is beaten and all that bet[357] of his side loose.[358]

They diet their cocks with oat bread, white bread, anise-seede bread, hard egs, in the summer onely the whites, in the winter the yolks to. The yolkes in summer would bee to hot.[359]

They lay their meat upon a soft place, as upon an old hat &c., to keepe their bills from beeing blunted.

If one of the cocks bee crammed with garlick, the other will run from him because of the smel. This is foule and if it bee discovered the cocks head is pulled up. They put pepper dust into their wings, which blinds the other cock, grease their wings &c., which is all foule.[360]

---

357. *bet*] interlineated over cancellation *lay*.

358. *loose*] follows cancellation *are beaten*.

359. *white bread ... bee to hot*] squeezed into space on page after cancellation *&c.*

360. *This is foule ... which is all foule*] later addition, squeezed into space on page.

They have a tradition, that hen egs hatched under ravens will breed good fighting cocks. **X**   But this is a story. **X**   The egs must bee spotted like a ravens, & taken away as soone as they are hatched, else the raven wil eate them.[361]

The severall sorts of cocks: common dung hill cocks, Freeze-land cocks, the fighting breed of cocks &c.

The best breed is to breed of several kinds &c., those that are no kin one to another.

They arme the spurres with iron, silver &c. but silver is better, iron making   270
the wounds fester. **X X** Steele is as good as silver. When a spurre is broken or stands crooked, they cut it of allmost to the bottome, and arme it with a gaffle of silver or steele.

The bottome of the gaffle **E** is hollow to receive the stump that is left of the spurre, & from the sides come out 2 little plates **E C**, **E B**. The gaffle is thrust thorough a peice of leather, & the leather beeing tied upon the plates **E B**, **E C** about their legs fastens the gaffles. These are allso called Gablocks.

Sparring of Cocks is breathing them once in 3, 4 or 5 daies, making them fight one with another, upon straw, a hey mow, or any soft place. To keepe them from hurting one another they put Huts upon their spurres. Huts are made of fingerstalls, allwaies filled up with wool quilted hard downe, & onely a hole left big enough for the spurres with strings on the sides to ty them fast about their legs.

(Aves Pugnaces would make as good sport as fighting cocks. **X**) **X**

When they are wearie & hot with beeing sparred, they stive them. Stives are baskets made of straw allmost like beehives, bigger in the middle then at both ends. The cock as soone as hee has done fighting is presently put into the stive, for fear of catching cold, with straw put quite round about him & the lid pegd downe. The stive beeing stuffed thus with straw makes the cock sweat. Hee must sweat for 12 houres or thereabouts, then they take him out & feed him with hot meat, white bread boiled with hony & ale, & then put them againe into the stive, open the lid & let them coole by degrees.

To make a cock that has bene cowed fight they allwaies carrie a hen with him & turne them out togather. In the midst of their sparring or fighting they give

---

361. *But this is a story ... wil eate them*] later addition, squeezed into space on page.

them herb of grace, hissop, rosemary & violet leaves, shredded[362] & roled up in a pellet of butter. They set them downe againe & let them fight a while after. This makes them scoure in their hives.

They fight allso dogs &c. for wagers.

They give fighting cocks sack to drink. *X   X*

Sparring & sweating makes their flesh hard. The harder his flesh is, the better order hee is to fight in.

---

362. *shredded*] follows cancellation *pound*.

Bull Bating

A bull is tied to a stake, fast driven into the ground, with a rope or chaine.

They bate him with great mastifs, the mastif striving to catch the bull by the nose or eare, and the bull to tosse up the dog with his hornes. When a dog has hung on a good while & made the bull roare, they draw him of, pulling him by the taile & legs. Bulls that grow cunning with having bene often bated will stand by their stakes, that they may have the full lenght of their chain to run at the dogs. Sometimes they will scrape a hole to put their noses in. Butchers throw pepper into the noses & eares of the bulls to make them madder.

Bare Bating

Blank space on page after title, apparently left for insertion of further text.

If a bare rise as a dog is comming, the dog rises with him to catch him by the face. The bare grasps him with his fore feet. The danger is then of the bares bending backwards & breaking the dogs back.

Honie pegd in a bone & throwne among bares makes them fight one with another.

Crabs sets their teeth on edge & keeps them from biting. Striking bares upon the toes, or hurting them any where, makes them madder & more furious.

Men, horses, dogs, as greyhounds, hounds &c., run for wagers. They that kill the hare first or give the first turne &c. win.

Haukes fly for wagers.

273–4 *blank*; 275   **[Duelling, Wrestling &c.][363]**

Men wrestle.

Blank space left for further text to be added.

Fight at Fisties Cuffes is fighting with their hands clutched.

With cudgels.[364] The cudgels are made of hard short staves.

They strike with the end **C**. At the other end is a hilt of straw &c., left open on one side for them to put their hands into, to hold the middle of the cudgel **n**. They strike with one cudgel in the right hand, and keepe of blowes with another cudgel in the left hand. Hee that bleeds first is beaten.

Back Sword when they fight with swords, striking as they doe with cudgels.

Single Rapier, which is the ordinary way of fighting in duels, is when they dont strike but thrust at one another with rapiers or tucks. Every thrust is called a Passe.

Sword & Buckler. They hold the buckler to defend themselves with the left hand & strike with a sword in their right. A staffe goes crosse the hollow of the buckler in the inside, the middle of which, **o**, they grasp with their left hands.

276   Seconds either fight themselves, or onely stand by and see faire play, & are readie with salves &c. to dresse the wounds.

277–378

Pages 290–379 incorrectly paginated in MS as follows: pp. 290–91 (280–81); 292–3 (291, 290); 294–316 (292–314); 317 (304); 318 (315); 319 (306); 320–27 (317–24); 328 (324); 329–79 (326–75).

---

363. Although the notes on this page are incomplete, Willughby's Index supplies the title of what was intended on page 275.

364. *with*] inserted in left margin.

[Superstitions and Customs][365]   379

Page 379 incorrectly paginated as 376 in MS.

Making of Crosses for good luck.

Setting up a stick perpendicularly and letting it fall of it selfe, when a man is indifferent to two designes. The falling of the stick determines him.

Throwing up the silver coloured *[blank in manuscript]*[366] under the row in herrings to the seeling,[367] to see whither a woman ly streight in her bed. If that light streight, then she lys streight &c.[368]

Ill luck to heare a pie chatter, or a signe of strangers [369]

If the first lambe you see bee with his face towards you, it is a signe of[370] good luck; with his taile, of ill luck.[371]

Th[e] flying of birds on the left hand, crossing of hares before you, is ill luck.[372]

Whats one is doing the first time hee heares the cuckow shall bee the most of his imployment all the yeare.[373]

Incorrectly paginated as 377–9 in MS.   380–82 *blank*

Blank; not paginated in MS.   383

---

365. The following notes on superstitions and customs are at the end of the volume, separated from the body of the text by almost 100 blank pages. The material is not referred to in Willughby's classified index. The heading has been added by the editors.

366. The space left for the identification of the part of the herring in question (the glutineous membrane located under the backbone) is curious in the light of Willughby's expert knowledge of fish dissection.

367. *to the seeling*] interlineated.

368. The divinatory use of the herring is attested from the nineteenth century: girls would cast the silvery coloured membrane against the wall, the shape in which it adhered being taken to indicate the appearance of their future husbands (Opie and Tatem 1989: 198).

369. A superstition recorded by Bourne (1725: 71) and Brand (1777: 93); cf. Opie and Tatem (1989: 235).

370. *a signe of*] interlineated.

371. This superstition survived into the nineteenth and twentieth centuries; see Opie and Tatem (1989: 156–7).

372. For superstitions pertaining to the flight of birds, see Bradford and Radford (1961: 50), Opie and Tatem (1989: 111, 113–14); on hares see Bourne (1725: 70), Brand (1777: 87), Opie and Tatem (1989: 190–91).

373. A superstition still current in the nineteenth century; see Opie and Tatem (1989: 113).

384

On the last page of the volume there is a figure made with a compass,
apparently illustrating perpetual motion.

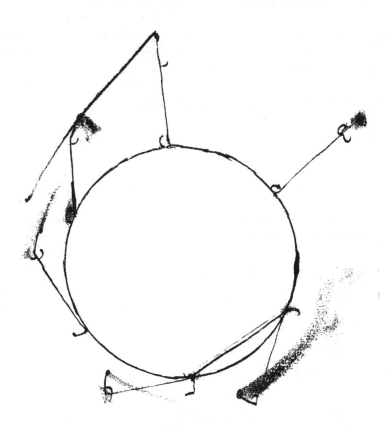

Appendices

1

The Flyleaf to the Book of Games

The first page of the Book of Games, which by its omission from Willughby's pagination seems to have originally served as a blank flyleaf, bears scribbled jottings of the names of various games, clearly used in the production of the text. The games are in random order, some written with the volume turned through 90° or 180°. The majority are in Francis Willughby's own hand, but vary in style and formality of composition, indicating that the notes were made on a number of different occasions. They appear occasionally to have been written in groups, apparently reflecting one session of work, rather than the structured grouping of particular types of games. In a few cases, games appear twice in different parts of the page. A small number of entries are in the child's hand which is responsible for many of the childhood games in the text itself. The possible importance of this page as evidence of the development of the work is discussed in the Introduction (above, Section 2.3). Identification of the games in question is frequently difficult. Many entries have been crossed out (which can make them difficult to read); on the evidence of the Book of Games itself, such cancellation can usually be taken to indicate that the game in question had been dealt with, although illegibility or the use of variant names for games sometimes leaves an uncertainty. This is increased in the few cases on the margin where the paper has suffered water damage and loss of paper.

Games which are named on the flyleaf and which either appear in the Book of Games itself or can clearly be identified are all listed in the Glossary of Games. This includes probable identifications where the name on the flyleaf has a fairly obvious association with a group of games, though not commonly known under Willughby's given title (e.g. Drop Pinne). Footnotes to the text below are limited to the few cases where a game has not even this approximate identification, or to points of obscurity in the text. In this transcription, italic is used for the entries in the child's hand, and a strikethrough identifies the games which are crossed out.

	~~Hummers~~	~~Charter House~~	
Capce dixere[1]	~~Whole Almon~~	~~Hurling Mr Scippon~~[6]	
	~~Double Tick, Ir:~~[ish][3]~~&c.~~		~~Scotch Hopper~~
		~~Matches Bottons~~[7]	
		~~Double [ha]nd nod[de]~~	
Throing up		~~Faher Fitchard~~	~~CopsHole~~
Bookes[2]			
		~~England & Ireland~~	
		~~Drawing Dun~~	~~Charter House 3 times~~
		~~Trusse a Feale~~[8]	~~Kicking~~ *X X*
		~~Hop Frog~~	~~Kibble Heft~~
		~~Whole Almon~~[9]	
~~Shittlecock~~[4]		~~Charter Hous~~	
~~Cropping Oaks~~		~~Hummers~~	~~Stealing 5 Colts~~[16]
~~Buying Bees~~			
~~Buying Mustard~~		~~Shovel Board~~	~~Bare Bating~~
~~Mill Stones~~			
~~Hockcockles~~		~~10 Pegs~~	
~~Handiback~~		~~9 Holes~~	~~Hunting a Dear~~
~~Throwing a Cocks~~		~~Chock Stone~~	~~in my Lords Parke~~
		~~Trole Madame~~	
			~~Tick Tack~~
	~~Fistie Cuffes, Cudgels, Rapier~~		
	~~Back Sword, Sword & Buckler~~		
		Chock Stone	
		H:[eads and][10] ~~points~~ *X X*	
		Tricks with Paper	~~Selling of~~
~~Crosse Sticks~~[5]		Strings &c. *X*	~~Bargaines~~
		~~Pennie Prick~~	~~Crossing of Proverbs~~
		~~Drop Glove~~	
		~~Barly Breaks~~	~~Crosse Questions~~
Tiring Irons			~~Riming~~
			~~Capping of Verses~~
		~~Hannikin canst abide it~~	
		~~Kitcat~~	
		~~Dan[c]ing Top~~[11]	~~Robin [Ali]fe~~
		~~A Foole who Bobed~~	~~Riddles~~
			~~X-mass G[ambols]~~
Preye Dame Coales			*Drop Pinne*
Lend me your		[Knave No]dde[12]	*[Slider] Pinne*[17]
Skimer			Shewing the
		~~Horsing~~	Wild Colt
Cook Stoole		Jo: By Jo:[13]	Whirlie Gigs 22[3][18]
		~~Jack art a sleep~~	
		Milking	*Fire and [no]*
		C[orm]Buck[14]	*Smoke*
		Herne[15]	

1.   Unidentified; possibly a garbled Latin reference to Capping of Verses.

2.   Unidentified.

3.   The abbreviation has been expanded.

4.   This and the next six entries below are written with the book inverted.

5.   Written with the book inverted.

6.   The text on Hurling in the Book of Games (p. 155/i) was supplied by Philip Skippon.

7.   Unidentified; possibly two separate entries. 'Matches' could refer to the making of matches from playing cards described on p. 52 of the manuscript; buttons were used for a number of children's games in place of counters or marbles.

8.   Beneath 'Trusse a Feale' is a single illegible word, heavily crossed out.

9.   This and the two entries below are written with the book inverted.

10. Abbreviation has been extended to suggest probable identification of the game.

11. Unidentified; possibly 'Dan[c]ing Top'; see Top in the Glossary of Games.

12. Unidentified; possibly a variant form of Noddy, see Glossary of Games.

13. 'By' inserted between the words 'Jo: Jo:'

14. Unidentified; possibly a variant form of Cambuc, an early name for Bandy Ball.

15. Unidentified; perhaps the underlying word is 'horn', see Horn Billets in the Glossary of Games.

16. Unidentified; written at 90° to the rest of the text.

17. Unidentified; see Drop Pin and Put Pin in the Glossary of Games.

18. The description of Whirlie Gigs appears on p. 223.

2

Willughby on the Rebounding of Tennis Balls

These observations on the effect of 'spin' on the rebounding of tennis balls are from Willughby's Commonplace Book (NUL Mi LM 15/1, p. 350). They occur in a section containing a variety of material relating to geometry, the range of which indicates that Willughby's mathematical interests in games included experimental concerns about the mechanical laws which underlie the physical aspects of games, as well as more abstract speculation concerning the numerology of games and its putative connection with ancient astronomical lore, which recurs throughout the Book of Games. In the same section of the Commonplace Book there is a related cross-reference: 'V: mr Jessops lettres de Angulo contactus 11. 12. 13. 14. & Dr Wallises Book of that subiect' (p. 338): the letters are presumably by Francis Jessop but have not been identified; the book by John Wallis is almost certainly his *Mechanica: sive De motu, tractatus geometricus* (1670). As we have seen, Willughby also involved himself in debate with members of the Royal Society on the general theory of motion (above, Introduction, Section 1.4 and 4.2).

If a tennis ball be so strooke with the racket that besides the direct motion forwards it get a verticity about its own center, when it has once reflected from the floore of the tennis court at **B** & coming afterwards to rebound from the wall at
C it rebounds contrarie to the rules of reflection and towards the same side from which it comes.

Q: The cause.[1] **Q:** Whither it reflect at **B** as it would doe had it no verticity. *X X X*

Whither the reflection at **B** bee any thing to the contrary reflection at **C** and whither it would not doe so though it never touched the ground. If it comes streight upon the wall at **C** it falls downe to **D** without rebounding at all.

---

1. cause] *replaces cancellation* reason.

The reason must bee[2] from the verticity about the center for in this onely it differs from another ball. The ball then strooke from **A** and mooving towards **C D** with a verticity allso turning the same way and rebounding at **C**, it would be carried towards **A** had it no verticity. But the verticity beeing now against the direct notion and carriing it still towards **C D**, if the verticity carry it just as fast forwards as the direct motion after the rebound dos backwards, it will fall directly downe to **D**. But if the direct motion bee a little stronger it will come out a little towards **B**. If weaker, and the wall **C D** did not stop it, it would bee carried beyond **C D** the same way. *X X*

Experiments should bee made with round Boules thrown hard against a wall, *X X* with tennis balls reflected at all angles and an exact calculation made of the difference of the angles, *X X* and whither a ball strooke with a contrarie verticity would not rebound[3] as other balls but with a bigger angle *X* & would have[4] a contrarie effect. *X X X*

2.   must bee] *replaces cancellation* seems to bee that all the while.

3.   rebound] *replaces cancellation* reflect.

4.   have] *followed by cancelled* quite.

Skippon on Games

These observations are from Philip Skippon's travel diary *A Journey through Part of the Low-Countries, Germany, Italy and France* (Skippon 1732) recording the continental expedition he made in the company of Willughby and Ray. Skippon was a collaborator in more than one of Willughby's projects: he also helped to collect language samples on the continental trip using Willughby's prompt-list (above, Introduction, Section 1.3). It is perhaps significant for the 'local' scope of the Book of Games that Skippon was asked to supply materials on Billiards, Tennis and Hurling but was not tapped for records of games brought back from the Continent, some of which presumably Willughby himself must have witnessed, but does not specifically include.

Ridotto[1]

In the carnival time there is a publick allowance of playing at cards in the ridotto, a great hall where, in the night, we saw many large rooms fill'd with gamesters. Several *Venetian* noblemen sate before a table and a heap of gold; and many that play'd with them were in masquerade. In a cloister underneath were many porters and water-men playing. The game is basset, after this manner: he that keeps the bank or stock of money, shuffles the cards; then any one that stakes what he pleases, names a card, as ace, two, &c. no matter of what suit; then the banker turns the cards with their faces upwards, and deals two at a time, laying them down by him till the card comes, which, if first of the pair, the dealer wins; but if the second of the pair, the other wins. When that card is dealt out, another card is named, and so on till they be dealt; and if the card call'd for be the last of the first pair, the banker loses nothing; but if it be the first of the first pair, he wins two thirds of the stake, which is the advantage the dealer has by a fasard (this being so call'd). As many as will, may play at a time; but they must carefully mark their card. If the card named be in the first pair before the pack be turned with

---

the faces upwards, it is no fasard, for either the dealer or the other wins, as the card is first or last. Many that play, come in masquerade, win or lose a great deal of money, go away and never speak a word. The banker is obliged to pay as far as his bank will; but if he hath not enough, he leaves his bank to the winner, and goes his way.

Che gioco guadagna, che melle perde, che taglia ariecha, is a proverb.

The cards in use here are the same in number with ours, and are divided into four suits, *viz.* 1. *Spadi,* 2. *Bastioni,* 3. *Denari,* 4. *Copi,* being differently painted from ours. The king is known by his crown; the cavallo, or a man on horseback, is instead of the queen; and the fanti or footman instead of the knave.

Gioco d'amore[2]

The Italians have a sport which they call *Gioco d'amore (digitorum lusus seu micatio)* which is thus: two stand together with their hands clutch'd, and both of them, just at the same time, jerk out their hands, and stretch out what number of fingers they please, each of the players naming a number; and he that chances to name the number of the fingers thrown out by both parties, wins, *Ex. gr.* if one throws out three, and the other two, and says five, he wins; but if both hit on the same number, and say five, neither win. A game or set is to win the first five, ten, &c. All the art is in speaking the number, jerking out the hand, and stretching out the fingers in the same instant of time; for if they should not do so, he that can see the others finger first stretched out, might always win. Three, four, or more may play together; but usually there are but two, tho' many will very attentively look on.

This was a sport among the old *Romans,* for *Cicero,* in his offices, page 129, speaks of a common proverb; *Cum enim fidem alicujus, bonitasque laudant, dignum esse dicunt, qui in tenebris Mices (i.e. Mices digitis)* i.e. such a one is a very honest man, you may trust him.

Making of Cards[3]

The making of cards was observ'd by us in this place: First they take a sheet of fine pastboard, and upon that lay a pastboard of the same bigness, which hath holes cut in it where they should paint; for the several colours they have such a pastboard; after they are press'd, cut and smooth'd, they take sheets of papers printed with a lyon, or any other figure, as often as there are cards in the pastboard, and these sheets being cut into the bigness of the cards, they press and cut smooth, and after that starch one to each card on the backside,

---

2.   From the section on Venice (Skippon 1732: 520–21).

3.   From the section on Padua (Skippon 1732: 533); see Glossary of Games under 'Cards'.

and then smooth them and press them a great many times together between two smooth plates of iron. A pack of these cards is sold for 20 soldi.

4

Ray on Hurling

This description of hurling is taken from John Ray's account of the journey to Cornwall in 1662 on which he was accompanied by Willughby ('Itinerary III', Derham 1760: 290–92, reprinted in Lankester 1846: 193–4). The entry is for Saturday, 5 July. Ray's description of hurling can be compared with that of Philip Skippon, which is included in Willughby's Book of Games (p. 155/i), and with the 'larger account' by Richard Carew in his *Survey of Cornwall* (1602: 73ᵛ–75ᵛ), to which Skippon refers.

We had an Account of the *Hurling-Play* much used in Cornwall. There are two kinds of *Hurling*, the *In-hurling* and the *Out-hurling*. In the first there are chosen 20 or 25 of a side, and two Goals are set up; then comes one with a small hard Leather Ball in his Hand, and tosses it up in the midst between both Parties; he that catches it endeavours to run with it to the furthermost Goal; if he be stopped by one of the opposite Side, he either saith I will stand, and wrestles with him, letting fall the Ball by him, (which one of the opposite Side must not take up, but one of his own) or else throws away the Ball to one of his own Side, (if any of them can catch it). He that is stopped may chuse whether he will wrestle, or throw away the Ball, but it is more generous to wrestle. He that stops must answer, and wrestle it out. When any one wrestles, one of his Side takes up the Ball, and runs with it towards the Goal, till he be stopped, and then, as before, he either wrestles or throws away the Ball, so that there are commonly many Pairs wrestling at once. An *Out-hurling* is played by one Parish against another, or eastern Men against western, or *Devonshire* Men against *Cornish*; the manner they enter upon it is as follows. Any one that can get Leave of a Justice, &c. goes into a Market-Town, with a little wooden Ball in his Hand, plated over with Silver, and there proclaims the *Hurling*, and mentions the Time and Place. They play in the same manner as in the other, only they make the Churches their Goals, that Party which can cast the Ball into, or upon a Church, wins. In an *Out-hurling* they have not a set Number on each Side, but each have as many as they can procure. An *Hurler*, to help him in running, may catch hold on an Horseman's Stirrup. No Horsemen play.

Glossaries

1

Glossary of Games

This glossary is intended to offer a brief orientation to the history and morphology of the games mentioned by Willughby, to elucidate Willughby's descriptions where necessary, and to provide guidance for readers who may wish to investigate the games further. Page references in the manuscript are given for each entry, with the primary description of each game given in **boldface**. Headword spellings are normalized where a clear modern equivalent exists; manuscript spellings are noted in square brackets. Headwords in *italics* indicate names not used in the manuscript. 'FL' indicates the occurrence of a word on the flyleaf.

Modern works on the history of games are numerous but uneven. The material in this glossary is suggestive rather than exhaustive; where possible it emphasizes sources that will lead the reader to further bibliography. A variety of resources have been mined for the purpose. There exist a number of valuable modern studies on the history of games. Joseph Strutt's *Sports and Pastimes of the People of England* (1903 [1801]) is quite dated, but ultimately underlies much of the subsequent work in the field. Henri-Réné d'Allemagne's series of profusely illustrated volumes on various classes of pastimes is a valuable resource focusing on Continental sources. Most other key modern sources focus on specific types of games; see for example the bibliographies below on Ball Games, Cards, Chess, Children's Games, Tables and Tennis.

Historians investigating early games and sports have made use of a diverse range of primary sources. In addition to texts specifically on games, discussed in Chapter 3 of the Introduction, a variety of incidental sources are helpful, including court records (both civil and ecclesiastical); allusions in poetry, plays and in moralizing literature; and personal diaries, a genre increasingly common in Willughby's century. One of the most accessible resources for bringing the researcher into instant contact with primary resource material is the *Oxford English Dictionary*, heavily cited in this glossary for its inclusion of passages from early texts that elucidate the history of specific games; the *Middle English Dictionary* can be used in a similar fashion. Games have also left a substantial body of visual and physical evidence, in contemporary depictions of games and their equipment, and in surviving artifacts. The former are readily accessible through the kinds of sources cited in this glossary; the latter are for the most part scattered across the published records of archaeological sites and museum collections.

A Fool Who Bobbed Thee
[A Foole Who Bobed, A Foole Who Bobed Thee: FL, **231**]
This is probably to be identified with the games of Bob-and-Hit and Bob-Fool, attested in sixteenth- and seventeeth-century texts; it resembles the French game of *Qui féry*. Medieval English sources refer to similar games called Bobbed and Abobbed. As described in one early fifteenth-century manuscript, Bobbed resembled Hot Cockles in that the victim lay in a prone position, but he was struck on the head as in A Fool Who Bobbed Thee. The game has obvious echoes of the Buffetting of Christ.

Brewster (1959: 20); *MED* **bobet, abobbed**; Mehl (1990: 112–14); *OED* **bob** v¹; Owst (1961: 510)

See also **Blindman Buff**; **Hock Cockles**

Archery
See **Shooting**

Babies
See *Toys*

Back Sword
See **Duelling**

Backgammon
[Back Gammon, Backgammon: 1, **43**; double hand Backgammon: **43**]
This English game appears to have been an early seventeenth-century innovation, combining the initial set-up of Irish with the rule in some other Tables games, such as Doublets, by which a roll of doubles was played twice or entitled the player to an extra turn.

Cotton (1930: 75–6); Holme (2001: iii.16.2.29a.); Murray (1952: 122); *OED* **backgammon**

See also **Doublets, Irish, Tables**

Ball
[1, 3/iii^v, 13/i^r ff., 14/i^r ff., 15/i^r ff., 155, **167–9**, etc.]
Ball games are very ancient, having been known to the ancient Egyptians as well as to the Greeks and Romans. The ordinary solid ball described by Willughby on p. 167 was sometimes called a 'hand ball' or 'yarn ball'. The tennis ball as described by Skippon is similar in construction (p. 15/i^v). The

combination of the hard packthread around a springy woollen core gave the ball a degree of bounce; similar balls are still used in Real Tennis. Solid wooden balls were used in such games as Bowls, Ten Pegs, and Pell Mell; solid ivory balls featured in Billiards and certain forms of Bowls. The inflated ball, described by Willughby in his account of Football (p. 155), consisted of a bladder encased in leather. The bladder was blown full of air and tied off at the mouth.

Willughby's description of the catching of a ball on pages 168–9 is somewhat difficult to interpret. The most coherent explanation would have the left hand held parallel to the horizon, thumb away from the body, with the right hand vertical, fingers pointing up, and the heel resting on the little-finger side of the left hand; catching a ball would involve clapping the fingers of the right hand down on the thumb of the left. Such a position would seem to allow for little flexibility in the arms, but it would stop the ball with the heel and palm of the right hand, preventing harm to the fingers. Willughby's observation that ball players fold the cuffs of their gloves over to protect their hands (p. 167) is predicated on the design of seventeenth-century gloves, which typically had long, flaring cuffs.

D'Allemagne (1902: 300); D'Allemagne (1903: 145 ff., 157, 161–2); Henderson (1947: 19–21, 63, 117); Holme (2001: iii.16.2.41, 42); Hyde (1694a: 250 ff.); *OED* **hand-ball, yarn-ball**; Scaino (1984: 95–6, 102); Souter (1622: 205 ff.); Strutt (1903: 80–82, 83)

See also **Bandy-Ball**; **Billiards**; **Bowls**; **I Call and I Call**; **Football**; **Hurling**; **Nine-Holes**; **Pell-Mell**; **Stoolball**; **Stowball**; **Ten Pegs**; **Tennis**

Bandy-Ball
[Bandie Ball: 1, **170**]
Versions of this game are well attested from the Middle Ages onward, and it continues to be played under the name Hockey or Field Hockey. The name Bandy, Bandy-Ball, or Ball and Bandy appears between the seventeenth century and the nineteenth. The game also existed on the Continent; it was known in French as *la crosse*.

D'Allemagne (1903: 152, 207); Gomme (1894–98: i, 16, 55, 98, 216–18; ii, 191–2); Henderson (1947: 39–46, 85–90, 114–20); Holme (2001: iii.16.5.91a); Hyde (1694a: 250–53); Jusserand (1901: 284 ff.); *MED* **camboke, campen**; *OED* **bandy, cammock**; Stella (1969: 41); Strutt (1903: 97–8)

See also **Ball**; **Billiards**; **Football**; **Hurling**; **Pell-Mell**

Barley-Breaks
[Barly Breaks, Barly Breakes: FL, 1, **148–9**]
This game is attested in the *OED* from the mid-sixteenth to the seventeenth century; the nineteenth-century Scots game Barla-Brake was more akin to Willughby's Lilman. Sixteenth- and seventeenth-century authors often allude to this game, especially in the context of rustic flirtation. Some, like Sir Philip

Sidney, suggest that the middle couple was required to keep their hands linked during the chase; others, like Nicholas Breton, imply a version closer to Willughby's. Willughby does not mention that the couples were commonly, perhaps invariably, of mixed sex: with the changing of partners each time, not to mention the chasing and grabbing in between, one can see how the game acquired its erotic connotations. Although Barley-Breaks enjoyed only a relatively brief popularity, there exist a range of comparable running and catching games (Opie and Opie 1969: 124–6, 128–30; Gomme 1894–98: ii, 88–9). The name seems to have had a peculiarly lasting influence: a comparable modern game is called How Many Miles to Barley Bridge (Gomme 1894–98: i, 231–8; Opie and Opie 1969: 125–6), and 'Barley' was recorded in the twentieth century as a truce-word in Tick (Opie and Opie 1969: 62–3).

Breton (1607); Gomme (1894–98: i, 21–3); Holme (2001: iii.16.5.91a); Newell (1883: 52–3); OED **Barley-break**; Opie and Opie (1969: 129–30); Sir Philip Sidney ('Lamon's song', ll. 205 ff., in Sidney 1962: 247 ff.); Sir John Suckling ('A Barley Break', in Suckling 1971: 18–19)

See also **Lilman**; *Running and Races*; **Tick**

Bearbaiting, Bullbaiting, *Dogfights*
[Bare Bating: FL, **271**; Bull Bating, Bul Bating, Bull Batings: 1, 269, **271**; they fight … dogs: 270]
The spectator sport of baiting bears and bulls with dogs had been known in England since the Middle Ages, and was not finally outlawed until the mid-nineteenth century. In the seventeenth century baiting was popular in both urban and rural areas; onlookers laid wagers on the outcome of the fights. Bullbaiting was often organized by butchers, as it was thought to make the meat tender prior to slaughter. Willughby's description of the sport is rather neutral in tone, but in his account of his travels in Spain he is more forthcoming on the subject of Spanish bullfighting:

The most noble sport in Spain is the *Jeu de Taureau*, or Bull-fighting, practised at *Valentia, Madrid*, &c. At *Madrid* 3 times in the year, where in the Market-place a brave Don on horseback, and a great many pages on foot fight with a wild Bull: When one Bull is killed or much wounded they turn in another. Seldom but some of the pages are killed. And with these cruel and bloody spectacles the people are much delighted, as were the *Romans* of old in the times of Heathenism.

(Willughby in Ray 1673: 499)

Billett (1994: 25 ff., 29–30); Brand and Ellis (1913: 533–5); Brewster (in Avedon and Sutton-Smith 1971: 29–30); Crosfield (1935: 85); D'Allemagne (1905: 172–4); Leggatt (1991); MED **baiten**; OED **bear-baiting, bull-baiting**; Scott (1974: 134–5); Strutt (1903: 204–9); Vale (1977: 128–30, 132–3)

See also **Cockfighting**; **Throwing at Cocks**

Beast
[Beast, Beste, Best, Le Beste: 1, 57, **79–81**]
This game first appears in England in the latter half of the seventeenth century. The earliest reference in English appears to be in Urquhart's translation of Rabelais from 1653 (Rabelais 1653: 93). The game appears to have been a recent French import, as Willughby suggests. Beast seems to have died out by the end of the eighteenth century, although the element of the beast survived in the related games of Ombre and Quadrille.

Cotton (1930: 73); Depaulis (1987: 46–8); Holme (2001: iii.16.2.47); La Marinière (1665: 72–4); *OED* **Beast 8. a.**; Parlett (1991: 196 ff.)

See also **Cards**

Billiards
[Biliards, Billiards: 1, **14/i**ʳ **ff.**, 167]
Billiards is a game of Continental origins, first attested in England in the late sixteenth century. It ultimately derives from an outdoor game akin to Golf and Croquet. In fact, the billiard stick described by Skippon was closer in shape to a golf-club than to a modern billiards cue, being curved, with a broad rectangular head. Billiards was principally a game of the wealthy, a feature of the game not mentioned by Willughby or Skippon. The game of Trucks was also played on a billiards-table in this period.

Anon. (1696: 324–32); Brewster (1959: 30); Cotton (1930: 12 ff.); D'Allemagne (1903: 256 ff.); Diderot and D'Alembert (1778–79: s.vv. **belouses, masse, queue, table de billard**); Henderson (1947: 121–3); Holme (2001: iii.5.8.147; iii.16.2); Howlet (1684: 184–202); Jusserand (1901: 320 ff.); La Marinière (1654: 117–21); *OED* **billiards, trucks**; Strutt (1903: 239–40)

See also **Ball**; **Bandy-Ball**; **Pell-Mell**

Blindman Buff, Blind Buck a Davie
[Blindmanbuffe, Blind Mans Buffe: 3, **221**; Blind Buck a Davie: **221**]
This ancient and widely international game was not exclusively a children's pastime (cf. Pepys 1970–83: v, 357). It was particularly popular during the Christmas season. The name Blindman Buff first appears in the sixteenth century, but versions are well attested in medieval art. The game has been known by many names: Willughby's variant Blind Buck a Davy survived into recent times as Blind Bucky-Davy in Somerset and Cornwall. The 'fantastical names' given to the players in Willughby's version are echoed in the modern game of Animal Blindman's Buff, in which the players caught must make animals noise to help the catcher identify them (Brewster 1953: 16).

Brewster (1953: 12–16); Brewster (1959: 30); Cotgrave (1611: s.vv. **clignemusset, savate**); D'Allemagne (1905: 218–30); Endrei and Zolnay (1986: 89); Gomme (1894–98: i, 36–40, 285); Holme (2001: iii.16.5.91a); Hyde (1694a:

265–7); Newbery (1967: 78); Newell (1883: 162–3); *OED* **blind-man's-buff**, **hoodman-blind**; Opie and Opie (1969: 118–20); Strutt (1903: 308)

See also **A Fool Who Bobbed Thee**; **Handiback**; **Hock Cockles**

Bowls

[Boules: 1, 3/ii^r, 3/iii^v, 14/i^v, 167, **240–4**, 251]
This game is well attested from the Middle Ages onwards. It was widely spread across Europe in the seventeenth century, and continues to be played as Bowling in England, *pétanque* in France, and *bocce* in Italy. The game was often the subject of legal prohibitions, more because of its encouragement of gambling and idleness among commoners than for any immorality inherent in the game itself. In fact, as Willughby hints, the game was sufficiently gentle to be enjoyed by women as well as men (p. 244).

Brewster (in Avedon and Sutton-Smith 1971: 31–2); Cotton (1930: 22); D'Allemagne (1903: 239 ff.); Holme (2001: iii.16.2.46–7); Howlet (1684: 129–32); Markham (1615: 108–9); Mehl (1990: 51 ff.); Strutt (1903: 216–19)

See also **Ball**; **Nine Holes**; **Ten-Pegs**

Bullbaiting
See **Bearbaiting, Bullbaiting**

Bum to Busse
[**231**]
The tumbling-trick described by the juvenile hand of the manuscript was known in French as *pet-en-gueule*, and is well attested in continental sources of the sixteenth and seventeenth centuries. Urquhart's translation of Rabelais (1653) renders *pet-en-gueule* as 'Bum to Busse, or nose in breech' (Rabelais 1973: 103; Rabelais 1653: 96), which is as close as we can come to an English name for the trick. The term 'Christmas gambol' seems normally to have meant a kind of tumbling trick associated with Christmas festivities, as mentioned in *The Taming of the Shrew* (Ind.ii.134): 'Is not a comonty [i.e. comedy] a Christmas gambol, or a tumbling-trick?' Such acrobatics could also be called Yule games, as in Randle Cotgrave's gloss for *pet-en-gueule*, 'The name of an Yew-game' (Cotgrave 1611).

D'Allemagne (1903: 23, 328–34); Endrei and Zolnay (1986: 27); *OED* **Christmas**; Stella (1969: 34)

See also **Christmas Gambols**

Buying Bees
[Buying Bees, Buying of Bees: FL, **229**]
The buzzing and striking in this game recall the game *la mouche* in Jacques Stella's *Jeux et plaisirs d'enfance* (1657) (cf. **Buying Mustard**), but overall the game more closely resembles a family of Continental games including the

Italian *civetino* and Spanish *abejón*. Illustrations of *civetino* show three boys in a row, the one in the centre with his hands held palms together, sometimes in front of his mouth as if making some sort of noise into them; the other two meanwhile hold one hand out as if to strike him, while leaning backwards to avoid a blow. Minsheu describes the game of *abejón* ('Hornet') in terms very similar to Willughby's Buying of Bees. In French the game is called *abattre le chapeau*: some illustrations show the middle boy wearing a hat, evidently a target to be knocked off by the other two. Versions of this game are also illustrated in the early fourteenth-century Flemish *Romans d'Alexandre* (Bodleian MS 264, ed. James 1933: f. 98ʳ, 125ʳ), in one case with the boys sitting on stools.

D'Allemagne (1905: 243–6); Endrei and Zolnay (1986: 90, 92); Minsheu (1617: s.v. **abejón**)

Buying Mustard

[Buying Mustard, Buying of Mustard: FL, **229**]

This game resembles *la mouche* in Jacques Stella's *Jeux et plaisirs d'enfance* (1657). Stella's engraving depicts one *putto* holding out a round platter and another reaching towards it; the caption reads *Pendant qu'il croque le marmot,/ l'autre, tournant autour du pot,/ Bourdone & contre-fait la mouche;/ N'estant pas encor satisfait,/ Si la peur qu'on a de la touchè/ ne fait plus de mal que leffet* ('While one waits, the other, going round the platter, buzzes and mimics a fly, not yet being sure whether the fear one has of the blow does not hurt more than the real thing') (Stella 1969: 40). The game is echoed in the nineteenth-century Cornish game called Scat, in which one player holds a paper-knife or a thin slip of wood on his palm, which the other tries to snatch away. It also bears a slight resemblance to the nineteenth-century game known as Twirl the Trencher, Spin the Trencher, Turn-Trencher, or Truckle the Trencher.

Brewster (1953: 32); D'Allemagne (1905: 179–80); Gomme (1894–98: ii, 182)

See also **Buying Bees**

Call and I Call
See **I Call and I Call**

Capping of Verses

[Capping of Verses, Capping Verses: FL, 235, **239**]

This pastime is mentioned in texts from the seventeenth century to the nineteenth. As Willughby's description implies, it was used as a Latin exercise in school.

Brewster (1959: 41); Brinsley (1917: 300); Langston (1675); *OED* **cap**, **capper**, **capping**, **Horatian**; Ross (1647); Watson (1968: 95)

See also **Drollery**

Cards
[Cards, Cardes: 1, 3/ii^r, 3/iii^r, **49 ff.**, 150]
Cards seem to have been imported into Europe from western Asia in the fourteenth century. They are not attested in England prior to the early fifteenth century, and English texts on card games do not begin to appear until the latter half of the seventeenth. Willughby's extensive discussion of the subject is the first of its kind in English. As Willughby's description implies, seventeenth-century cards were unwaxed and had no pattern on the back; because the backs eventually acquired natural markings, it was common to replace the cards regularly, which is why they were often recycled as matches. There were no numbers or letters on the cards, and the figures of the court cards were full length, not mirrored images as on modern cards.

Beal (1988); Benham (1957); Cotgrave (1662: 353–71); Cotton (1930: 39 ff.); D'Allemagne (1906); Depaulis (1994; 1997: 11 ff.); Diderot and D'Alembert (1778–79: s.v. **cartier**); Duhamel de Monceau (1984); Dummet (1980); Hargrave (1930); Hoffmann (1973); Holme (2001: iii.16.2.46–7); Horr (1892); Jessel (1905); La Marinière (1651); La Marinière (1654: 1–31); La Marinière (1665: 1–100); *MED* **carde** n.², **carder** n.²; Mehl (1990: 152 ff.); Minsheu (1599: 25 ff.); Parlett (1991); Parlett (1992); Souter (1622: 222–3)

See also **Beast; Cribbage; Gleek; Ging; Hannikin Canst Abide It; Laugh and Lie Down; Loadum; Noddy; One-and-Thirty; One-and-Thirty Bon Ace; Post and Pair; Put; Ruff; Ruff and Trump; Trump; Whehee**

Charter House
[Charter House, Charter Hous, Charter House 3 times, Running 3 times thorough the Charter House: FL (2x), **150**, 157]
This version of 'running the gauntlet' is named after the school in London. The cloister of this former Carthusian monastery, a gallery about 70 yards long and 9 wide, was at least in later years the scene of a vigorous version of football that involved a good deal of shin-kicking.

Magoun (1938: 81–2)

See also **Horsing;** *Running and Races*

Cherry-Stone, Cherry-Pit
[Cherrie-Stone, Cherrie Pit: 3/iii^r, **220**]
A game by these names is attested in the *OED* in the sixteenth and seventeenth centuries; versions were still being played under various names in the nineteenth century, using money, leaden counters, marbles or buttons instead of cherry pits. French illustrations of the sixteenth and seventeenth centuries show a similar game called *la fossette* played with nuts.

Brewster (in Avedon and Sutton-Smith 1971: 32); D'Allemagne (1903: 229, 242); Gomme (1894–98: i, 66, 51, 54–5); Mehl (1990: 103–4); Newell (1883: 87); *OED* **cherry-pit, cherrystone**; Stella (1969: 16)

Chess

[Chest, Chests, Chesse: 3/ii[r], 3/ii[v], 3/ii[r], 17, 150, 255, 256]

Willughby refers to a planned section on Chess (p. 17), and the reference on p. 255 suggests that he may have envisioned placing it with Nine Men's Morris and Fox and Geese; but the section was never actually written. Given the substantial body of prior literature on the subject, he may have found the task rather daunting, or perhaps simply less worthwhile, since the field was already well tilled. By the late seventeenth century Chess had taken essentially its modern form.

Beale (1656); Caxton (1860 [1474]); Cotgrave (1662: 372–87); Cotton (1930: 29 ff.); D'Allemagne (1905: 13–48); Damiano (1562); Furno (1903: 110); Holme (2001: iii.5.8.148; iii.16.2.30–37; iii.16.9.120–22); Hyde (1694a; 1694b); La Marinière (1665: 276–84); Mehl (1990: 32–3); Murray (1913); Souter (1622: 3 ff.); Vale (1977: 137)

Children's Games

[The First Games That Children Learn: 1; Plaies … used most by children: 3/iii[r]; Childrens Plays: **217 ff.**]

Willughby's treatise appears to be the oldest substantial treatment of children's games in any European language, although the subject had been a popular theme in art since the Middle Ages. It is difficult to tell precisely how much of the manuscript Willughby intended to include under the heading 'Children's Plays' on p. 217. In addition to the toys of very young children described at the beginning of this section, the following are clearly included: Put Pin, Heads and Points, Even and Odd, Upper or Nether Choose You Whither, Cross and Pile, Cob Castle, Cobnut, Cherry Pit, Hide and Seek, King Heywood's Park, Hunting a Deer in My Lord's Park, Blindman's Buff, Hummers, Hot Cockles, Tick, Tops, Gigs, Whirligigs.

Several of the subsequent groupings may be intended as subsections of the children's games. The 'Tricks to Abuse and Hurt One Another' (Buying Mustard, Cropping Oaks, Buying Bees, Selling Millstones, Robin Alive) are in the juvenile hand, and the players in Selling Millstones and Robin Alive are explicitly described as boys. The Christmas Gambols (apparently including Bum to Busse, A Fool Who Bobbed Thee, Shoeing the Wild Colt, and the Christmas customs on p. 232), and the games Fire and No Smoke and Jack Art Asleep, were also contributed by the juvenile hand. The games of Drollery, with which Willughby's hand resumes (Selling of Bargains, Riddles, Purposes, Cross Purposes, Gliffs, Capping of Verses, Riming), may also be intended as a continuation of this section, although of these only Selling of Bargains and, arguably, Capping of Verses were primarily children's games.

Other games elsewhere in the manuscript might also be characterized as children's games, although Willughby's alteration of the category 'Used only by children' to 'Used most by children' on p. 3/iii[r] warns us of the difficulty of drawing clear distinctions between juvenile and adult games. Kit-Cat appears to have been primarily a children's game, and some of the games mentioned on the flyleaf (e.g. Chockstones, Truss a Fail) would probably also fall in this category. Whehee, Dust Point, and Penny Prick are in the juvenile hand, although there is evidence that they were sometimes played by adults. The juvenile hand also contributes part of the text on Nine Men's Morris, although this game was also played by adults. Willughby describes a number of the activities of exercise and running as being played by boys (Charter House, Drawing Dun, England and Ireland, Copsole, Kibble Heft, Hop Frog, Tick), and he explicitly states that Father Fitchard is played only by boys.

On the other hand, not all of the games included by Willughby under the heading of children's games were played exclusively by children – Blindman's Buff and Hot Cockles, for example, were also played by adults. Many games were more or less equally associated with children and adults – many of the running games, ball games, and comparable sports would fall into this category.

Ariès and Margolin (1982: 469–621); Brewster (1953); Gomme (1894–98); Holme (2001: iii.16.2.42; iii.16.5.91a); Newell (1883); Opie and Opie (1969); Sorel (1657: i, 204 ff.); Stella (1969); Strutt (1903: 300–13)

See also **Christmas Gambols**; **Drollery**; *Toys*; **Tricks to Abuse and Hurt One Another**

Chock-Stone
[Chock Stone: FL]
Willughby does not describe this game, which appears twice on the flyleaf – once crossed out along with Ten Pegs, Nine Holes and Troll Madam, and once uncancelled, in the company of Put Pin, Tricks with Paper, and Penny Prick. The cancellation presumably took place when Willughby noticed that this game was mentioned twice on the page.

The game probably belongs to the 'Hucklebones' family, which includes Check-Stone, Chuckie Stanes, and Jackstones. In these games a number of pebbles or comparable objects are deposited on a flat surface, and the player tosses a stone, ball or similar object into the air. The object of the game is to manipulate the pebbles in some manner (e.g. picking up a certain number), and then catch the ball before it hits the ground; the specific rules vary greatly.

However, the game could belong to the same family as Cherry-Pit (q.v.), as in the nineteenth-century game of Chock or Chock Hole, which involved throwing marbles at a hole in the ground.

Brewster (1953: 136–42); D'Allemagne (1905: 75 ff.); Gomme (1894–98: i, 66, 67–8, 69, 122–9, 239–40, 259); Holme (2001: iii.16.5.91a); *OED* **check-stone**

Christmas Gambols
[Christmas Gambolls, X mass Gambols(?): FL, **231 ff.**]
The term 'Christmas gambol' seems normally to have meant a kind of tumbling trick associated with Christmas festivities (see *Bum to Busse*). In this case, however, Willughby's juvenile informant seems to extend the term 'Christmas gambol' to include a variety of games played at Christmas. The

Christmas season was traditionally a time for the playing of games: legal restrictions on games were eased at Christmas, and the respite in work between Christmas and Twelfth Day allowed time for playing them.

It is not clear which games Willughby's juvenile informant meant to include as Christmas gambols under the heading 'these and those which follow'. The game immediately preceding, Robin Alive, seems likely to be a Christmas game, and Selling of Millstones could conceivably be played indoors. Of the games which follow, A Fool Who Bobbed Thee and Shoeing the Wild Colt both seem to be intended as Christmas sports, particularly since they are followed by a specifically Christmas tradition. In fact, both have documentable Christmas associations: the former closely resembles Hot Cockles, which is known to have been popular at Christmas, and the latter is listed among Christmas sports in a text of the mid-seventeenth century. The following game, Fire and No Smoke, seems a bit too vigorous for indoors, and may therefore break up the Christmas theme, even though Jack Art Asleep, Gliffs and Selling of Bargains are all indoor entertainments which could have been enjoyed at Christmas.

Several other games in the text, such as Blindman Buff, Inch Pinch, and Hot Cockles, as well as games at cards and dice in general, were also common at Christmas, although this is not mentioned in the manuscript.

Furnivall (1877, 1882: 316–17); *OED* **Yule**, **Christmas**; Strutt (1903: 267 ff.)

See also **A Fool Who Bobbed Thee**; **Blindman Buff**; *Bum to Busse*; **Hock Cockles**; **Inch Pinch**; **Robin Alive**; **Shoeing the Wild Colt**

Cob-Castle
[Cob Castle: **219**]
This game is described in Randle Cotgrave's French-English dictionary: '*chastelet*: … the childish game at Cobnut; or (rather) the throwing of a Ball at a heape of Nuts, which done, the thrower takes as many as he hath hit, or scattered' (Cotgrave 1611). Cotgrave seems to agree with Willughby that Cobnut was a different game. Gomme mentions versions of the same game under the names Castles, Cockly Jock, Cogs, Paip and Pyramid. It appears as *la rangette* in Stella (1969: 15).

Gomme (1894–98: i, 60, 72, 76, 77, ii, 36, 89)

See also **Cobnut**

Cobnut
[Cobnut: **219**]
A game by this name is attested in the *OED* as early as 1532; it also appears in the seventeenth century as Jobnut. Variants in later centuries perpetuated such details as the use of the hat and the identification of the nut by the number of its conquests. There are also nineteenth- and twentieth-century analogues for Willughby's verse, used by players to establish priority of play,

such as this one from Cheshire (which clarifies the pronunciation of Willughby's 'hobblete'): 'Cobblety cuts, Put down your nuts' (Gomme 1894–98: i, 78). Cobnuts are a variety of hazelnut: the game is now generally played with horse-chestnuts.

Gomme (1894–98: i, 71–2, 77–9, 297); *OED* **cobnut, job** n.[3]; Opie and Opie (1969: 227–32)

See also **Cob-Castle**

Cockfighting
[1, **268 ff.**]
This internationally practised spectator sport had been known in England since the Middle Ages; in the seventeenth century it was enjoyed by both commons and aristocracy, and had acquired a literature of its own. Cockfighting was condemned by moralists as early as the sixteenth century, but was not made illegal in Britain until the mid-nineteenth, and was still being practised surreptitiously in the twentieth. As with other animal sports, gambling was an essential part of the game. It is unclear what birds Willughby may have had in mind as *aves pugnaces* (p. 270), but versions of the sport used quails.

Billett (1994: 47 ff.); Blome (1686); Brand and Ellis (1913: 325–9); Brewster (in Avedon and Sutton-Smith 1971: 33, 42); Cotton (1930: 100); D'Allemagne (1905: 172–4); Holme (2001: ii.9.5.89); Howlet (1684: 33, 54–4); Markham (1614); Norris and Palmer (1995); Scott (1957); Souter (1622: 217–20); Strutt (1903: 224–6); Vale (1977: 130, 133–4); Wilson (1607)

See also **Bearbaiting, Bullbaiting**; **Throwing at Cocks**

Cook Stool
[Cook Stoole: FL]
The meaning of this is uncertain. The expression was commonly used in the seventeenth century to refer to a 'cucking stool' or 'ducking stool', used to punish petty malefactors by ducking them in the water. In later dialect usage it could mean a chair where misbehaving children were confined as a form of punishment. Whoever added 'Cook Stool' to the flyleaf may have had in mind some form of mock punishment (cf. **Charter House**; **Horsing**), or perhaps a game in which a person was seated over a tub of water; such entertainments are illustrated in medieval manuscripts.

Brand and Ellis (1913: 527, [#26, 35]); *OED* **cuck-stool**; Strutt (1903: 309–10)

Copshole
[Copshole, Copsole: FL, **157**]
Versions of this game can be traced as far back as the Middle Ages: the game is illustrated in the fourteenth-century *Romans d'Alexandre* (Bodleian MS 264, ed. James 1933: f. 100[r]) and in Stella (1969: 36). Paradin in the sixteenth

century calls it *le jeu de la panoye*; Stella calls it *le court baston*. The game was known as Sweer Tree in nineteenth-century Scotland; it was still being played in the twentieth century, as Lifting in England, and as Pulling Swag in the USA. A 'copsole' was a U-shaped iron fitted with a pin through the ends, used to attach tackle to a pole, most notably as part of a plough.

Brewster (1953: 175); Gomme (1894–98: ii, 222); *OED* **copsole**; Opie and Opie (1969: 213–14); Paradin (1989)

See also **Drawing, Lifting, and Throwing**

Cribbage

[Cribbidge, single hand Cribbidge: 1, 3/iiiʳ, 52, 57, 60, 66, 67, 68, **69–70**; a new Cribbidge: **69**; double hand Cribbidge: **70**, 71]
This English card game is first attested in the *OED* in 1630; it was a variant on Noddy invented (according to John Aubrey in the late seventeenth century) by Sir John Suckling. Cribbage was principally an aristocratic game in the seventeenth century, but had become a more ordinary pastime by the eighteenth. The modern game is usually played with six cards rather than Willughby's five.

Cotgrave (1662: 369–71); Cotton (1930: 51); Holme (2001: iii.16.2.47b); Parlett (1991: 128–31)

See also **Cards**; **Noddy**

Cropping Oaks

[Cropping Oaks, Cropping of Oakes: FL, **229**]
This game is not well attested elsewhere, but a version is illustrated in the early fourteenth-century Flemish *Romans d'Alexandre* (Bodleian MS 264, ed. James 1933: f. 3ʳ): two boys are depicted sitting on stools, each with his left hand extended to hit the other, and his right hand protecting his own face.

Cross and Pile

[Crosse & Pile, Crosse or Pile: 3/iiʳ, 15/iᵛ, 164, 175, **218**, 243]
This simple, ancient, and ubiquitous game can be traced to at least the thirteenth century in England. Willughby's principal description of it is as a children's game, but he also records many instances of its use in establishing priority of play in various sports. The game was played on the Continent under various names reflecting the design of the local coinage; the Romans knew it as *caput aut navis*.

D'Allemagne (1905: 146–7); Endrei and Zolnay (1986: 31); Furno (1903: 110); Gomme (1894–98: i, 82); *OED* **cross 21**; Strutt (1903: 266)

See also **Drawing Cuts**

Cross Purposes, Cross Questions

[Crosse Purposes: **237**; Crosse Questions: FL]

These appear to have been interchangeable names for the same game. The names are first attested in English in the seventeenth century; versions persisted into the twentieth century. Willughby seems to categorize this as a children's game, but it was played by adults as well, especially during the Christmas season.

Anon. (1658: 1); Augarde (1984: 167–8); Brewster (1953: 37); Chope (1893); Gomme (1894–98: i, 82); *OED* **cross-purpose, cross-question**

See also **Christmas Gambols; Drollery; Purposes**

Cross Sticks
[FL]
Identity unknown.

Crossing of Proverbs
[FL]
This pastime is alluded to by numerous authors of the sixteenth and seventeenth centuries, beginning with Shakespeare, who calls it 'capping' rather than 'crossing'. The basic structure appears to have been for each participant in turn to produce a proverb which contradicted the previous one.

OED **cap** v., **cross** v, **crossing, master**

See also **Capping of Verses; Drollery**

Cudgels
See **Duelling**

Dice
[17, **19, 21,** 22, **35,** 50, 88, etc.]
Willughby describes dice and their use in the context of games at Tables. He almost entirely omits mention of games played with the dice alone: the sole exception is the allusion to In and In on p. 3/ii^r. The techniques of cheating at dice had been the subject of its own literary genre since the mid-sixteenth century (cf. Cardano 1663: ch. 7; Kinney 1990: 59 ff., 175–6; Rid 1612; Cotton 1930: 6–8). A version of the quaint names for the casts appears in a mid-seventeenth-century collection of proverbs:

Proverbs used at Dice, very frequent among the Western Inn-keepers.
Twelve quoth *Twatt* when it rung noon.
Am's ace, Ambling *Annes*, and trotting *Joan.*
Size deuz, Si Deus nobiscum, quis contra nos?
Sice cinque, When a Queen shites, she needs must stinke.
Quatre tray, Katherine Gray.
Tray deux ace, Passage cometh apace.
Two sixes, Black is my hole quoth *Nan Bentley.*
Foure and five, Whom Fortune favoureth he will thrive.
Cinque tray, Some stood, and some ran away.

Two fives, Two thiefs besides the caster.
Six foure, We shall be all merry within this houre.
Six three, Six Trees will make two pair of Gallowes.
Cinque tray, Some fought, and some run away.

> (Howell 1659: 19; cf. the similar names used by seventeenth-century roofers for various sizes of slates as given in Holme 2001: iii.5.8.150)

Brewster (in Avedon and Sutton-Smith 1971: 33–4); Cotton (1930: 80–84); D'Allemagne (1905: 62–74); Holme (2001: iii.16.2.28–9); Hyde (1694a: 17 ff., 30 ff., 101 ff.); La Marinière (1665: 274–6); Mehl (1990: 76 ff.); Strutt (1903: 245–8)

See also **In and In**; **Tables**

Dogs
See **Bearbaiting, Bullbaiting,** *Dogfights*

Double Backgammon; Double-Hand Cribbage; Double-Hand Noddy; Double-Hand Ruff; Double Irish; Double Ticktack
See **Backgammon**; **Cribbage**; **Noddy**; **Ruff**; **Irish**; **Ticktack**

Doublets
[Dublets: 1, 22, **23 ff.**]
This was also known as Queen's Game: all references to Doublets in the *OED* come from the seventeenth century, but Queen's Game is attested as early as 1554. Versions existed in France under different names. A game called *doblet* occurs in Alfonso X's book of games: it is similar in some respects to this game, although the pieces are played onto the board rather than off.

Alfonso X (1941: 310–13, fol. 74ʳ); Cotgrave (1611: s.vv. **renette, tables rabbatues**); Cotton (1930: 78); Holme (2001: iii.16.2.29a); Murray (1952: 121); *OED* **doublet, Queen 15.**

See also **Tables**

Draughts
[1, 255, 259]
Willughby has a heading for a section on Draughts on page 259, and has even included it in his table of contents, but the section was never written. The game, essentially a combination of the pieces from Tables with the board from Chess, had been in use since the Middle Ages, and is attested in English literature as early as the fourteenth century. The game was also known on the Continent, for example as French *dames* and Spanish *damas*, and there had been some continental literature on the subject prior to Willughby. The game as played in the seventeenth century was essentially the same as the modern version. It is of course known as Checkers in North America.

D'Allemagne (1905: 48–61); Holme (2001: iii.5.8.148c; iii.16.2.37c); Hyde (1694a: 173–95); Mehl (1990: 146 ff.); Murray (1913: 615–16, 733); Murray (1952: 72 ff.); *OED* **draught 22, jeu**

Drawing Cuts

[164]

Drawing cuts, or drawing straws, is a simple form of lottery well attested from the Middle Ages onwards. Willughby mentions it only as a means of choosing the first player in Scotch Hopper, but it was used in a wide variety of contexts.

D'Allemagne (1905: 149); *MED* **cut** n.²; *OED* **cut** n.¹; Opie and Opie (1969: 25)

See also **Cross and Pile**

Drawing Dun Out of the Mire

[Drawing Dun, Drawing Dun Out of the Mire: FL, **157**]

This game may be alluded to by Chaucer, and was still known in the nineteenth century. Other descriptions have the players pulling a stump instead of a person. 'Dun' in this game represents a carthorse.

Brand and Ellis (1913: 537); Brewster (1971: 34); Gomme (1894–98: i, 108–9); Nares (1822: s.v. **dun**); *OED* **dun** n.¹ **5**.; Strutt (1903: 312–13)

Drawing, Lifting, Throwing

[Drawing: 1, **157–8**; Lifting: 1, **157–60**; Throwing: **160**; Pitching the Barre: 1, **160**]

The drawing and lifting games listed on pages 157–8 appear to have been boys' pastimes, but the 'lifting great weights' and similar exercises on p. 160 refer to adult athletics. Various sorts of throwing games had been practised in England since the Middle Ages: objects thrown included stones, hammers (often called 'sledges'), iron bars and pikes. These and other feats of strength had been practised by the medieval warrior aristocracy; by the seventeenth century they seem to have fallen out of favour with the élite, but they were still being practised by country folk, and were featured in Robert Dover's Cotswold Games (Dover 1636: frontispiece).

Holme (2001: iii.16.5.91); *OED* **bar**, **sledge**; Strutt (1903: 61–3, 64–5); Vale (1977: 118–19)

See also **Copsole**; **Drawing Dun out of the Mire**; **England and Ireland**; **Kibble Heft**; **Leaping, Vaulting**; **Wrestling**

Drollery

[Drollery, Drolery: 1, **234 ff.**]

This is the general heading Willughby offers for word games – he specifically mentions Selling of Bargains, Riddles and Purposes, and may also have envisioned Gliffs, Capping of Verses and Rhyming as belonging to the same category.

See also **Capping of Verses**; **Gliffs**; **Purposes, Cross Purposes**; **Riddles**; **Rhyming**; **Selling of Bargains**

Drop Glove
See **Hunting a Deer in My Lord's Park**

Drop Pin
[Drop Pinne: FL]
Identity unknown. For the use of pins in games, cf. **Put-Pin**.

Drudge Cat
See **Horn Billets**

Duelling
[Duelling: 1; Cudgels, cudgel play: FL, 53, **275**; Back Sword, Sword & Buckler, Rapier, Single Rapier: FL, **275**]
Willughby offers only a cursory glimpse of an ancient and popular sport which already had quite a fully developed literature and culture of its own.

The backsword was the traditional English weapon, and characteristically had only one cutting edge; it involved a fighting style based primarily on blows. The rapier was thinner, often longer, and relied more heavily on the point. The sword and buckler was a particularly ancient fencing combination: it had been the characteristic form of sport fencing in the Middle Ages. Cudgels were also termed wasters, single-billets, and sometimes backswords; in later centuries they were called single-sticks. They were similar in use to the backsword. Willughby's list of weapons is not exhaustive: other popular styles of combat included sword and dagger, quarterstaff, and falchion. These sports were used both as private exercises and as public entertainments, with prize monies and betting commonly involved.

A. (1639); Anglo (2000); Hale (1614); Holme (2001: iii.16.5.91; iii.19.1b.22); OED **backsword, billet, cudgel, single-stick, waster**; Swetnam (1617)

See also **Fisticuffs**; **Wrestling**

Dust Point
[Dust Pointe, Dust Point: 1, **236**]
The name Dust Point is attested in the OED only in the seventeenth century. Cotgrave's description of the French game *darde* (1611) offers a description of Dust-Point similar to Willughby's:

Darde. A play, wherein boyes hauing layded a heape of points vnder a stone, and made a circle about them, dard at them with a rod, and win as many as they driue out of that circle; (Our boyes laying their points in a heape of dust, and throwing at them with a stone, call that play of theirs, Dust-Point).

Points, the laces used in tying up clothing, were commonly used by children in gambling, being small and plentiful objects of some small value. There were a number of other games played with points, among them Blow-Point, Spurn-Point Yert-Point and Point in the Hole.

Gomme (1894–98: i, 119); Holme (2001: iii.16.5.91a); *OED* **dust point, spurn point, yert point**; Peacham (1641: 32); Strutt (1903: 312)

England and Ireland
[FL, **157**]
Tug-of-War was known in the nineteenth century as French and English, a name also applied to a chasing game. In the sixteenth century John Higgins mentions a version of the game by the name Sun and Moon. Similar tugs-of-war occurs in the games of Oranges and Lemons and Through the Needle Eye Boys (Gomme 1894–98: ii, 25–35, 289).

Brewster (1953: 176–7); Gomme (1894–98: ii, 183–4, 221); *OED* **French B. 2. b.**; Opie and Opie (1969: 235–6)

Even and Odd
[Even & Odde: **218**]
An ancient game, corresponding to the Roman *par vel impar*, Greek αρτιαζειν; versions have existed across Europe and North America, and were still being recorded in the twentieth century. It was proverbially a children's pastime.

Brewster (1953: 7–8); Furno (1903: 110); Gomme (1894–98: ii, 14); Holme (2001: 16.5.91a); Hyde (1694a: 261); *OED* **even** adj. **15. d.**, **odd** adj. **2. d.**; Souter (1622: 225); Strutt (1903: 305)

Father Fitchard
[FL, 1, **187**]
A version of this game was known as Peg-Fiched in western England in the nineteenth century; another is the twentieth-century American game of Stick, or King Stick. Related games were known on the Continent. The name is apparently connected with the French *fiche*, as in Cotgrave (1611): 'Fiche. A Gardneres dible, or setting yron'.

Brewster (1953: 157–8); Endrei and Zolnay (1986: 123); Gomme (1894–98: ii, 38)

Fencing
See **Duelling**

Fire and No Smoke
[FL, **233**]
This game has a long and successful history under a variety of names, including Round Tag, Fox and Goose, Faggots, Tertia, Touch-Third and Twos and Threes. It has counterparts on the Continent, such as the French *tiers*, *jeu de paquets* and *jeu de fagots*, apparently datable as far back as the fourteenth century.

Brewster (1953: 93–5); D'Allemagne (1903: 64–7); Gomme (1894–98: ii, 144–5, 307); Mehl (1990: 111–12); Opie and Opie (1969: 82–4)

Fisticuffs
[Fistie Cuffes, Fisties Cuffes: FL, **275**]
Willughby's allusion to boxing is rather early. Although fistfighting was practised as a sport in the Classical world, it is virtually unattested in England before the late seventeenth century, and does not appear to have become widely popular until the eighteenth century.

Billett (1994: 44–5); D'Allemagne (1903: 334 ff.); Holme (2001: iii.16.5.91a); *OED* **cudgel**

See also **Duelling**; **Wrestling**

Football
[Football, Foot Ball: 1, **155**, 167, 170]
Football was already a popular game in the Middle Ages. Perhaps the earliest English reference is the *lusus pilae celebrem*, 'the well-known ball-game', played by Londoners on Shrove Tuesday according to William FitzStephen in the twelfth century. The game is well attested in sources of the fourteenth century and later, although many instances could refer either to 'handling' Football, in which the ball may be carried (cf. **Hurling**), or a 'no-handling' version in which it may only be kicked (as in Willughby's description). The earliest certain example of a no-handling version appears in a late medieval account of miracles attributed to Henry VI, which describes Football as a game 'in which young men, in country sport, propel a huge ball not by throwing it into the air but by striking and rolling it along the ground, and that not with their hands but with their feet' (Magoun 1938: 14).

By the seventeenth century, Football seems generally to have implied a no-handling game. This is suggested both by Willughby and by his countryman Richard Lassels, who visited Florence in the middle of the century, and described the Florentine *giuoco di calcio* as 'a play something like our football, but that they play with their hands' (Heywood 1904: 173). Yet even in subsequent centuries the name was also applied to handling games.

Football was distinguished from other ball games of the period not only in being played with the feet, but also in that the ball was filled with air (see **Ball**). Other sources mention a ball filled with beans or peas (Magoun 1938: 19), but such balls would have been hard to kick effectively, and may imply a handling game. Willughby's detail of the quicksilver inside the bladder also features in a trick in a sixteenth-century conjuring book (Hill 1581: C ij^v; also Cotgrave 1655: 133).

Football is one of the games for which Willughby omits mention of social implications well attested by contemporaries. It was a particularly vigorous game, often chaotic, and even downright violent. Willughby's emphasis on the art of tripping is reflected in numerous writings of the sixteenth and seventeenth centuries which suggest that this was an integral part of the game. The violence of the game met with the disapproval of many authors, such as the Puritan Stubbes, who thought the game 'may rather be called a freendly kinde of fight, than a play, or recreation; A bloody and murthering practise, then a felowly sporte or pastime' (Stubbes 1583: 184).

In part perhaps because of the energetic and violent disorder involved, football was often seen as a sport better suited to the multitude than to the gentleman. Aristocrats were sometimes known to play (Magoun 1938: 34, 37–8; Marples 1954: 54–5), but many, like James I, thought the game ill-suited for an aristocrat (Magoun 1938: 92). The game had strongly rustic connotations as a pastime for 'countrey swaines' (Peacham 1969: 81; see also Magoun 1938: 19, 54, 55), although it was also played in urban settings.

Willughby likewise omits mention of Football's seasonal associations. Contemporary allusions to the game suggest that it was characteristically a winter sport, probably because the vigorous exercise involved was best suited for cold weather (Magoun 1938: 19, 24, 32, 33, 39, 54, 57). In particular, it was often featured in Shrovetide festivities. As noted above, Shrovetide football may be indicated by FitzStephen as far back as the twelfth century. Shrove Tuesday football was well established in Chester by 1533 (Magoun 1938: 101–2); the custom persisted in some communities even into the twentieth century (Magoun 1938: 19 ff., 99 ff.).

Bascetta (1978: i, 119–62); Brewster (in Avedon and Sutton-Smith 1971: 36); D'Allemagne (1903: 154 ff.); Gomme (1894–98: i, 134–7); Henderson (1947: 39–46, 79–82); Holme (2001: iii.16.5.91a); Jusserand (1901: 265 ff.); Magoun (1938); Marples (1954); Mehl (1990: 68 ff.); Mulcaster (1581: 111); *OED* **football**; Strutt (1903: 93–7)

See also **Ball**; **Bandy-ball**; **Hurling**; *Running and Races*

Fox and Goose
[1, 255, **256 ff.**]
The name Fox and Goose is attested in the *OED* from 1633 onwards, but the game was already well known in the Middle Ages; the earliest reference in English, dating to the fifteenth century, calls the pieces foxes and hounds. The game had at least a slight history of literature prior to Willughby, most notably in Alfonso X's thirteenth-century treatise on games.

Alfonso X (1941: 364–7, fol. 91ᵛ); Gomme (1894–98: i, 141–2); Holme (2001: iii.16.2.39); Murray (1913: 617); Murray (1952: 101 ff.); *OED* **fox 16. d.**

Gig
See **Top**

Ging
[Ging: 1, 57, **87–8**; 7 Cards: 87]
This very unusual game has left very little trace elsewhere; the only known instance may be a reference to 'Seven Cardes' in the list of card games included in Thomas Crosfield's diary in 1629 (Crosfield 1935: 38). The various hands in this game somewhat recall those of Poker and related games, but as

Willughby remarks, it is a game of pure chance, lacking Poker's element of competitive gambling. The name probably derives from *OED* **ging**, 'company, crew'.

See also **Cards**

Gleek
[Gleek, Gleeke: 1, 3/iii^r, 50, 51, 52, 57, 72, **73 ff.**]
This game is clearly a relative of Ruff and Trump. It is first attested in England in the early sixteenth century, but seems to have fallen out of favour by the mid-eighteenth, when Goldsmith classed it among games 'now exploded, [that] employed our sharping ancestors' (Goldsmith 1762: 56). The French equivalent, *glic*, is attested as early as the mid-fifteenth century.

Cotgrave (1662: 365–8); Cotton (1930: 44); De Lannoy (1875: 241); Depaulis (1990, 1991); Godefroy (1881–90: sv. 1. *glic*); Holme (2001: iii.16.2.47); Lucas (1930: 152); McTear (1899); *OED* **gleek** n.^1; Parlett (1991: 93–5)

See also **Cards**; **Ruff and Trump**

Gliffs
[Gliffes: 1, **234**]
The word 'gliff' is not attested in the standard dictionaries in this sense, but it appears in *The Mysteries of Love & Eloquence* (Anon. 1658: 3). It could derive from Middle English *gliffen*, 'to slip', sometimes used with reference to making a slip in reading. However, this sense is not attested after the fourteenth century. Alternatively, Willughby may be correct in his derivation from Latin *griphus*, 'a riddle'.

The history of the tongue-twister is largely obscure: the *Oxford Guide to Word Games* claims that it came into fashion in the nineteenth century, and cites only one tenuous seventeenth-century example. However, the appearance of tongue-twisters in both Willughby and in *Mysteries of Love & Eloquence* demonstrates that they were a well-established entertainment long before they left any substantial trace in the written record. Other examples may be found in seventeenth-century rounds, including the following example from *The Pinder of Wakefield*:

Three Geese in a pudle, Gigle gagle, gigle gagle,
Three Puddings in a ladle, Wible wable, wible wable.

(Anon. 1632: D2^v; cf. also Ravenscroft 1611: #17)

The Pinder also includes a list of verbal entertainments featuring riddles, tales, catches, and saying 'hard things one after another' (77). The verse on tobacco is included in the second edition of John Ray's *Proverbs* (Ray 1678: 296). Halliwell collected some nineteenth-century versions:

Tobacco wick! tobacco wick!
When you're well, 'twill make you sick;

Tobacco wick! tobacco wick!
'Twill make you well when you are sick.

(Halliwell 1970b: 151)

Tobacco hic,
Will make you well
If you be sick.

(Halliwell 1970a: 170–71)

The line 'Three blue beans in a blue bladder' also appears in a mid-seventeenth-century round (Hilton 1652: 3); a bladder filled with peas was often used as a rattle at the time. The phrase 'Rattle bladder rattle' is mentioned in Ben Jonson's *Bartholomew Fair* (Jonson 1640: i.iv.70), in terms that probably imply its use as a tongue-twister.

Anon. (1658: 3); Augarde (1984: 160 ff.); *MED* **gliffen**; Wallis (1653: 164–5)

See also **Drollery**

Half Almond, Whole Almond
[Halfe Almonde: **161**; Whole Almon, Whole Almond: FL (2x), **161**]
The Half Almond and Whole Almond may take their name from the sixteenth-century dance known from its reputedly German origin as an Almain. The basic step in the dance consisted of three steps forward and a hop – very much as described by Cotgrave, and similar enough to Willughby's whole and half almonds to make the derivation plausible.

The last *OED* instance of the Half Almond is dated ante-1701, but the game itself persisted under other names. The Half Almond appears as Hop, Step, and Jump in Newbery's *A Little Pretty Pocket-Book* (Newbery 1967: 83); in nineteenth-century Norfolk the same game was known as Half-Hammer (Gomme 1894–98: i, 187). Other nineteenth-century versions included Hick, Step and Jump, and Hitch Jamie (Gomme 1894–98: i, 211, 216). A similar jumping game existed on the Continent in the late Middle Ages (Endrei and Zolnay 1986: 139), and Scaino's sixteenth-century treatise on Tennis mentions jumping *a l'alemano* as a sport (Scaino 1984: 275).

See also **Leaping, Vaulting**

Holme (2001: iii.16.5.91); Hyde (1694a: 253–4); *OED* **almain**

Handiback
See **Hockcockles**

Hannikin Canst Abide It
[Hannikin Canst Abide It, Hanikin Canst Abide it: FL, 1, **60**]
This game, essentially a variant of One-and-Thirty, has left very little trace, but a game called Anakin is included in a list of card games in Thomas Crosfield's diary in 1629 (Crosfield 1935: 38), and a French game called *hanequin* appears in a list of card games from 1464 (De Lannoy 1875: 241).

See also **Cards**; **One-and-Thirty**

Hawks
See *Running and Races*

Heads and Points
[FL, **218**]
This juvenile game was known both in England and on the Continent: Randle Cotgrave (1611) mentions '*Bechevet, Teste a teste Bechevet*, the play with pins, called, heads and points'. Versions were recorded in the nineteenth century under the names Headick and Pinticks, Prickey Sockey, and (in Cornwall) Pednameny.

D'Allemagne (1905: 96-7); Gomme (1894–98: i, 199–200; ii, 37, 78); Holme (2001: III.16.5.91a)

Hide and Seek
[Hide & Seeke: **220**]
This ancient game has many international versions. The name Hide and Seek is not attested in the *OED* until 1672, but Hide and Find occurs in Randle Cotgrave's French–English dictionary, and versions were played in the late sixteenth century under the name All Hid; the game was also called King By Your Leave. The fifteenth-century game of Buck-Hide seems to have been similar.

Brewster (1953: 42–6); Brewster (in Avedon and Sutton-Smith 1971: 37); Cotgrave (1611: s.v. **iouer au clot**); D'Allemagne (1903: 68 ff.); Gomme (1894–98: i, 1); Holme (2001: 16.5.91); Hyde (1694a: 266); *MED* **buk-hide**; Newbery (1967: 75); *OED* **hide** v.¹ **1.e**; Opie and Opie (1969: 149–55)

Hockback
[**221**]
Meaning unknown; possibly another term for 'piggy-back' (cf. German *Huckeback*).

Hock Cockles, Handiback
[Hockcockles, Hock Kocles, Hockockles: FL, 3, **221**, 231; Handiback, Handie Back: FL, **221**]
The name Hotcockles is attested from the mid-sixteenth century, but there is visual evidence for this game from the Middle Ages. It was known on the Continent as well as in England: it is known in French as *frappe-main* or *la main chaude*. It seems to have been a game with rustic connotations – Sir Philip Sidney in *Arcadia* mentions it in a list of shepherds' pastimes. The name Handiback seems to be unattested elsewhere; as with the French names, it may imply a version in which the victim holds his hand behind him to be slapped. A vestige of the name Handiback apparently survived in the nineteenth-century version of the game in the Orkneys and Shetlands, called Handy-Croopen (Gomme

1894–98: i, 188–9). Although Willughby does not specify it, other sources suggest that in at least some versions of the game the player looked up after each blow, hoping to read mischief in the eye of the guilty party.

D'Allemagne (1905: 230–43); Gomme (1894–98: i, 229–31); Holme (2001: iii.16.5.91); OED **hot cockles**; Opie and Opie (1969: 292–4); Strutt (1903: 308)

See also **A Fool Who Bobbed Thee; Blindman Buff**

Hop-Frog
[FL, 1, **162**]
There is little classical or medieval evidence for this game. It is attested in the OED from 1599 onward, under the names Leap-Frog and Hop-Frog; it is also well documented on the Continent from the sixteenth century onwards.

Brewster (1953: 103–6); Brewster (in Avedon and Sutton-Smith 1971: 38); D'Allemagne (1903: 319–23); Gomme (1894–98: i, 223, 327–8; ii, 440–41); Hyde (1694a: 241–2); OED **Leap-frog**; Opie and Opie (1969: 247–9); Stella (1969: 38)

Horn Billets, Drudgecat
[Horne Billets, Horn Billets, Hornebillets: 1, 174, **175**; Drudge Cat: **175**]
The second element of this name is evidently OED **billet** n.², 'a thick piece of wood'. The first element may refer to the material horn: in the nineteenth century, the similar Scottish game of Hornie Holes was played with a kit-cat made of horn. It could also refer to the shape of the kit-cat, which is essentially a billet shaped into a horn at each end. Billet was still the name for the game of Kit-Cat in nineteenth-century Derbyshire (Gomme 1894–98: i, 28).

Horn Billets clearly bears a formal relation to Cricket (see **Stoolball**). An Italian engraving of the eighteenth century depicts a version of this game, which D'Allemagne describes under the name *bâtonnet*. Nineteenth-century versions included Cat, Cat and Dog, Cat i' the Hole, Cudgel, Hornie Holes, Lobber, Munshets, Pize Ball, Tip Cat, Trunket, Waggles, and Cat and Dog Hole. The game also resembles the Scottish game Sow in the Kirk (Gomme 1894–98: ii, 209–10), the Irish game Stones (Gomme 1894–98: ii, 216–17), and the American game Sooey (Brewster 1953: 159–60).

D'Allemagne (1903: 27–8); Gomme (1894–98: i, 60, 63–4, 84–5, 228, 331, 407–8; ii, 45, 295, 310, 329, 409–10)

See also **Kit-Cat**

Horse Races
See *Running and Races*

Horsing
[FL, **232**]
The term 'horse' or 'horsing' has been applied over the centuries to a variety of punishments, both ritual and real. Soldiers from the

seventeenth century to the nineteenth were punished by forcing them to sit astride a narrow wooden beam or pole termed a horse, and victims of beating or flogging were sometimes said to be 'horsed' upon someone who held them on his back during the punishment. The horsing used here in Christmas revels particularly recalls the element in some English versions of the ritual *charivari* in which the victim (in person or in effigy) was carried astride a pole. *The Pinder of Wakefield* includes in a list of entertainments Tending the Mare, 'which was a great wooden horse, which carryed all that had not tasted of my Lords beere to the buttery' (Anon. 1632: 76).

Barrett (1895); *OED* **horse**; Thompson (1992)

See also **Charter House**

Hummers
[FL, **221**]
These correspond to the nineteenth-century 'Bummers' and 'Thun'er spell'.

Gomme (1894–98: i, 51, ii, 291)

See also **Toys**

Hunting a Deer in My Lord's Park
[Hunting a Deer in My Lords Parke, Hunting a Deere in My Lords Parke, Hunting a Dear in My Lords Parke: FL, 1, **220**; Drop Glove: FL]
A common game, with variants occurring under diverse names, among them Hunt the Squirrel, Cat after Mouse, Allicomgreenzie, and Drop Handkerchief; there are also continental analogues, and there may be some medieval evidence for some version of it. Games of this sort were not exclusively for children: a similar game, played with a napkin, is played by young men and women in Breton's *Barley Breake*, where it affords an opportunity for flirtatious contact.

'More sacks to the mill' was the name of a rough nineteenth-century game, in which the cry 'Bags to the mill!' was a call for all to pile onto some hapless boy (Gomme 1894–98: i, 390). 'More sacks to the mill' also occurs in *Love's Labours Lost* (iv.iii.81), in a context suggesting that a children's game is the basis of the allusion.

Drop Glove, which appears cancelled on the flyleaf but is not mentioned in the text, is probably a similar game, if not an alternative name for the same one. Holme's *Academy of Armory* includes Drop Glove in a list of children's games. The game of Drop Glove was recorded by Halliwell in the nineteenth century along lines similar to Willughby's Hunting a Deer in My Lord's Park. Willughby's description of Hunting a Deer specifically mentions the dropping of a glove.

Brewster (1953: 91–3); Brewster (in Avedon and Sutton-Smith 1971: 38); D'Allemagne (1903: 24–6); Endrei and Zolnay (1986: 23); Gomme (1894–98: i,

7, 64, 109–12, 188); Halliwell (1970a: 118–19); Holme (2001: iii.16.5.91a); Opie and Opie (1969: 115, 198–202, 204); Strutt (1903: 302)

See also **King Heywood's Park**; *Running and Races*

Hurling
[FL, 1, 3/iii^v, **155/i**^r]

Skippon's description of Hurling resembles that found in John Ray's *Itinerary* (see Appendix 4), but in spite of a number of verbal echoes, the two are not close enough to suggest a direct textual connection between them.

Cornish Hurling should not be confused with the Irish game known as Hurley or Hurling. Hurley most resembles Hockey or Lacrosse, whereas Cornish Hurling is essentially a variant of the 'handling' version of Football (q.v.). The *OED*'s earliest reference to the sport dates to about 1600, although it could easily be much older. References from the late eighteenth and early nineteenth centuries suggest that the game had all but vanished by that time.

The principal distinctive feature of Hurling relative to other forms of no-handling Football was the element of wrestling. Wrestling was a favoured pastime among the Cornish, which probably accounts for its role in Hurling. Skippon's description of the role of wrestling seems a bit garbled; according to both Carew and Ray, if a player chose to wrestle, he threw the ball to a teammate, but if he refused, his opponents had liberty to intercept the throw.

The silvered ball, which according to Skippon and Ray was a part of the ceremony for arranging a match, was at least in some cases used in the game itself, to judge by Carew and in two accounts of a hurling-match played by Cornishmen in London on Mayday, 1654 (Scott 1974: 129). This ball was apparently made of wood, in which it resembled the very similar Welsh game of *Cnapan*.

Carew (1602: 73–5); Gomme (1894–98: i, 56–58, 245–6); Henderson (1947: 85–90); Marples (1954); Norden (1966: 23); *OED* **hurling**; Owen (1892: 264); Strutt (1903: 91–3)

See also **Ball**; **Football**; *Running and Races*; **Wrestling**

I Call and I Call
[Call & I Call, I Call and I Call: 1, **168**]

This was apparently considered one of the most basic games at ball: Randle Holme's list of games includes 'Ball play, or call at a call' (Holme 2001: iii.16.5.91a). Herrick apparently alludes to the game in his lyric 'I call and I call': 'I call, I call, who doe ye call? The Maids to catch this Cow-slip ball' (Herrick 1956: 112). American boys in the nineteenth century were still playing a version under the name Call Ball. Other parallel games of the nineteenth century include the English game Monday Tuesday, and the Scottish game Burley-Whush; the latter even involved a punishment very similar to Pilloring.

Endrei and Zolnay (1986: 99); Gomme (1894–98: i, 52, 199, 389–90); Newell (1883: 181)

See also **Ball**; **Tennis**

In and In
[Inne & In: 3/ii^r]
This was a game at dice; all instances in the *OED* date to the seventeenth century, and Goldsmith in the mid-eighteenth century classed it among games 'now exploded, [that] employed our sharping ancestors' (Goldsmith 1762: 56). The player would roll four dice, trying to roll one or two pairs, and winning or losing stakes accordingly. The game resembles *la riffa* (Raffle) in Alfonso X's thirteenth-century treatise (1941: 294–7 [fol. 68^r]), except Alfonso's game is played with three dice.

Cotton (1930: 80–81); Holme (2001: iii.16.2.29d); *OED* **In and In**

See also **Dice**

Inch Pinch
[161]
This game is mentioned by Samuel Harsnet in 1603 in a list of Christmas games, under the name 'Hinch pinch and laugh not'; Randle Cotgrave also gives it this name. A nineteenth-century English pinching game was called Inchy (or Hinchy) Pinchy; the same phrase occurs in a children's rime recorded in nineteenth-century Liverpool.

English Dialect Dictionary s.v. **inchy pinchy**; Gomme (1894–98: i, 214); *OED* **Hinch Pinch**

See also **Leaping, Vaulting**

Irish
[1, 22, 25, **37 ff.**, 43; double hand Irish: FL, **43**]
This game flourished in the sixteenth and seventeenth centuries; thereafter it seems to have given way to its faster paced derivative Backgammon. During its day it was esteemed among the best games at Tables. In spite of the name, it represented one of the most international forms of Tables, corresponding to Spanish *Todas Tablas* (in Alfonso X's treatise), French *Toutes Tables*, Italian *Tavole Reale* and many Asian forms of the game.

Alfonso X (1941: 322–5 [fol. 77^v]); Cotton (1930: 75); Holme (2001: iii.16.2.29a–b); Murray (1952: 120, 122); *OED* **Irish, Queen 14. b.**

See also **Backgammon**; **Tables**

Jack Art Asleep
[Jack Art Asleepe, Jack Art a Sleep: FL, **233**]
This game does not appear to be attested elsewhere. It bears a slight

resemblance to the game of Leap-Candle, attested as early as the seventeenth century and still surviving in the nineteenth. Perhaps the two games may be further associated through the nursery rhyme 'Jack Be Nimble'.

Gomme (1894–98: i, 327); Halliwell (1970a: 15); Opie and Opie (1952: 226–7)

Kibble Heft
[FL, **157**]
This sport does not seem to be mentioned in other sources; the description suggests an acrobatic feat rather than a competitive game. 'Kibble' is a dialect word for a bucket used to pull ore up from a mine (*OED* **kibble** n.³).

See also **Christmas Gambols**; **Drawing, Lifting, Throwing**

Kicking
[FL]
This entry is cancelled on the flyleaf, but there is no heading for Kicking in the text. Willughby may have been thinking of some form of the game of Kick-Shins, attested in the nineteenth and twentieth centuries, in which two contestants traded kicks to the shins until one acknowledged himself beaten (cf. Ditchfield 1907: 315). However, the reference may simply allude to activities in which kicking was featured, such as the Charter House, which appears next to Kicking on the flyleaf.

See also **Charter House**

King Heywood's Park
[220]
The identity of this game is uncertain, but it may be akin to Hunting a Deer in My Lord's Park (q.v.), which occurs on the same page of the manuscript. The park is a common theme in circle games. The nineteenth-century games of Bull in the Park, Garden Gate, and Letting the Buck Out all involved one player being enclosed in a ring by the other players and trying to get out. In this case, the name may be related to Heywood Park at Great Haywood in Staffordshire.

Gomme (1894–98: i, 50, 146–7, 329)

Kit-Cat
[Kitcat, Kit Cat: FL, 1, 13/iʳ, **173–4**]
The name Kit-Cat is attested in the *OED* from the mid-seventeenth century to the early nineteenth, Tip-Cat from the late seventeenth to the early nineteenth. There is a reference to 'pleying … at the cat' as early as the mid-fifteenth century. In the nineteenth century Gomme records the name Kit-Cat as referring to a game akin to Willughby's Horn Billets.

Versions of Kit-Cat existed on the Continent as well as in England: French *bâtonnet* is mentioned as early as 1347, and there are also German, Danish, Swiss, Austrian and Italian versions.

Brewster (1953: 160–62); D'Allemagne (1903: 27–8); Gillmeister (1977a: 211–14 and pl. 9); Gomme (1894–98: i, 310–11; ii, 37, 294–5); Holme (2001: iii.16.5.91a); *MED* **cat**; Newbery (1967: 92); *OED* **cat, tip-cat, kit-cat**; Stella (1969: 42); Strutt (1830: 109–10)

See also **Horn Billets, Drudgecat**

Laugh and Lie Down

[Laugh & Ly Downe: 1, 57, **61–3**]

This game is attested in the *OED* in the sixteenth century, and was still known in some parts of England in the nineteenth. It belongs to the family of 'fishing' games such as Cassino, Scopa and Tablanette, a type relatively rare in Western Europe, and otherwise unattested in seventeenth-century England. There existed a similar French game at the time by the name of *le culbas*.

La Marinière (1674: 314–15); *OED* **laugh** v. **1. d.**; Parlett (1991: 133 ff.)

Leaping, Vaulting

[Leaping: 1, **161**; Vaulting: 1, **162**; Leaping with a Staffe: **162**; Standing Jumpe, Running Jumpe: **161**]

Leaping contests were a regular feature of English country entertainments; they were featured, for example, in Robert Dover's Cotswold games (Dover 1636: frontispiece). Vaulting had a long history as a virile skill among the aristocracy – in the Middle Ages it had served to train men-at-arms to mount a horse quickly even when burdened by armour. By the seventeenth century there were many who felt that such pastimes were beneath the dignity of a gentleman, but the sport still had its advocates. Pole vaulting may be attested in the early fourteenth-century *Roman d'Alexandre* (Bodleian MS 264, ed. James 1933: f. 126^r).

Bascetta (1978: i, 1–118); D'Allemagne (1903: 300 ff.); Holme (2001: iii.16.5.91a); Stokes (1641); Strutt (1903: 187–8); Vale (1977: 118–19)

See also **Drawing, Lifting, Throwing; Half Almond, Whole Almond; Hop Frog; Inch Pinch; Jack Art Asleep**; *Running and Races*; **Scotch Hopper**

Lend Me Your Skimmer

[Lend Me Your Skimer: FL]

The identity of this game is unknown, but the name has many echoes in other games. Rabelais mentions *Compere prestez-moy vostre sac* (Rabelais 1973: 102); games collected in the nineteenth and twentieth centuries included Neighbour Lend Me Your Hatchet and Lend Me Your Key (Gomme 1894–98: i, 328–9; Brewster 1953: 175; Opie and Opie 1969: 208–9).

See also **Pray Dame Coals**

Lifting
See **Drawing, Lifting, Throwing**

Lilman
[Lilman, Lil Man: 1, **154**]
This game belongs to a large family of aggregative chasing games; nineteenth- and twentieth-century versions are found under such names as Devil's Den, Jockie Rover, Barla-Bracks, Stacks, Black-Man's Tig, Boggle about the Stacks, Booman, Cock, Stag and King Caesar. Willughby's name for the game actually survived in the nineteenth-century New England variant Lil Lil (Newell 1883: 165). Particular features of Willughby's Lilman can be found in some other games of the family. The nineteenth-century American game of Red Lion began with the verse 'Red Lion, Red Lion, Come out of your den, Whoever you catch Will be one of your men' (Newell 1883: 250–51). The Scots game of Hunt the Staigie opened with the line 'Ailleman, ailleman, aigie' (Gomme 1894–98: i, 242–3). The detail of spitting over the defeated antagonist's head appears in the game of Stocks (Gomme 1894–98: ii, 216; cf. also Brewster 1953: 68–9).

Brewster (1953: 53); Gomme (1894–98: i, 22, 34, 42, 43, 72–3, 150, 227–8, 299, 300, 325–6; ii, 211–12, 214, 374, 435–6); Opie and Opie (1969: 89)

See also *Running and Races*

Loadum
[Loadum, Lodum, Losing Loadum, Losing Lodum: 1, 6, 51, 57, **83 ff.**; Winning Loadum: 1, **85**]
Loadum is attested in the *OED* from the late sixteenth century to the mid-eighteenth. The game was often called Losing Loadum; it is unclear whether Winning Loadum actually existed, or was merely Willughby's own extrapolation. Loadum belongs to a family of trick-avoidance games, like the French game of Reversis, popular in the seventeenth and eighteenth centuries.

OED **loadum**; Parlett (1991: 301–2)

See also **Cards**

Long Laurence
[1, **47**]
This game is alluded to by Willughby's contemporary John Wilson in his play *The Cheats* (1607: iv.i.46); it was still in use in the nineteenth century. It closely resembles the game of the tee-totum and its relatives, including the Jewish dreidel, which are essentially the same device in the form of a polyhedral top. A similar four-sided stick is used as a die in India.

Avedon and Sutton-Smith (1971: 71); Gomme (1894–98: i, 326–7; ii, 203–4); Strutt (1903: 305)

Ludus Astronomicus
[3/iii^r]

Games based on Ptolomaic astronomy had been known in Europe since the Middle Ages, apparently as imports from the Arabic world. Willughby probably has in mind the version described by William Fulke in *Ouranomachia* (1571): Fulke's game seems to have had some currency in the seventeenth century, since it is alluded to in Burton's *Anatomy of Melancholy* (1990: 81). The game is vaguely reminiscent of Chess: the players move pieces corresponding to the Ptolomaic luminaries about a board which represents the zodiac, defeating or capturing opposing pieces according to the astrological conjuctions generated.

Alfonso X (1941: 370–83 [fol. 95^r–97^r]); Fulke (1571); Murray (1913: 343, 349, 569); Murray (1952: 156–7)

Milking
[FL]

The identity of this game is unknown. There existed a game in the nineteenth century called Milking Pails (Gomme 1894–98: i, 376–88; ii, 446), but this was a mimetic game for girls, a type not otherwise represented in Willughby's treatise.

Mill Stones
See **Selling of Millstones**

Nine Holes, Troll Madam
[Nine Holes: FL, 1, **249**; Troll Madam, Trole Madame: FL, 1, **249**]

This game is attested in the *OED* from the late sixteenth century onwards under such names as Bridgeboard, Trunks, Small Trunks, The Hole, and Pigeon-Holes. Versions existed on the Continent as well, and the game was probably an import, since Troll Madam is a corruption of the game's French name, *Trou Madame*. Nine Holes was an indoor sport, and particularly favoured by women; another version was played outdoors on the ground. The number of holes was not fixed at nine – other versions are attested with 11 or 13 holes.

Randle Holme uses the name Nine Holes for Three Men's Morris.

Brewster (in Avedon and Sutton-Smith 1971: 47); D'Allemagne (1905: 140–46); Gomme (1894–98: i, 45, 81, 413–14); Holme (2001: iii.16.5.91a); *OED* **Bridgeboard, hole 10 a.**, **Nine-Holes**, **Pigeon-Holes**, **Troll-Madam**, **Trunks**; Strutt (1903: 304)

Nine Men's Morris, Three Men's Morris
[Nine Mens Maurice: 1, **254/i^r ff.**, 255; 3 Mens Maurice: 1, **254/ii^r**, 255, 256]

Nine- and Three-Men's Morris are ancient and widely international games; they had been known in England since the Middle Ages, and had been included in some of the previous European games literature, most notably the thirteenth-century book of games of Alfonso X. The name Morris first appears in the sixteenth century, as a corruption of the older name Merels.

Alfonso X (1941: 362–671 [fol. 91ʳ–93ʳ]); Brewster (in Avedon and Sutton-Smith 1971: 39); Furno (1903: 110); Gomme (1894–98: i, 122, 414–19); Holme (2001: iii.16.2.38); Hyde (1694a: 202–14); Mehl (1990: 149–51); Murray (1913: 613–15, 618 ff., 643–4, 702–3, 733); Murray (1952: 37 ff.); *OED* **merels, morris**

See also **Fox and Goose**

Nine Pegs
See **Ten Pegs**

Noddy
[Nodde, Noddie, single hand Nodde: 1, 60, **65 ff.**, 70; ?Knave Nodde: FL; double hand Nodde: FL, **70**, 71; a new Nodde: **69**]
This English card game is first attested in the late sixteenth century. By the nineteenth it seems to have been displaced by its seventeenth-century derivative, Cribbage; however, a few local variants persisted, one of which is reported to survive still in parts of Lancashire.

Brewster (in Avedon and Sutton-Smith 1971: 40); Holme (2001: iii.16.2.47); *OED* **noddy** n.², **noddy-board**; Parlett (1991: 131); Parlett (1992: 173–4)

See also **Cards**; **Cribbage**

One-and-Thirty
[One and Thirtie: 1, 3/iiʳ, 6, **59**]
This appears to be one of the oldest European card games: a game so named is attested in England from the mid-sixteenth century, and on the Continent from the mid-fifteenth. Versions were still circulating regionally in the nineteenth century. The similarity to modern Pontoon or Blackjack is obvious.

Brewster (in Avedon and Sutton-Smith 1971: 40); De Lannoy (1875: 241); Holme (2001: iii.16.2.47); La Marinière (1665: 82–3); *OED* **thirty-one**; **one 2. b.**; Parlett (1991: 80–81)

See also **Cards**; **Hannikin Canst Abide It**; **One-and-Thirty Bon Ace**

One-and-Thirty Bon Ace
[1, **60**]
This variant of One-and-Thirty is attested in the *OED* from the early seventeenth century to the early eighteenth.

Cotton (1930: 62); Holme (2001: iii.16.2.47); *OED* **bone-ace**

See also **Cards**; **One-and-Thirty**

Pelmel
[167]
This early relative of Croquet was imported from France; it appears in

Scottish contexts in the sixteenth century, and in England in the seventeenth. English sources indicate that it was quite fashionable with the upper classes. Cotgrave (1611) describes it as follows:

Palemaille. A game, wherein a round box bowle is with a mallet strucke thorugh a high arch of yron (standing at either end of an alley one) which he that can do at the fewest blowes, or at the number agreed on, winnes.

Anon. (1696: 360–69); D'Allemagne (1903: 196 ff., 252–6); Jusserand (1901: 304 ff.); La Marinière (1665: 195–202); Lang (1910); Lauthier (1717); *OED* **closh, mall, pall-mall**; Prior (1872)

See also **Stowball**

Penny Prick
[Pennie Prick: FL, 1, **241**]
This game is attested as early as 1311 under the name 'halfpenny prick', and still played in the early nineteenth. A few similar games were also recorded in the nineteenth century, such as All in the Well and Skyte the Bob.

Gomme 1894–98: i, 2, ii, 39, 204–5; *MED* **peni-prik, halpeni**; *OED* **penny-prick, prick** n. **vii. 21**

Pitching the Bar
See **Drawing, Lifting, Throwing**

Post and Pair
[Post & Pare: 57]
A card game called Post is attested by the *OED* from the early sixteenth century to the seventeenth; Post and Pair is attested in the seventeenth century, but may have survived longer in local versions – Cotton mentions that the game was particularly popular in the west of England. Willughby gives no rules for the game, but Holme and Cotton describe it as a three-stake game similar to Brag. Each player was dealt three cards, with the final card upwards: one stake was taken by the player whose cards were closest to but not over a certain total, the second stake by the player with the best matching cards, or who could outvie the others into ceding him the stake, and the third by the player who held the highest card.

Cotton (1930: 71–2); Holme (2001: iii.16.2.47); *OED* **post** n.⁴; Parlett (1991: 88, 102–3)

See also **Cards**

Pray Dame Coals
[Preye Dame Coales: FL]
The identity of this game is unknown, but the name is echoed in the nineteenth-century game Pray Pretty Miss (Gomme 1894–98: ii, 65–7), and probably refers to the borrowing of hot coals as a quick means of starting a fire.

See also **Lend Me Your Skimmer**

Prison Bars
[Prison Barres: 1, 150, **153**, 222]
This is one of the most enduring of all games, and appears in many international versions. A game by the name of Bars or Base is attested in medieval England from the early fourteenth century onward. The name Prison Bars or Prison Base is first attested at the end of the sixteenth century and beginning of the seventeenth. In England at least it seems to have been characteristically a children's game, and could have rustic connotations; however, there are eighteenth- and nineteenth-century examples of adults playing the game.

Brewster (1953: 56–9); Brewster (in Avedon and Sutton-Smith 1971: 41); D'Allemagne (1903: 54–60); Endrei and Zolnay (1986: 86); Gomme (1894–98: ii, 79–83); Holme (2001: iii.16.5.91a); Hyde (1694a: 240–41); *MED* **barre 8.**, **bas**; Mehl (1990: 65 ff.); *OED* **prisoners' bars**, **bar** n.[1] **17.**; Opie and Opie (1969: 143–6); Peacham (1641: 31); Strutt (1903: 67–9)

See also *Running and Races*

Purposes
[1, 234, **237**]
This game is mentioned in Burton's list of winter entertainments in *The Anatomy of Melancholy* (Burton 1990: 79); in Cotgrave's dictionary (1611): '*Opinion* … the prettie game which we call Purposes'; and in Edward Chamberlayne's list of entertainments favoured by the English aristocracy (Chamberlayne 1669: 86). A similar game appears in Sorel's *Les Récréations Galantes* under the name *jeu des propos interrompus* (Sorel 1671: 71–2).

OED **purpose 4. a.**

See also **Cross Purposes**; **Drollery**

Put
[1, 57, **89–90**]
This game is first attested in the sixteenth century; during the sixteenth and seventeenth centuries it appears to have been regarded as a rather low pastime. The game seems to have died out in the nineteenth century.

Cotton (1930: 62); Holme (2001: iii.16.2.47); *OED* **put** n.[3]; Parlett (1991: 169–70)

See also **Cards**

Put-Pin
[3/iii[r], **218**]
This proverbially childish and trivial pastime is attested in the *OED* under the name Put-Pin from the late sixteenth to the mid-seventeenth century, Push-Pin from the late sixteenth to the nineteenth. It somewhat resembles the

nineteenth-century Scottish games of Hattie and Pop the Bonnet (Gomme 1894–98: i, 199; ii, 64). The game was also known on the Continent.

Brewster (in Avedon and Sutton-Smith 1971: 42); D'Allemagne (1905: 96–100); Gomme (1894–98: ii, 86); Holme (2001: iii.16.5.91a); *OED* **push-pin**, **put-pin**; Stella (1969: 6)

Puzzle of the Ship
[3/iii^v–3/vi^r, 101]
This mathematical puzzle had been circulating since the Middle Ages, in a variety of guises. It is ultimately of Arabic origin; as originally formulated, 15 Muslims and 15 Christians are aboard a sinking ship, and must be arranged such that by counting around by a fixed number, all the Christians will be thrown overboard and the Muslims saved. The puzzle appears in a number of seventeenth-century texts. The puzzle is discussed by Hyde in his treatise on chess under the name 'Circulus Muslimorum et Christianorum' (Hyde 1689: 'Prolegomena curiosa'), and appears as problem three in the 'Sports and Pastimes' appended to contemporary editions of Wingate's *Arithmetic*. Willughby has notes on the puzzle in his Commonplace Book (NUL Mi LM 15/1 p. 360), cross-referenced on 3/iii^v of the Book of Games.

Cotgrave (1655: 103–5); Hunt (1631: 266–9); Hyde (1694a: e2); Murray (1913: 280, 620, 622, 643); Wingate (1671: 498)

See also **Tricks**

Quoits
[1, 3/ii^r, 3/iii^r, **240–41**]
This game is well attested from the fourteenth century onwards. It seems to have been particularly popular among country folk, perhaps because of the relative simplicity of the equipment involved – Burton and Peacham both list it among common country sports (Burton 1990: 72; Peacham 1641: 31). The game was also played on the Continent; its French name is *le palet*.

Brewster (in Avedon and Sutton-Smith 1971: 43); D'Allemagne (1903: 139 ff.); Holme (2001: iii.16.5.91a); *MED* **coit**; *OED* **quoit**; Stella (1969: 21); Strutt (1903: 76–7); Vale (1977: 119)

See also **Bowls**

Races
See *Running and Races*

Rapier
See **Duelling**

Rattles
See *Toys*

Riddles
[FL, 1, 234, **238**]

Riddles are a pastime of considerable antiquity, and most of the examples Willughby cites had enjoyed a long history of their own. The riddle about Abel may be the oldest – a part of it appears in a text of the ninth century (Tupper 1903: #78; Roy 1977: #8; Anon. 1617: #61). 'What God never sees' has a long and very international history; it appears in Germany in 1505, and versions were still circulating in the nineteenth century (Taylor 1951: #1715–20; Opie and Opie 1952: 190; Halliwell 1970a: 133–4). The fish riddle appears in the medieval romance of Apollonius of Tyre, and was still known in the nineteenth century (Taylor 1951: #906; Roy 1977: #45). The riddle about the arrow had also existed since the Middle Ages (Roy 1977: #173; Tupper 1903: #141). The moon riddle was still circulating in the twentieth century (Taylor 1951: #90–94). The riddle about the cuckold is used in John Marston's *The Malcontent* (i.iii.88).

The curious riddle 'Item deriditum' seems to have been quite enduring in spite of its opacity: it has been recorded in several nineteenth-century versions, with various renditions of the initial nonsense words, substantially divergent contents (although green is usually a central element), and a variety of answers. The following is one of the more elaborate versions, having as its answer 'a holly tree':

Itum Paradisum all clothed in green,
The king could not read it, no more could the queen.
They sent for the wise men out of the East,
Who said it had horns, but was not a beast.

(Taylor 1951: #601–3)

A 'Book of Riddles' is included in the catalogue of the Willoughby library catalogue (NUL Mi I 17/1, Item T67).

Augarde (1984: 1 ff.); Bryant (1983); Opie and Opie (1952: 15–16); Roy (1977); Taylor (1939); Taylor (1951); Tupper (1903)

Rhyming
[FL, **239**]

Rhyming-games are alluded to in Continental texts of the Middle Ages; the version described by Willughby was known as Crambo, under which name it is well attested in sources of the seventeenth and eighteenth centuries. Versions of the verse riming 'porringer' were well known at the time, and continued to circulate into the nineteenth century.

B. (1865); Endrei and Zolnay (1986: 81–2); Halliwell (1970b: 9); *OED* **crambo**; Opie and Opie (1952: 354); Sorel (1657: 342–3)

Robin Alive
[FL, **230**]

Versions of this game are well attested across Europe. Nineteenth-century

English names included Jack's Alive and Dan'l My Man. In nineteenth-century Cornwall the game was still known as Robin's Alight, and in America as Robin's Alive. Several versions of the accompanying verse also survived, of which the American is closest to Willughby's: 'The bird is alive (or 'Robin's alive'), and alive like to be, If it dies in my hand you may back-saddle me' (Newell 1883: 135). The laying of furniture on the player's back occurs in several versions of the game. The text following this game in the manuscript suggests that it may have been considered a Christmas game.

Gomme (1894–98: i, 256–9; ii, 413); Newell (1883: 135–6); Opie and Opie (1952: 227)

See also **Christmas Gambols**

Ruff and Trump; Trump and Ruff; Ruff; Trump
[Ruffe and Trump: **71–2**; Trumpe and Ruffe: 1; Ruffe: 71, 73, 75, 79, 83; double hand Ruffe: 71, 72; single hand Ruffe: 71; 4-hand Ruffe: 72; Trump, Trumpe: 1, 72]
The game of Ruff and Trump belongs to a family of variants on a single game with overlapping names. Willughby's account differs from the variant described by Cotton and Holme under the name Ruff and Honours – in Cotton's version, the ruff as defined by Willughby is omitted, and the element of honours (as in Whist) is added. According to Cotton, Ruff and Honours was also called Slamm; according to Holme, it was called Trump 'among the vulgar', but Holme also calls it simply Ruff. Randle Cotgrave uses Ruff as a synonym for Trump. Willughby, on the other hand, offers the reasonable speculation that the name Trump may once have designated a simple trick-taking game unadorned by the element of the ruff or the honours. Some version of the game seems to have been around by the mid-fifteenth century, to judge by a reference to the game of *roufle* in the letter of Jan de Lannoy (De Lannoy 1875: 241). Versions of this game seem to have been among the principal forms of card games in the sixteenth and seventeenth centuries, but by the end of the eighteenth century they had been displaced by their derivative Whist.

Cotton (1930: 55–6); Holme (2001: iii.16.2.47); Mehl (1990: 173); *OED* **ruff** n.[3]; **trump** n.[2]; Parlett (1991: 216)

See also **Cards**; **Gleek**

Running and Races
[running, running of races: 1, 3/iii[v], **151**, 272; horse races, horses … run: **151**, 272; dogs … run: **272**; haukes fly: 272]
Racing on foot or on horse was a popular entertainment in the late seventeenth century. Horse racing was an ancient form of aristocratic entertainment in England – the sport is alluded to as early as *Beowulf* (864–7, 916–17). It seems to have become increasingly formalized in the seventeenth

century, which witnessed the establishment of permanent racing tracks and the emergence of a body of literature on the subject.

Racing with greyhounds was called coursing, and involved flushing out a quarry (usually a hare) and letting the dogs slip from the leash when the quarry had a certain lead. The victor was the dog that either caught the hare, or was in front of the other when they got close enough to cause the hare to make a sharp change in direction (called 'giving the hare a turn').

Billett (1994: 123 ff.); Blome (1686: ii, 8–9, 94–95); Cotton (1930: 95–8); Cox (1674: 65–71); D'Allemagne (1903: 51–4); Davis (1989: 107–22; Gomme (1894–98: ii, 220–21); Holme (2001: iii.3.2.27; iii.9.1b.30; iii.9.4a.58; iii.16.5.91a; iii.18b); Howlet (1684: 26–33); Markham (1615: 79–86, 97–106); Pepys (1970–83: i, 218; iv, 160, 243, 255; viii, 167; ix, 209, 473); Strutt (1903: 32 ff., 65–7); Turberville (1575: 244–8)

See also **Barley Break; Charter House; Football; Hunting a Deer in My Lord's Park; Hurling; Lilman; Leaping, Vaulting; Prison Bars; Tick**

Scotch Hopper
[FL, 1, **163–4**]
The name Hop Scotch first appears in the *OED* in 1801, but Scotch Hoppers can be documented as early as 1677. 'Scotch' in this context means 'a score, an incised line'. It is consistently identified as a children's game. A variety of international versions exist.

Brand and Ellis (1913: 547); Brewster (1953: 107–15); D'Allemagne (1903: 313 ff.); Gomme (1894–98: i, 223–7; ii, 182–3); Holme (2001: iii.16.5.91a); *OED* **hopscore**, **hopscotch**, **scotch**; Stella (1969: 18)

See also **Leaping, Vaulting**

Selling of Bargains
[Selling of Bargaines: FL, 1, 234, **235**]
This description of children's verbal competitions may make them seem a bit more formalized than they were in practice. For the name, compare Cotgrave: '*Bailler foin en corne*. To deceiue, gull, cousen, sell a bargaine, giue a gudgeon.'; '*Sorner*. To ieast, boord, frumpe, gull, sell bargains, speake merrily, talke idly.'

Selling of Mill Stones
[Selling of Mill Stones, Mill Stones: FL, **230**]
Aspects of this game are echoed in the modern game of Honey Pots and its relatives. In Honey Pots, one child plays a shopkeeper, another a customer, while the rest crouch in a row with their hands clasped under their knees at 'pots': the customer tests the pots by lifting, swinging or shaking them, trying to break their grip. The game was extremely popular in the nineteenth century, and has French and Italian versions. The detail of leading the boys by their ears recalls the nineteenth-century Scottish game of Luggie (Gomme 1894–98: i, 361–2).

Gomme (1894–98: i, 219–21); Opie and Opie (1969: 243–5)

See also **Christmas Gambols; Tricks to Abuse and Hurt One Another**

Seven Cards
See **Ging**

Shewing the Wild Colt
See **Shoeing the Wild Colt**

Shittlecock
[Shittlecock, Shittle Cock, Shickle Cock: FL, 1, 150, **177**]
The name *shittel cocke* is attested in the *OED* as early as 1522, but the game is illustrated in a manuscript of the fourteenth century (Strutt 1903: pl. 37 [facing p. 306]). No early reference or illustration suggests the use of a net or any equivalent; the game would seem to have been quite loosely structured, and may only have involved batting the shuttlecock back and forth. This game is obviously the ancestor of Badminton. It was also known on the Continent; its French name was *le volant*. Visual evidence suggests that Shuttlecock was often played indoors, and that it was popular with women as well as with men.

D'Allemagne (1903: 210 ff.); Gomme (1894–98: ii, 192–6); Holme (2001: iii.16.2.44–5; iii.16.5.91a); Hyde (1694a: 251); Newbery (1967: 79); *OED* **battledore, shuttlecock**; Strutt (1903: 243–4)

Shoeing the Wild Colt
[Shoeing the Wild Colt, Shewing the Wild Colt: FL, **232**]
Several seventeenth-century texts mention Shoeing the Wild Mare as a Christmas sport (Brand and Ellis 1913: 272; Scott 1974: 54). A variant name appears in Thomas Thomas's Latin dictionary (1587):

oscillatio … A tottering or hanging motion, which is a kinde of game commonlie vsed of children and contrifolkes, wherein the ends of cords being tied hard to a beame or tree, they clime or swinge, as it were houering in the aire: some take it for a gamboll called the haltring of Hix mare.

The connection between the two entertainments mentioned by Thomas may be clarified by the nineteenth-century Scots game of Shooing the Auld Mare, or Shoeing the Wild Boar, in which a board was slung between two ropes, and a boy had to sit on it and perform various actions without falling off.

   This game may be quite old: various medieval manuscripts depict a youth seated on a makeshift bench and performing diverse actions, suggesting some version of the same game (Brand and Ellis 1913: 527 [#35]; Strutt 1903: pl. facing p. 312).

Brewster (in Avedon and Sutton-Smith 1971: 43); Cotgrave (1611: s.vv. **baccoler, bacule**); Gomme (1894–98: ii, 192, 383); Halliwell (1970a: 89–90); Halliwell (1970b: 136, 206); Mehl (1990: 481)

See also **Christmas Gambols**; **Cook-Stool**

Shooting
[1, 3/iii^v, **181**]

Willughby offers a minimal description of the venerable and subtle sport of archery, which had already been the subject of a few treatises. Since the fourteenth century, the English government had sought to foster archery for military preparedness, in part by forbidding other forms of outdoor sports, but the effectiveness of these efforts declined over time. By Willughby's day archery was a relatively specialized pursuit, but it was still cultivated by an enthusiastic if diminished following, and continued to be performed for public entertainment.

Ascham (1545); Bascetta (1978: ii, 351–78); Brand and Ellis (1913: 528–9); Brewster (in Avedon and Sutton-Smith 1971: 28–9); Cotton (1930: 99–100); Hardy (1976); Heath (1971); Holme (2001: iii.16.5.91a); Howlet (1684: 121–8); Markham (1615: 107); Markham (1634); Parker (1950); Souter (1622: 232–4); Strutt (1903: 55–8)

See also **Father Fitchard**

Shovel Board
[FL, 1, 243, **251–2**, 253]

This game is attested as early as the late fifteenth century under such names as Shove-Groat, Shove-Board, Slip-Groat, Shovel-Board, Shovel-a-Board, Shuffle-Board, Slide-Groat, and (perhaps in jest) Slidethrift; it seems to have been quite popular between the sixteenth and eighteenth centuries, but to have fallen out of favour thereafter. The game was often the object of official sanction, in part because of the heavy gambling involved. The shillings and half-crowns Willughby mentions as being used in this game were about 3 cm (1¼ ins) in diameter (Sutherland 1973: pl. 99; Ruding 1840: iii, pls 33, 34). The game was known on the Continent as well.

Brewster (in Avedon and Sutton-Smith 1971: 44); Hartley and Elliot (1929: pl. 29a); Holme (2001: iii.16.5.91a); *OED* **shoveboard**, **shovegroat**, **shovelboard**, **slidegroat**, **slidethrift**; Strutt (1903: 238–9, 242)

Single Rapier
See **Duelling**

Skittle Pins
See **Ten Pins**

Span-Counter
[1, **253**]

This was a boy's game, attested from the mid-sixteenth century onward. The game was also called Span-Farthing. Analogous games are Banger and, in the

USA, Spans. It is related to the games of Chuck-Farthing and Pitch and Hustle. Versions were also played on the Continent in the seventeenth century. The sixpence mentioned by Willughby measured about 2.5 cm (1 ins) across (Sutherland 1973: pl. 99).

Brewster (in Avedon and Sutton-Smith 1971: 44–5); D'Allemagne (1903: 139 ff.); Furno (1903: 110); Gomme (1894–98: i, 17; ii, 210); Holme (2001: iii.16.5.91a); *OED* **span-counter**, **span-farthing**; Strutt (1903: 304); Stella (1969: 19)

Stoolball, Tutball
[Stoole Ball: 1, 3/iii^v, 167, **169–70**; Tutball: 170]
A game called Stoolball is attested as early as the fifteenth century. It has traditionally been supposed that this game was akin to Cricket, and essentially identical with the Stoolball played in the eighteenth and nineteenth centuries. In Willughby's treatise, the closest relative of Cricket is actually Horn Billets. Willughby's Stoolball is simply a ball-throwing game, and there is no defence of the stool. This does not exclude the possibility that there did exist a seventeenth-century version of the game in which the stool was defended; such a version certainly existed within half a century of the writing of this treatise.

Tuts or Tutball is attested in the *OED* between 1519 and the late nineteenth century. Willughby clearly distinguishes between Stoolball and Stowball, two games which have sometimes been confused by modern authors (see **Stowball**).

There is a suggestive similarity between Willughby's Stoolball and the New England game of Schoolball as collected by Newell in the nineteenth century: 'The ball is tossed by the *teacher* to the head of the class, and, after being returned by the latter, sent to the next of the row, and so on. If any girl misses, she must go to the foot, and if the *teacher* misses, the *first scholar* takes her place' (Newell 1883: 182).

Contemporary references suggest that Stoolball was considered a rustic pastime, and one of the few sports in which women freely took part. It seems to have been especially associated with Easter.

Crosfield (1935: 63); Gomme (1894–98: ii, 218–20, 314); Grantham (1931); Henderson (1947: 70–78, 128–31); Holme (2001: iii.16.5.91a); *MED* **stol**; Newbery (1967: 88); *OED* **stoolball**, **tut**; Peacham (1641: 31); Strutt (1903: 100–101)

See also **Ball**, **Horn Billets**, **Stowball**

Stowball
[Stowball, Stow Ball: 1, 3/ii^r, 3/iii^v, **13/i^r ff.**, 167]
Stowball is one of the few games in the treatise which can be clearly localized. According to John Aubrey in 1685:

Stobball-play is peculiar to North Wilts., North Gloucestershire, and a little part of

Somerset near Bath. They smite a ball, stuffed very hard with quills and covered with soale leather, with a staffe, commonly made of withy, about 3 and a halfe long. Colerne-downe is the place so famous and so frequented for stobball playing. The turfe is very fine, & the rock (freestone) is within an inch and a halfe of the surface which gives the ball so quick a rebound. A stobball-ball is of about four inches diameter, and as hard as a stone. I doe not heare that this game is used anywhere in England but in this part of Wiltshire and Gloucestershire adjoining.

(Aubrey 1847: 117)

Stowball is the only game recorded on one of Willughby's small notepads, and the account may have been among the earliest portions of the text, written during Willughby's visit to the west in 1662 or 1667 (see Introduction, Section 1.3).

As Willughby's description of the game is less than lucid, a summary may be helpful. Stowball is quite distinct from Stoolball, although the two games are sometimes confused by modern authors (e.g. Gomme 1894–98: i, 217–18). Stowball is essentially a vigorous cousin of Golf and Croquet. The players at the lay pin have the task of driving the ball, blow by blow, around the course, from the lay pin around the boot pin and back to the lay pin. Their opponents attempt to hit the ball back each time; each new blow begins where the ball stopped. When the ball comes close to the end, one of the players of the first side stands by the lay pin to catch it. The object for each side was to get the ball around in as few blows and ending as close to the lay pin as possible.

In addition to being localized, Stowball seems to have enjoyed a relatively brief life – the *OED* records it only in the sixteenth and seventeenth centuries. However, there have been comparable games at other times and places. The stakes as targets at each end recall similar stakes in Dutch *kolven* (as well as in modern Croquet); in *kolven* the ball had to be driven right to the stake. The efforts of the opposition to drive the ball back resemble the north-eastern French and Walloon game of *la chole*, in which the opposing party drives the ball back after every three blows (Browning 1955: 15; Henderson 1947: 116). The game also has some resemblance to the nineteenth-century Scottish games of Han' and Hail, and Troap (Gomme 1894–98: i, 187–8; ii, 308–9).

The *OED* suggests that the name may derive from 'stob', meaning 'stick, stake'. Based on Willughby's description, it may be conjectured that the first element of the name is actually 'stop', since this is what the player does to the ball at the lay pin. In fact, the *OED*'s earliest reference to the game, in 1634, renders the name as 'Stopball'.

Willughby's description of the ball as being entirely of wood or leather disagrees with both Aubrey and with Littleton's *Dictionary*, which defines *paganica* as 'A goff-ball, a stow-ball, stuffed with feathers'. If these other two sources are correct, Willughby's error may reflect the circumstances under which the description was composed: his itinerary may not have allowed time to examine the ball very closely, or he may simply not yet have had sufficient experience in observing games to have obtained this information.

Gomme (1894–98: ii, 217); *OED* **stow-ball**

See also **Pell-Mell**; **Stoolball**

Sword and Buckler
See **Duelling**

Tables
[1, 3/ii^r, 3/iii^r, **17 ff.**, 150]
This game was already well known in Greco-Roman Europe, and versions are widely disseminated around the Old World. In the English-speaking world, the game of Backgammon is the only surviving example of a wide range of games played on a backgammon board, or tables. These games were already quite popular in the Middle Ages, and were the subject of some of the earliest surviving European games literature. Willughby's account of these games appears to be the oldest in English.

Anon. (1696: 370 ff.); Fiske (1905: 161–5); Holme (2001: iii.16.2.26–7, 29a–c); Hyde (1694a: 1 ff., 20 ff., 35 ff.); Mehl (1990: 135 ff.); Murray (1913: 619ff., 643–4, 702–3); Murray (1941); Murray (1952: 117 ff.); Souter (1622: 3 ff.)

See also **Backgammon**; **Doublets**; **Irish**; **Ticktack**

Ten Pegs, Nine Pegs, Skittle Pins
[Ten Pegs: FL, 1, **245 ff.**; Nine Pegs, Skittle Pins: 245]
This game seems to have evolved from the medieval game of Kayles or Loggats, in which an array or row of pins were knocked over with a casting stick. From the sixteenth century onward, versions of this game using a ball instead of a stick are well attested across Europe. Additional names for versions of this game are Nine-Pins, Ten-Pins, Skittles, Kittle-Pins and Skayles.

The 'Madg' (i.e. 'Madge') is also mentioned in a description of the game by Holme, who terms it the 'Margery'. This detail of the game does not appear to be mentioned elsewhere, but may be implied in versions where the game is called Ten-Pins (modern American Tenpins involves a triangular layout of the ruck, which does not seem to be attested in sources from this period). The name may be related to 'Madge', a term for a small owl (Cotgrave 1611: s.v. **cheveche**), or it may be a play on 'peg' and 'Peg'.

Both Burton and Peacham list this game as typical of country folk (Burton 1990: 72; Peacham 1641: 31), but it was also popular with the upper classes – it is frequently mentioned by Pepys (1970–83: i, 118, 119, 121, iv, 144, etc.).

Brewster (in Avedon and Sutton-Smith 1971: 38); Cotgrave (1662: 126); D'Allemagne (1903: 279 ff.); Gomme (1894–98: i, 332; ii, 115–16); Holme (2001: iii.16.2.48; iii.16.5.91a); Jones (1773); Mehl (1990: 55 ff.); *OED* **kayles**, **kittle pins**, **loggat**, **nine 6.**, **nine-pins**, **ten-pins**, **skayles**; Strutt (1903: 220–21)

Tennis
[1, 3/ii^r, 3/iii^r, 14/i^v, **15/i^r ff.**, 167]

The game as described by Skippon, still sometimes found today under the name Court Tennis, Royal Tennis or Real Tennis, was the normal form of the game until the invention of Lawn Tennis in the late nineteenth century. Tennis appears to have evolved in medieval France some time before the fourteenth century; the earliest known reference in English dates to about 1400. The French name for the game was *le jeu de la paume*, and the name Palm sometimes appears in English as well.

Neither Skippon nor Willughby mention one of the most obvious features of Tennis: because of the expensive equipment involved, this was very much a game for the privileged classes, and in Willughby's day was much favoured by the king and court, although there were also outdoors versions played by ordinary people.

Shaver's Hall, also called Pickadilly, was a fashionable gaming house in what is now Piccadilly, an area of relatively recent development on the outskirts of seventeenth-century London. It was listed as having a tennis court in a survey of 1651. Other tennis courts were built in the area in about 1673, and lasted nearly two centuries (Kingsford 1925: 81–2, 91).

Aberdare (1951); Anon. (1696: 333 ff.); Brewster (in Avedon and Sutton-Smith 1971: 45–6); D'Allemagne (1903: 165 ff.); Furno (1903: 110); Gillmeister (1977a); Gillmeister (1997b); Henderson (1947: 47–69); Holme (2001: iii.5.8.149; iii.16.2.41, 43; iii.16.5.91a); Howlet (1684: 133–7); Jusserand (1901: 240 ff.); La Marinière (1654: 125–62); *MED* **paume 5.**, **tenis**; Mehl (1990: 31 ff.); *OED* **palm 6.**; Potter (1994); Scaino (1984); Strutt (1903: 82–90); (Vale 1977: 100–107)

See also **Ball**; **Call and I Call**

Thirty-One
See **One-and-Thirty**

Three Men's Morris
See **Nine Men's Morris**

Throwing
See **Drawing, Lifting, Throwing**

Throwing at Cocks
[FL, 3, **269**]
Shrovetide Throwing at Cocks is first attested in England in the early sixteenth century, although medieval sources indicate that cocks were sometimes used as the targets in archery practice. The sport persisted into the nineteenth century.

Billett (1994: 60–61); Brand and Ellis (1913: 37–40); Fishwick (1914: 25); Holme (2001: iii.16.5.91a); *OED* **cock, cock-shy, cock-throwing**; Strutt (1903: xlvii, 226–7, 292)

See also **Cockfighting**; **Drawing, Lifting, Throwing**

Tick
[154, **222**]

This is one of the simplest of running games, and has been known by a variety of names. 'Tick' is first attested in the seventeenth century, and is now the normal name in the west Midlands and north Wales – which corresponds suggestively with Willughby's Warwickshire background. Willughby is correct to suppose that 'tick' is an old word meaning 'to touch' (*MED* **tiken**).

Gomme (1894–98: ii, 291, 293); *OED* **tick** n.³ 1. b, **tig** n.¹ 2.; Opie and Opie (1969: 62–8)

See also *Running and Races*

Ticktack
[FL, 1, 22, **27 ff.**, 37; double Ticktack, double hand Ticktack: FL, **43**]

This game is attested as early as the mid-sixteenth century, but in England it does not appear to have survived the eighteenth. It corresponds to the French *trictrac*, and is probably named from the sound of the pieces clicking on the board. It is comparable to the game *emperador* in Alfonso X's book of games, and to the *ludus Anglicorum* in a fourteenth-century English manuscript.

Alfonso X (1941: 316–19 [fol. 75ᵛ–76ʳ]); Anon. (1696 370 ff.); Brewster (in Avedon and Sutton-Smith 1971: 46); Cotton (1930: 76); D'Allemagne (1905: 3–13); Holme (2001: iii.16.2.29); La Marinière (1654: 32–116); Murray (1952: 124–5); *OED* **tick-tack**

See also **Tables**

Tiring Irons
[FL]

Tiring Irons were a puzzle which continued to enjoy some currency into the nineteenth century; the earliest known reference in English dates to 1601. As described in the nineteenth century, they consisted of a strip of metal pierced by a line of holes, usually seven or ten, and an oblong metal loop of the same length. In each hole was anchored a wire which passed through the loop and attached to a ring which sat around the loop; each wire except the last also passed through the ring attached to the next wire before passing through the loop. The object of the puzzle was to remove all the rings from the loop. Seventeenth-century sources also refer to the puzzle as 'tarriers' or 'tarrying irons'. The various names are quite apt: the ten-ring version of the puzzle requires no less than 681 distinct moves to detach all the rings.

Clarke (1834: 216–17); Endrei and Zolnay (1986: 84); Gomme (1894–98: ii, 296); *OED* **tiring-irons, tarrier**³; Scriba (1998: 100–110)

Top, Gig
[Top: **222**; Gig: **222**]

Tops are widely attested across Europe since the Middle Ages; the earliest

English reference may date to the eleventh century. In Willughby's day they were used in specific games such as Peg Farthing, in addition to their use as a simple toy.

Willughby seems to imply that the whirligig is a distinct form of top, but it is unclear from other sources where the distinction lay, if indeed it was generally observed.

Brewster (1953: 149–51); Brewster (in Avedon and Sutton-Smith 1971: 46–7); D'Allemagne (1903: 35 ff., 41 ff.); Gomme (1894–98: ii, 299–303); Holme (2001: iii.16.5.91a); Hyde (1694a: 259–61); Newbery (1967: 81); *OED* **gig** n.¹, **top** n.²; Souter (1622: 230–31); Stella (1969: 3); Strutt (1903: 304–5)

See also **Toys**; **Whirligig**

Toys
[whistles, rattles, babies, corall, bores tush: **217**]
Willughby's account of toys on p. 217 is specifically focused on those of infants, evidently as a means of approaching the earliest manifestations of play as precursors to an interest in games. The whistle described by Willughby is well attested in contemporary sources, and some fine examples survive. Of the diverse toys used by older children in the seventeenth century, Willughby mentions only hummers and various forms of tops.

D'Allemagne (1902: 21 ff., 96 ff.); Fournier (1889); Fraser (1966); *OED* **baby**, **clout** n.¹ **4. c.**, **coral 3.**, **poppet**, **rattle**; Stella (1969)

See also *Children's Games*; **Hummers**; **Tiring Irons**; **Top**; **Whirligig**

Tricks
[Tricks at Cards: 1, **101**; Tricks with Paper, Strings, &c.: FL]
Conjuring is a very old practice, and the literature of conjuring was already well established by the late seventeenth century. Both card tricks and tricks with paper, string, and other materials can be found in such seventeenth-century texts as Thomas Johnson's *Dainty Conceits* (1630), John Cotgrave's *Wit's Interpreter* (1655) and the unattributed *Sports and Pastimes* (1676). The trick involving split cards is mentioned by both Rid and Holme, and a surviving seventeenth-century example of such cards is illustrated in Hargrave's history of playing-cards. Willughby's Commonplace Book describes one example of a trick with paper:

The Art of Cutting White Paper into Trees, Landskips, &c.
It requires a steady hand, little fingers. Women are most expert at it. They hold their sizzars in one hand and the paper they cut in the other and have nothing to rest either hand upon. When a peice is finished, to make it keepe and looke better, they fasten it upon isinglasse.

(NUL Mi LM 15/1 p. 479)

Cotgrave (1655: 102 ff., 130, 143–8); Hall (1957); Hall (1972); Hargrave (1930:

71 and pl. p. 38); Holme (2001: iii.12.2); Johnson (1630: A3v ff.); M. (1676: 14–15, 28–9, 38–9); Rid (1614: D3ᵛ–D4); Toole-Stott (1976)

See also *Puzzle of the Ship*

Tricks to Abuse and Hurt One Another
[1, **229 ff.**]
This grouping may be intended as a subsection of children's games, and pretty certainly includes Buying Mustard, Cropping Oaks and Buying Bees. The next games in the manuscript, Selling Millstones and Robin Alive, have elements of pain and abuse, but seem rather to be grouped with the Christmas Gambols. Several of the games elsewhere in the manuscript could also fall under the heading of tricks to abuse and hurt, such as Hot Cockles, Blindman Buff, A Foole Who Bobbed Thee (although these seem to have been less specifically children's games), and perhaps Selling of Bargains.

See also *Children's Games*; **Christmas Gambols**

Tricks with Paper, Strings, etc.
See **Tricks**

Troll Madam
See **Nine Holes**

Trump; Trump and Ruff
See **Ruff and Trump**

Truss-a-Fail
[Trusse a Feale: FL, 162]
This is probably not the same as Hop Frog. Cotgrave (1611) glosses *cheval fondu* as 'A kind of play like our trusse'. *Cheval fondu* was a game like Buck-Buck or Hi Jimmy Knacker, in which one team would bend over as a chain, each grabbing the one before, the foremost grabbing a tree or similar sturdy support; the other team would leap onto their backs, the object being to make the chain collapse.

Brewster (1953: 116–18); D'Allemagne (1903: 323 ff.); Endrei and Zolnay (1986: 87); Gomme (1894–98: i, 46-8, 52; ii, 147, 199–200); Holme (2001: iii.16.5.91a); *OED* **truss 7.**, **truss-a-fail**; Opie and Opie (1969: 255–61); Stella (1969: 23)

Tutball
See **Stoolball**

Upper or Nether Choose You Whether
[Upper or Nether, Chuse You Wither: 218]
This game is best known in English by the name Handy-Dandy. It may be

alluded to as early as the late fourteenth century in *Piers Plowman*, although the most secure examples date to the sixteenth century or later. Willughby's name for the game was doubtless recited as part of the game itself; numerous parallels exist from the nineteenth century, as in this example from Halliwell:

Handy dandy riddledy ro –
Which will you have, high or low?

(Halliwell 1970b: 216)

A similar verse is apparently alluded to by Chapman in 1598:

Why loe heere we are both, I am in this hand, and hee is in that, handy dandy, prickly prandy, which hand will you haue?

(Chapman, *The Blind Beggar of Alexandria* ii.90–92, in Chapman 1961: i, 14)

Gomme (1894–98: i, 189–90, 410–11); Halliwell (1970a: 104–5); *OED* **handy-dandy**; Opie and Opie (1952: 197–8)

Vaulting
See **Leaping, Vaulting**

Whehee
[1, **90**]
Whehee resembles the modern game My Bird Sings or My Ship Sails. It is the only card game in the juvenile hand of the manuscript, and the rules suggest a game primarily for children, although it may have been related to the game My Sow (Has) Pigged mentioned by Thomas Crosfield and John Taylor in the early seventeenth century (Crosfield 1935: 38; Taylor 1630: ii, 54 [Ee 3/2ᵛ]), suggesting that children were not the only players. The name Whehee could have originated in imitation of the squealing of piglets.

Foster (1916: 253); Parlett (1991: 141)

See also **Cards**; *Children's Games*

Whirligig
[Whirlie Gigs: FL, 223]
Willughby may have used this word to indicate some form of top, although since he already has a heading for tops which includes gigs, he may instead have been thinking of the pinwheel on a stick often represented in contemporary art, sometimes referred to as a 'windmill'.

OED **whirligig**; Strutt (1903: 307)

See also **Top**; **Toys**

Whistles
See *Toys*

Whole Almond
See **Half Almond, Whole Almond**

Winning Loadum
See **Loadum**

Wrestling
[1, 3/iii^v, 275]
This ancient sport had long been popular in England, although by the seventeenth century it seems to have fallen out of favour among the upper classes, at least as a participatory activity. As with other combat sports, wrestling was especially popular as a form of spectacle. Holme's description of wrestling reveals it to be a subtle art, with a fully developed vocabulary of its own. As described by Holme, each wrestler strove to cast his opponent flat on his back or on his neck and shoulders. North- and west-country men were particularly reputed for their skill at wrestling; the sport was particularly popular in Cornwall; Carew describes the Cornish version in some detail.

Anglo (2000: 172–201); Brewster (in Avedon and Sutton-Smith 1971: 47); Carew (1602: 75–6); Holme (2001: iii.5.3.64; iii.16.5.91a); Parkyns (1727); Strutt (1903: 69–73); Vale (1977: 118–21)

See also **Duelling**; **Hurling**

2

Glossary of Technical and Obsolete Terms

This glossary is intended to cover two categories of words: expressions or spellings not readily recognizable to the modern reader, and technical terms relating to games, regardless of their familiarity. Since the purpose of this glossary is lexical rather than orthographic, the form of the headword has been modernized as appropriate, with cross references where necessary. Where the word cannot be readily found in the *Oxford English Dictionary*, an *OED* headword or other etymon is added in square brackets. Page references are by page of the manuscript.

4edrical see **tetraedrical**
ace *n.* a roll of one on a die, or the side of a die with one spot, 19, 29, 35, etc.; the ace in cards, 49, 51, 53, etc.; **ace point**, see **point**. See also **bon ace**.
aequicrural *adj.* of a triangle: isosceles, 19.
aequinoctial *n.* the equinox, 5; *adj.* pertaining to the equinox, 53; **aequinoctial hours**, in the system of unequal hours: hours lasting as long as hours at the equinox, 5.
again *adv.* back, in response, 268.
a living a dog would not have it *phr.* a roll of six and five on two dice, 35.
ambling Annice *phr.* a roll of one and one on two dice, 35.
amsace *n.* a roll of one and one on two dice, 35 (*OED* **ames-ace**).
ar *conj.* or, 232.
arch see **port**
auntiant *adj.* ancient, 3/ii^v.
aves pugnaces (Latin) fighting birds, 270.
baby *n.* a doll, 217.
back lurch see **lurch**
back side *phr.* the blank side of a playing card, 49, 58.
backward *adv.* at Billiards: through the port from the direction opposite the king, 14/i^r, 14/i^v.
bandy *v.* in Tennis: ?to hit the ball over the line to the far wall of the court without attempting to score, 15/i^r.
bar *n.* at Prison Bars, Lilman, Father Fitchard, Hide and Seek: a base, 153, 154, 187, 220.

bar the suit *phr.* at Loadum: to forbid an exchange of the same suit, 84.

bare see **bear**

bare shoulders *phr.* at Ging: a hand with no court cards, 87.

basetting stick *phr.* meaning unknown: perhaps a curved stick used in stuffing fabric items to be basted? (Cf. the upholsterer's 'stuffing stick' in Holme 2001: iii.5.13.172), 171.

basis *n.* the base of a triangle or cone, 19, 222.

bate *v.* to reduce, subtract, 15/ii^r; ? = **bait**, to wrangle with an animal (used figuratively), 79.

battle cock see **cock**

be *v.*: **be one** (**five, seven**), to have scored one point (five points, seven points), 168.

bear *v.* at Tables: to play a piece off the board, 23, 43, etc.; also **bear off**, 37; also **play off**, 22, 23, 25.

bearded *adj.* tipped (with iron), 187.

beast *n.* at Beast: the stakes in the pot, 79; *v.* at Beast: to foil the player who initiated play or the counterer, compelling him to add as many stakes to the beast as are currently in it, 79, 80, 81.

beere *n.*: **take beere**, to get a running start, 161, 162 (*OED* **birr**).

beeves *n. pl.* cattle, 245.

bent *contr.* be not, 3/iv^r.

better *adj.*: **have the better**, to have the advantage, 39, 256.

bias side *phr.* the larger or heavier side of an assymetric bowl, 243.

biased *adj.* of a bowl: assymetrically shaped or weighted to follow an oblique course, 243.

bind *v.* at Tables: to play a piece onto a point occupied by one of one's own pieces, 27, 31; **bind up tables**, to bind all of one's own first six points, 39, 41, 43.

biske *n.* at Tennis: a free stroke that may be claimed at will once in the set, awarded to even the odds, 15/ii^r (*OED* **bisque**).

blackt *p. ppl.* blacked, covered with blacking, 15/i^r.

blank *n.* the blank side of a Long Laurence, 47.

blind *v.* to cover someone's eyes, 231; to blindfold, 221.

blot *n.* at Tables: a point having only one man on it and within range to be taken by the opponent, 29; *v.*: to create a blot, 39; **blot of a die**, a blot which can be reached by the opponent with the roll of a single die, 29, 31; **set a blot**, to create a blot, 31, 39; **hit a blot**, see **hit**.

board *n.* at Tennis: the lower hazard on the server's side, made of wood, 15/i^r.

bon ace *phr.* at One-and-Thirty Bon Ace: the ace of hearts, 60 (*OED* **bone-ace**).

booby *n.* a fool, 52; **play booby**, at cards: to make a secret deal with another player to collaborate, 52, 81.

boot pin *phr.* at Stowball: the post that marks the far side of the field from the starting point, 13/i^r, 13/i^v, 13/ii^v, 13/iiii^r. (Cf. *OED* **bout** n.^{2} 'circuit'.)

bowl (boule) *n.* a ball used for bowling games, 243, 245, 249, etc.; *v.* at Bowls: **bowl narrow**, to bowl too much toward the bias side of the ball, 243; **bowl wide**, to bowl too much away from the bias side, 243.

box *n.* at Billiards: one of the six hazards around the edge of the table, 14/i^r, 14/i^v; **give to the box**, at cards: to give a small part of the winnings to the butler or the one who provided the cards, 52.

brazil (brasell, brasil) *n.* brazilwood, 14/i^r, 19, 181, 243.

breadth *n.*: **of breadth**, along the breadth dimension, 15/i^r.

break *v.* at Tables: when a player's home table is bound up, to remove all men but one from one of the home points, 39, 41; also **break tables**, 39; also **open (tables)**, 39.

breathe *v.* to exercise (a horse, a cock) briskly, 151, 270.

brickwall *v.* at Tennis: to strike a ball against a side wall, causing it to rebound in an unexpected direction when it hits the floor, 15/i^r.

bridge see **port**

brimstone *n.* sulphur, 52.

bullet *n.* a small round ball, possibly of lead, 167, 168, 174, 219.

buttery *n.* a store room for drinks, 232.

buy the stock see **stock**

buz *n.* at Horn Billets: a cylindrical version of the **kitcat**, q.v. (?Cf. *OED* **buzz** *n.*^{2}, 'a plant-bur; a kind of beetle'.)

call for *phr.* at Gleek: to claim the points for (a gleek), 75.

capt *v.* ?error for **cap**, 235

carry good heels *phr.* of a fighting cock: to be an effective killer, 268.

cast *n.* the number rolled on a die or dice, 21, 22, 23, etc.; at Bowls or Quoits: the throwing of a bowl or quoit, 240; at Bowls, Penny Prick: one round of throwing by each player, 241, 243, 244. See also **single**, **double**.

cat see **kitcat**

cats are grey *phr.* a roll of four and three on two dice, 35.

challenge *v.* at Gleek: to question whether a player has the gleeks he called for, 75, 77; at Loadum: to compel another player to prove that he is not out, 83.

change *v.* to exchange, 84, 90.

charta (Latin) paper, 53.

chase *n.* at Tennis: a situation in which a player fails to return the ball after one bound, or the value assigned to the point on the court where the ball landed on the second bound, 15/i^v, 15/ii^r.

cinque *n.* a roll of five on a die, or the side of a die with five spots, 19, 22, 35, 49, etc.

clout *n.* a piece of cloth, a rag, 217.

club *n.* a card in the suit of clubs, or the symbol of the suit of clubs on a card, 49, 53.

coat *n.* at cards: a face card, a knave, queen, or king, 49, 52, 59, 75, 84, 87; also **coat card**, 49, 51, 87.

cobber *n.* at Cobnut: a nut which has broken other nuts, 219.

cob castle *phr.* at Cob Castle: the pyramidal pile of nuts that serves as a target, 219.

cock *n.*: **battle cock**, a fighting cock set to fight in an arranged match with another of comparable quality, 268; **dunghill cock**, an ordinary barnyard cock, as opposed to a fighting cock bred and trained for combat, 269; **Friesland cock**, a breed of cock, 269 (see Willughby 1678: 156); **game cock**, a cock bred and trained for fighting, a fighting cock, 268.

cod *n.* scrotum, 155.

cog *v.* to contrive to roll a particular number on the dice, 21.

conceit *n.* an idea, a concept, 7.

conoide *n.* a cone-shaped object, 222.

cotton *n.* a cotton cloth or (more likely) a kind of coarse woollen cloth, 15/i^v.

counter *v.* at Beast: to undertake to win against the player, 80; **counterer**, at Beast: one who counters, 80, 81.

court *n.*: **over the court**, at Tennis: ?to the far wall of the court, 15/i^r, 15/i^v.

crab *n.* a crabapple, 271.

crib *n.* at Cribbage: four cards laid out by the players, two by each, at the beginning of a game, 69, 70.

cropper *n.* one who has won victory at Cropping of Oaks, 229.

cross strings see **strings**

crow *n.* a bar of iron for the sport of bar-casting, 160.

cut *v.* at cards: to cut a pack of cards, 58; at Tennis: to give the ball a swift spin when hitting it with the racket, causing it to rebound contrary to its normal direction, 15/i^r, 15/iii^r.

cuts see **draw**

d. *abbrev.* penny, pence, 15, 244, 269, etc.

dead see **lie**

deal *v.* at cards: to deal, 49, 52, 55, etc.; **dealer**, at cards: the one who deals, 52, 55, 58, etc. See also **lose, lift**.

deck *n.* at cards: a pack of cards, 49, 51, 53, 59, etc.; also **pack**, 49, 101 (cancelled).

demonstration *n.* a mathematical proof, 50; at Beast: a hand in which a player has three cards sure to win their tricks, 80.

deuce (duce, dewce) *n.* a roll of two on a single die, or the side of a die with two spots, 19, 22, 35, etc.; at cards: a two, 49, 51, 73, 84, 89, etc.; at Tennis: a score of thirty-thirty, 15/i^v; at Shovelboard: a piece cast such as to score two points, 252.

diamond *n.* a card in the suit of diamonds or the symbol of the suit of diamonds on a card, 49, 51, 53. See also **picks**.

dib *v.* to coat with daub, 187; **dibbing**, clay or mud used as daub, 187.

die see **hell**

dies Lunae (Latin) Monday, 5.

dog, dogstaff *n.* the staff used in Horn Billets and Kit-Cat, 173, 175, 269.

double *adj*: **double game**, a victory which yields double the original stakes to the winner, 14/i^v, 29, 43, 59, 69, etc; **double cast**, at Bowls, Quoits, etc.: a throw that scores two points, 240; **double hand**, see **hand**; **double perryal**, see **perryal**. Cf. **single, treble**.

doublets *n.* a roll of doubles on two dice, 23, 25, 43.

down, downwards *adv.* at Stowball: toward the boot pin, 13/i^r, 13/iii^r; at Stoolball: into the field, 169 (cf. **up**).

draw *v*. at cards: to ask for or take a card from the deck, 59, 60; **draw cuts**, to draw lots, draw straws, 164; **draw stakes**, see **stake**.

duce see **deuce**

dun *n*. a generic name for a horse, 156.

dunghill cock see **cock**

eight *adj*. eighth, 233.

either *pron*. each, 21.

elder *adj*. at cards: having priority in play from having received cards before another player, usually through being located closer to the dealer's left, 55, 59, 67, etc.; **eldest**, at cards: having received the first card in the deal, 55, 59, 60, 61, etc. Cf. **younger**.

enter *v*. at Tables: to play a piece onto the tables, 37, 39, 41; of a piece: to be played onto the tables, 37, 39, 41.

face *n*. the face side of a card, 49, 53, 55, etc.

fall down *phr*. to get down, crouch down, 246.

fellow *n*. at Laugh and Lie Down: a card of matching value to another card, 61, 62; *v*. at Laugh and Lie Down: to play a matching card to a card on the table, 61.

few *interj*. a cry used by bowlers to encourage the ball to go faster, 244. (Origin unknown. Cf. 'flee' in Holme 2001: iii.16.2.46d.)

fifteen *n*. at Noddy, Cribbage: a combination of cards totalling 15 points, 65, 66, 69, etc.

find *v*. to provide, 52, 155/i^r.

fingerstall *n*. a cover or protection for the finger, 270.

first come at two *phr*. at Tennis: a situation in which, both players being one game away from winning the set, they agree that they will play until each wins a game, and the player who wins the next game afterwards wins the set, 15/iii.

fitchard *n*. the sharpened stick used in the game of Father Fitchard, 187.

five madg, five peg see **madg**

flush *n*. at cards: several cards of the same suit, 65, 66, 70.

follow suit see **suit**

forbear *v*. omit, refrain from, 15/i^r.

fore game see **game**

fore lurch see **lurch**

form *n*. a bench, 229, 232.

forward *adv*. at Billiards: through the port from the direction of the king, 13/i^r.

foul *adj*. cheating, unfair, 21, 55, 219, 268, 269.

fox *n*. the large mobile piece in Fox and Geese, 256.

freestone *n*. fine-grained sandstone or limestone, 15/i^r.

Friesland cock see **cock**

gablock see **gaffle**

gaffle *n*. at cockfighting: an artificial spur of metal, 270; also **gablock**, 270.

gallery *n*. at Tennis: the arcade where the spectators stand, 15/i^r, 15/ii^r.

game *n*. at Tennis: a unit of play achieved when a player wins four strokes, four games constituting a set, 15/i^v, 15/ii^v, 15/iii; at Billiards: a victory or defeat that scores a point for one of the players, five or seven games constituting a set, 14/i^v (cf. **loss**); at cards: the combination of cards held by the player or a specific combination of cards that scores points, 59, 65, 66, 67; as *adj.*, at Tennis: having won four strokes, 15/i^v, 15/ii^r; **fore game**, at Irish: a game in which the player plays his pieces off the board without having had any of them removed by his opponent, 39; **latter game**, at Irish: a situation in which a player leaves blots on purpose in order to incite the opponent to take them off the board, so that they can be played onto the board again and impede the opponent's progress, 39; at Noddy: a game in which the victor does not reach thirty-one points, 67. See also **single**, **double**, **treble**.

game cock see **cock**

gamester *n.* a player, 15/i^r, 21, 49, 241, etc.

gaol see **goal**

gentile *adj.* genteel, fashionable, 53, 244.

gentlemen *n.* at Ging: a hand containing only court cards, 87.

geometrical proportion see **proportion**

ging *n.* at Ging: a hand containing a total of thirty-seven points in any one suit, 87, 88 (?cf. *OED* **ging** 'company, crew, pack').

give *v.* **give over**, to stop, stop playing, give up, 21, 73, 149, 175, 187; **give ground**, see **ground**; **give to the box**, see **box**; **give a turn**, see **turn**.

gleek *n.* at cards: three of a kind, 57, 75, 77, 80, 83; also **perryal**, q.v.

gliff *n.* a tongue-twister, 234 (?cf. *OED* **gliff** v. 'to make a slip in reading').

goal, gaol *n.* at Football, Hurling, Bandy Ball: a goal at or through which points are scored, 155, 155/i^r, 170; at Hide and Seek: a base, 220.

goose *n.* one of the smaller pieces at Fox and Geese, 256.

great planet see **planet**

ground *n.*: **give ground**, at Bowls: to set one's foot at a spot on the ground to indicate where one's teammate should aim, 243; **hit one's ground**, at Bowls: to roll one's bowl to the target spot indicated by a teammate, 243.

grill *n.* at Tennis: a form of upper hazard covered by a grate, 15/i^r.

guarded *adj.* at Loadum, of a high card: protected by the presence of a low card of the same suit in the same hand, 84.

habiliments *n. pl.* clothing, 51.

half-crown *n.* a coin worth 2 shillings 6 pence, 251; **half a crown**, the value of 2 shillings 6 pence, 33.

half-dozens *n.*: **toss (play) half-dozens**, at Tennis: ?to play a simple version of the game involving smothering and bandying, 15/i^r. Cf. **set**.

hams *n. pl.* hips, 158.

hand *n.* at cards: a hand of cards, 58, 63, 79, etc.; **double (single) hand**, at Tables, cards: a game played with two people (one person) on a side, 43, 70, 71, 72.

hand kerchier *n.* handkerchief, 151.

hard *p. ppl.* heard, 51.

hast *n.* haste, 14/i^r.

have it *phr.* at Thirty-One: to take another card, 59.

hazard *n.* at Tennis: one of four targets at the corners of the court, 15/i^r, 15/i^v; at Billiards: one of six targets located around the billiards table, 14/i^r; **hazarding**, at Billiards: attempting to knock an opponent's ball into a hazard, 14/i^v; also called **holing**, 14/i^v; **hazard side**, at Tennis: the end of the court occupied by the one who receives the serve, 15/i^v.

head *n.* at Ruff and Trump: the four cards left over after the deal, 71; **on (of) their own heads**, independently, 72, 241; **take a point on a man's head**, see **take**.

heart (hart) *n.* a card in the suit of hearts or the symbol of the suit of hearts on a card, 49, 51, 53, etc.

heigth, heighth *n.* height, 15/i^r.

hell *n.* the central position in Barley Breaks, 148, 149; **die in hell**, to be in hell at the end of the game, 149.

herb of grace *phr.* the plant rue, Ruta graveolens, 270 (*OED* **herb-grace**).

hexaedrical *adj.* six-sided, 22 (cf. *OED* **hexahedricall** sv. **hexahedral**).

hip skip *phr.* at Nine Men's Morris: a state of play in which a player has only three pieces left, and can move them anywhere on the board without regard to contiguity, 254/i^v, 254/ii^v (cf. *OED* **hip** v^1 'to hop').

hit *v.* at Tables: to play a piece onto (an opponent's blot), 29, 31, 37, 41; **hit one's ground**, see **ground**.

hitter *adj.* at One-and-Thirty or Hannikin Canst Abide It: having reached exactly the number needed to win, 59, 60.

hive *n.* the hat in Buying of Bees, 229; see also **stive**.

hog *n.* at Shovel Board: a piece which stops short of the first scoring line, worth no points, 251.

hoist see **stock**

holing see **hazard**

home *n.* at Tables: the first point on a player's side, 27, 29, 37, etc.; *adv.*, at Tables: to the player's first six points, 37, 39, 41, 43; at various games: to the starting or finishing point, 153, 163, 164; **play at home**, at Tables: to play one's pieces in one's first twelve points, 27.

homewards *adv.* at Tables: toward the player's first point, 37.

honour *n.* at Gleek: the ace and face cards of trumps, which are worth extra when counting up points, 51, 77.

hoodwink *v.* to blindfold someone, 221; to hide someone's eyes, 221, 230.

hoodwinke *adj.* having one's eyes hidden, 220.

hot *p. ppl.* of **hit** 37, 39.

hut *n.* in cockfighting: a protective cover placed over a fighting cock's spur to prevent it causing injury in sparring, 270 (*OED* **hot** sb^3).

in *adv.* in a round of play, not out, 59, 84. Cf. **out**.

insist *v.* to stand, rest, 19.

interchangeably *adv.* in alternation, 19.

is *poss. pron.* his, 230.

jack *n.* in Quoits or Bowls: the quoit or bowl at which the others are cast, 240, 241, 243, 244.

jockey *n.* a rider of race horses, a jockey, 151.

kater *n.* a roll of four on a die, or the side of a die with four spots, 19, 22, 35, etc. (*OED* **cater**).

keeper *n.* at Tennis: one who keeps a tennis court, 15/ii^r; at Bowls: one who keeps a bowling green, 244.

kersey *n.* a kind of woollen cloth, 15/i^v.

king *n.* at Billiards: the standing target on a billiards table, 14/i^r, 14/i^v.

kitcat *n.* a wooden cylinder, sometimes tapering on the ends, used in the games of Kit-Cat and Horn Billets, 173, 174; also **cat**, 173, 174, 175.

knack see **knock**

knatch *v.* ?to snatch, ?to knock, 229 (orig. unknown; ?cf. *OED* **knetch**, 'knock').

knock, knack *v.* to knock, 187; at Bowls: to aim one's bowl at an opponent's bowl to knock it away from the target, 243; **knocking of dogstaffs**, at Horn Billets: the act of two players knocking their staves together over one of the holes, required for the last three points of the game, 175.

knots or flats *phr.* at Tennis: the two sides of a racket, used in a toss to determine priority of play, 15/i^v.

latter game see **game**

latus *n.* the measurement of a side, 19.

law *n.* a rule in a game, 27, 53, 81, 155.

lay *n.* at Stowball: the distance a player can reach with his staff from his planted foot, 13/i^v, 13/ii^r, 13/ii^v, 13/iii^v; **within (without) the compass of four lays**, within (outside) a radius of four lays, 13/ii^r; **lay pin**, the post at which the players begin, 13/i^r, 13/i^v (?cf. *OED* **lay** n.^{7}). Cf. **pin**.

lead *v.* at Bowls: to throw the jack onto the pitch, 243, 244; at cards: to play the first card of a trick, 79, 89; also **lead about**, 71; **lead out**, at Prison Bars: to step away from contact with the base, 153.

lenght *n.* length, 17, 35, 173, etc.; **at length**, at Tables: using the total of both dice, 22, 27.

lenghten *v.* to lengthen, 53.

lesser planet see **planet**

lie dead *phr.* at Bowls, Shovel Board: to count for nothing, score nothing, 241, 252.

lift *v.*: **lift (for dealing)**, at cards: to lift cards from the deck to determine who will deal first, 53.

lilman *n.* at Lilman: the player who guards the base, 154.

line *n.* at Tennis: the cord stretched across the middle of the court, 15/i^r, 15/i^v, 15/ii^r; **over line**, at Tennis: over the line, 15/i^v; **under line**, at Tennis: under the line, 15/i^r, 15/i^v; **turn line**, at Tennis: to exchange ends of the court, 15/i^v.

loader *n.* at Losing Loadum: a card that counts against the person holding it at the end, 83, 84; at Winning Loadum: a card that counts in favour of the one holding it, 85.

long rest *phr.* at Tennis: a long sequence of hits back and forth, 15/i^v.

looker see **trea**

lose, loose *v*.: **lose dealing**, at cards: to misdeal, 52, 87; **losing of men**, at Irish: a situation in which some of one's pieces are trapped in the opponent's tables and one is obliged to accumulate the rest on one's own first points, 41.

loss *n*. at Billiards: an event which causes a player to lose a game, 14/i^r, 14/i^v.

love *n*. at Tennis: a score of zero, 15/i^v, 15/ii^r.

lurch *n*. at Cribbage: a situation in which a player reaches sixty-one points before the opponent reaches forty-five, 69; at Bowls: a situation in which one side loses before scoring any points (also **fore lurch**), or a side wins by getting all its points at once or in succession (also **back lurch**), 244; **be lurched**, at Bowls: to be defeated through a lurch, 244

make *v*.: to allow (a certain way of winning a game), 31; **make aloft**, to cause something to rise, 15/i^r.

madg *n*. at Ten-Pegs: a small pin placed halfway between the trig and ruck, 245, 246, 247; also **five madg, five peg**, 245. (?Shortened form of **Margery**; cf. **jack**; ?also cf. *OED* **madge**, 'barn owl'.)

main strings see **strings**

making for a set see **set**

man *n*. at Tables, Nine Men's Morris, Three Men's Morris: a playing piece, 22, 251/i^v, 254/ii^r, etc.

match *n*. a piece of cardboard soaked in sulphur to take flame from a tinderbox, 52.

maumsay *n*. a roll of one and one on two dice, 35 (?cf. **maumsie**, var. of *OED* **malmsey**).

measured *adj*. divisible, 5.

mend *v*. to improve, 80.

mice *phr*. a roll of one and one on two dice, 35.

mistress *n*. a fixed target in bowling or quoits, 241, 243. See also **sweetheart**.

more *adv*.: **as much more as**, as many again as, 29, 69.

murnivall *n*. four of a kind at cards, 50, 57, 61, etc.; also **double perryal**, see **perryal** (*OED* **mournival**).

musical proportion see **proportion**

nick *n*. at Tennis: the angled corner at the base of the end walls of the court, 15/i^r, 15/ii^r (?cf. *OED* **nick** sb^1 'notch').

nip *v*. at Tables: to take a man with the roll of one die, and move onward with the roll of the other, 37.

nodde *n*. at Noddy: the Knave, 65, 66, 67; also **nodde knave**, 66.

nor *conj*. neither, 67.

nothing *n*.: **stand for nothing, signify nothing**, to do nothing, have no effect, 13/ii^r, 55, 83, 148, 251.

obtusangle *adj*. obtuse-angled, 49.

of *adv*. off, 17, 23, 25, etc.

one *num*.: **be all one**, to be the same, not to matter, 43, 148.

open see **break**

out *adv*. at Tables: ?out of the player's first six points, 29; at various games: out of a round of play, 59, 163, 169, 175, etc. (cf. **in**); at Losing Loadum: having reached thirty-one points or more, 83, 84; **lead out**, see **lead**.

outbid *v.* at cards: to offer increasing bids against one another, 73.

outbowl *v.* at Bowls: to play the jack farther away than another player can bowl, 244.

outdare *v.* to outbluff, 75.

outtop *v.* to rise above, 268.

overhand *adv.* overhand, 168; also **upper hand**, 177.

overplus *n.* surplus, 72.

oversee *v.* to overlook, 33, 62.

packthread *n.* a heavy thread or twine used for packing and bundling, 15/i^v.

pair *n.* at cards: two cards of the same value, 57, 62, 65, etc.; **pair royal**, see **perryal**.

parallelogrammon *n.* a parallelogram, 49 (Greek).

parallelopipedon *n.* a solid figure whose faces are six parallelograms, each parallel to its opposite, 47 (Greek; cf. *OED* **parallelcpiped**).

pass *n.* at fencing: a thrusting attack with a rapier, 275.

pass *v.* at Beast: to decline to undertake to win a round of play, 79, 80; at Ruff and Trump: to decline to bid for the ruff, 73, 75.

pat *v.* to strike, 167; ? = **put**, 175.

pease *n. pl.* peas, 217.

pee *n.* the central stake at Ging, 87; the center hole at Three Men's Morris, 254/ii^r (cf. *OED* **pee** sb^2 'the intersection of two veins in mining').

peep *n.* a pip on a playing card, 49, 51, 71, etc.

peg *n.* a bowling pin, 245, 246, 247; **five peg**, see **madg**; **ten peg**, the large pin in the middle of the ruck at bowling, 245, 246; also **ten**, 247.

pegged *p.ppl.* sealed into a hole by means of a peg, 271.

penthouse *n.* the slope-roofed structure lying around two sides of a tennis court, 15/i^r, 15/i^v.

pepper dust *phr.* ground pepper, 269.

perryal *n.* at cards: three of a kind, 57, 62, 65, 70, 101; also **pair royal**, 57; also **gleek**, q.v.; **double perryal**, four of a kind, 57, 62, 65; also **murnivall**, q.v. (*OED* **pair-royal**).

pescod *n.* a peascod, pea-pod, 238.

picks *n. pl.* at cards: a rustic name for the suit of diamonds, 53.

pile *n.* the downy part of a feather, 177; the point of an arrow, 177; the 'head' side of a coin, 218.

pillored *p.ppl.* at I Call and I Call: subjected to a kind of game punishment (see text), 168 (?cf. *OED* **pillor** 'pillory').

pin *n.* at Stowball: one of two sticks planted in the ground to mark the course, 13/i^r, 13/i^v, 13/ii^r, 13/ii^v, 13/iii^r. See also **boot**, **lay**.

pitching *ger.*: **pitching off the arm**, a form of casting the bar in which the bar is thrown one-handed like a javelin, 160; **pitching off the shoulder**, a form of casting the bar in which the bar is thrown two-handed from an upright position, like a caber, 160.

planet *n.*: **great planets**, the sun and moon, 7; **lesser planet**, any of the other planets from Mercury to Saturn, 7, 9.

plate see **silver**

play *n.* a game, 3, 3/ii^r, 3/iii^r, etc.; *v.* at cards: to lay down a card in play, 55, 62, 67, etc.; at Beast: to initiate play, 79, 80; at Tables: to move a man, 22, 27, 31, etc.; to move a man according to (a roll on the dice), 22, 27, 28; **play off**, see **bear**; **play upon**, at Tables: to move a piece onto a point, to move a piece onto a point occupied by another piece, 27, 29; **play down**, at Doublets: to play down a piece from its stack, 23, 25; also **put down**, 23.

player *n.* at Beast: one who initiates play, 80, 81.

playstered *p. ppl.* plastered, 15/i^r.

point *n.* a lace with metal ends, used to secure clothing, 236 (see Glossary of Games sv. **Dust Point**); at Tables: any of the triangular spaces on the board, 19, 21, 22, etc.; **ace point**, at Tables: a player's first point on the board, 41. See also **take**.

porch see **port**

port *n.* at Billiards: the arched target on the billiards table, 14/i^r, 14/i^v; also **porch**, 14/i^r; also **arch**, 14/i^r, 14/i^v; also **bridge**, 14/i^v.

post *v.* to toss a ball up with one hand and hit it with the other, 168, 169, 170 (?cf. *OED* **post** v.^{1} sense 4. 'dispatch, send in haste'; ?cf. Italian *posta*, 'a volley in Tennis').

pound *n.* at Nine Men's Morris: the circle in the centre of the board into which pieces are put when they are removed from play, 254/i^r; *v.*, at Nine Men's Morris: to remove an opponent's piece from play, 254/i^v, 254/ii^r, 254/ii^v.

praecedent *adj.* previous, 5.

prime *n.* at Beast: a hand with one of each suit, 81.

prison *n.* at Prison Bars: the area where captured players are kept until released by a teammate, 153; at Father Fitchard: the base to which a player must run when his fitchard is dug up from the ground, or if he tries and fails to dig up another player's fitchard, 187.

proportion *n.*: **geometrical proportion**, the relationship between a series of numbers in which the ratio between each adjacent pair of numbers remains constant, 66, 70; **musical proportion**, the relationship between a series of numbers whose reciprocals are in arithmetic proportion (so that in the sequence a:b:c, $1/b - 1/a = 1/c - 1/b$), 70.

pull up *phr.* to kill a fighting cock by pulling on (its head), 269.

punctual *adj.* precise, detailed, 15/ii^v.

put *n.* at Put-Pin: a pushing of one's pin, 218.

put *v.* at Put: to say 'Put', thereby offering to stake the entire game on the current hand, 89, 90; **put out**, at cards: to remove a card from the deck or one's hand, discard, 57, 71, 73, etc.; **put down**, see **play**.

quadrant *n.* a quarter, a fourth part, 7.

quaere (Latin) 'question, inquire, investigate', 3/iii^r, 7, 15/i^r, etc.

quasi (Latin) 'as if, as it were' (used to suggest etymologies), 13/ii^v, 234.

racket *n.* a tennis racket, 15/i^{r-v}, 15/iii^r.

rake *v.* at Tennis: to hit (a ball), 15/i^r (?cf. *OED* **rake** v.^{1} or v.^{2}).

ramper *n.* a fighting cock who bears his head high, 268. (Cf. *OED* **ramp** v.^{1} 'rear up'.)

rapd *p.* of **wrap** *v.*, 238.

rectangle *adj.* right-angled, 49.

refuse *v.* at cards: to decline to see a vie, 75.

relieve prisoners *phr.* at Prison Bars: to release one's teammates from prison by touching them, 153.

remove *v.* to move a playing piece or marker, 67, 254/i^v, 254/ii^r; *n.*, a move of a playing piece, 254/ii^r, 256.

renounce *v.* at cards: to play a card which is not of the suit led, 80, 83.

request *n.*: **come in request**, to come into vogue, 5.

revie *v.* at Ruff and Trump: to increase a vie, 73, 75; **seeing and revying,** at Ruff and Trump: meeting and increasing a bid for the ruff, 73.

rim *v.* to move pieces at Nine Men's Morris, 254/i^v, 254/ii^v (cf. *OED* **rime** v. 4, 'remove, clear away').

roll (roul) *v.* to pass a heavy roller over a bowling green in order to even it, 243.

rose *n.* at Tennis: one of four images of a rose marked on the court, used in reckoning chases etc., 15/i^v, 15/ii^r.

rovers *n.* at Ticktack: the situation of getting a man into the twelfth and thirteenth points, if none of the player's other men are 'out' (q.v.), thereby winning a double game, 29, 31, 33 (?cf. *OED* **rover** n.^{1} 'a wanderer'; cf. also the name 'boveries' given to the same situation in Cotton 1930: 77).

rub *n.* at Bowls: an impediment on the surface of the green or alley, 244; also, as *interj.*, a cry used by bowlers to encourage the ball to slow down; *v.* at Ruff and Trump: to take in the head, 71, 72.

ruck *n.* at Ten Pegs: the body of pins standing together, 245, 246, 247 (*OED* **ruck** n.^{1} 'heap, throng').

ruff (ruffe, rufe) *n.* at cards: the stage at which the players bet on whether they have the largest point-value of cards in a single suit, or the cards so held or the points scored for them, 51, 55, 71, 72, etc.

run *p. pl.* of run, 35.

running hazards *phr.* at Tennis: ?a simple version of the game in which there is no bandying or smothering, 15/i^r. Cf. **set**.

running rotchet, running ratchit *phr.* at Nine Men's Morris: a situation in which a player has three pieces in a row on three of the inner points of the board, 254/i^v, 254/ii^v.

s. *abbrev.* shilling, 71, 73.

save *v.* at Tables: to bring a piece out of the opponent's tables, 41.

scape *n.* the shaft of a feather, 177.

scour *v.* to be purged through diarrhea, 270.

see *v.* at Gleek: to meet a vie or revie, 73, 75; at Put: to meet a put, 89; at Ticktack: to meet a vie, 33. See also **revie**.

septemplal *adj.* generated from a set of seven possible alternatives, 88; ?also as *n.*, 88.

sequence (sequens) *n.* a series of cards in numerical sequence, a straight, 52, 65, 66, 69, 70; also as *adj.*, 52.

serve *v.* at Tennis: to initiate play by hitting the ball over the court, 15/i^v;

serving end, at Tennis: the end from which the ball is served, 15/ii^r. Cf. **hazard**.

service *n.* at Tennis: the serving of the ball, 15/i^r.

set *n.* at Tennis: a unit of play achieved by winning four games, 15/i^v, 15/ii^r, 15/ii^v, 15/iii^r; at Billiards: a unit of play achieved by winning five or seven games, 14/i^v; at Ruff and Trump: a unit of play that wins the stake, 71; at Noddy, Cribbage, Put: a game, 68, 69, 70, 71, 89; **making for a set**, at Tennis: a situation in which both players have three games each, and the winner of the last chooses **first come at two** or **two for it**, 15/iii^r; **play a set**, at Tennis: to play a full version of the game involving winning four 'games' to make a 'set', 15/i^v (cf. **half-dozens**, **running hazards**).

set *v.*: **set down**, to score, 67, 71, 169, 173, 241, 245, etc.; **set the cards**, at cards: to stack the deck, 58; **set on**, ?error for **set down**, 89. See also **blot**.

setter *n.* at cockfighting: an official in charge of matching cocks against one another, 268.

seven cards *phr.* at Ging: a hand containing seven cards of a single suit, 87, 88.

sextant *n.* a sixth part, 7.

shakebag *n.* at cockfighting: a cock kept in a bag prior to the contest so that it can be brought out to fight another sight unseen, 268.

sharpen round *phr.* to sharpen to a conical point, 173.

shelve *phr.* to project, 174, 232.

shovel *v.* to shuffle, slide, 241.

shuffle *v.* at cards: to shuffle cards, 58.

shut *p.ppl.*: **get shut of**, to get rid of (a card), 83.

silver plate *n.* silver plating, 155/i^r.

sing Alse and I'll whistle *n. phr.* a roll of five and one on two dice, 35.

single *adj.*: **single game**, a game which yields a single stake to the winner, 14/i^v, 29, 33, 43, 59, etc.; **single cast**, at Stoolball: a throw that scores one point, 169; **single hand**, see **hand**. Cf. **double**, **treble**.

sise *n.* a roll of six on a die, or the side of a die with six spots, 19, 22, 35, 49, etc.

sixt *adj.* sixth, 3/iii^v.

slight *n.* a trick, secret, special art of doing something, 101, 155, 162, 168 (*OED* **sleight**).

slur *v.* at dice: to roll a particular number by throwing the die such that it does not tumble, 21.

smother *v.* at Tennis: to hit a ball under line to the nick, causing it to rebound upward, 15/i^r.

solstitial *adj.* pertaining to the solstice, 53.

some fought, some ran away *phr.* a roll of five and three on two dice, 35.

soope *v.*: **soope all**, the side of a Long Laurence with several crosses on it, indicating that the player takes up the entire pot, 47 (*OED* **soop** v. 'sweep').

sow *v.* to sew, 15/i^v, 155, 167, 217.

spade *n.* a card in the suit of spades or the symbol of the suit of spades on a card, 49, 51, 53.

span *n.* the breadth of a hand, 253.

spar *v.* to set fighting cocks to engage in practice combat, 270; of a fighting cock: to engage in practice combat, 270.

sphaerula (Latin) a small sphere, a ball, 3/iii^v.

squared *p. ppl.* made square in cross section, 14/i^r.

staff *n.* a billiards staff, 14/i^r, 14/i^v.

stake *n.* a stake played for in a game, 21, 33, 63, etc.; *v.* to place a stake in the pot, 47, 61, 79, etc.; **draw stakes**, to withdraw everything staked on a match, 268.

stich *n.* a stick, 232.

stick *v.* at One and Thirty, Hanikin Canst Abide It, etc.: to stop taking cards, 59, 60.

stive *n.* a straw container resembling a beehive, serving to keep a fighting cock warm, 270; also **hive**, 270; as *v.*, to place a cock in a stive, 270.

stock *n.* at cards: the cards left over after all hands are fully dealt, 52, 59, 73, etc.; **buy the stock**, at Gleek: to take the stock by bidding, 73, 75; **hoist the stock**, at Gleek: to raise the bidding on the stock without intending to take it in, 73.

straight *adj.* tight, 220.

string *n.*: **cross strings**, the horizontal strings on a tennis racket, 15/i^v; **main strings**, the vertical strings on a tennis racket, 15/i^v.

stroke, strocke *n.* at Tennis: the smallest unit of scoring, an event which scores, 15/i^v, 15/ii^r; also, a hitting of the ball, 15/ii^r.

strooke *p. ppl.* struck, 155.

suit (suite, sute) *n.* a suit of cards, 49, 51, 55, etc; **follow suit**, to play a card of the suit led, 55, 80.

superficies *n.* surface, 174.

sure card *phr.* at Laugh and Lie Down: a card that the player can be certain to have for himself, 62.

sute see **suit**

swallow *v.* at Loadum: to take by mistake a trick which has been trumped by another player, 83, 84.

sweetheart *n.* at Ticktack: **keep your sweetheart**, to keep two men on one's first point, 31; also **keep your mistress whole**, 33; **break (lose) your sweetheart**, to be compelled to move a man out of one's first point, 31.

table *n.* one half of the hinged board used for games at Tables, 17, 21, 22, etc.; see **bind, break, open**.

tailor's shreds *phr.* scraps of woollen cloth, 15/i^v.

take *v.*: **take a point,** at Tables: to place two men upon a point so that the opponent cannot move there, 27, 29, 31, etc.; **take a point upon a man's head**, at Tables: to take a point occupied by a single opponent, 37; **take bar**, at Prison Bars: to touch base, 153; **take in**, at cards: to take (cards) into one's hand, 71, 73, 77, etc.; **be taken**, at Gleek: to put out better cards than one takes in when taking the stock, 73. See also **beere**.

tatching end *phr.* a shoemaker's waxed thread, pointed with a hog's bristle, 219 (*OED* **tache** v^2).

ten *v.* at Gleek: to play a card worth ten points to a card led, 77; **ten peg**, see **peg**.

tetraedrical *adj.* tetrahedral, 22, 48.

then *conj.* than, 5, 7, 9, etc.

thorough, thorow *prep.* and *adv.* through, 14/iʳ, 14/iᵛ, 21, etc.

throw *v.* to throw a die or dice, 21, 22, 23, etc.; **throw for the dice**, at Tables: to throw dice to determine order of play, 21, 53; **throw down**, knock down, 14/iʳ, 14/iᵛ; **throw up the cards**, at cards: to turn in the cards and deal new hands, 89, 90.

Tib *n.* at Gleek: the ace of trumps, 77.

tick *v.* at Tick: to tag, 222.

tie *n.* at Put: a tied trick, 89.

tip *n.* at Kit-Cat: a stroke at the kitcat, 173.

tipt *p. ppl.* furnished with a tip, tipped, 14/iʳ.

titch *n.* ?error for **stitch**, 167.

to *adv.* too, 15/iiʳ., 15/iiᵛ, 41, etc.

Tom *n.* at Gleek: the knave of trumps, 77.

toots *n.* at Ticktack: taking all the points in one section of the table, worth a double game, 29, 31, 33, etc. (*OED* **tout** n.³).

toss half-dozens see **half-dozens**

tossing of balls *phr.* a pastime in which balls are bounced back and forth, 167.

toucher *n.* at Bowls, Quoits: a ball or quoit which touches the jack or mistress, 240.

traduce me not *phr.* a roll of three and two on two dice, 35.

traies see **trea**

trash and trumpery *phr.* a roll of three and one on two dice, 35.

trea (pl. **treas**, **traies**) *n.* a roll of three on a die, or the side of a die with three spots, 19, 22, 35, 43, etc.; at cards: a three, 49, 65, 73, etc.; at Shovelboard: a piece so cast as to project over the edge of the board, scoring three points, 252; also **looker**, 252.

treble game *phr.* a game that yields three times the original stakes to the winner, 43. Cf. **single**, **double**.

trencher *n.* a wooden plate, 87, 221, 229, 230, 232.

trick *n.* a series of cards played in sequence by each player, a trick, 52, 55, 89, etc.; **trick, trick, and tie**, at Put: a situation in which each player wins one trick and they tie for the third, 89.

trig *n.* at Bowls: a metal marker used to indicate the point at which the players place their rear feet, 243.

tripping up of heels *phr.* at Football: tripping up an opponent while he is running, 155.

trompe see **trump**

tromper (French) to deceive, 55.

trull *v.* to roll a ball, 167.

trump, trompe *n.* at cards: the card which is turned up to determine the trump suit, 55, 71, 72, etc.; any card of the trump suit, 55, 57, 71, etc.

tuck *n.* a thrusting sword, 275.

tup *n.* ?a ram, 35 (*OED* **tup** n.).

turn *n.* **give the first turn**, at coursing, of a greyhound: to cause the hare to change direction sharply to evade capture, 272.

turn line see **line**

tush *n.* a tusk, 217.

tut *n.* the target in Tutball or Stoolball, 171.

twenty-five *n.* at Noddy: a combination of cards totalling twenty-five, 65, 66.

two for it *phr.* at Tennis: a situation in which, the players having each won three games, the winner of the last decides that whoever can win two games before the other player gets one will win the set, 15/iii^r; also **two games**, 15/iii^r.

two tailors *phr.* a roll of three and three on two dice, 35.

two thieves beside the caster *phr.* a roll of five and five on two dice, 35.

Tyde *n.* at Gleek: the four of trumps, 75 (*OED* **Tiddy**).

underhand *adv.* underhand, 168, 177.

up *adj.* having reached the number to which a game is being played, 89, 173, 244, 246; as *n.*, the number required to be up, 55, 71, 89, 241, etc.; as *adv.*, at Stowball: towards the lay pin, 13/i^v, 13/iii^r; at Stoolball: to the upper end of the field (where one defends the stool), 169 (cf. **down**).

upper hand see **overhand**

use to *phr.* to be accustomed to do something, 33, 150, 169, etc.; accustom (someone) to (something), 217; **there uses to be**, there is commonly, 81.

valor *n.* at cards: the worth or point-value of a card, 51, 57.

vauntage *n.* at Tennis: a score of forty-thirty, 15/i^v, 15/ii^r (*OED* **vantage**).

verticity *n.* rotation, 222, 241.

vide (Latin) see, 5, 13/iii^v, 21, etc.

vie *n.* at Tables: an increasing of the stakes by a factor of one, 33; at Gleek: a bid for the ruff, 75; *v.* at Tables: to propose to increase the stakes by a factor of one, 33; at Gleek: to bid for the ruff, 73, 75.

vollee *n.* at Tennis: a stroke which hits a ball before it bounces, 15/ii^r (*OED* **volley**).

wattles *n.* the fleshy appendages hanging from the head or neck of a fighting cock, 268.

wheehee *adj.* at Wheehee: having all three of one's cards of the same suit, 90.

whitleather *n.* a soft, light-colored leather, 15/i^v, 222.

why not *phr.* at Ticktack: a loss incurrred when the player fails to see that he has a win or the opportunity for a win, 33.

win *v.* at cards: to beat (a card), 51, 55, 60, etc.; to take (a trick), 52, 55, 71, etc.; **win of**, to win a stake from (someone), 59, 60, 73.

windore *n.* window, 21, 238.

wink *v.* to hide one's eyes, 220.

wither, whither *conj.* whether, 3/iii^r, 7, 9, etc.

wrangler *n.* a quarreller, 55.

yard *n.* a roll of six and six on two dice, 35.

younger *adj.* at cards: having lower priority in play due to having received one's cards after another player, usually due to sitting closer to the right side of the dealer, 55, 59, 67; **youngest**, having lowest priority in play, 55, 81, 87. Cf. **elder**.

Bibliography

A

Francis Willughby's Literary Remains

1 Books

Francisci Willughbeii de Middleton in agro Warwicensi, Armigeri, e Regia Societate, Ornithologiæ libri tres: In quibus aves omnes hactenus cognitæ in methodum naturis suis convenientem redactæ accuratè describuntur, Descriptiones iconibus elegantissimis & vivarum avium simillimis, Æri incisis illustrantur / Totum opus recognovit, digessit, supplevit Joannes Raius; Sumptus in Chalcographos fecit Illustriss. D. Emma Willughby, Vidua. Londini: Impensis Joannis Martyn, Regiæ Societatis Typographi, ad insigne Campanæ in Cæmeterio D. Pauli, 1676.

The Ornithology of Francis Willughby: in three books wherein all the birds hitherto known being reduced into a method suitable to their natures are accurately described. The descriptions illustrated by … LXXVIII copper plates. Translated into English, and enlarged with many additions throughout the whole work. To which are added, three considerable discourses, I. Of the art of fowling: with a description of several nets in two large copper plates. II. Of the ordering of singing birds. III. Of falconry / by John Ray. London: Printed by A.C. for John Martyn, printer to the Royal Society, at the Bell in St. Paul's Church-Yard, 1678.

De historia piscium libri quatuor, in quibus non tantum De Piscibus in genere agitur, sed & species omnes, tum ab aliis traditae, tum novae & nondum editae bene multae, naturae ductum servante methodo dispositae, accurate describuntur. Earumque effigies, quotquot haberi potuere, vel ad vivum delineatae, vel ad optima exemplaria impressa artifici manu elegantissime in aes incisae, ad descriptiones illustrandas exhibentur. Cum appendice historias & observationes in supplementum operis collatas complectente. Totum opus / recognovit, coaptavit, supplevit, librum etiam primum & secundum integros adjecit Johannes Raius e Societate Regia. Oxonii: E Theatro Sheldoniano, 1686.

2   Contributions to the *Philosophical Transactions of the Royal Society*

'Experiments Concerning the motion of the *Sap* in Trees, made this Spring by Mr *Willughby*, and Mr *Wray*', *Phil. Trans.* 1669: vol. iv, no. 48, 963–5.

'A prosecution of the formerly begun Inquiries, Directions and Experiments, Concerning the Motion of Sap in Trees', [In reply to Dr *Ezerel Tonge*] *Phil. Trans.* 1670: vol. v, no. 57, 1167.

'An Extract of a Letter Written by *Francis Willoughby* Esquire to the Publisher, containing some Observations of his made on some *Sycamore-Trees*, the *Black-Poplar*, and the *Walnut*. As also his thoughts about the *Dwarf-Oaks*, and the *Stellar Fish* described in *Numb. 57*', *Phil. Trans.* 1670: vol. v, no. 58, 1200–1201.

'Extracts of two Letters, written by *Francis Willoughby* Esquire, to the Publisher, from *Astrop*, August 19th and from *Middleton*, Sept. 2d., 1670 Containing his Observations on the Insects and Cartrages, described in the precedent Accompt', *Phil. Trans.* 1671: vol. v, no. 45, 2100–2210

'Extract of a Letter, Written to the Publisher by *Francis Willoughby* Esq., from his House at *Middleton* in *Warwickshire* March 16 1670/1 relating to some particulars, above mention'd in Mr *Lyster*'s Communications of *Feb. 15. 1670/1*', *Phil. Trans.* 1671: vol. v, no. 70, 2125–6.

'An other Extract of a Letter from *Middleton* in *Warwickshire* to the Publisher, July 10th by *Francis Willughby* Esquire; about the Hatching of a kind of Bee, lodged in Old Willows', *Phil. Trans.* 1671: vol. vi, no. 74, 2221.

'A Letter of *Francis Willoughby* Esquire, of August 24, 1671. Containing some considerable Observations about that kind of Wasps, called *Vespæ Ichneumones*; especially their several ways of Breeding, and among them, that odd way of laying their Eggs on the Bodies of Caterpillars, &c.', *Phil. Trans.* 1671: vol. vi, no. 76, 2279–81.

3   Contributions to other publications

'Tables of animals'
> Part II, chapter IV of John Wilkins's *Essay* (1668: 121–161).
> In the Epistle to the Reader, Wilkins thanks Willughby for his 'special assistance' with these tables, Ray being similarly credited with the section 'Of Plants' (Part II, chapter IV).

'Relations of a voyage made through a great part of Spain by Francis Willughby Esq; containing the chief observations he met with there, collected out of his notes', In J. Ray (1673) *Observations topographical, moral and physiological made in a journey through part of the Low-Countries, Germany, Italy and France: … Whereunto is added a brief account of Francis Willughby Esq; his voyage through a great part of Spain*, London: John Martyn, pp. 466–99.

'Tables of insects'
> Ray's summary taxonomy of insects, *Methodus Insectorum* (1705), includes

two classification schemes which are wholly attributed to Willughby: the table of intransmutable insects (pp. 1–6) and the table of aquatic insects (pp. 11–13). These, along with numerous other scattered observations, are reprinted in Derham's subsequent edition of this work as the *Historia Insectorum* (1710).

4   Manuscripts

The following list includes both surviving manuscripts by Willughby and those which are described by his daughter Cassandra in her account of her father's library. She describes some by subject or title, also making more general reference to his 'many manuscripts'. In a few cases the contents of these other unlisted works can be deduced from Willughby's own cross-references to them. In his Commonplace Book, for instance, he refers to descriptions of the preparation of woad to be found both in the account of his journey into Cornwall with Ray (Mi LM 15/1 p. 481) and in the 'Worcester journey with Mr Courthope' (Mi LM 15/1 p. 486); he also refers to what appears to have been a separate book of experiments (Mi LM 15/1 p. 351 '*lib. exper.*'). Although some lost works can in this way be suggested, there is insufficient evidence to reconstruct his *nachlass* in its entirety.

'A Book of Games'
>   The present text. Probably the item referred to in the library catalogue (see below) as 'Book of Plaies'
>   NUL Mi LM 14

'Mathematical Observations on the Theory of Motion'
>   A holograph tract in Latin entitled 'Animadversiones in novam Theoriam motus a binis clarissimis D^{no} Christophoro Wren et D^{no} Christiano Hugenio nuper exhibitam'. This was sent to Oldenburg and read to the Royal Society, as an anonymous contribution, on 10 June 1669. Willughby's covering letter, but not the text of the tract itself, is printed in Oldenburg (Oldenburg 1965–86: 571–2).
>   Royal Society Classified Papers III (I) no. 54.

'Commonplace Book'
>   A volume containing notes on many subjects, including extracts from books read, notes of experiments, and speculations about different topics. It survives together with many loose papers of a similar nature.
>   NUL Mi LM 15

'Word lists'
>   Comparative Latin/vernacular vocabularies collected by Willughby and Skippon on the Continent, together with English/Welsh word list.
>   NUL Mi 4/149a/3/1–16

'Memoirs and observations taken out of old minniments videlicet, deeds, fines, accounts, court roles, and all sorts of old writings, which were found the most of them either at Wollaton or Middleton chiefly concerning

Pedigrees, Marriages, Titles of land, Purchases and sales, Suits in all courts, of the Familie of the Willughbies'

A manuscript notebook primarily in the hands of Willughby and John Ray. The majority of the documents extracted survive and bear endorsements by Willughby and Ray.

NUL Mi LM 13

'Upon ye Sherifs office'

Unidentified. The work is said by Cassandra Willoughby to have been written by her father and to include 'his opinion of ye Oaths of Allegience & Supremacy'. Some notes by Willughby on his duties as Sheriff 1670–71 do survive, and the work in question may refer to some or part of them or to further materials lost from these very decayed papers (NUL Mi O 12 and Mi O 10 *passim*).

'Games of Chance'

Unidentified. Described by Cassandra Willoughby as a work 'wch shews ye Chances of most Games', this is not, apparently the present 'Book of Games' but another text, possibly the unidentified 'Book of Dice' to which Willughby himself refers in his descriptions of board games.

'Descriptions of work'

Unidentified. Mentioned by Cassandra Willoughby as a text which 'describes ye mannor of doing most sorts of Work'. It seems likely that this was related to Francis Willughby's involvement in the Royal Society's Committee on Trades.

5   Collections of research materials

Listed here are the materials preserved in the Middleton Collection at the University of Nottingham. Further details about these are supplied in Welch (1972). On Willughby's collection of natural history specimens in collaboration with Ray, see Raven (1950 *passim*).

'Illustrations of birds'

Watercolour drawings and engravings collected by Willughby mainly on the Continent, and bearing labels by him and his collaborators.

NUL Mi LM 24

'Illustrations of fishes'

Watercolour and pen and ink drawings, oil paintings and engravings from different sources, purchased or created at least in part by Willughby and his associates during his continental journey. Survive with some examples collected after his death, and a number of proof plates for the *Historia Piscium* annotated by John Ray.

Together with a small number of drawings of mammals and lizards, some at least of which were probably purchased by Willughby in Rome, and bear his identifications.

NUL Mi LM 25

'Illustrations of plants'

Watercolour drawings from different sources, apparently continental and possibly from the late sixteenth century. It is assumed that these were collected at least in part by Willughby during his continental journey.

NUL Mi LM 22

'Specimens of plants. First series'

A volume of dried plants sewn onto the pages of a book which bears the name of Dominico Zanetti. It was presumably purchased by Willughby on his visit in 1663–64 to Padua, where Zanetti had been Keeper of the Botanic Gardens.

NUL Mi LM 23

'Specimens of plants. Second series'

A collection of dried plants apparently made by Willughby, Ray and their fellow enthusiasts, and by unidentified late seventeenth- or early eighteenth-century collectors. The specimens are interleaved on coarse paper within the disbound pages of John Ray's *Historia Plantarum*, vols I and II (London, 1686, 1688), almost certainly by Thomas and Cassandra Willughby, and possibly before the publication of volume 3 in 1704.

NUL Mi LM 17–21

'Observations Anatom. Patavii 1663'

Account of human dissection and anatomical lectures at Padua, dating from Willughby's visit to the city. Although the two hands that are responsible for the text are unknown, it bears marginal annotations and corrections by Willughby.

NUL Mi LM 15/2

'Library Catalogue'

A volume, very damaged and incomplete, originally used by Francis Willughby as a notebook, in which the library of his son Thomas Willoughby was subsequently recorded. Although the published works date into the eighteenth century, many imprints are earlier and the catalogue at least in part can be taken to describe the working library of Francis Willughby himself.

NUL Mi I 17/1

6   Correspondence

Omitted from this examination are legal, financial or routine administrative papers which lie within the family archive.[1]

Note that in the following tables all dates are given in New Style.

---

1. No substantial series of correspondence survives for this period but instructions and reports on estate management issues are scattered through series and bundles in the family papers at the University of Nottingham.

6.1   LETTERS FROM WILLUGHBY

Very little of Francis Willughby's personal correspondence is extant. Relatively few original manuscripts have survived, and published editions of lost manuscripts sometimes only give selective extracts. The following list collates the known texts, and uses internal and secondary evidence to suggest possible dates for undated items. Manuscript references have been given for the letters in the Danny Collections at East Sussex Record Office, as their published forms do not fully cite the location of the originals. Originals of letters to Oldenburg, some of which include items published in *Philosophical Transactions*, lie in the Royal Society archives. Their appearance in Birch (1756–57), in extracted or paraphrased form, is not noted here.

Date	From	To	References
Undated [late 1650s–early 1660s]	Willughby	Courthope	East Sussex Record Office ACC 5653/1/6; Gunther (1937: 343–4)
Undated	Willughby	Courthope	East Sussex Record Office ACC 5653/1/1; Gunther (1937: 344)
[Summer 1660]	Willughby	Courthope	East Sussex Record Office ACC 5653/1/3; Gunther (1937: 344)
[October 1661]	Willughby	Courthope	East Sussex Record Office ACC 5653/1/2; Gunther (1937: 345)
Summer 1662	Willughby	Ray	Derham (1718: 9); Lankester (1848: 5–6)[2]
[March 1663]	Willughby	Courthope	East Sussex Record Office ACC 5653/1/5; Gunther (1928: 36)
[*c.* April 1664]	Willughby	Ray	Lankester (1848: 7–8)
29 May 1669	Willughby	Oldenburg	Oldenburg (1965–86: v, 571–2)
21 June 1669	Willughby	Oldenburg	Oldenburg (1965–86: vi, 63–4)
23 July 1669	Willughby	Oldenburg	Oldenburg (1965–86: vi, 150–51)
29 January 1670	Willughby	Oldenburg	Oldenburg (1965–86: vi, 451–3)
12 March 1670	Willughby	Oldenburg	Oldenburg (1965–86: vi, 554–6)
16 April 1670	Willughby	Oldenburg	Oldenburg (1965–86: vi, 635–6)
8 May [1670 or 1671]	Willughby	Courthope	East Sussex Record Office ACC 5653/1/4; Gunther (1928: 36–7)

---

2.   One paragraph from this letter is quoted in Brown (1882: 209).

7 June 1670	Willughby	Oldenburg	Oldenburg (1965–86: vii, 29–30)
[July 1670]	Willughby	More	Hutton (1992: 303) *Text not extant; mentioned in letter from More to Lady Anne Conway.*
4 July 1670	Willughby	Oldenburg	Oldenburg 1965–86: vii, 53–5
19 July 1670	Willughby	Oldenburg	Oldenburg 1965–86: vii, 89–90
19 August 1670	Willughby	Oldenburg	Oldenburg 1965–86: vii, 136–9
2 September 1670	Willughby	Oldenburg	Oldenburg 1965–86: vii, 148–50
13 January 1671	Willughby	Oldenburg	Oldenburg 1965–86: vii, 383–4
16 March 1671	Willughby	Oldenburg	Oldenburg 1965–86: vii, 519–20
21 April 1671	Willughby	Oldenburg	Oldenburg 1965–86: viii, 9–10
10 July 1671	Willughby	Oldenburg	Oldenburg 1965–86: viii, 153–5
24 August 1671	Willughby	Oldenburg	Oldenburg 1965–86: viii, 209–11

6.2   LETTERS TO WILLUGHBY

Although Willughby clearly conducted an extensive correspondence, the family archive no longer contains any series of in-coming letters to him. While letters received would normally be excluded from a writer's own papers, the scarcity of evidence about Willughby's correspondence gives a special value to any material of this nature. The following list collates surviving references where either a text still exists or, in the case of the Oldenburg correspondence, where notes by the recipient shows the nature and frequency of communications.[3]

Date	From	To	References
25 February 1660	Ray	Willughby	Derham (1718: 355); Lankester (1848: 1–3)
17 March 1660	Courthope	Willughby	Derham (1718: 357)
14 September 1661	Ray	Willughby	Derham (1718: 358–9); Lankester (1848: 3–4)
26 March 1662	Barrow	Willughby	Derham (1718: 360)
5 June 1664	Skippon	Willughby	Derham (1718: 361)

3. Oldenburg gives the dates of his replies to Willughby's correspondence, but the text is rarely available (Oldenburg 1965–86; *passim*).

5 October 1665	Barrow	Willughby	Derham (1718: 362–5)
20 October 1666	Wilkins	Willughby	Derham (1718: 366)
undated	Ray	Willughby	Derham (1718: 369); Lankester (1848: 4–5)
[5 January 1667][4]	Jessop	Willughby	Derham (1718: 367–8)
6 May 1668	Henry Barnard	Willughby	Wood (1958: 111–12)
15 June 1669	Oldenburg	Willughby	Oldenburg (1965–86: vi, 35–6)
9 July 1669	Oldenburg	Willughby	Oldenburg (1965–86: vi, 103–4)
20 January 1670	Oldenburg	Willughby	Oldenburg (1965–86: vi, 437–8)
17 February 1670	Oldenburg	Willughby	Oldenburg (1965–86: vi, 508) *Text not extant*
19 March 1670	Oldenburg	Willughby	Oldenburg (1965–86: vi, 578) *Text not extant*
3 May 1670	Oldenburg	Willughby	Oldenburg (1965–86: vii, 3) *Text not extant*
17 May 1670	Oldenburg	Willughby	Derham (1718: 370); Oldenburg (1965–86: vii, 18)
28 June 1670	Oldenburg	Willughby	Oldenburg (1965–86: vii, 51) *Text not extant*
9 July 1670	Oldenburg	Willughby	Oldenburg (1965–86: vii, 59) *Text not extant*
5 August 1670	Oldenburg	Willughby	Derham (1718: 372); Oldenburg (1965–86: vii, 103) *Text not extant; extract in Derham*
10 September 1670	Oldenburg	Willughby	Oldenburg (1965–86: vii, 158) *Text not extant*
3 January 1671	Oldenburg	Willughby	Oldenburg (1965–86: vii, 347–8) *Text not extant*
21 January 1671	Oldenburg	Willughby	Oldenburg (1965–86: vii, 409–10)
18 February 1671	Oldenburg	Willughby	Oldenburg (1965–86: vii, 463) *Text not extant*
4 April 1671	Oldenburg	Willughby	Oldenburg (1965–86: vii, 545) *Text not extant*
18 April 1671	Oldenburg	Willughby	Oldenburg (1965–86: vii, 577) *Text not extant*

---

4. Letter undated, but a contemporary writer, who makes other authoritative changes, supplies the date '5 January 1666' to a copy of Derham in the Bodleian Library (Lister L 86). This is presumed to be Old Style. A later date might be suggested by comparison of the content of the letter with one which Jessop sends to Ray on 25 November 1668: see Lankester (1848: 33–4).

29 April 1671	Oldenburg	Willughby	Oldenburg (1965–86: viii, 32–3) *Text not extant*
16 May 1671	Oldenburg	Willughby	Oldenburg (1965–86: viii, 56–7) *Text not extant*
13 July 1671	Oldenburg	Willughby	Oldenburg (1965–86: viii, 158) *Text not extant*
27 July 1671	Oldenburg	Willughby	Oldenburg (1965–86: viii, 178)
31 August 1671	Oldenburg	Willughby	Oldenburg (1965–86: viii, 252) *Text not extant*
11 October 1671	Oldenburg	Willughby	Oldenburg (1965–86: vii, 288) *Text not extant*
[Early 1672]	Lettice Wendy	Willughby	NUL Mi Av 143/37/1
9 April [1672]	Lettice Wendy	Willughby	NUL Mi Av 143/37/2
20 April [1672]	Lettice Wendy	Willughby	NUL Mi Av 143/37/3
6 July 1672	Oldenburg	Willughby	Derham (1718: 109–11); Oldenburg (1965–86: ix, 147–8)

B

General References

A., G. Pallas Armata (1639), *The Gentleman's Armorie, wherein the right and genuine use of the rapier and of sword is displaied*, London: John Williams.

Aberdare, Clarence Napier Bruce, 3rd baron (1951), *Rackets, Squash Rackets, Tennis, Fives, and Badminton*, The Lonsdale Library 16, London: Seeley Service and Co.

Alberti, Leon Baptista (1565), *L'architettura di Leon Batista Alberti*, Nel Monte Regale: Appresso Lionardo Torrentino.

Aldrovandi, Ulisse (1602), *De animalibus insectis libri septem*, Bonon.: apud Ioan: Bapt: Bellagambam.

—— (1606), *De reliquis animalibus exanguibus libri quatuor, post mortem eius editi: nempe de mollibus, crustaceis, testaceis, et zoophytis*, Bonon.: apud Ioan: Bapt: Bellagambam.

—— (1610–13), *Ornithologiæ, hoc est, De auibus historiæ libri XII*, Francofurti: Typis Wolffgangi Richteri, impensis Ioannis Bassæi.

Alfonso X, (1913 [1283]), *Das spanische Schachzabelbuch des Königs Alfons des Weisen vom Jahre 1283*, Leipzig: Hiersemann.

—— (1941 [1283]), *Libros de Acedrex, Dados e Tablas. Das Schachzabelbuch König Alfons des Weisen*, Geneva and Zürich-Erlenbach: Librairie E. Droz and Eugen Rentsch Verlag.

Anglo, Sydney (2000), *The Martial Arts of Renaissance Europe*, New Haven, CT: Yale University Press.

Anon. (1617), *The Booke of Merrie Riddles*, London: Roger Jackson.

Anon. (1632), *The Pinder of Wakefield*, London: E. Blackamore.

Anon. (1658), *The Mysteries of Love & Eloquence, Or, the Arts of Wooing and Complementing*, London: printed for N. Brooks.

Anon. (1680), *A Leter from a Minister to his Friend concerning the Games of Chesse*, single sheet, London: Thomas Parkhurst and Joseph Collier.

Anon. (1696), *Divertissements innocens, contenant les règles du jeu des eschets, du billiard, de la paume, du palle-mail, et du tric-trac*, La Haye: A. Moetjens.

Ariès, Philippe and Margolin, Jean-Claude (eds) (1982), *Les Jeux à la Renaissance*, Paris: J. Vrin.

Armytage, W.H.G. (1952), 'Francis Jessop, 1638–1691: a seventeenth-century Sheffield scientist', *Notes and Queries*, 197, 343–6.

Ascham, Roger (1545), *Toxophilus, the Schole of Shootinge conteyned in Two Bookes*, London: E. Whytchurch.

—— (1570), *The Scholemaster. Or a plaine and Perfite Way of Teachyng Children, to Vnderstand, Write and Speake, the Latin Tong*, London: I. Daye.

Aubrey, John (1847 [1685]), *The Natural History of Wiltshire*, ed. John Britton, London: J. B. Nichols and Son.

—— (1881), *Remaines of Gentilisme and Judaisme 1686–87*, ed. James Britten, Publications of the Folklore Society, 4, London: published for the Folklore Society by W. Satchell, Peyton, and Co.

—— (1898), *Brief Lives, chiefly of Contemporaries*, ed. Andrew Clark, 3 vols, Oxford: Clarendon Press.

Augarde, Tony (1984), *The Oxford Guide to Word Games*, Oxford and New York: Oxford University Press.

Avedon, Elliott M. and Sutton-Smith, Brian (1971), *The Study of Games*, New York, London, Sydney and Toronto: John Wiley and Sons.

Aydelotte, F. (1913), *Elizabethan Rogues and Vagabonds*, Oxford: Clarendon Press.

B., W.C. (1865), 'Uncommon rhymes', *Notes and Queries*, 3rd ser., 8, 329–30.

Bacon, Francis (1620), *Fransisci de Verulamio sumi Angliæ Cancellaris Instauratio magna*, London: apud Joannem Billium.

—— (1887–1901), *The Works of Francis Bacon: Philosophical Works*, eds J. Spedding, R.L. Ellis and D.D. Heath, London: Longmans.

Baker, John Hamilton (1990), *The Third University of England: The Inns of Court and the Common-law Tradition*, London: for the Seldon Society.

Balmford, James (1623), *A Modest Reply to certaine Answeres, which Mr Gataker BD in his Treatise of the Nature & Vse of Lotts, giveth to Arguments in a Dialogue concerning the Unlawfulnes of Games consisting in Chance. Imprinted 1623*, London: E. Boyle.

Bardi, Giovanni de (1580), *Discorso sopra il giuoco del calcio fiorentino / del Puro accademico alterato*, Firenze: nella stamperia de' Giunti.

Barrett, C.R.B. (1895), 'Riding Skimmington and Riding the Stang', *Journal of the British Archæological Association*, n.s. 1, 58–68.

Barrow, Isaac (1655), *Euclidis Elementorum Libri XV breviter demonstrati*, Cambridge: William Nealand.

Bascetta, Carlo (1978), *Sport e Giuochi. Trattati e Scritti dal XV al XVIII Secolo*, Milan: il Polifilo.

Beal, George (1988), *Playing Cards and Tarots*, Shire Album 217, Princes Risborough, Bucks.: Shire Publications.

Beal, Peter (1987), *Notions in Garrison: The Seventeenth-Century Commonplace Book*, London: Renaissance English Text Society.

Beale, Francis (1656), *The Royall Game of Chesse-play … Being the study of Biochimio the famous Italian*, London: Henry Herringman.

Bell, Robert Charles (1960; 1969), *Board and Table Games from many Civilizations*, London Oxford University Press, 2 vols (single-volume reprint, New York: Dover Books, 1979).

Bellhouse, D.R. (1988), 'Probability in the sixteenth and seventeenth centuries: an analysis of puritan casuistry', *International Statistical Review*, 56, 63–74.

Benham, W. Gurney (1957), *Playing Cards*, London: Spring Books.

Billett, Michael (1994), *A History of English Country Sports*, London: Hale.

Birch, Thomas (1756–57), *The History of the Royal Society* (reprinted New York and London: Johnson Reprint Company, 1968).

Blome, Richard (1686), *The Gentlemans Recreation … The Second Part, Treats of Horsmanship, Hawking, Hunting, Fowling, Fishing, and Agriculture. With a Short Treatise of Cock-Fighting*, London: R. Blome.

Boissière, Claude de (1556), *Le tresexcellent et ancien ieu Pythagorique, dict Rythmomachie, fort propre & tres util à la recreation des esprits vertueux, pour obtenir vraye & prompte habitude en tout nombre & proportion*, Paris: Chez Guillaume Cauellat.

—— (1556), *Nobilissimus et antiquissimus ludus Pythagoreus (qui Rythmomachia nominatur … Per Claudium Buxerium Delphinatum illustratus*, Paris: apud Gulielmum Cauellat.

Bolgar, R.R. (1954), *The Classical Heritage*, Cambridge: Cambridge University Press.

Bomhard, Anne-Sophie von and Yoyotte, Jean (1999), *The Egyptian Calendar: A Work for Eternity*, London: Periplus Publishing.

Boulger, George Simonds (1900), 'Francis Willughby', in Sidney Lee (ed.), *Dictionary of National Biography*, London: Smith, Elder & Co, vol. 59, pp. 525–8.

Bourne, Henry (1725), *Antiquitates Vulgares; or the Antiquities of the Common People*, Newcastle: for the author.

Boyle, Robert (1666a), 'General heads for a natural history of a country, small or large', *Phil. Trans.*, i, 11, 186–9.

—— (1666b), 'Inquiries concerning mines', *Phil. Trans.*, i, 19, 330–44.

Bradford, Edwin and Radford, Mona Augusta (1961), *Encyclopaedia of Superstitions*, ed. and revd Christina Hole, London: Hutchison.

Brailsford, Dennis (1969), *Sport and Society: Elizabeth to Anne*, Toronto: University of Toronto Press/London: Routledge, Kegan and Paul.

Brand, John (1777), *Observations on Popular Antiquities; Including the whole of Mr. Bourne's Antiquitiates Vulgares*, Newcastle: J. Johnson.

Brand, John and Ellis, Henry (1913 [1777]), *Observations on Popular Antiquities*, London: Chatto and Windus.

Brathwait, Richard (1630), *The English Gentleman*, London: R. Bostock. (Facs. reprint, English Experience 717, Amsterdam/Norwood, NJ: Theatrum Orbis Terrarum, 1975)

Breton, Nicholas (1607), *Barley-Breake, or a Warning to Wantons*, London: Simon Stafford.

Brewster, Paul G. (1953), *American Nonsinging Games*, Norman, OK: University of Oklahoma Press.

—— (1959), *Games and Sports in Shakespeare*, FF Communications No. 177. Helsinki: Academia Scientiarum Fennica (reprinted in Avedon and Sutton-Smith, 1971, pp. 27–47).

Brinsley, John (1917 [1612]), *Ludus Literarius: or, The Grammar School*, London: for T. Man (ed. E.T. Champagnac, Liverpool: University Press, 1917).

Briquet, Charles-Moïse (1968), *Les filigranes: Dictionnaire historique des marques du papier dès leur apparition vers 1282 jusqu'en 1600; A facsimile of the 1907 edition with supplementary material contributed by a number of scholars*, ed. Allan Stevenson, Amsterdam: Paper Publications Society.

Broadway, Jan (1999), *William Dugdale and the Significance of County History in Early Stuart England*, Dugdale Society Occasional Paper 39, Dugdale Society.

Brown, Cornelius (1882), *Lives of Nottinghamshire Worthies and Remarkable Men of the County*, London: H. Southeran; Nottingham: Ch. Wheatley.

Browne, Thomas (1835–36), *Sir Thomas Browne's Works: Including his Life and Correspondence*, ed. Simon Wilkin, 6 vols, London: William Pickering.

Browning, Robert (1955), *A History of Golf: The Royal and Ancient Game*, London: A. and C. Black.

Bryant, Mark (1983), *Riddles Ancient and Modern*, London: Hutchinson.

Burke, Peter (1994 [1978]), *Popular Culture in Early Modern Europe*, London: Temple Smith.

Burton, Robert (1990 [1621]), *The Anatomy of Melancholy*, eds N.K. Kiessling, T.C. Faulkner and R.L. Blair, 3 vols, Oxford: Clarendon Press.

Butler, Martin (1984), *Theatre and Crisis 1632–1642*, Cambridge: Cambridge University Press.

Calendar of State Papers, Domestic Series, March 1st 1677 – February 27th 1678, Preserved in the Public Record Office, ed. F.H. Blackburne Daniell, London: HMSO, 1911.

Cardano, Girolamo (1555), *In Cl. Ptolemæ ... iiii de astrorum iudiciis ... libros commentaria*, Lugduni: apud Theobaldum Paganum.

—— (1663), *De Ludo Aleae*, in *Hieronymi Cardani Mediolanensis Opera Omnia*, ed. Carolus Sponius, Lugduni: sumptibus Ioannis Antonii Huguetan, vol. i, pp. 262–76.

Carew, Richard (1602), *The Suruey of Cornwall*, London: J. Jaggard.

Castliglione, Baldassare (1987 [1528]), *Il Libro del Cortegiano*, ed. Amedeo Quondam, Milan: Garzanti.

Cats, Jacob (1657), *Kinder-Lustspiele*, Zürich: n.p.

Caxton, William (1860 [1474]), *The Game of the Chesse by William Caxton, reproduced in facsimile from a copy in the British Museum*, London: John Russell Smith.

Chamberlayne, Edward (1669), *Angliæ Notitia, or, The Present State of England*, 2nd edn, London: John Martyn.

Chapman, George (1961), *The Plays of George Chapman: The Comedies*, ed. Thomas Marc Parrott, 2 vols, New York: Russell and Russell.

Chope, Richard Pearse (1893), 'Cross purposes', *Notes and Queries*, 8th ser., 3, 275.

Clarke, William (1834), *Boy's Own Book*, Boston, MA: Munroe and Francis.

Cliffe, J.T. (1984), *The Puritan Gentry: The Great Puritan Families of Early Stuart England*, London: Routledge and Kegan Paul.

Cocles, Bartholomæus (1550), *La Geomantia*, Venice: n.p.

Cokayne, George Edward (1904), *Complete Baronetage*, vol. 4, 1665–1705, Exeter: W. Pollard.

Comenius, Johann Amos (1658), *Orbis Sensualium Pictus. Hoc est omnium fundamentalium in mundo rerum and in vitâ actionum pictura et nomenclatura*, Noribergae: sumptibus Michaelis Endteri.

Cotgrave, John (1655; 1662²), *Wits Interpreter: The English Parnassus, or, A sure guide to those admirable accomplishments that compleat our English Gentry, in … discourse or writing*, London: N. Brooke.

Cotgrave, Randle (1611), *A dictionarie of the French and English tongues*, London: printed by A. Islip.

Cotton, Charles (1669), *The Nicker Nicked, or, The cheats of games discovered*, London: n.p. (published under the pseudonym 'Leathermore').

—— (1930 [1674]), *The Compleat Gamester: or, Instructions how to play at billiards, trucks, bowls, and chess. To which is added. The art of riding, racing, archery, and cock-fighting*, London: R. Cutler (reprinted in *Games and Gamesters of the Restoration*, ed. C.H. Hartmann, 1930, London: Routledge English Library).

Coumet, E. (1970), 'La théorie du hasard est-elle née par hasard', *Annales; Economies, Sociétés, Civilisations*, 25, 574–98.

Couturat, Louis and Leau, Léopold (1903), *Histoire de la langue universelle*, Paris: Hachette.

Cox, Nicholas (1674), *The Gentleman's Recreation, in Four Parts, viz. Hunting, Hawking, Fowling, Fishing*, London: Maurice Atkins and Nicholas Cox.

Cram, David (1990), 'John Ray and Francis Willughby: universal languages schemes and the foundations of linguistic field research', in Werner Hüllen (ed.), *Understanding the Historiography of Linguistics: Problems and Projects*, Münster: Nodus Publikationen, pp. 229–39.

—— (1991), 'Birds, beasts and fishes *versus* bats, mongrels and hybrids: the publication history of John Ray's *Dictionariolum* (1675)', *Paradigm*, 6, 4–7.

—— and Awbery, Gwenllian M. (2001), 'Francis Willughby's catalogue of Welsh words (1662)', *Cylchgrawn Llyfrgell Genedlaethol Cymru/The National Library of Wales Journal*, 32, 1–55.

—— and Maat, Jaap (2001), *George Dalgarno on Universal Language: The Art of Signs, 1661, The Deaf and Dumb Man's Tutor, 1680, and the Unpublished Papers*, Oxford: Oxford University Press.

Crosfield, Thomas (1935), *The Diary of Thomas Crosfield M.A., B.D. Fellow of Queen's College Oxford*, ed. Frederick S. Boas, London: Oxford University Press.

Cummins, John G. (1988), *The Hound and the Hawk: The Art of Medieval Hunting*, New York: St. Martin's Press.

D'Abana, Pietro (1550), *La Geomantia*, Venice: n.p.

D'Allemagne, Henri-Réné (1902), *Histoire des jouets*, Paris: chez l'auteur.

—— (1903), *Sports et jeux d'adresse*, Paris: Hachette.

—— (1905), *Récréations et passe-temps*, Paris: Hachette.

—— (1906), *Les cartes à jouer du XIVe au XXe siècle*, Paris: Hachette.

Damiano, da Odemira (1562), *The Pleasaunt and Wittie Playe of the Cheasts, renewed with instructions, tr. by I. Rowbothum*, London: R. Hall for I[ames] Rowbothum. (Another translation in 1597: *Ludus Scacchiae: Chesse-play; translated out of the Italian tongue*, London: H. Jackson.)

Daneau, Lambert (1586), *A Treatise touching Dice-play and prophane Gaming ... Written in Latine by Lambertus Danæus: Englished by Tho: Newton*, London: Abraham Veale.

David, Florence Nightingale (1962), *Games, Gods and Gambling: The Origin and History of Probability and Statistical Ideas from the Earliest Times to the Newtonian Era*, London: Charles Griffin and Co.

Davies, Natalie Zemon (1975), 'Proverbial wisdom and popular errors', in N.Z. Davies, *Society and Culture in early Modern France: Eight Essays*, London: Duckworth, pp. 227–67.

Davis, Ralph Henry Carless (1989), *The Medieval Warhorse: Origin, Development, and Redevelopment*, London: Thames and Hudson.

Davison, Dennis (1956), 'Francis Jessop', *Notes and Queries*, 201, January, 20–23.

De Lannoy, Jan (1875), 'Les Lettres du Seigneur de Lannoy', *Cabinet Historique*, 21, October–December: 225–42.

Depaulis, Thierry (1987), 'Un peu de lumière sur l'hombre (3)', *The Playing Card*, 16.2, 44–53.

—— (1990, 1991), 'Pochspiel: an international card game of the 15th century', *The Playing-Card*, 19.2: 52–67; 20.3: 77–87; 20.4: 109–17.

—— (1994), *Les lois du jeu: bibliographie de la littérature technique des jeux de cartes en français avant 1800, suivie d'en supplément couvrant les années 1800–1850*, Paris: Cymbalum mundi.

—— (1997), *Histoire du Bridge*, Paris: Bornemann.

Derham, William (1718), *Philosophical Letters between the late learned Mr Ray and several of his ingenious correspondents. To which are added those of Francis Willughby Esq*, London: W. and J. Innys.

—— (1760), *Select Remains of the Late Learned John Ray, M.A. and F.R.S., with the Life*, London: G. Scott. (Reprinted in Lankester 1846.)

Descartes, René (1657–67), *Lettres de Mr Descartes: Où sont traittées les plus belles Questions de la morale, physique, medecine, et des mathematiques*, ed. Claude Clerselier, 3 vols, Paris: Chez Charles Angot.

—— (1668), *Renati Descartes Epistolae, partim ab auctore Latino sermone conscriptae, partim ex Gallico translatae*, London: impensis Joh: Dunmore, & Octaviani Pulleyn.

—— (1996), *Œuvres de Descartes publiées par Charles Adam et Paul Tannery*, Paris: Librairie Philosophique J. Vrin.

Diderot, Denis and D'Alembert, J. (1778–79), *Encyclopédie, ou Dictionnaire Raisonnée des Sciences, des Arts, et des Métiers*, 3rd edn, Geneva: Pellet.

Ditchfield, Peter Hampson (ed.) (1907), *The Victoria County History of Berkshire*, vol. 2, London: Archibald Constable.

Dover, Robert (1636), *Annalia Dubrensia; Vpon the yeerely Celebration of mr. Robert Douer's Olympick games vpon the Cottswold-hills*, London: Mathewe Walbancke.

Du Cange, Charles du Fresne (1678), *Glossarium ad Scriptores Mediæ & Infimæ Latinitatis*, Lutetiæ Parisiorum: Ludovicus Billaine.

Dugdale, William (1730 [1656]), *The Antiquities of Warwickshire. second edition, revised by William Thomas*, London: printed for J. Osborn and T. Longman.

Duhamel de Monceau, Henry Louis (1762), *Art du Cartier* (Descriptions des arts et métiers, faites au approuvées par messieurs de l'Académie royale des sciences) Paris: Académie royale des sciences.

Dummet, Michael A.E. (1980), *The Game of Tarot*, London: Duckworth.

Duport, James (1660), *Homeri Poetarum omnium saeculorum facile Principis Gnomologia. Duplici Pallelismo illustrata*, Cambridge: John Field.

—— (1676), *Musæ Subsecivæ seu Poeta Stromata*, Cambridge: Ex Officina Joann. Hayes.

Elyot, Thomas (1531), *The Boke Named the Gouernour*, London: T. Berthletet. (Facs. edn, Scolar Press, 1970.)

Emery, Frank V. (1959), 'A map of Edward Lhuyd's *Parochial Queries in Order to a Geographical Dictionary, etc. of Wales.* (1696)', *Transactions of the Honourable Society of Cymmrodorion*, 45–57.

Endrei, Walter and Zolnay, László (1986), *Fun and Games in Old Europe*, trans. Károly Ravasz, Budapest: Corvina.

English Dialect Dictionary (1898–1905), ed. Joseph Wright, 6 vols, London: Henry Frowde.

Evelyn, John (2000), *Elysium Britannicum, or the Royal Gardens*, ed. John E. Ingram, Pennsylvania: University of Pennsylvania Press.

Fenner, Dudley (1590), *A Short and Profitable Treatise of lawfull and vnlawfull Recreations, and of the right vse and abuse of those that are lawfull*, Midleburgh: Richard Schilders. (Facs. edn, English Experience 870, Amsterdam, 1977.)

Firth, Charles Harding and Rait, Robert Sangster (1911), *Acts and Ordinances of the Interregnum, 1642–1660*, London: HMSO.

Fishwick, Henry (1914), 'Shrovetide throwing at the cock', *Notes and Queries*, 11th ser., 10, 25.

Fiske, Daniel Willard (1905), *Chess in Iceland and Icelandic Literature, with Historical Notes on Other Table-Games*, Florence: Florentine Typographical Society.

Florio, John (1591), *Florios Second Frutes*, London: Thomas Woodcock.

Forbet, J. (1592), *L'Vtilité qvi provient dv ieu de la pavme*, Paris: T. Sevestre.

Foster Joseph (1889), *The Register of Admissions to Gray's Inn, 1521–1889*, London: Hansard.

—— (1892), *Alumni Oxonienses*, Oxford: Parker and Co.

Foster, R.F. (1916), *Foster's Complete Hoyle. An Encyclopedia of Games*, New York: Frederick A. Stokes.

Fournier, Edouard (1889), *Histoire des jouets et des jeux d'enfants*, Paris: E. Dentu.

Fox, George (1998), *The Journal*, ed. Nigel Smith, Harmondsworth: Penguin.

Foxe, John (1572), *Pandectae locorum communium, praecipua rerum capita & titulos, complectens*, London: J. Dayus.

Fraser, Antonia (1966), *A History of Toys*, London: Weidenfeld and Nicolson.

Frischlin, Nicodemus (1600), *Nomenclator Trilinguis, Graeco-Latinogermanico, continens omnium rerum, quae in probatis omnium doctrinarum auctoribus inveniuntur, appellationes*, Francofurti ad Moenum: impensis Iannis Spiessii.

Fulke, William (1571), *Ouranomachia, hoc est, Astrologorum ludus*, London: T. Eastum and H. Middletonum.

—— (1578), *Metromachia, sive Ludus geometricus*, London: T. Vautrollerius.

Furnivall, Frederick James (1877, 1882), *Phillip Stubbes's Anatomy of the Abuses in England in Shakspere's Youth, A.D. 1583*, London: N. Trübner for the New Shakespeare Society.

Furno, Albertina (1903), 'Un codice di giuochi populari fiorentini del secolo XVI', *Rivista delle Biblioteche e degli Archivi*, 14.7–8, July–August, 97–110.

Gataker, Thomas (1619), *Of the Nature and Use of Lots: A Treatise Historical and Theologicall*, London: William Bladen.

—— (1623), *A Iust Defence of Certain Passages in a former Treatise concerning the Nature and Use of Lots, against such exceptions ... as haue beene made ... by mr. I.B[almford]*, London: R. Bird.

Gellius, Aulus (1984), *The Attic Nights of Aulus Gellius*, trans. John C. Rolfe, 3 vols, Cambridge, MA: Harvard University Press; London: Heinemann.

Gesner, Conrad (1604), *Historiae animalium liber iv. Qui est de piscium & aquatilium animantium natura*, Francofurti: In Bibliopolio Andreae Cambieri.

Gillmeister, Heiner (1977a), 'Über Tennis und Tennispunkte', *Gladion: Journal of the History of Sport and Physical Education*, 3, 187–229.

—— (1977b), *Tennis: A Cultural History*, London and Washington: Leicester University Press.

Glanvill, Joseph (1662), *Lux Orientalis, or An Enquiry into the Opinion of the Eastern Sages, Concerning the Præexistence of Souls: Being a Key to unlock the Grand Mysteries of Providence, In relation to mans sin and misery*, London: Printed and are to be Sold at Cambridge, and Oxford.

Godefroy, Frédéric (1881–90), *Dictionnaire de l'ancienne langue française*, Paris: F. Vieweg.

Goldsmith, Oliver (1762), *The Life of Richard Nash, Esq., late master of ceremonies at Bath*, London: J. Newbery.

Golius, Theophilius (1579), *Onomasticon Latinogermanicum, in usum scholae Argentoratensis*, Strassburg: n.p.

Gomme, Alice Bertha (1894–98), *The Traditional Games of England, Scotland, and Ireland*, Dictionary of British Folklore, Part 1, vols 1–2 (reprinted London: David Nutt, 1904).

Govett, Lionel Arthur (1890), *The King's Book of Sports, a History of the Declarations of James I. and Charles I. as to the Use of Lawful Sports on Sundays, with a reprint of the declarations*, London: Elliot Stock.

Grantham, W.W. (1931), *Stoolball and How to Play It*, London: Tatersall.

Graunt, John (1662), *Natural and Political Observations mentioned in a following Index and made upon the Bills of Mortality*, London: John Martin, James Allestry and Tho: Dicas.

Gronovius, Jacobus (1697–1702), *Thesaurus Græcarum Antiquitatum*, Leyden: Petrus et Baldinus Vander Aa.

Gunther, Robert William Theodore (ed.) (1928), *Further Correspondence of John Ray*, London: Ray Society.

—— (1937), *Early Science in Cambridge*, Oxford: for the author.

Hale, George (1614), *The Private Schoole of Defence*, London: John Helme.

Hall, A. Rupert (1966–67), 'Mechanics and the Royal Society 1668–1670', *British Journal of the History of Science*, 3, 24–38.

Hall, Trevor (1957), *A Bibliography of Books on Conjuring in English from 1580 to 1850*, Lepton: Palmyra Press.

—— (1972), *Old Conjuring Books*, London: Duckworth.

Halliwell, James Orchard (1970a), *Popular Rhymes and Nursery Tales of England*, London, Sydney and Toronto: Bodley Head.

—— (1970b), *The Nursery Rhymes of England*, London, Sydney and Toronto: Bodley Head.

Hardy, Robert (1976), *Longbow: A Social and Military History*, Cambridge: Stephens.

Hargrave, Catherine Perry (1930; 1966²), *A History of Playing Cards*, New York: Dover Publications.

Hartley, Dorothy and Elliot, Margaret M. (1929), *Life and Work of the People of England. A Pictorial Record from Contemporary Sources. The Seventeenth Century*, New York and London: Putnam's.

Heal, Felicity and Holmes, Clive (1994), *The Gentry in England and Wales 1500–1700*, London: Macmillan.

Heath, E.G. (1971), *The Grey Goose Wing*, Reading: Osprey Publishing.

Heidfeld, Johann Gottfried (1601), *Sphinx Philosophica*, Herbornae Nassoviorum: Christophorus Corvinus.

Henderson, Robert W. (1947), *Bat, Ball, and Bishop. The Origin of Ball Games*, New York: Rockport Press.

Herrick, Robert (1956), *The Poetical Works of Robert Herrick*, ed. L.C. Martin, Oxford: Clarendon Press.

Heywood, William (1904), *Palio and Ponte: An Account of the Sports of Central Italy from the Age of Dante to the XXth Century*, London: Methuen.

Hill, Christopher (1964), *Society and Puritanism in Pre-Revolutionary England*, London: Secker and Warburg.

—— (1972), *The World Turned Upside Down: Radical Ideas During the English Revolution*, Harmondsworth: Penguin Books.

Hill, Thomas (1581), *A Briefe and Pleasaunt Treatise Entituled, Naturall and artificiall Conclusions: written by scholers of Padua and now Englished by T. Hill*, London: Abr. Kitson.

Hilton, John (1652), *Catch that Catch Can*, London: J. Benson and J. Playford.

Hindman, Sandra (1981), 'Peter Bruegel's *Games*, folly, and chance', *Art Bulletin*, 63, 447–75.

Hoffmann, Detlef (1973), *The Playing Card: An Illustrated History*, trans. C.S.V. Salt, [Leipzig]: Edition Leipzig.

Hole, Christina (1949), *English Sports and Pastimes*, London: B.T. Batsford.

Holme, Randle (1688), *An Academie of Armory, Or, a Storehouse of Armory and Blazon*, Chester: for the author.

—— (1905), *The Academy of Armory, Or, A Storehouse of Armory and Blazon*, London: Roxburghe Club.

—— (2001 [1688]), *Living and Working in Seventeenth-Century England. An Encyclopedia of Drawings and Descriptions from Randle Holme's original manuscripts for* The Academy of Armory *(1688)* [CD-ROM], ed. N. W. Alcock and Nancy Cox, London: British Library.

Hooke, Robert (1705), 'A general scheme, or idea of the present state of natural philosophy, and how its defects may be remedied by a methodical proceeding in the making experiments and collecting observations', in *The Posthumous Works of Robert Hooke*, ed. Richard Waller, London: Sam. Smith and Benj. Walford, pp. 1–70.

Hoole, Charles (1657), *Vocabularium Parvum Anglo-Latinum. / A little vocabulary English and Latin*, London: Joshua Kirton.

Horr, Norton T. (1892), *A Bibliography of Card-Games and of the History of Playing-Cards*, Cleveland, OH: Charles Orr.

Houghton, Walter E. (1941a), 'The history of trades: Its relation to seventeenth-century thought: as seen in Bacon, Evelyn, and Boyle', *Journal of the History of Ideas*, 2, 33–60.

—— (1941b), 'The English virtuoso in the seventeenth-century', *Journal of the History of Ideas*, 3, 51–73.

Howell, James (1659), Παροιμιογραφια. *Proverbs, or Old Sayed Savves & Adages in English*, London: printed by J.G.

—— (1660), *Lexicon Tetraglotton, an English-French-Italian-Spanish Dictionary: whereunto is adjoined a large nomenclature of the proper terms (in all the four) belonging to several arts and sciences, to recreations, to professions both liberal and mechanick, &c*, London: Cornelius Bee.

Howlet, Robert (1684), *The School of Recreation*, London: H. Rodes.

Hoyle, Edmond (1742), *A short treatise on the game of whist. Containing the laws of the game: and also some rules, … Calculations for those who will bet the odds. By Edmund Hoyle, gent*, London: for the author.

—— (1754), *An Essay towards making the Doctrine of Chances easy to those who understand Vulgar Arithmetick only. To which is added, some useful Tables on Annuities for Lives*, London: J. Jolliff.

Hugh of Saint-Victor (1939), *Hugonis de Sancto Victore Didascalicon de Studio Legendi*, ed. Charles Henry Buttimer, Catholic University of America Studies in Medieval and Renaissance Latin X, Washington, DC: Catholic University Press.

Hüllen, Werner (1989), *'Their Manner of Discourse': Nachdenken über Sprache im Umkreis der Royal Society*, Tübingen: Gunter Narr.

—— (1999), *English Dictionaries 800–1700: The Topical Tradition*, Oxford: Oxford University Press.

Hunt, Nicholas (1631), *Newe Recreations*, London: Luke Faune.

Hunter, Michael (1982), *The Royal Society and its Fellows 1660–1700. The Morphology of an Early Scientific Institution*, London: British Society for the

History of Science (2nd edition, Stanford in the Vale: British Society for the History of Science, 1994).

Hutton, Sarah (1992), *The Conway Letters: The Correspondence of Anne, Viscountess Conway, Henry More, and their Friends 1642–1684*, ed. M.H. Nicolson, revd edn S. Hutton, Oxford: Clarendon Press.

Huygens, Christiaan (1657), 'De Ratiociniis in Ludo Aleae', in Fransiscus à Schooten, *Exercitationum Mathematicarum libri quinque*, Lugd. Bat.: ex officina Johannis Elsevirii, pp. 517–34.

—— (1692), *Of the laws of chance, or, A method of calculation of the hazards of game plainly demonstrated*, trans. J. Arbuthnot, London: Randall Taylor.

—— (1703), 'De motu corporum ex percussione', in *C. Hugenii opuscula postuma*, ed. B. de Volder and B. Fullenius, Leiden: apud Cornelium Boutesteyn, pp. 369–98 (reprinted in *Oeuvres complètes*, The Hague: M. Nijhoff, 1888–1950, xxix, 29–136).

Hyde, Thomas (1665), *Tabvlæ long. ac lat. stellarum fixarvm, ex observatione Ulugh Beighi, Tamerlanis Magni*, Oxford: sumptibus authoris.

—— (1689), *De Historia Shahiludi*, Oxford: e Theatro Sheldoniano.

—— (1694a), *De Historia Nerdiludii*, Oxford: e Theatro Sheldoniano.

—— (1694b), *De Ludis Orientalibus Libri Duo*, Oxford: e Theatro Sheldoniano. (Partial English translation in *Chess, its Origins: A translation with Commentary of the Latin and Hebrew in Thomas Hyde's De ludis orientalibus*, trans. Victor Keats, Oxford: Oxford Academia Publishers, 1994.)

Inner Temple (1877), *Students Admitted to the Inner Temple 1547–1660*, London: Clowes.

Ionides, Stephen and Ionides, Margaret (1939), *One Day Telleth Another*, London: Arnold.

Isidore, of Seville (1985 [1911]), *Isidorii Hispalensis Episcopi Etymologia sive Originum libri xx*, ed. W.M. Lindsay, Oxford: Clarendon Press.

James I (1603 [1599]), *Basilikon Doron: His maiesties instructions to his dearest sonne, Henry the prince*, London: I. Norton.

James, Montague Rhodes (ed.) (1933), *The Romance of Alexander: A collotype facsimile of MS Bodley 264*, Oxford: Clarendon Press.

Jessel, Frederic Henry (1905), *Bibliography of Works in English on Playing Cards and Gaming*, London: Longmans, Green and Co.

Jessop, Francis (1687), *Propositiones hydrostaticæ ad illustrandum Aristarchi Samii systema destinatæ et quædam phænomena naturæ generalia*, London: Sam. Smith and Hen. Faithorn.

Johns, Adrian (1998), *The Nature of the Book. Print and Knowledge in the Making*, Chicago and London: University of Chicago Press.

Johnson, Thomas (1630), *Dainty Conceits*, London: Henry Gosson and Francis Coules.

Jones, A. (1773), *The Art of Playing at Skittles*, London: for the author.

Jonson, Ben (1640), *The Workes of Benjamin Jonson. The second volume. Containing these playes, viz. 1. Bartholomew fayre. 2. The staple of newes. 3. The divell is an asse*, London: R. Meighen.

Junius, Hadrianus (1585), *The Nomenclator, or Remembrancer of Adrianus Iunius*

Physician, divided in two Tomes, conteigning proper names and apt termes for all things under their convenient Titles ... Now in English by Iohn Higins, London: Ralph Newberie and Henrie Denham.

Jusserand, Jean Jules (1901), *Les sports at jeux d'exercice dans l'ancienne France*, Paris. Plon-Nourrit et cie. (Geneva: Slatkine Reprints, 1986).

Kingsford, Charles Lethbridge (1925), *The Early History of Piccadilly, Leicester Square, Soho, and Their Neighbourhood*, Cambridge: Cambridge University Press.

Kinney, Arthur F. (1990 [1973]), *Rogues, Vagabonds and Sturdy Beggars*, Barre, MA: Imprint Society.

Kinsley, Shaw (1999), Willughby's Fishes: a publishing venture of the early Royal Society, unpublished MSc dissertation, University of Oxford.

Kusukawa, Sachiko (2000), 'The *Historia Piscium* (1686)', *Notes and Records of the Royal Society of London*, 54, 179–97.

La Marinière, Denis de (1651), *The Royall and Delightful Game of Picquet. Written in French and now Rendred into English out of the last French Edition*, London: J. Martin, and J. Ridley.

—— (1652), *Le Ieu dv Piquet Plaisant et Recreatif*, Paris: chez Iean Promé.

—— (1654), *La Maison Académique. Contenant vn recveil général de tous les Ieux diuertissans pour se réjouyr agreablement dans les bonnes Compagnies. Par le Sieur D L M*, Paris: chez Robert De Nain et Marin Leche.

—— (1665), *Maison des Ieux Académiques, contenant un recueil général de tous les Ieux diuertissans pour se réjoüir, & passer le temps agreablement*, Paris: chez Estienne Loyson.

—— (1674), *La Maison Académique*, Lyon: chez André Olyer.

—— (1718), *Académie Universelle des Jeux*, Paris. English translation *The Academy of Play*, by Gilles Colson Bellecour, 1768.

Lang, Andrew (1910), *New Rules for the Game of Mail*, St Andrews: n.p.

Langston, John (1675), *Lusus Poeticus Latino-anglicanus in usum scholarum. Or, The more eminent sayings of the Latin poets collected; and for the service of youth in that exercise commonly called capping of verses, alphabetically digested*, London: Henry Eversden.

Lankester, Edwin (ed.) (1846), *Memorials of John Ray*, London: Ray Society.

—— (ed.) (1848), *The Correspondence of John Ray*, London: Ray Society.

Lauthier, Joseph (1717), *Nouvelles règles pour le jeu de mail*, Paris: C. Huguier and A. Cailleau.

Lechner, Joan Marie (1962), *Renaissance Concepts of the Commonplaces*, Westport CT: Greenwood Press.

Leggatt, Alexander (1991), 'Shakespeare and bearbaiting', in *Shakespeare and Cultural Traditions*, eds Tetsuo Kishi, Roger Pringle and Stanley Well, Newark, NJ: University of Delaware Press, pp. 43–53.

Leibniz, Gottfried Wilhelm (1882), *Die Philosophischen Schriften von Gottfried Wilhelm Leibniz*, ed. C.J. Gerhard, Berlin: Weidmannsche Buchhandlung.

—— (1981), *G.W. Leibniz's New Essays on Human Understanding*, eds and trans Peter Remnant and Jonathan Bennett, Cambridge: Cambridge University Press.

Lever Ralph (1563), *The most ancient and learned playe, called the philosophers game ... set forth ... by R. Lever ... augmented by W.F*, London: Iames Roubothum.

Littleton, Adam (1678), *Linguae Latinae Liber Dictionarius Quadripartitus*, London: T. Basset, J. Wright and R. Chiswell.

Lucas, Theophilus (1930 [1714]), 'Memoirs of the lives, intrigues, and comical adventures of the most famous gamesters', in *Games and Gamesters of the Restoration*, ed. Cyril Hughes Hartman, London: Routledge, pp. 117–269.

M., J. (1676), *Sports and Pastimes; or Sport for the City and Pastime for the Country*, London: John Clark.

MacRay, William D. (1984), *Annals of the Bodleian Library*, 2nd edn, Oxford: Bodleian Library.

Magoun, Francis Peabody (1938), *History of Football from the Beginnings to 1871*, Bochum-Langendreer: H. Pöppinghaus.

Manning, Percy (1923), 'Sport and pastime in Stuart Oxford', in H.E. Salter (ed.), *Surveys and Tokens, Oxford Historical Society*, vol. 75, pp. 83–135.

Marinus of Naples (1625), *Euclidis Data, C. Hardy ed., Lat. vertit, scholijs(que) illustrauit. Adiectus est Marini commentarius Græcè & Latinè*, Lutetiæ Parisiorum: impensis Melchioris Mondiere.

Markham, Gervase (1614), *The Pleasure of Princes*, London: John Browne.

—— (1615), *Country Contentments, in Two Bookes: The first, containing the whole Art of Riding Great Horses in very short Time, by G.M. The second intituled, The English huswife*, London: R. Jackson.

—— (1634), *The Art of Archerie*, London: Ben Fisher.

Marples, Morris (1954), *History of Football*, London: Secker and Warburg.

Marshall, Julian (1878), *The Annals of Tennis*, London: 'The Field' Office.

McIntosh, Peter C. (1963), 'The puritans and sport', in *Sport in Society*, ed. Peter C. McIntosh, London: Watts, pp. 35–45.

McMahon, Susan (2000), 'John Ray (1627–1705) and the Act of Uniformity, 1662', *Notes and Records of the Royal Society of London*, 54, 153–78.

McTear, John Smith (1899), 'Gleek: a forgotten old game', *Gentleman's Magazine*, 287, October, 358–67.

Mehl, Jean-Michel (1990), *Les jeux au royaume de France du XIIIe au début du XVIe siècle*, n.p.: Fayard.

Mendyk, Stan A.E. (1989), *Speculum Britanniae: Regional Study, Antiquarianism, and Science in Britain to 1700*, Toronto, Buffalo and London: University of Toronto Press.

Merret, Christopher (1666), *Pinax rerum naturalium Britannicarum continens vegetabilia, animalia et fossilia, in hac insula reperta inchoatus*, London: impensis Cave Pulleyn.

Meursius, Joannes (1622), *De Ludis Græcorum*, Lugduni Batavorum: Ex officina Isaaci Elzeviri.

Middle English Dictionary (1956–2001), eds Hans Kurath and Sherman M. Kuhn, Ann Arbor, MI: University of Michigan Press.

Milan, Luis (1951 [1535]), *Libro de Motes*, Barcelona: Ediciones Torculum.

Minsheu, John (1599), *Pleasant and Delightful Dialogues in Spanish and English*, in Richard Perceval, *A Spanish Grammar*, London: E. Bollifant.

—— (1617), *Vocabularium Hispanicolatinum et Anglicum*, in *Ductor in linguas, The Guide into Tongues*, London: J. Browne.

Moivre, Abraham de (1711), 'De mensura sortis, seu, de probabilitate eventuum in ludis a casu fortuito pendentibus', *Phil. Trans.*, xxvii, no. 329, 213–64.

—— (1718), *The Doctrine of Chances. Or, A Method of Calculating the Probability of Events in Play*, London: for the author.

—— (1725), *Annuities upon lives, or, The valuation of annuities upon any number of lives, as also, of reversions: to which is added, an appendix concerning the expectations of life, and probabilities of survivorship*, London: Frances Fayram, Benj. Motte and W. Pearson.

More, Henry (1653), *An Antidote against Atheisme: or an Appeal to the Natural Faculties of the Minds of Man*, London: Roger Daniel.

—— (1660), *An Explanation of the Grand Mystery of Godliness: or, A true and faithfull representation of the everlasting gospel*, London: W. Morden.

Morton, Charles (1684), *The Gaming-humor Considered, and Reproved. Or, The Passion-Pleasure, and Exposing Money to Hazard, by Play, Lot, or Wager, Examined*, London: Tho. Cockerill.

Moss, Ann (1996), *Printed Commonplace-Books and the Structuring of Renaissance Thought*, Oxford: Clarendon Press.

Mulcaster, Richard (1581), *Positions Wherin those Primitive Circumstances be Examined, which are Necessarie for the Training vp of Children*, London: T. Vautrollier. (Facs. edn, English Experience 339, Amsterdam, 1971.)

Murray, Harold James Ruthren (1941), 'The medieval games of tables', *Medium Ævum*, 10, 57–69

—— (1952), *A History of Board Games other than Chess*, Oxford: Clarendon Press.

—— (1962 [1913]), *A History of Chess*, Oxford: Clarendon Press.

Nares, Robert (1822), *A Glossary*, London: R. Triphook.

Newbury, John (1967), *A Little Pretty Pocketbook* [1744, 1767], intro. M. F. Thwaite. *Milestones in Children's Literature*, New York: Harcourt, Brace and World.

Newell, William Wells (1883), *Games and Songs of American Children*, New York: Harper and Brothers.

Norden, John (1966), *Speculi Britanniæ Pars. A Topographicall and Historical Description of Cornwall*, Newcastle upon Tyne: Frank Graham.

Norris, John and Palmer, John (1995), *A Bibliography of Gamecocks and Cockfighting*, Christchurch, NZ: Arnold Books.

Northbrooke, John (1579), *A treatise wherein Dicing, Dauncing, vaine Plaies or Enterludes with other idle Pastimes, &c commonly vsed on the Sabboth day, are reproued*, London: T. Dawson for G. Bishoppe.

Obelkevich, James (1987), 'Proverbs and social history', in Peter Burke and Roy Porter (eds), *The Social History of Language*, London: Cambridge University Press, pp. 43–72.

Ochs, K.H. (1985), 'The Royal Society of London's history of trades programme: an early episode in applied science', *Notes and Records of the Royal Society of London*, 39, 129–58.

Oldenburg, Henry (1965–86), *The Correspondence of Henry Oldenburg*, eds and trans A. Rupert Hall and Marie Boas Hall, Madison, WI: University of Wisconsin Press.

Opie, Iona Archibald and Opie, Peter (1952), *The Oxford Dictionary of Nursery Rhymes*, Oxford: Clarendon Press.

—— (1969), *Children's Games in Street and Playground*, Oxford, New York, etc.: Oxford University Press.

—— and Tatem, Moira (1989), *A Dictionary of Superstitions*, Oxford: Oxford University Press.

Ore, Øystein (1953), *Cardano the Gambling Scholar, with a translation of Cardano's book on games of chance by S.H. Gould*, Princeton, NJ: Princeton University Press.

Owen, George (1892 [*c.* 1603]), *The Description of Pembrokeshire*, ed. Henry Owen, Cymmrodorion Record Series, no. 1, London: Honourable Society of Cymmrodorion.

Owst, G.R. (1961 [1933]), *Literature and Pulpit in Medieval England*, Oxford: Blackwell.

Oxford English Dictionary (1989), 2nd edn, prepared by John Andrew Simpson and Edmund Simon Christopher Weiner, Oxford: Oxford University Press.

Pappus, of Alexandria (1588), *Pappi Alexandrini Mathematicae Collectiones à Federico Commandino Urbanite in Latinum conversae, at Commentariis illustratae*, Pisauri. (Trans. *La Collection Mathématique*, ed. Paul Ver Eecke, Paris: Blanchard, 1982.)

Paradin, Claude (1989 [1557]), *Les Devises Heroïques*, Aldershot: Scolar Press; Brookfield, VT: Gower Publishing.

Parker, Clement C. (1950), *Compendium of Works on Archery*, Philadelphia, PA: G.S. MacManus.

Parkyns, Thomas (1727), *Progymnasmata. The Inn-Play; or, Cornish-Hugg Wrestler*, London: T. Weekes.

Parlett, David (1991), *A History of Card Games*, Oxford and New York: Oxford University Press.

—— (1992), *A Dictionary of Card Games*, Oxford and New York: Oxford University Press.

Peacham, Henry (1622), *The Compleat Gentleman*, London: F. Constable. (Facs. edn, English Experience 59, Amsterdam, 1968.)

—— (1641), *The Worth of a Peny: or, A Caution to keep Money*, London: by R. Hearne.

—— (1969 [1612]), *Minerva Britanna 1612*, English Emblem Books no. 5, Menston, Yorks.: Scolar.

Pearce, Robert R. (1855), *A Guide to the Inns of Court and Chancery: with notices of their ancient discipline, rules, orders, and customs, readings, moots, masques, revels, and entertainments*, London: Butterworths.

Pepys, Samuel (1970–83), *The Diary of Samuel Pepys: A New and Complete*

Transcription, eds Robert Latham and William Matthews, 11 vols, London: Bell and Hyman.

Perkins, William (1608), *A Discourse of the Damned Art of Witchcraft*, Cambridge: C. Legge.

Petty, William (1927), *The Petty Papers: Some Unpublished Writings of Sir William Petty Edited from the Bowood Papers by the Marquis of Lansdowne*, 2 vols, London: Constable and Co.

Plot, Robert (1676), *The Natural History of Oxford-shire, Being an Essay towards the Natural History of England*, Oxford and London: Moses Pits and S. Millers. (Facs. reprint, Chicheley, Buckinghamshire: Paul B. Minet, 1972.)

Pollux, Julius, of Naucratis (1608), *Iulij Pollucis Onomasticon. Adiecta interpretatio Latine Rodolphi Gualtheri; & notæ, studio atque operâ W. Seberi*, Francofurti: apud Claudium Marnium, & heredes Iohan. Aubrii.

Potter, Jeremy (1994), *Tennis and Oxford*, Oxford: Unicorn Club.

Prior, Richard Chandler Alexander (1872), *Notes on Croquet and Some Ancient Bat and Ball Games Related to It*, London and Edinburgh: Williams and Norgate.

Purver, Margery (1967), *The Royal Society: Concept and Creation*, London: Routledge and Kegan Paul.

Quarles, Frances (1643), *Emblemes*, 4th edn, Cambridge: Frances Eglesfield.

Rabelais, François (1653), *The First Book of the Works of Mr. Francis Rabelais*, trans. Thomas Urquhart, London: Richard Baddeley.

—— (1973), *Œuvres Complètes*, ed. Guy Demerson, Paris: Du Seuil.

Ratcliff, Sidney Charles and Johnson, H.C. (1941), *Quarter Sessions Indictment Book Easter 1631 to Epiphany 1674*, Warwick County Records, vol. 6, Warwick: L.E. Stephens.

Raven, Charles E. (1942; 1950^2), *John Ray, Naturalist: His Life and Works*, London: Cambridge University Press.

Ravenscroft, Thomas (1611), *Melismata*, London: Thomas Adams.

Ray, John (1660), *Catalogus Plantarum circa Cantabrigiam nascentium*, Cambridge: impensis Gulielmi Nealand.

—— (1670), *A Collection of English Proverbs*, Cambridge: W. Morden (2nd expanded edn, Cambridge: W. Morden, 1678).

—— (1673), *Observations topographical, moral and physiological made in a journey through part of the Low-Countries, Germany, Italy and France: ... Whereunto is added a brief account of Francis Willughby Esq; his voyage through a great part of Spain*, London: John Martyn.

—— (1674), *A Collection of English Words not generally used*, London: T. Burrell (2nd edn, 'With an account of the preparing and refining such metals and minerals as are gotten in England', London: Christopher Wilkinson, 1691).

—— (1675), *Dictionariolum trilingue, secundum locos communes, nominibus usitatioribus Anglicis, Latinis, Græcis, ordine παραλληλωσς dispositis*, London: Thomas Burrel. (Facs. edn, ed. William T. Stearn, London: Ray Society, 1981.)

—— (1686), *Historia Plantarum*, London: apud H. Faithorne (vol. ii, 1688; vol. iii, 1704).

—— (1690), *Synopsis Methodica Stirpium Britannicarum*, London: Sam Smith.

—— (1691), *The Wisdom of God Manifested in the Works of the Creation*, London: Samuel Smith.

—— (1700), *A Persuasive to a Holy Life: from the Happiness that attends in both this World and in the World to come*, London: Sam. Smith and Benj. Walford.

—— (1705), *Methodus Insectorum seu Insecta in Methodum aliqualem Digesta*, London: Sam. Smith and Benj. Walfold.

—— (1710), *Historia Insectorum*, ed. William Derham, London: A. and J. Churchill.

Reay, Barry (ed.) (1985) *Popular Culture in Seventeenth-Century England*, London: Croom Helm.

Rid, Samuel (1612), *The Art of Jugling*, London: George Eld.

Ringhieri, Innocentio (1551), *Cento Giuochi Liberali*, Bologna: per Anselmo Giaccarelli. (Abridged French version, *Cinquante Ieus Divers*, trans. Hubert Philippe de Villiers, Lyon: par Charles Pesnot, 1555.)

Robertson, James Craigie (ed.) (1875–85), *Materials for the History of Thomas Becket, Archbishop of Canterbury*, Rolls Series 67, 7 vols, London: HMSO.

Roget, Peter Mark (1852), *Thesaurus of English words and phrases, classified so as to facilitate the expression of ideas*, London: Longmans, Brown, Green and Longmans.

Ross, Alexander (1647), *Gnomologicon Poëticum; hoc est, sententiæ veterum poëtarum insigniores, in ordinem alphabeticum digestæ*, London: impensis Joan Marshæ.

Roy, Bruno (1977), *Devinettes Françaises du Moyen Âge*, Montreal and Paris: Bellarmin.

Ruding, Rogers (1840), *Annals of the Coinage of Great Britain*, 3 vols, London: J. Hearne.

Rühl, Joachim G. (1984), 'Religion and amusements in sixteenth- and seventeenth-century England: "Time might be better bestowed, and besides wee see sin acted"', *British Journal of Sports History*, 1, 125–65.

Salmon, Vivian (1974), 'John Wilkins' *Essay* (1668): Critics and continuators', *Historiographia Linguistica*, 1, 147–63.

Scaino da Salo, Antonio (1984 [1555]), *Treatise on the Game of the Ball [Trattato del Giuoco della Palla]*, trans. W.W. Kershaw, London: Raquetier Productions.

Scot, Reginald (1584), *The Discoverie of Witchcraft*, London: n.p.

Scott, Arthur Finley (1974), *Every One a Witness: The Stuart Age*, London and New York: White Lion.

Scott, George R. (1957), *The History of Cockfighting*, London: C. Skilton.

Scriba, Christoph J. (1998), 'Zwei Beispiele für die Andwendung der Algebra auf technische Fragestellungen im 17. Jahrhundert', in Günter Bayerl and Wolfhard Weber (eds), *Sozialgeschichte der Technik: Ulrich Troitzch zum 60. Geburtstag*, Münster: Waxmann, pp. 95–110.

Seymour, Richard (1719), *The Court Gamester: or, full and easy Instructions for Playing the Games now in Vogue, after the best Method; as they are play'd at court*, London: E. Curll.

Shaw, William A. (1906), *The Knights of England*, 2 vols, London: Sherrat and Hughes.

Sidney, Philip (1962), *The Poems of Sir Philip Sidney*, ed. William A. Ringler, Jr, Oxford: Clarendon Press.

Sieveking, A. Forbes (1917), 'Sports and pastimes: games', in Sidney Lee and Charles Talbut Onions (eds), *Shakespeare's England*, Oxford: Clarendon Press, pp. 451–83.

Sieveking, A. Forbes (1923), 'Evelyn's 'Circle of Mechanical Trades', *Transactions of Newcomen Society for the History of Engineering and Technology*, 4, 40–47.

Skippon, Philip (1732), *A Journey through Part of the Low-Countries, Germany, Italy and France. By Philip Skippon, Esq; (afterwards Knighted) in company with the celebrated Mr Ray, Mr Lister, Mr Willughby, Mr Henry Massingberd, &c*, in *A Collection of Voyages and Travels*, eds A. and J. Churchill, London: by Assignment from Messrs Churchill. For John Wathoe [and others], vol. 6, pp. 359–736.

Slaughter, Mary M. (1982), *Universal Languages and Scientific Taxonomy in the Seventeenth Century*, Cambridge: Cambridge University Press.

Smith, Richard S. (1961), 'A woad growing project at Wollaton in the 1580s', *Transactions of the Thoroton Society*, 65, 27–44.

—— (1964), The Willoughbys of Wollaton 1500–1643, with special reference to early mining in Nottinghamshire, unpublished PhD thesis, University of Nottingham.

—— (1967), 'Sir Francis Willoughby's ironworks, 1570–1610', *Renaissance and Modern Studies*, 11, 90–140.

—— (1988), *Sir Francis Willoughby of Wollaton Hall*, Nottingham: City of Nottingham Arts Department.

—— (1989), *Early Coal-Mining around Nottingham 1500–1650*, University of Nottingham, Department of Adult Education.

Sorel, Charles (1657), *La Maison des Jeux. Où se trouvent les Divertissemens d'une Compagnie, par des Narrations agreables, & par des Ieux d'Esprit, & autre Entretiens d'une honneste conversation. Dernière Edition Reveuë, Corrigée, & Augmentée*, 2 vols, Paris: chez Antoine de Sommaville.

—— (1671), *Les Récréations Galantes ... Suite & Seconde Partie de la Maison des Jeux*, Paris: chez Estienne Loyson.

—— (1672), *Les récréations galantes*, Paris: Jean-Baptiste Loyson.

Souter, Daniel (1622), *Palamedes; sive de tabula lusoria, alea, et variis ludis: libri tres*, Lugduni Batavorum: ex officina Isaaci Elzeviri.

Sprat, Thomas (1667), *History of the Royal Society of London, for the Improving of Natural Knowledge*, London: J. Martyn and J. Allestry.

Stella, Jacques (1657), *Games and pastimes of childhood / Engr. by Claudine Bouzonnet.* (Facs. edn, New York: Dover Publications, 1969.)

—— (1969 [1657]), *Games and Pastimes of Childhood*, New York: Dover.

Stevenson, William Handforth (1911), *Report of the Manuscripts of Lord Middleton Preserved at Wollaton Hall, Nottinghamshire*, London: Historical Manuscripts Commission.

Stokes, William (1641), *The Vaulting Master: or, The art of vaulting*, London: by I. Okes.

Stow, John (1912 [1598]), *Stow's Survey of London*, ed. H.B. Wheatley, London: Dent; New York: Dutton.

Strutt, Joseph (1903 [1801]), *The Sports and Pastimes of the People of England … A New Edition … by J. Charles Cox*, London: Methuen (revised edn, ed. W. Hoone, 1830).

Stubbes, Phillip (1583), *The Anatomie of Abuses*, London: R. Jones.

Suckling, John (1971), *The Works of Sir John Suckling. The Non-Dramatic Works*, ed. Thomas Clayton, Oxford: Clarendon Press.

Sutherland, C.H.V. (1973), *English Coinage 600–1900*, London: Batsford.

Swetnam, Joseph (1617), *The Schoole of the Noble and Worthy Science of Defence*, London: Nicholas Okes.

Taylor, Archer (1939), *Bibliography of Riddles*, Helsinki: Suomalainen Tiedeakatemia, Academia Scientiarum Fennica.

—— (1951), *English Riddles from Oral Tradition*, Berkeley and Los Angeles, CA: University of California Press.

Taylor, Jeremy (1660), *Ductor Dubitantium: Or, The Rule of Conscience in all her General Measures; Serving as a great Instrument for the Determination of Cases of Conscience*, London: Richard Royson.

Taylor, John (1630), *All the Works of Iohn Taylor the Water-Poet*, London: James Boler.

Thomas, Keith (1964), 'Work and leisure in pre-industrial society', *Past and Present*, 29, 50–66.

Thomas, Thomas (1587), *Dictionarium linguæ Latinæ et Anglicanæ*, Cambridge: T. Thomas; London: R. Boyle.

Thompson, E.P. (1992), 'Rough music reconsidered', *Folklore*, 103.1, 3–26.

Thoroton, Robert (1677), *The Antiquities of Nottinghamshire*, London: Henry Mortlock.

Tilley, Morris Palmer (1950), *A Dictionary of the Proverbs in England in the Sixteenth and Seventeenth Centuries*, Ann Arbor, MI: University of Michigan Press.

Tillotson, John (1694), *Six Sermons, I. Of Steadfastness in Religion, II. Of Family-Religion, III.IV.V. Of the Education of Children, VI. Of the Advantages of an early Piety*, London: B. Aylmer and W. Rogers.

Todhunter, Isaac (1865), *History of the Mathematical Theory of Probability from the Time of Pascal to that of Laplace*, Cambridge and London: Macmillan and Co.

Toole-Stott, Raymond (1976), *A Bibliography of English Conjuring 1581–1876*, Derby: Harpur and Sons.

Trevisa, John (1975), *On the Properties of Things: John Trevisa's translation of Bartholomeus Anglicus' De Proprietatibus Rerumm*, ed. M.C. Seymour, 2 vols, Oxford: Oxford University Press.

Tupper, Frederick (1903), 'The Holme Riddles (MS Harl. 1960)', *Publications of the Modern Language Association*, 18, 211–72.

Turberville, George (1575), *The Noble Arte of Venerie*, London: C. Barker.

Vale, Marcia (1977), *The Gentleman's Recreations: Accomplishments and Pastimes of the English Gentleman, 1580–1630*, Studies in Elizabethan and Renaissance Culture 1, Cambridge and Totowa: Brewer, Rowman and Littlefield.

Vanden Branden, Jean-Pierre (1982), 'Les jeux d'enfants de Pierre Bruegel', in P. Ariès and J.-C. Margolin (eds), *Les Jeux à la Renaissance*, Paris: J. Vrin, pp. 499–524.

Venn, John Archibald (1927), *Alumni Cantabrigienses*, Cambridge: Cambridge University Press.

Visscher, Roemer (1949 [1614]), *Sinnepoppen*, ed. L. Brummel, 's-Gravenhage: Martinus Nijhoff.

Vives, Juan Luis (1970 [1538]), *Tudor School-Boy Life: The Dialogues of Juan Luis Vives*, trans. Foster Watson, London: Frank Cass.

Walker, Gilbert (1552), *A manifest detection of the more vyle and detestable vse of diceplay*, London: A. Vele. (ed. J.O. Halliwell for the Percy Society, vol. 29, London, 1850).

Wallis, John (1653), *Grammatica Linguae Anglicanae*, Oxford: John Crosley.

—— (1670), *Mechanica: sive, De motu, tractatus geometricus*, London: impensis Mosis Pit.

—— (1685), *A Treatise of Algebra, both historical and practical*, London: John Playford for Richard Davis.

Watson, Foster (1968), *The English Grammar Schools to 1600: Their Curriculum and Practice*, London: Frank Cass.

Webster, Charles (1975), *The Great Instauration. Science, Medicine and Reform, 1626–1660*, London: Duckworth.

—— (1982), *From Paracelsus to Newton: Magic and the Making of Modern Science*, Cambridge: Cambridge University Press.

Webster, John (1937), *The Complete Works of John Webster*, ed. F.L. Lucas, Oxford: Oxford University Press.

Welch, Mary A. (1972), 'Francis Willughby F.R.S. (1635–1672)', *Journal of the Society for the Bibliography of Natural History*, 6, 71–85.

—— (1977), 'Francis Willughby of Middleton, Warwickshire and Wollaton, Nottinghamshire: a seventeenth century naturalist', *Transactions of the Thoroton Society of Nottinghamshire*, 81, 33–40.

—— (1981), 'Francis Willughby', in *Dictionary of Scientific Biography*, ed. Charles C. Gillispie, New York: Scribner's Sons, vol. 14, pp. 412–14.

Wilkins, John (1668), *An Essay towards a Real Character, and a Philosophical Language*, London: John Martyn.

—— (1675), *Of the Principles and Duties of Natural Religion*, London: T. Basset, H. Browne, R. Chiswell.

Willughby, Francis: For publications by Francis Willughby, see section A of this Bibliography, 'Francis Willughby's Literary Remains'.

Wilson, George (1607), *The Commendation of Cockes and Cock-fighting*, London: Henrie Tomes.

Wilson, John (1664), *The Cheats. A Comedy. Written in the Year 1662*, London: G. Bedell and T. Collins.

Wingate, Edmund (1671), *A Treatise of Common Arithmetic […] revised by John Kersey*, London: for Robert Stephens.

Withals, John (1602), *A Dictionary in English and Latine for Children and young beginners*, London: Thomas Purfoot.

Wither, George (1634), *A Collection of Emblemes*, London: printed by A. Mathewes.

Wollaton Hall Sale Catalogue (1925), *Catalogue of Valuable Books Selected from the Library at Wollaton Hall, Nottingham … Which Will be Sold by Auction by Messrss. Christie, Manson & Woods … On Monday, June 15, 1925*.

Wood, A.C. (ed.) (1958), *The Continuation of the History of the Willughby Family by Cassandra Duchess of Chandos*, Windsor: Shakespeare Head Press for the University of Nottingham.

Wood, Anthony (1691), *Athenae Oxonienses: An Exact History of all the Writers and Bishops who have had their Education in the University of Oxford, to which are added, the Fasti, or Annals, of the said University*, 2 vols, Oxford: Tho. Bennet (2nd edn, ed. Philip Bliss, London: Rivington, 1813–20).

Wright, Thomas and Wülker, R.P. (1884 [1857–73]), *Anglo-Saxon and Old English Vocabularies*, Darmstadt: Wissenchaftliche Buchgesellschaft.

Wymer, Norman George (1949), *Sport in England: A History of Two Thousand Years of Games and Pastimes*, London: Harrap.

Index of Names

The following index is limited to significant personal names mentioned in the text. Cross-references to Francis Willughby (1635–1672) are abbreviated to 'FW'.

For a comprehensive index to names of games and associated terms see the Glossary of Games and the Glossary of Technical and Obsolete Terms.